FLASH HACKS ™

Other resources from O'Reilly

Related titles

Essential ActionScript 2.0

ActionScript Cookbook

ActionScript for Flash MX: The Definitive Guide

ActionScript for Flash MX Pocket Reference

Flash Remoting: The Definitive Guide

Hacks Series Home

hacks.oreilly.com is a community site for developers and power users of all stripes. Readers learn from each other as they share their favorite tips and tools for Mac OS X, Linux, Google, Windows XP, and more.

oreilly.com

oreilly.com is more than a complete catalog of O'Reilly books. You'll also find links to news, events, articles, weblogs, sample chapters, and code examples.

oreillynet.com is the essential portal for developers interested in open and emerging technologies, including new platforms, programming languages, and operating systems.

Conferences

O'Reilly brings diverse innovators together to nurture the ideas that spark revolutionary industries. We specialize in documenting the latest tools and systems, translating the innovator's knowledge into useful skills for those in the trenches. Visit *conferences.oreilly.com* for our upcoming events.

Safari Bookshelf (*safari.oreilly.com*) is the premier online reference library for programmers and IT professionals. Conduct searches across more than 1,000 books. Subscribers can zero in on answers to time-critical questions in a matter of seconds. Read the books on your Bookshelf from cover to cover or simply flip to the page you need. Try it today with a free trial.

FLASH
HACKS™

Sham Bhangal

O'REILLY®

Beijing · Cambridge · Farnham · Köln · Sebastopol · Tokyo

Flash Hacks™

by Sham Bhangal

Copyright © 2004 O'Reilly Media, Inc. All rights reserved.
Printed in the United States of America.

Published by O'Reilly Media, Inc., 1005 Gravenstein Highway North,
Sebastopol, CA 95472.

O'Reilly books may be purchased for educational, business, or sales promotional use. Online editions are also available for most titles (*safari.oreilly.com*). For more information, contact our corporate/institutional sales department: (800) 998-9938 or *corporate@oreilly.com*.

Editor:	Bruce Epstein	**Production Editor:**	Marlowe Shaeffer
Series Editor:	Rael Dornfest	**Cover Designer:**	Hanna Dyer
Executive Editor:	Dale Dougherty	**Interior Designer:**	Melanie Wang

Printing History:

June 2004:   First Edition.

ISBN: 978-0-596-00645-7
[LSI]

[2010-11-30]

Contents

Foreword

About seven years ago, I started working with Macromedia Flash—Version 2.0 to be precise. The client for my first Flash project was Levi's Canada, the world-famous apparel company. Levi's was looking for the proverbial "really cool web site." I guess corporations, like any other living entity, have an aversion to death, and Levi's was keen to renew its lease on life by attracting a new generation of customers (read: teenagers). But kids, said Levi's, don't like clothing web sites; to a kid, a clothing web site is a boring shopping catalog with a Buy button. The solution? Make the new Levi's site an interactive comic strip, where the stories of the characters lead to Levi's products. Fill the comic with action, romance, drama, and intrigue...kids love that stuff.

At the initial project meetings, the creative director presented the animated web site concept while we, the HTML jockeys and web designers, shuddered at the thought of trying to implement it. As envisioned, the site even included—hold onto your hat—actual sounds for the characters' voices! (Remember this was 1997; audio and animation on web sites was almost unheard of.) In our first technical plan for the site, we proposed the use of animated GIF images, WAV sound files, and JavaScript image rollovers. We knew the site wouldn't be as spectacular as the creative director had described, but we were accustomed to playing the developer scapegoat. We would be the ones to break the news to the client: web browsers can't really do animated cartoons; the creative director's description of the site was conceptual, intended merely as inspiration, not to be taken literally.

But the creative director had seen animations on the Web; he was sure of it. He asked us how Disney's web site did its cartoons. We told him with Macromedia Flash. For him, the name of the software and technical details were irrelevant. The Levi's site had to be animated at any cost. So we did the Levi's site in Flash (see it at *http://moock.org/webdesign/portfolio/levisite*).

Shortly after we completed the Levi's site, the web design industry went crazy over Gabocorp and EYE4U, two self-promotional web agency sites with animated Flash interfaces. By today's standards, these two sites look comically simple and naïve. (See for yourself—as of April 2004 the original EYE4U site is still live at *http://www.eye4u.com*.) Gabocorp and EYE4U consisted of nearly no programming, arguably gaudy design, some moving shapes, and some balls flying around the screen. So what made them popular?

Like the Levi's site, they proved that you could hack the system.

As a browser add-on, Flash is one of the largest scale hacks of the past decade. Since its inception, Flash has breathed life into the somewhat sterile web browser. Flash lets the creative community explore what the Web can be: a cartoon network, a game platform, an OS-style environment for connected applications, an electronic art gallery, a video chat, a collaborative multiuser environment, a remote meeting room, an MP3 music player—or pretty much anything you can dream up. Fitting that ideal, Macromedia used "What the Web can be" as its marketing slogan a few years back.

Accordingly, it's no surprise that Flash is pervasively flexible, a veritable hacker's playground. In fact, Flash's "hackability" is arguably the key to its success. Here, I'm using the word "hack" to mean "a creative exploration, using any means possible (even ugly), that leads to some desirable (even exhilarating) result." Flash grew from a humble animation toy to the expansive "Rich Internet Application" tool it is today, largely in response to the hacks introduced by the development community.

I remember people using Flash 3 to create games like Whack-a-Mole, Leo's Great Day (*http://www.pepworks.com/leoenglish.swf*), and even crude prototypes of Pacman and chess. Mind you, all without a single line of code. Flash 3 had no scripting language! In response to this hacked demand for greater interactivity, Macromedia introduced a very simplistic version of Action-Script in Flash 4. Little did they know it would fuel a motion graphics movement that would influence design in print, television, and movies for years. Months after Flash 4 shipped, sites like Mono-craft (*http://www.yugop.com*), PrayStation (*http://www.praystation.com*), Levitated Design & Code (*http://www.levitated.net*), and Presstube (*http://www.presstube.com*) became famous for their creative explorations in real-time audio/visual expression (in other words, for their hacks!).

People use Flash to explore things that are hard or impossible to do in other media. It's hard to do motion graphics in HTML, but you can dream about a motion graphics web with Flash. It's hard to do expressive, customized user interfaces in traditional desktop applications, but you can see branded Flash applications today on thousands of web sites. As I write this foreword, I'm finishing up a web site in which you can observe other connected users interacting with the site's interface (see *http://moock.org/unity/clients/ uPresence*). Meanwhile Marcos Weskamp is working on Version 2 of his remote control car application (*http://www.marumushi.com/apps/ remotedriver2*), in which anyone in the world can drive a physical remote control car via a Flash-based web interface. It's hard to imagine building these things with any tool but Flash.

So Flash is a hacker's paradise. It lets you play. It gives you the freedom to explore your ideas. And it forces you to pull some zany tricks to get what you want. For a long time, the tricks and hacks of Flash have circulated throughout the online development community. Many of them, new and old, are now committed to print in this book, in a quality and style deserving of the O'Reilly name.

I consider this book both a service and a challenge.

The service: use what you find in these pages to your advantage on whatever you're building. There's tons of great info here, bound to be of help on nearly any project. You'll benefit from Sham Bhangal's considerable experience in the field and a clarity of expression I truly believe only Bruce Epstein (this book's editor) can guarantee.

The challenge: remember that exploration and invention are your greatest tools. Before there were books on Flash and before there were established tricks and methodologies, there was a vision of what could be and the clever, bullish, tinkering desire to make it so.

—Colin Moock
April 2004

Credits

About the Author

Sham Bhangal began on the route to web design in 1991, designing and specifying information screens for safety-critical computer systems, as used in places like nuclear power plant control rooms. He soon discovered more conventional interface design, animation, and multimedia tools, such as 3D Studio Max, Photoshop, and Flash. He has been writing books on them since the turn of the century.

Contributors

The following people contributed their hacks, writing, and inspiration to the book:

- Anthony "Ant" Eden (a.k.a. arseiam) has worked for several high-profile clients including Microsoft, Disney, and Adobe. He spends his spare time creating wild and quirky effects with ActionScript, which can be sampled at *http://www.arseiam.com*.

- Zeh Fernando has been working with Macromedia Flash since Version 2. Currently working at Brazilian-based design studio Grafikonstruct (*http://www.grafikonstruct.com.br*), he creates real-world Flash-based web sites daily and is searching for better ways to do it in his free time.

- Edwin "XemonerdX" Heijmen is a professional Flash developer living in the Netherlands who also moderates several ActionScript forums. He enjoys combining mathematics and code, some results of which can be seen at *http://www.poeticterror.com*. Besides ActionScript, he also enjoys coding PHP, ColdFusion, Python, and every obscure language he can get his hands on. Other passions include his wonderful girlfriend, underground metalcore, open source software, Russian literature, and his friends.

- Adam Phillips is the award-winning animator behind biteycastle.com, hitchHiker, and the Brackenwood series of Flash movies. He was a Flash Forward Cartoon category winner in NYC 2003 and again a finalist in SF 2004. With a desire to tell stories and more than 10 years of traditional 2D animation experience with the Walt Disney Company, Adam continues to produce his own short movies, 13 of which can be found at *http://www.biteycastle.com*.

- Grant Skinner (*http://www.gskinner.com*) is an internationally recognized Flash developer with experience fusing code, interface design, usability, marketing, and business logic. He works with top agencies and progressive corporate clients on Flash application conceptualization, architecture, and implementation. Grant has won multiple top Flash awards, has had work featured in the SIGGRAPH Web Expo of "The finest web-graphics work of 2003," and participates regularly in numerous conferences and publications.

- Stickman has asked that his real name be kept secret to protect the innocent, but we can divulge that he works in web design for a large content site in the UK and is also a freelance writer. Oh, he is also tall and thin. You can catch up with his online persona at *http://www.the-stickman.com*.

Acknowledgments

This book has been a long time in the making, and thanks go out to all who stayed on for the ride. I guess it's been a strange trip for all involved!

Thanks, of course, go to Macromedia for creating Flash and to the contributors for contributing hacks.

Thanks to Colin Moock (*http://www.moock.org*) for his great books, technical assistance, and insightful Foreword.

Thanks to the review team for querying and correcting: Marc Garrett, David Humphreys, Chafic Kazoun, Marc Majcher, Sam Neff, Darron Schall, Jesse Warden, and Edoardo Zubler.

Thanks also to the folks at O'Reilly, including Tim O'Reilly for the initial comments and Rael Dornfest for putting the "hack" into *Flash Hacks*. Thanks also to Brian Sawyer and Claire Cloutier for production assistance, to Rob Romano for converting the numerous screenshots, and to Norma Emory for her detailed copy editing. Special thanks to Bruce Epstein for his death-defying nerves of steel in the face of insurmountable deadlines, superhuman editing strength, and time for a chat. Thanks also to my agent, Carole McClendon, at Waterside Productions.

Thanks to the designers within the Flash community who have provided helpful advice on third-party tools, including Igor Kogan, Dave Hayden, Damian Morten (Flasm), and Alex Blum (Flash Plugin Switcher). Thanks to Alessandro Capozzo (*http://www.ghostagency.net*) for allowing me to reproduce some of his images created in Processing. Thanks also to the large number of developers, designers, and dreamers whose work has directly or indirectly inspired portions of this book; they include Josh Davis (*http://joshdavis.com*), Branden Hall (*http://waxpraxis.org*), Erik Natzke (*http://www.natzke.com*), James Paterson (*http://www.presstube.com*), Amit Pitaru (*http://www.pitaru.com*), and Hardino (*http://www.hardino.com*).

Finally, thanks to Brian Molko and company (*http://www.brian-molko.com*) for the first four lines of "Pure Morning." Stuff like that keeps me smiling all day as I'm writing. Pure genius.

Preface

Macromedia Flash's ancestor started out as a core component of the pen computer, a keyboardless machine that used a pen stylus for input, making it much more portable than traditional keyboard-based designs and ideal for handheld devices. The system featured a vector-based drawing engine, which was more suited to input via a pen than more traditional bitmap-based systems.

The idea didn't take off, but a new avenue was beginning to present itself—the Web. The pen-based vector drawing program became FutureSplash, which was released around 1995 as a web-centric vector animation tool. FutureSplash was soon bought by Macromedia, and the first version of the renamed application, Flash, was released in 1996.

Late in 2003, Macromedia released Flash MX 2004 (and Flash MX Professional 2004) and the corresponding Flash Player 7 browser plugin and ActiveX control. In recent years, Flash has gained a number of important features, including multimedia handling capabilities (sound, images, video) and a full-fledged scripting language (ActionScript) to create nonlinear animation or client-side processing, as well as interfacing with remote data or server-side scripts.

Flash is now the standard web multimedia delivery platform. The Flash Player (the browser plugin that plays back Flash SWF files) is ubiquitous, and Flash can also create desktop applications. Web design continues to move away from traditional HTML and toward the interactivity and multimedia features offered by Flash. And Macromedia continues to expand the Flash platform with products like Macromedia Central (a personal browser for occasionally connected Flash-based content), Flash Communication Server MX (a real-time video and audio server), and Flash Remoting (enhanced remote connectivity to web services and server-side applications).

Why Flash Hacks?

The term *"hacking"* has a bad reputation in the popular media. They use it to refer to breaking into systems or wreaking havoc using computers as weapons. Among people who write code, though, the term *"hack"* refers to a quick and dirty solution to a problem or a clever way to get something done. And the term *"hacker"* is taken very much as a compliment, referring to someone as being creative and having the technical chops to get things done. The Hacks series is an attempt the reclaim the word, document the good ways people are hacking, and pass the hacker ethic of creative participation on to the uninitiated. Seeing how others approach systems and problems is often the quickest way to learn about a new technology.

Flash Hacks is about coming up with new ideas for your Flash web designs, ActionScript, and Flash content.

Flash authoring is all about creativity, in both design and coding, and pushing the envelope of what is possible. Although multimedia scripting has become more structured and formalized, there is still plenty of room (and need) for hacks and workarounds when the standard routes fail.

When I first opened up the Flash application and started reading the official documentation, it took me a while to understand how Flash is really supposed to be used, and from feedback I have received since, this is a common problem.

Flash is thus an area in which experimenting, hacking around limitations, and knowing a lot of design tricks is part of the workflow because the aim is often to create something original and engaging. Reading the Macromedia Flash documentation will take you only so far before you need to start looking for clever hacks and inside tricks that overcome many of Flash's limitations.

Therefore, this book is not just about showing you some interesting hacks, it is about showing you some of the nonobvious techniques and ideas that will make your Flash designs more original and your applications more effective.

Of course, this also means that you won't be using many of the hacks presented here as-is, but instead will use them as starting points for further exploration and development. Experimentation is to be promoted—it is what Flash and the Flash community are all about. This book borrows much from the rich tradition of the Flash community but also presents many original ideas to teach, entertain, and inspire you.

Who This Book Is For

Okay, let's face it. O'Reilly is better known for its technical references than for edgier books like the Hacks series. O'Reilly has published some of the most advanced books on ActionScript development available, including the well-respected *ActionScript for Flash MX: The Definitive Guide* and the hardcore object-oriented programming guide *Essential ActionScript 2.0*, both by Colin Moock. O'Reilly's *ActionScript Cookbook*, by Joey Lott, presents more than 300 practical recipes for a wide range of ActionScript problems, and *Flash Remoting: The Definitive Guide*, by Tom Muck, covers high-end application development and remote connectivity.

I think it is safe to say that this book is substantially different from those books, which is appropriate since the books serve different purposes, even if their audiences overlap. Whereas those are serious, traditional programming books speaking to well-structured code and best practices, this tome is full of exploration and whimsy. Whereas those books speak of productivity to experienced programmers, this book speaks of adventure to the young at heart. If you're new to Flash, this book is as tantalizing as the aroma of a warm apple pie. If you are experienced with Flash, and perhaps a bit bored with it, it might remind you why you fell in love with Flash in the first place. That said, hard-core developers will find lots of serious coding advice, optimization techniques, and tips and tricks for application development.

Frankly, if you've never used Flash, some of the hacks will confuse you, but many will not, as there is something here for everyone. In early chapters, I make an effort to explain occasional operational basics, such as creating a new empty layer (Insert → Timeline → Layer) and attaching code to a frame (select the frame in the Timeline panel and open the Actions panel using F9 or Window → Development Panels → Actions). We'll be placing most of our scripts on a dedicated *actions* layer [Hack #80] but some scripts must go in external *.as* files [Hack #10].

Because this book is predominantly geared toward readers with some familiarity with Flash, if you've never used Flash, you should probably pick up one of the many fine tutorial books available from (gasp!) other publishers. (O'Reilly is coming out with a Flash tutorial book—*Flash Out of the Box* by Robert Hoekman—in the second half of 2004.) If you don't have a copy of the Flash authoring tool, you can download a trial version from Macromedia (*http://www.macromedia.com/cfusion/tdrc/index.cfm?product=flash*) and go through some of the included tutorials to learn the basics, too.

That said, many of the hacks in this book can be appreciated even if you've never picked up Flash. I certainly hope this book inspires the uninitiated to try Flash and those who know Flash to appreciate it anew.

If you're a traditional programmer new to Flash or a serious application developer, be forewarned. This book isn't about best practices or object-oriented programming or Rich Internet Application (RIA) development. And if you're prejudiced against Flash, the large number of hacks covering animation, drawing, and motion graphics may turn you off to Flash forever. That would be a shame. What is presented here is but a small slice of the Flash universe, my own personal corner in fact (with a little help from friends and contributors). Skip around and you'll find not just eye candy and ear candy but lots of ActionScript examples, too. You'll learn something, even if it wasn't what you set out to learn.

The Flash universe is both vast and diverse and this book doesn't try to be all things to all people. But almost every developer, whether an experienced Flasher, a beginning scripter, or a hard-core coder, will find more than a few interesting techniques and tips. If you were ever a child, if you were ever in love, if you like drive-in movies or howling at the moon, this book will remind you a little bit of all those things. And that, to me, seems like a very good thing.

So read all the other Flash and ActionScript books you can get your hands on, but leave a place on the shelf or your desk for this one, too.

How to Use This Book

If you read the book from cover to cover, you'll find many technical tidbits in unlikely places that you'd miss if you judge a hack by its title alone. For those who prefer to pick an interesting hack from the table of contents and dive right in, be sure to skim the remaining hacks to see what you might be missing. Be sure to read through the chapter headings regardless of whether you are a newbie or an expert in a given topic, as you're sure to find something both useful and interesting at almost every turn.

If you want to get some quick ideas for new directions in your designs, the first four chapters look at the core techniques that affect the look and feel of a site, such as drawing, animation, and effects. Chapters 5, 6, 7, and 8 revolve around media and content, so visit them for inspiration and information pertaining to 3D, text, sound, or UI elements. Chapters 9, 10, 11, and 12 cover specialized topics such as browser integration, optimization, and security (plus a healthy dose of ActionScript for good measure). You should peruse them for answers to question like, "How do I center the Flash Stage in the browser?" or "Someone ripped off my site design! How can I prevent it from happening again?"

How This Book Is Organized

Flash is a versatile authoring tool and consists of a number of separate areas that usually need to be combined to produce the finished effect or piece, so don't take the chapter titles and synopses as anything other than broad headings. For example, many chapters contain some element of animation, and most hacks contain ActionScript because it lets you do some really cool things. Regardless, we have straitjacketed the 100 hacks into something resembling sensible groupings. So there are chapters on drawing, sound, optimization, and a whole lot more.

Chapter 1, *Visual Effects*
> This chapter looks at ways you can make your graphic content more interesting by adding various snazzy effects and transitions.

Chapter 2, *Color Effects*
> The savvy designer uses color in addition to animation. Color is often overlooked, but this chapter shows how color changes can transform the atmosphere of a piece or add video-like effects, such as fades and wipes.

Chapter 3, *Drawing and Masking*
> Combining Flash's graphic animation facilities with ActionScript increases your creative horizons considerably. This chapter shows graphic effects created at both authoring time and runtime. Masking, which underlies many of the graphics tricks and techniques, is also discussed.

Chapter 4, *Animation*
> The hacks in this chapter offer content creation shortcuts for manually drawn animation, plus ways to optimize animation created under ActionScript control.

Chapter 5, *3D and Physics*
> This chapter provides a number of hacks that bypass Flash's performance limitations to add physics simulations and 3D effects to your repertoire.

Chapter 6, *Text*
> This chapter covers ways to store, display, and manipulate text, as well as create animated text effects.

Chapter 7, *Sound*
> Without sound, your carefully crafted content will feel flat and uninspired. This chapter helps the audio-challenged create and manipulate sound effects and music.

Chapter 8, *User Interface Elements*
> This chapter covers hacks related to user interface issues, such as buttons, scrollbars, and mouse input.

Chapter 9, *Performance and Optimization*
> This chapter includes hacks to keep your filesizes small and your applications speedy.

Chapter 10, *ActionScript*
> Although almost every hack in the book includes some ActionScript, this chapter covers ways to get the most out of ActionScript, including undocumented goodies.

Chapter 11, *Browser Integration*
> This chapter looks at ways of maximizing browser compatibility so you can maximize the audience and enhance their enjoyment of your content.

Chapter 12, *Security*
> This chapter provides a few ways to protect your content and designs, despite the vulnerability of the SWF format.

Conventions Used in This Book

The following typographical conventions are used in this book:

Plain text
> Indicates menu titles, menu options, menu buttons, and keyboard accelerators (such as Alt and Ctrl).

Italic
> Indicates new terms, function names, method names, class names, event names, package names, layer names, URLs, email addresses, filenames, file extensions, pathnames, and directories. In addition to being italicized in the body text, method and function names are also followed by parentheses, such as *setInterval( )*.

Constant width
> Indicates code samples, movie clip instance names, symbol names, symbol linkage identifiers, frame labels, commands, variables, attributes, properties, parameters, values, objects, XML tags, HTML tags, the contents of files, or the output from commands.

Constant width bold
> Shows commands or other text that should be entered literally by the user. It is also used within code examples for emphasis, such as to highlight an important line of code in a larger example.

Constant width italic

Shows text that should be replaced with user-supplied values. It is also used to emphasize variable, property, method, and function names referenced in comments within code examples.

Color

The second color is used to indicate a cross-reference within the text.

 This icon signifies a tip, suggestion, or general note.

 This icon indicates a warning or caution.

The thermometer icons, found next to each hack, indicate the relative complexity of the hack:

 beginner moderate expert

Using Code Examples

This book is here to help you get your job done. In general, you may use the code in this book in your programs and documentation. You do not need to contact us for permission unless you're reproducing a significant portion of the code. For example, writing a program that uses several chunks of code from this book does not require permission. Selling or distributing a CD-ROM of examples from O'Reilly books *does* require permission. Answering a question by citing this book and quoting example code does not require permission. Incorporating a significant amount of example code from this book into your product's documentation *does* require permission.

We appreciate, but do not require, attribution. An attribution usually includes the title, author, publisher, and ISBN. For example: "*Flash Hacks,* by Sham Bhangal. Copyright 2004 O'Reilly Media, Inc., 0-596-00645-4."

If you feel your use of code examples falls outside fair use or the preceding permission, feel free to contact us at *permissions@oreilly.com*.

Getting the Code Examples Working

The most common reason for being unable to get a code example to work (assuming you haven't made any typos) is a failure to set up the Flash file according to the instructions. Reread the surrounding text and follow the steps carefully. Be sure to place the code where it belongs (usually in the first frame of the *actions* layer or in an external *.as* file). Be sure you've set the compiler version to ActionScript 2.0 under File → Publish Settings → Flash → ActionScript Version.

Any code example that accesses movie clips, buttons, or text fields via ActionScript won't work unless you set the item's instance name properly. To set the instance name for a movie clip, button, or text field, select it on stage and enter the instance name on the left side of the Properties panel (Window → Properties) where you see the placeholder "<Instance Name>".

Another common source of problems is failure to set a symbol's linkage identifier properly, as is necessary when accessing Library symbols from ActionScript. To set the linkage identifier for a symbol, check the Export for Actionscript and Export in First Frame checkboxes in the Symbol Properties or Linkage Properties dialog box. (These are accessible by selecting a symbol in the Library (Window → Library) and choosing either Properties or Linkage from the Library panel's pop-up Options menu.) Then enter the identifier in the field labeled Identifier (which isn't active until Export for ActionScript is checked).

Read the instructions carefully to make sure you haven't confused a movie clip instance name with a symbol linkage identifier.

If you still can't get it working, download the examples from this book's web site, contact O'Reilly book support, or check the book's errata page. If all else fails, get a tutorial book on Flash or ask an experienced Flasher for help.

 Many of the longer examples and sample files can be downloaded from this book's web page at *http://examples.oreilly. com/flashhks*.

ActionScript 1.0 Versus ActionScript 2.0

Many of the hacks presented in this book are written in ActionScript 2.0, which requires the Flash MX 2004 or Flash MX Professional 2004 authoring environment. You can use either of these authoring tools (see *http:// www.macromedia.com/software/flash/productinfo/features/comparison* for a comparison of the two) because we don't use any features that are exclusive to the Professional edition. To make sure the examples compile, you should set the ActionScript Version to ActionScript 2.0 under File → Publish Settings → Flash. All examples have been tested in Flash Player 7.

Where noted, ActionScript 2.0 class definitions must be placed in external *.as* files. For example, the custom *Transform* class [Hack #10] must be placed in an external plain-text file named *Transform.as* (both the capitalization of the name and the *.as* extension are mandatory). You can create and edit such a file in Flash MX Professional 2004 if you select File → New → ActionScript File. If using Flash MX 2004, you'll need an external text editor [Hack #74].

We can't give a full course on object-oriented programming (OOP) and ActionScript 2.0 here, although we do try to provide pointers throughout the book. For many more details on ActionScript 2.0 classes and object-oriented development, see *Essential ActionScript 2.0* by Colin Moock (O'Reilly).

Most examples can also be exported in Flash Player 6 format from Flash MX 2004 (standard or Professional edition), by setting the Export format to Flash Player 6 under File → Publish Settings → Flash.

However, methods that are new to Flash MX 2004 and Flash Player 7 won't work if you are exporting to Flash Player 6 format. For example, where we use *MovieClip.getNextHighestDepth( )* in the code examples, you'll have to substitute it with a unique depth or it won't work in Flash Player 6.

The previous version of the Flash authoring tool, Flash MX, does not support ActionScript 2.0. However, many of the hacks and example code will work in Flash MX. If you have Flash MX and want to try out an ActionScript 2.0 hack, you can convert most of the examples to ActionScript 1.0 by simply removing the ActionScript 2.0 datatyping as shown next.

For example, here is the ActionScript 2.0 code using datatypes (shown in bold):

```
// ActionScript 2.0 with datatypes
// Requires Flash MX 2004 authoring environment
// configured to compile ActionScript 2.0
function myFunction(x:Number):Number {
  var y:Number = 2 * x;
  return y;
}
var myString:String = "hello";
var myClip:MovieClip = this.createEmptyMovieClip("myClip", 0);
var double:Number = myFunction(2);
trace(double);
```

And here is the ActionScript 1.0 version without datatypes:

```
// ActionScript 1.0 (untyped)
// Works in Flash MX authoring environment (and later)
function myFunction(x) {
  var y = 2 * x;
  return y;
```

```
}
var myString = "hello";
var myClip = this.createEmptyMovieClip("myClip", 0);
var double = myFunction(2);
trace(double);
```

This book uses a lot of timeline-based code, which, although it is not necessarily a best practice, is supported for both ActionScript 1.0 and ActionScript 2.0. We made this choice because most of the examples don't lend themselves readily to custom ActionScript 2.0 classes. This also makes the examples easier to follow and implement in both Flash MX and Flash MX 2004.

Some of the class-based OOP examples written in ActionScript 2.0 won't compile in ActionScript 1.0 and require Flash MX 2004 (standard or Professional edition). If you are still using ActionScript 1.0 in Flash MX 2004, consider this as an opportunity to broaden your horizons. See Chapters 10 and 12 for additional details and resources on the ActionScript differences between Flash Player 6 and Flash Player 7.

Case-Sensitivity

Many developers continue to be confused by the case-sensitivity rules in Flash MX 2004. Realize first that we are talking about two different issues: compile-time case-sensitivity and runtime case-sensitivity. The ActionScript 1.0 compiler is not case-sensitive, whereas the ActionScript 2.0 compiler is. However, runtime case-sensitivity is a function of the version of the SWF file format to which you export, not the ActionScript version used at compile time nor the version of the Flash Player plugin in which the file is played.

Runtime case-sensitivity is summarized in Table P-1, reproduced from Colin Moock's excellent book, *Essential ActionScript 2.0* (O'Reilly).

Table P-1. Runtime case-sensitivity support by language, file format, and Flash Player version

Movie compiled as either ActionScript 1.0 or 2.0 and	Played in Flash Player 6	Played in Flash Player 7
Flash Player 6-format .swf file	Case-insensitive[a]	Case-insensitive[a]
Flash Player 7-format .swf file	Not supported[b]	Case-sensitive

[a] Identifiers (i.e., variable and property names), function names, frame labels, and symbols export IDs are case-insensitive in Flash Player 6-format .swf files. But reserved words such as *if* are case-sensitive, even in Flash Player 6.

[b] Flash Player 6 cannot play Flash Player 7-format .swf files.

Comments and Questions

Please address comments and questions concerning this book to the publisher:

O'Reilly Media, Inc.
1005 Gravenstein Highway North
Sebastopol, CA 95472
(800) 998-9938 (in the United States or Canada)
(707) 829-0515 (international or local)
(707) 829-0104 (fax)

We have a web page for this book, where we list errata, examples, and any additional information. You can access this page at:

http://www.oreilly.com/catalog/flashhks

To comment or ask technical questions about this book, send email to:

bookquestions@oreilly.com

For more information about our books, conferences, Resource Centers, and the O'Reilly Network, see our web site at:

http://www.oreilly.com

Visual Effects
Hacks 1–7

This book assumes you are familiar with the basics of using Flash to create visual effects and animations using the timeline. If you aren't comfortable with Flash, you might still find the techniques employed here interesting. Once you've learned some Flash basics via either Flash's online help or a tutorial book, you can revisit the hacks that piqued your curiosity. I considered beginning the book with tips on optimization, security, and similar topics. But I decided to defer those until later, hoping that the hacks in this chapter would get you excited about the book and expand your horizons while remaining true to the hacker ethic: "Show me the cool stuff first."

So, in this chapter, I've grouped hacks that show you how to achieve some effects you might not have known about or might have seen and not known how to reproduce. As with all the hacks presented in this book, I hope they educate and ultimately inspire you—not in the sense of "inspiration," as when one views a great piece of art, but in the sense of "motivation." Thus, I hope you are motivated to try these hacks and inspired to create some of your own.

The hacks in this chapter are grouped together because they are all loosely associated with visual effects. Later chapters in this book deal with additional visual effects using transitions and colorization, 3D, masking, and the Drawing API. This chapter includes pixel effects and converting from animated GIFs and Photoshop files to Flash *.fla* and *.swf* files (the source document and distribution formats used by Flash). I close the chapter with two hacks that show you how to generate a tree and make it sway in the breeze.

Although Chapter 3 makes the heaviest use of masks, masks are so ubiquitous in Flash [Hack #1] that hacks in other chapters use them as well. So for readers unfamiliar with masks, here is a brief introduction.

Flash animations are created by superimposing one or more layers in an animation (similar to layers as you'd find in Photoshop and other graphics programs). The Timeline panel contains the main timeline, which organizes the layers and displays their contents over time. Masks are traditionally used to create visual effects, such as a spotlight effect, in which one layer is viewed through the "hole" created by the masking layer. That is, the masking layer defines the area of the underlying masked layer that is visible (the remainder is "masked off" and therefore invisible). To create a masking layer (or simply "mask layer") in the authoring tool, insert a new layer in the timeline (using Insert → Timeline → Layer) in front of the layer you want masked. Then set the mask layer's Type to Mask in the Layer Properties dialog box, accessible under Modify → Timeline → Layer Properties. Then, on the mask layer, create the shape to use as the mask. In Flash, areas with pixels in the mask layer allow the masked layer to show through. Areas in the mask layer without pixels block (mask off) the masked layer. For example, if you want to create a spotlight effect in which the masked layer shows through the circle, you could use the drawing tools (Window → Tools) to create a black circle as the mask.

Flash MX added the ability to create scripted masks in which a mask defined by one movie clip is used to mask another movie clip's contents. A scripted mask, as the name implies, is a mask applied dynamically at runtime with ActionScript via the *MovieClip.setMask( )* method. Applying a runtime mask is akin to creating a mask layer during authoring time, except that it affords much more flexibility. The mask used over a given clip can be changed at runtime, and new masks can be created at runtime. Although you can animate a mask layer in the authoring tool, again, you can create more sophisticated animations by animating the mask at runtime via ActionScript. I hope this brief introduction to masking allows you to get the most out of the various hacks in this book that use author-time and runtime (scripted) masks. For more information on masks see the online Help topic How Do I → Basic Flash → Work with Layers → Add a Mask Layer, or search the online Help for the term "Mask."

Without further ado, on to the cool stuff.

Fake Per-Pixel Transitions

HACK
#1

Simulate pixel-based fades and wipes, as supported in Macromedia Director.

Flash doesn't have built-in support for pixel-based transitions. This hack can be used with other video-friendly hacks [Hack #8] to make your static bitmaps more interesting [Hack #3].

Flash uses a vector-based rendering engine, which doesn't allow direct access to the individual screen pixels. This hack depends on the fact that pixels are small, and when you make something small, it looks like anything else that is small.

The per-pixel transition effect is shown in Figure 1-1.

Figure 1-1. Simulated per-pixel transition, steps 1 through 4

The transition hides (masks) pixels in the first image over time so that the image disappears a few pixels at a time. Masking off the first image reveals a second image that is positioned below it, thus creating the transition effect from the first image to the second image. The masks used to create the preceding effect are shown in Figure 1-2. Note that for black pixels, the mask effect shows the first (topmost) image; for white pixels (no mask), it shows the second (bottom) image.

As we shallsee, we can make much more complex transitions with little change.

This hack requires three steps:

1. Make the fake pixel. In this hack we will create a little 4×4 rectangle.

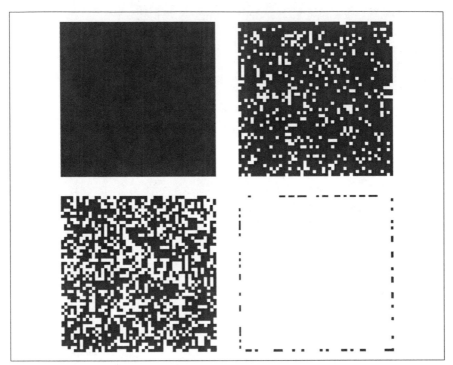

Figure 1-2. Masks for simulated per-pixel transition, steps 1 through 4

2. Find a way to make lots of fake pixels. This is done very easily in Flash using *MovieClip.attachMovie( )*.

3. Create a transition by creating a script that makes each dot disappear after a certain time. By using all the dots as a large mask, we create the transition between two images (or video clips), as seen in Figure 1-1.

The problem here is that we will have thousands of fake pixels, and we can't use anything as processor-extravagant as thousands of *onEnterFrame( )* scripts running every frame for the duration of the effect. Instead, we will use *setInterval( )*, which reduces our processing overhead significantly by running code only once per fake pixel for the duration of the effect.

Make the Pixels

Making a pixel mask is as simple as creating a rectangle:

1. Create a new Flash document (File → New → Flash Document).

2. Use Modify → Document to set the Stage area bigger than 200 × 200 pixels and specify a white background (any light color will allow you to see the black rectangle in Step 3).

3. Draw a black rectangle with no stroke (the stroke wouldn't be seen but would still slow down our effect).

4. Using the Properties panel (Window → Properties), set the rectangle's height and width to 4. Set the X and Y coordinates to 0. You can see the result just next to the registration point in Figure 1-3.

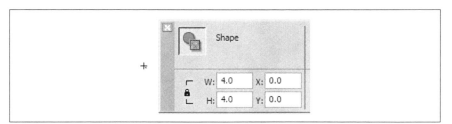

Figure 1-3. A 4×4 pixel mask with its registration point

ActionScript gurus might want to draw the mask using the Drawing API, but it would take too long for Flash to dynamically draw all the rectangles we would need for this effect.

5. Convert the rectangle into a movie clip symbol by selecting it (with the Selection tool) and pressing F8 (Modify → Convert to Symbol), which brings up the Symbol Properties dialog box. Name the movie clip symbol dot and make sure you have the export options set up as shown in Figure 1-4 (click the Advanced button if you don't see the Linkage options).

You can delete the movie clip instance from the Stage, since we will use the *MovieClip.attachMovie( )* method to dynamically attach the Library symbol to the main timeline at runtime. If you want to avoid creating and then deleting the movie clip from the Stage, you can use Insert → New Symbol (Ctrl-F8 or ⌘-F8) to create the movie clip symbol directly in the Library.

The effect uses a large mask consisting of these 4×4 squares. The mask is applied to the first image, and the effect works by masking additional rectangles over time, causing the second image (which is below the first) to show through the gaps.

Make Lots of Pixels

On the main timeline, add a new layer and name it *actions* [Hack #80].

In the *actions* layer of the main timeline, select frame 1 and attach the following script using the Actions panel (F9):

```
function drawGrid (theWidth:Number, theHeight:Number):Void {
  var initDot:Object = new Object( );
  var k:Number = 0;
```

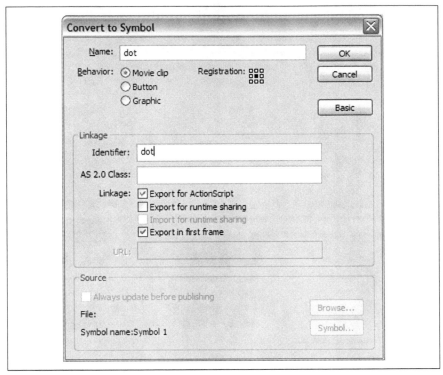

Figure 1-4. The Symbol Properties dialog box

```
for (var i:Number = 0; i < theWidth; i += 4) {
  for (var j:Number = 0; j < theHeight; j += 4) {
    var dotName:String = "dot" + i + "_" + j;
    initDot._x = i;
    initDot._y = j;
    this.attachMovie("dot", dotName, k, initDot);
    k++;
  }
 }
}
drawGrid(200, 200);
```

The preceding code creates a 200×200-pixel square consisting of our 4×4 movie clips (you can invoke the *drawGrid( )* function with different dimensions to create a grid of a different size). Each pixel is placed at position (i, j) and depth k on the Stage and has instance name dot*i_j*. The first instance name (situated at the top left of the square) is dot0_0 and the last one is dot199_199 (bottom right). You can see the movie clips created if you run the code in Debug Movie mode (Control → Debug Movie), but be aware that the debugger will take some time to display all your movie clips (although it may look as if Flash has hung up, give it a few seconds!).

This effect creates a large number of movie clips; $(200/4)^2 =$ 2500. Flash seems to become very sluggish if more than 3000 to 4000 movie clips appear on the screen at the same time (even if you are not moving the clips), so you are advised not to go far beyond 2500. If you need to mask a larger area than the one we are working with (200 pixels square), consider making the constituent rectangles bigger rather than adding more of them.

Control the Pixels

The trick now is to make the dots disappear on demand. The way to do this is via setInterval(*object*, *"method"*, *timer*), which invokes the function *object.method( )* every *timer* milliseconds. Add the following code after initDot._y = j; in the preceding script:

```
initDot.timer = 1000 + Math.ceil(Math.random( )*800);
```

The preceding line creates a property, timer, which stores an integer between 1000 and 1800 for each dot clip. The 1000 specifies the pause before the effect starts, and the 800 is the duration of the effect. Both values are in milliseconds, the standard measure of time in ActionScript.

This hack is based on a mask effect, but Flash allows only one mask per movie clip. The easy way around this limitation is to create all our dot movie clips inside another one that acts as the mask. We also pass in the name of the clip to be masked as a parameter to the *drawGrid( )* function (changes are shown in bold):

```
function drawGrid(theWidth:Number, theHeight:Number,
                  imageClip:MovieClip):Void {
  var initDot = new Object();
  var k:Number = 0;
  // Create a mask clip to hold all the dots
  this.createEmptyMovieClip("mask", 1);
  // Assign it as the masking clip
  imageClip.setMask(mask);
  for (var i:Number = 0; i < theWidth; i += 4) {
    for (var j:Number = 0; j < theHeight; j += 4) {
      var dotName:String = "dot" + i + "_" + j;
      initDot._x = i;
      initDot._y = j;
      initDot.timer = 1000 + Math.ceil(Math.random( )*800);
      // Place the masking dots within the container mask clip
      mask.attachMovie("dot", dotName, k, initDot);
      k++;
    }
  }
}
drawGrid(200, 200, image1_mc);
```

So now we have all our dot clips inside another movie clip named mask, which we use as the mask for a movie clip whose name is passed in as a parameter to the *drawGrid( )* function. In this case, we use a clip named image1_mc, which we create later in the section "Using the Effect." First though, let's finish off the dot movie clips.

Create the Timers

We already have a timer property for each dot movie clip. Now let's write the code to make our dots disappear.

Edit the *dot* movie clip symbol and add a new layer named *actions* (the first layer of a timeline is traditionally named *scripts* or *actions* and used exclusively to hold your timeline-based scripts).

In the first frame of the *actions* layer, add the following code:

```
removeMe = function () {
  clearInterval(countDown);
  this.removeMovieClip();
};
var countDown = setInterval(this, "removeMe", timer);
```

The last line of the preceding code uses *setInterval( )* to create a timer named countdown for each dot. It calls the *removeMe( )* function when the timer expires. The *removeMe( )* function clears the interval and then removes the current dot clip, which creates our "disappearing pixels" transition effect.

> If *setInterval( )* is passed a function reference as the first parameter, such as *setInterval(removeMe, timer);*, the value of the keyword this would be undefined within the *removeMe( )* function. Therefore we use the alternative form *setInterval(this, "removeMe", timer)* in which we pass an object and a method name as the first two parameters. (In this case, the keyword this is the object passed as the first argument.) When *removeMe( )* is invoked, the keyword this is in scope, so we can invoke *this.removeMovieClip( )* to remove the clip.

Using the Effect

To use the effect, you need to have the two things you want to transition between on two separate layers, with the first image or video clip on the top layer, as shown in Figure 1-5. You should give the first clip the instance name image1_mc using the Properties panel. The second image can be called anything since it is never referred to in the code.

You can see the effect in action by downloading *pixelMask.fla* from this book's web site.

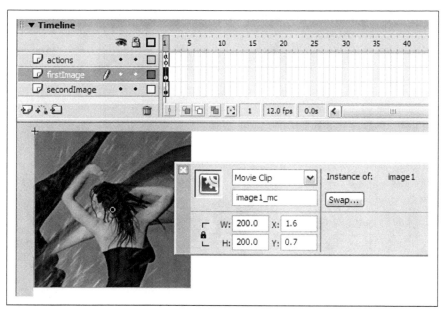

Figure 1-5. Setting up a transition between two layers

Extend the Effect

By changing the time interval before each dot disappears, you can create different transition effects. For example, changing the timer values based on the position of the dots serves as the basis for many common pixel-based transitions:

```
// Left-to-right wipe
initDot.timer = 1000 + (Math.random( )*(initDot._x)*10);
// Diagonal wipe
initDot.timer = 1000 + (Math.random( )*(initDot._x + initDot._y)*5);
```

Final Thoughts

Masking is a very underutilized feature of Flash. It's one of those features that seems to have no real use until you delve deeper. No surprise then that many of the coolest effects [Hack #21] seem to use it extensively!

Per-Pixel Text Effects

Create advanced text effects and transitions that operate on the per-pixel level.

The problem in simulating per-pixel effects in Flash is that potential performance degradation limits how many fake pixels you use. You have two ways to keep this number small: keep to small images (as we did in the per-pixel transition effect hack [Hack #1]), or use the effect on an image with lots of background pixels (which you can ignore to reduce the number of fake pixels needed).

Although it's probably obvious in hindsight, it took me ages to realize that text fits the "lots of background pixels" criterion. A quick trawl on the Web suggests that it really isn't obvious because nobody else seems to be using this hack.

In this hack, we'll make the text appear to coalesce from pixels spread out over the screen. Of course, you can implement various effects using different calculations for the mask pixels' positions.

The hack comes in two parts:

- Converting the text block's shape into 1×1 squares (i.e., our "fake pixels")
- Animating the fake pixels

Here are the steps:

1. Create a text field and enter some text.

2. Press Ctrl-B (Windows) or ⌘-B (Mac) or choose Modify → Break Apart twice to turn the text field into a primitive shape.

3. With the text still selected, press F8, and convert it into a movie clip symbol named **text**. Make sure the Export for ActionScript checkbox is checked and specify the linkage identifier as **text**. (Delete the clip instance from the Stage, as we'll be adding it at runtime from the Library with *MovieClip.attachMovie( )*.)

4. For the effect to work, the movie clip's registration point must be at the top left of the text. Enter Edit in Place mode by double-clicking the movie clip; then to select all the text choose Edit → Select All and enter 0 for X and Y values in the Properties panel, as shown in Figure 1-6.

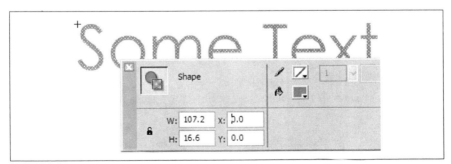

Figure 1-6. Setting the registration point for the selected text symbol

You must turn your text into a primitive shape for this hack to work using the Modify → Break Apart command (we'll see why later), which is not ideal because it adds to the filesize. For a lot of text, it can bloat the filesize considerably. One way around this is to include each letter in your font as a separate clip containing a primitive shape and form them into sentences at runtime. Although this sounds like a lot of additional bytes to add to your SWF, remember that Flash effectively does the same thing when you save font outlines to your SWF, which you have to do whenever you want to treat font characters as graphic elements.

You also need to create a second movie clip with linkage identifier dot. The dot clip should consist of a 1×1 rectangle, with X and Y positions both set to 0 as shown in Figure 1-7 (use the Properties panel to set these because the dot will be too small to see).

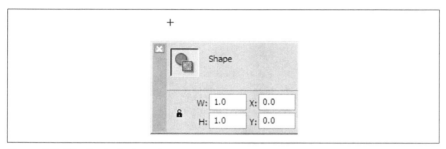

Figure 1-7. The 1×1 pixel mask

This code replicates the "zoom in from the sides with blur" effect, but this time the text really does blur (the effect is usually simulated with alpha), as shown in Figure 1-8, because we are splitting the text into pixels as part of the effect.

Figure 1-8. Per-pixel text effect, steps 1 through 4

```
function mover( ) {
  this._x -= (this._x - this.x) / 4;
  this._y -= (this._y - this.y) / 4;
}

function lastMover( ) {
  this._x -= (this._x - this.x) / 4;
  this._y -= (this._y - this.y) / 4;
  if ((this._x - this.x) < 0.1) {
    dotHolder.removeMovieClip( );
    textClip._visible = true;
  }
}
// Place the text on the Stage and hide it
textClip = this.attachMovie("text", "textClip", 0);
textClip._x = 200;
textClip._y = 100;
textClip._visible = false;
// Initialize variables, including height and width
var dots = 1;
var distance = 10000;
var stopDot = true;
var height = textClip._y + textClip._height;
var width  = textClip._x + textClip._width;
// Create a dot clip for every pixel in the text
var dotHolder = this.createEmptyMovieClip("holder", 1);
for (var j = textClip._y; j < height; j++) {
  for (var i = textClip._x; i < width; i++) {
    if (textClip.hitTest(i, j, true)) {
      var clip = dotHolder.attachMovie("dot", "dot" + dots, dots);
      if (stopDot) {
        clip._x = distance;
        clip.onEnterFrame = lastMover;
        stopDot = false;
      } else {
        clip._x = Math.random( ) * distance - distance/2;
        clip.onEnterFrame = mover;
      }
      // Store the position that the dot clip has
      // to get to (clip.x, clip.y) and move it off screen
      clip.x = i;
      clip.y = j;
      clip._y = j;
      dots++;
    }
  }
}
```

Ignoring the *mover( )* and *lastMover( )* function definitions for a moment, the remaining code places the text on the Stage and hides it. The code then initializes several variables, including those that define the height and width of our text.

The subsequent *for* loop uses *MovieClip.hitTest( )* to find all nonempty pixels in the text and create a dot movie clip corresponding to each. Each of these dots is given an *onEnterFrame( )* handler to animate the overall effect. (Instead, we could use *setInterval( )* to animate the effect [Hack #1].)

Two hacks are at work in this loop code.

The first hack, using *hitTest( )*, is the reason we had to break apart our text. The *hitTest( )* method always returns false when used with a dynamic text field (in which case it treats all pixels as empty).

The second hack is the way we check that all pixels are in their final positions. Most of our pixels are placed randomly on the screen and controlled by the event handler *mover( )*. The first pixel, however, is placed furthest away and also given a slightly more complicated event handler, *lastMover( )*. This event stops the effect when the associated pixel has moved to its final position, by which time the others will also have reached their final positions (given that they all have less distance to travel).

Although a bit of a kludge, this hack is far more performance-friendly than forcing each pixel to perform a similar check.

Final Thoughts

Although Flash text effects are all over the Web, I don't know of any that use per-pixel transitions. The cool thing about using our fake pixels is that you can use any other particle effect (such as the snow, waterfall, or star field effects [Hack #33]) for the pixel movement routine.

HACK
#3 Simulate Old Film Grain
Create the effect of old film grain using Photoshop and Flash.

Flash's vector graphic engine has a lot going for it, but sometimes you want something a little less clean-edged. Adding an old film grain effect is one of the easiest ways to add instant atmosphere or a grungy hard edge to an otherwise crisp and clean clip. It can be combined with video colorization [Hack #8] or sepia tone colorization [Hack #13] for more dramatic and specialized effects.

The most obvious way to add a film grain effect is to add random vector lines and dots to an image. That reproduces the effect, but it doesn't really reproduce the atmosphere of old film; we still end up with a crisp rendering. In this hack we use a bitmap, which allows us to avoid the clean effect of vectors.

The hack has two parts: creating the film grain bitmap in Photoshop and then importing and using it in Flash. (We could of course use Fireworks in place of Photoshop; the principles are the same.)

Create the Film Grain Bitmap

Dirt, scratches, and dropouts add a real-world edge to a photograph. Dust, dirt, and hair or lint that has made its way onto the film or negative appear as dark patches and lines. Scratches appear as white lines.

To begin adjusting the image in Photoshop:

1. Open Photoshop.
2. Press D to reset to the default background and foreground colors.
3. Press X to switch background and foreground colors. This will give you a background color of black and a foreground color of white.
4. Create a new Photoshop file called *grain.psd* using File → New. Select a bitmap size that is longer than it is wide. I created a file 800×400 pixels for demonstration purposes, but you can go much smaller (typically 400 ×200).
5. Check the Background Color option in the Contents section of the New Document dialog box, as shown in Figure 1-9. This creates a rectangular black canvas.

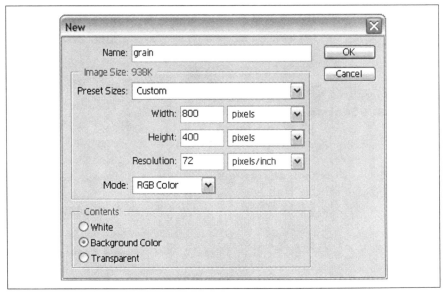

Figure 1-9. Setting the Background Color option in Photoshop

6. Add a new layer using the Create a New Layer icon at the bottom of the Layers tab. We will be drawing only on the new layer, so ensure *Layer 1* is always selected in the Layers tab, as shown in Figure 1-10.

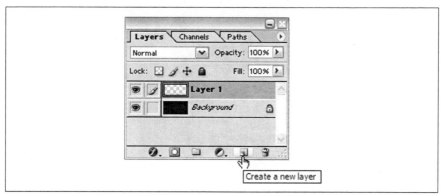

Figure 1-10. The newly created layer selected in Photoshop

We now need to draw our effects. Three types of noise are seen on old film:

Hairlines
    Hairlines are caused by dark strands in the film.

Dots and patches
    Dark dots are caused by specks of dirt or other material on the film, and light dots are caused by scratches or dropouts in the film.

Scratches
    These are caused by scratches in the film that erase part of the film image.

Using the Photoshop tools (typically the Pencil and Brush tools), add the three types of effect on *Layer 1*. In Figure 1-11, I have created small dots to the left, large patches in the middle, and scratches to the right. I have also created hairlines at the top and bottom.

Using Photoshop's Eraser tool with a medium opacity, fade some of your pixels. On real film, deep scratches and other effects appear white, but many imperfections affect the film surface only partially, and this is what we are simulating in Figure 1-12.

Although we have used only white, many effects on old film are black, so we also need to simulate those:

1. Select some areas of your white pixels using Photoshop's Selection tool.

2. Invert the selection using Image → Adjustments → Invert. Although your selected pixels will seem to disappear, this is because you are creating black pixels on a black background; they are still there, you just can't see them.

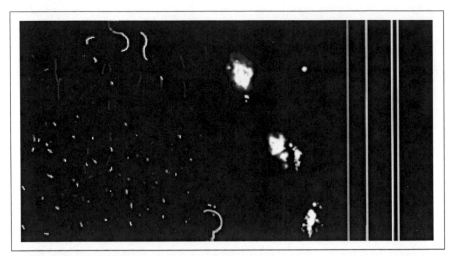

Figure 1-11. Simulated imperfections in Photoshop

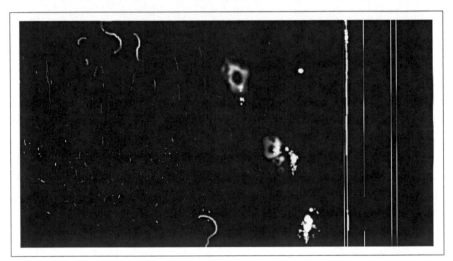

Figure 1-12. Simulating shallow scratches

3. Delete the background layer (click-drag it in the Layers tab, and release it over the trashcan icon at the bottom of the tab).

You should end up with something like the image shown in Figure 1-13 (the checkerboard background is Photoshop's way of representing zero alpha, or no pixels).

Save the image as a PNG file. Do not optimize it for the Web in any way.

Many designers optimize their graphics at this point, given that they are about to be loaded into a web design package (Flash). There is really no

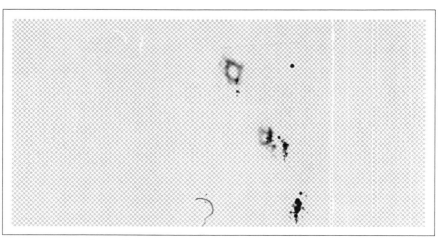

Figure 1-13. Simulating drop outs

need to do so; leaving the optimization until the point you create the SWF in Flash always gives you more flexibility.

For example, if the client decides she wants a high-bandwidth version of the site, you simply change the bitmap export settings in Flash. If you had optimized your bitmaps before importing them into Flash, you would have to go to Photoshop and reexport the images at the new setting. Then, you would have to swap all instances of the old bitmap on the Flash timeline for the new one. Obviously, then, importing full-quality bitmaps into Flash, and letting Flash optimize them, can be a real time-saver compared to the alternatives. For those who prefer working in Fireworks, its integration with Flash (i.e., its launch and edit feature) can also speed your workflow.

Using a Bitmap in Flash

Once you've exported the bitmap as a PNG file from Photoshop, you still need to use it in Flash:

1. Import the PNG file into Flash using File → Import → Import to Library.
2. Select the bitmap in the Library.
3. Right-click (Windows) or ⌘-click (Mac) in the Library panel, and select Properties from the context menu that appears (also known as the pop-up Options menu).
4. Change the Bitmap Properties, as shown in Figure 1-14: select a low JPEG compression ratio and remove smoothing (Flash handles bitmaps faster if you disable smoothing).

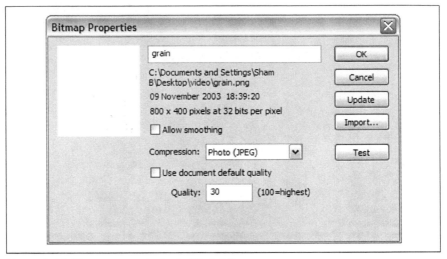

Figure 1-14. Bitmap properties in the Flash Library

Note that we have created an image that has both JPEG compression and an alpha channel! You cannot have a JPEG image with an associated alpha channel as a standalone file, but Flash doesn't seem to mind, which is very useful to know when you want to overlay Flash vectors with a bitmap.

Drag the bitmap onto the Stage, then press F8 (Modify → Convert to Symbol) and convert the bitmap into a movie clip symbol named *grain*.

All you have to do now is overlay a quick-moving version of our movie clip onto a video, bitmap, or vector animation. In Figure 1-15, I have overlain it over a static image, making the image appear as if it is a section of video.

I have also used a mask to hide areas of the grain clip that don't appear over the image. The final effect is shown in Figure 1-16 (or take a look at *grain.fla*, which is downloadable from this book's web site).

Final Thoughts

Not only can this technique add interest to a section of video that isn't doing much, it can also:

- Hide imperfections in the video (such as pixelation caused by high compression rates).

- Give movement to static images, making them appear as if they are a video clip.

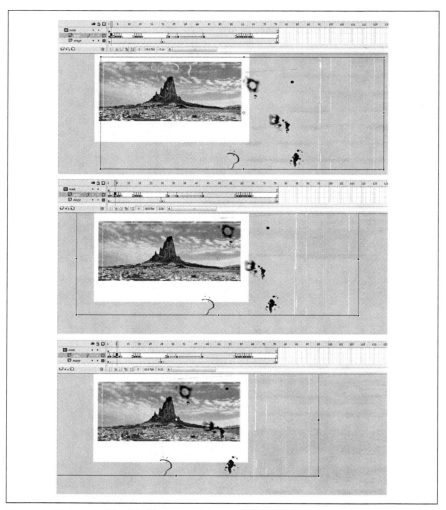

Figure 1-15. Simulating old video, steps 1 through 3

Figure 1-16. Using a mask to complete the effect

- Hide discontinuities. If you are mixing video and still images (such as a main video section and vector-based opening or closing titles), you can hide this by adding a grain effect over the whole production.

Create SWFs from Animated GIFs

#4   Quickly repurpose animated GIFs for use in Flash effects.

I thought it would be fun to show how you can enhance a GIF by reproducing it in Flash. So I went to the O'Reilly home page (*http://www.oreilly.com*) where I was greeted by the little critter—I'm told it's a tarsier—shown in Figure 1-17. The filename is *oreilly_header1.gif*, which is typical of slices created for an HTML-based table, so I knew I had a GIF I could work with. Anyway, I kept looking at him, given that he looks so cute, and then I blinked. He blinked back. After the surprise and obligatory double take, I realized he's an animated GIF.

Figure 1-17. The O'Reilly tarsier mascot on oreilly.com

So I started thinking...doing a Flash version of this critter would be a good example of the difference between Flash and traditional HTML design. This hack shows how you can reduce filesizes by using Flash instead of your animated GIFs. Once the 2D blinking tarsier animation is in Flash, you can modify it to simulate a 3D blinking tarsier [Hack #35].

The GIF Animated Critter

We can obtain a copy of our animated friend using a web browser's Save option. In Internet Explorer on Windows, for example, we right-click on the GIF and select Save Picture As from the pop-up menu to download the image to our local drive.

Another advantage of Flash animations over animated GIFs is that you can make them harder to steal than this critter was from O'Reilly's site by obfuscating the SWF [Hack #98] in the browser cache, which is where users ordinarily look for downloaded SWFs.

If you open the O'Reilly GIF file in an image editor (such as Fireworks or Photoshop/ImageReady), you will see that the blink animation runs every 12 seconds (the first frame has a delay of 12 seconds), and the animation is 12 seconds in total. One thing worth noticing is that an awful lot of pixels in the image don't change between frames—only the eyes do. So converting it to Flash and animating only the eyes should give us a big filesize advantage straight away.

Notice also that the animation is not interactive. In this case, the lack of interactivity is appropriate design—you don't want the critter's actions to distract the reader—but we will add interactivity for fun and show that the SWF will still be smaller than the original GIF.

Create the Animation Assets

The best way to import all the sections of our GIF animation is as a series of PNGs because these will not reduce the quality of the original (especially if we use PNG-24), and we can easily add an alpha channel. Although GIFs support transparency, it's really only a mask in which you can have pixels showing or not showing. The PNG-24 format supports true alpha, where transparency has a percentage value. Figure 1-18 shows the PNGs (as seen in Photoshop) ready for export into Flash.

I've used a couple of cool hacks here:

- I have cropped the image to separate the portion that animates (i.e., the eyes) from everything else.

- Although the original animation lasts six frames, three of them are repeated (the eye closing sequence is simply the reverse of the eye opening sequence), so we can significantly reduce the number of unique frames we need to re-create it in Flash, again reducing filesize.

- We can export with true alpha in PNG-24 format, which allows us to feather the edges of the image. If we place the critter in front of a jungle scene to make him more at home, we can blend his edge pixels rather than producing jaggies or a halo as we'd expect with a standard GIF.

To add transparency to an imported image in Photoshop:

1. In the Layers tab, copy the *Background* layer.
2. Delete the original *Background* layer. You will now end up with a single layer called *Background Layer Copy.*
3. When you use the Eraser tool on this layer, it creates an alpha channel. (Having deleted the *Background* layer, when you erase any pixels, there is no background to show through, so Photoshop instead gives you transparency.)

If you import the PNG images into Flash (using File → Import), you can rebuild the critter in the usual way, starting from the lowest layer up: first the eyeballs, then the pupils, followed by the eyelids, and finally the body, as shown in Figure 1-19.

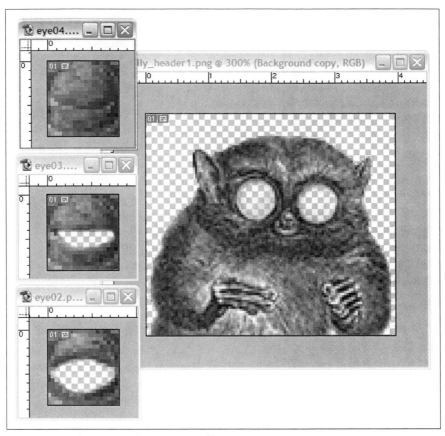

Figure 1-18. The animated GIF as PNG files

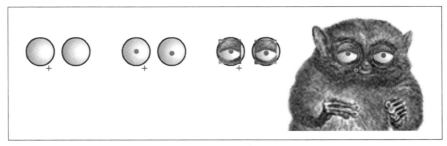

Figure 1-19. The eyeballs, pupils, eyelids, and body

Note that the eyeballs are vectors in this version. The blink sequence is implemented as a movie clip consisting of the three bitmaps with the eyes closing progressively and the same three bitmaps being reversed to reopen them.

The pupils are two dots named leftEye_mc and rightEye_mc. When controlled by the following script, they will keep a wary eye on the mouse cursor, as shown in Figure 1-20. As usual, you can add this code to the first frame of your *actions* layer on the main timeline.

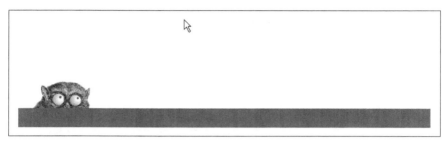

Figure 1-20. Tracking the mouse position

```
followMouse = function () {
  this.startX = this._x;
  this.startY = this._y;
  this.onEnterFrame = animateEye;
};

animateEye = function () {
  var distX = (_xmouse - this._x) / 50;
  var distY = (_ymouse - this._y) / 50;
  if (Math.abs(distX) < 5) {
    this._x = this.startX+distX;
  }
  if (Math.abs(distY) < 5) {
    this._y = this.startY+distY;
  }
};

leftEye_mc.onEnterFrame = followMouse;
rightEye_mc.onEnterFrame = followMouse;
```

The *followMouse( )* function is specified as the *onEnterFrame* event handler for both pupils. Once it is called, it simply captures the starting pupil position and changes the *onEnterFrame* event handler to *animateEye( )* for subsequent frames. This function moves the pupils a distance from the start position, based on the mouse position, giving the appearance that the critter is watching the mouse.

You can, of course, give your critter a much wider range of emotions than the animated GIF, as shown in Figure 1-21, but that's not a hack—that's what Flash is all about.

Figure 1-21. A sad tarsier and his drinking buddy

Final Thoughts

Although this is a fairly standard animation, the way it was (very) quickly converted from an existing animated GIF shows how easy it is to create a more versatile Flash animation. Bitmaps with transparency can be stacked above one another to create layered animations using the animated GIF bitmaps themselves. This trick is also a good way to export Photoshop *PSD* files into Flash; simply export each layer as a separate PNG-24, which will include transparency. You can then reassemble the PNGs in the correct order using Flash layers. The only difference, of course, is that you can then animate your layers!

Animate Photoshop PSD Files with Flash
#5   Import full Photoshop PSD files into Flash, then animate them.

This hack tells you how to re-create a Photoshop file with layers in Flash. We'll go through the details because they are instructive (and free!), but a third-party Photoshop plugin, called PSD2FLA (*http://www.medialab.com/ psd2fla*) from Media Lab, simplifies the process considerably. Director developers will recognize Media Lab as the maker of PhotoCaster, the well-respected and popular Xtra that imports PSD files into Director.

Assuming you have QuickTime 4.0 or higher installed, you can import a PSD file directly into Flash. Flash will most likely tell you that it cannot import the file, but it gives you the option of trying to import via QuickTime. Clicking Yes to this prompt imports your image.

Flash's file import description for *.psd* files is Photoshop 2.5, 3 Image; however, when importing via QuickTime, Flash can handle *.psd* files from much more recent versions of Photoshop.

The trouble with importing files using the QuickTime option is that the imported file becomes flattened, preventing you from accessing the separate PSD layers, seen in Figure 1-22. Given that the only real reason to import a PSD (as opposed to web formats such as JPEG) is to access the embedded layer information; this limitation makes QuickTime import less than ideal.

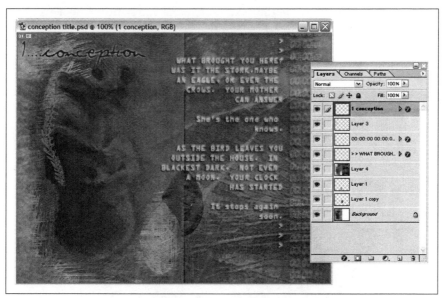

Figure 1-22. A Photoshop image with layers

This hack shows how to import a PSD in such a way that you can efficiently rebuild it in Flash for animation, complete with a significant amount of the original PSD layer information.

Starting in Photoshop, crop/resize the PSD so that you have an image with dimensions that make it suitable for the Web (i.e., no larger than 500×500 pixels).

You will get much better results if you scale a Photoshop image down in steps. For example, reducing a 1000×1000 image to 900×900, then 800×800, and so on, all the way down to 500×500 will give you a better final image and offer more options when you compress it later.

The other reason to keep the image size down is that Flash is not designed to handle bitmaps in the way we are going to use it; Flash is better suited to vectors. We can hack around this by making sure that we don't ask Flash to change too much on the screen per frame, and keeping the bitmap sizes modest gives us a head start.

The next step is to reduce the number of layers as far as possible by combining (flattening) as many layers as you can. You will get good performance in Flash if you can get down to no more than five or six layers. Also, consider removing all text layers or any layers that can be reproduced in Flash (you can re-create these later in Flash using the Flash drawing tools).

I decided to remove all of the text except the main title (top left). This removed text can be replaced by sharper vector text when we rework the image in Flash. The main title was retained as-is because it has Photoshop text effects applied that cannot be easily reproduced with vectors.

Figure 1-23 shows the simplified version with the text removed.

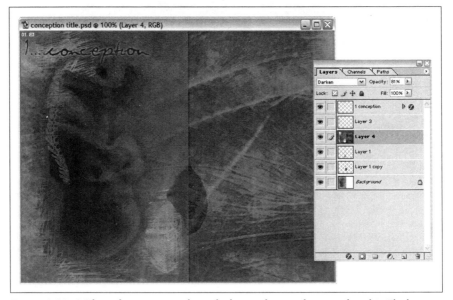

Figure 1-23. A Photoshop image without the layers that can be reproduced in Flash

The next step involves exporting each layer as a PNG. For each layer in the Photoshop document:

1. Hide all layers except the one to be exported.

2. Select File → Save As, and save the image as a PNG.

3. Once you have exported all your layers, reload any PNGs that have a substantial blank area around them, such as the leaf in Figure 1-24, and crop them so that the extraneous zero alpha pixels are cut, as shown in Figure 1-25.

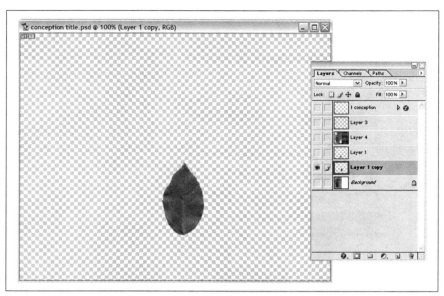

Figure 1-24. A layer that is a candidate to be cropped

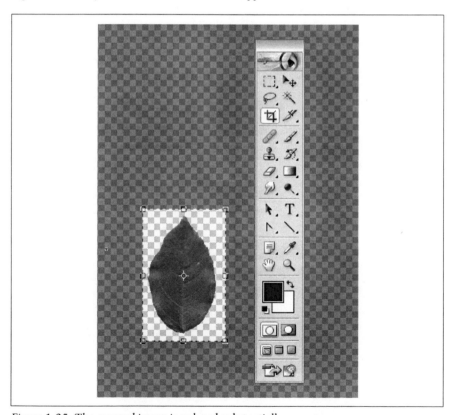

Figure 1-25. The cropped image is reduced substantially

Revert to the original PSD and leave Photoshop open (or take a screenshot of the image if you don't have enough memory to have both Flash and Photoshop open at the same time). You'll need to refer back to it later.

In Flash, set the Stage to the same size as the PSD, and import all the PNGs to the Library using File → Import → Import to Library (in Flash MX 2004) or File → Import to Library (in Flash MX).

To animate your bitmaps effectively, you are best advised to make each into a movie clip (i.e., wrap each bitmap in a movie clip, because you can then use the methods and animation transitions available to movie clips):

1. Drag each bitmap in turn from the Library onto the Stage.
2. Select the bitmap.
3. Press F8 with the bitmap selected, and create a movie clip symbol from it. To avoid confusion, it is a good idea to name the movie clips the same as the bitmaps but with the suffix "_mc."

When you have finished, you will end up with a series of bitmaps with transparent backgrounds, allowing you to position them on the Flash Stage in much the same way they appeared in the PSD original. Figure 1-26 shows the bitmaps in the Flash Library.

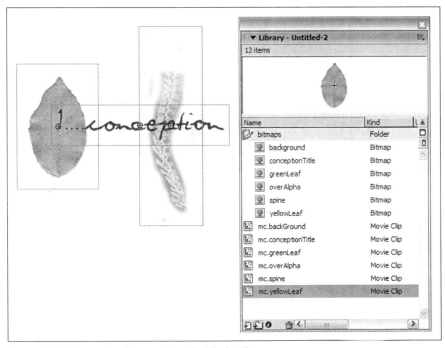

Figure 1-26. Importing bitmaps into the Flash Library

Manually place the movie clips on the timeline (or in another clip, depending on how you will be presenting them) in the same order and position that
they appeared in the original PSD. You can emulate Photoshop layer effects
(such as Darken, Multiply, and so on) using Flash color effects. Naturally,
you can make adjustments if you want the Flash web version, shown in
Figure 1-27, to be different from the Photoshop print version.

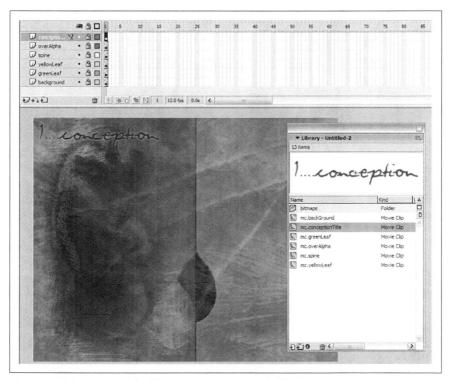

Figure 1-27. Re-creating the Photoshop composition in Flash

To finish your composition, you should optimize each bitmap separately by
right-clicking (Windows) or ⌘-clicking (Mac) each bitmap in the Library
and setting individual export settings. The settings for the best compromise
between size and appearance are usually:

- Photo (JPEG)
- No smoothing
- A quality setting in the range of 30% to 50%

When setting the quality for each bitmap, bear in mind that your bitmaps
are in a layered composition, and much of the noise introduced by high
compression rates will be hidden by the layers and semitransparencies. You

should look at the composition overall to judge how low you can go, in terms of quality. You may find that compression ratios of 20% or less look okay on some of the lower layers.

> Flash allows you to export a bitmap with an alpha channel at the same time you apply JPEG compression!

You now have your starting point for animation. Each element in your composition can now be:

- Animated using tweens (by setting the Properties panel's Tween option to Motion)
- Given an instance name and animated dynamically using ActionScript

You can also add the missing text and vectors that the original had (or create new vector content for the Flash version).

As mentioned previously, Flash can get sluggish when animating bitmaps, although experience shows that you can get good results as long as you either animate only one layer at a time or keep the number of things changing between any two frames modest, in terms of size.

Final Thoughts

As long as the animations you want to create are not seriously processor-intensive or do not require a large image area (in which case you need to start thinking about Director), you can use the PSD-layers-to-PNGs-to-Flash route shown here. This route also has merit if you want to mock up a site using Photoshop visualizations or print-based assets. In that case, you might also consider PhotoWebber (*http://www.photowebber.com*) from the makers of PSD2FLA.

Experience with this technique also shows that the final SWF filesize can be remarkably low, considering the original filesize of the PSD. Typically, the size of the animated SWF version is of the same order of magnitude as a static, medium- to high-quality JPEG.

A Tree Grows in Brooklyn
HACK #6
Create a random tree generator.

This hack creates a natural-looking tree using the usual suspects (fractals/recursion/repeat-and-scale algorithms). In the next hack, we'll create movement using an embedded hierarchy of movie clips.

For those of us who prefer speaking English, we're going to grow a tree and make it sway in a breeze [Hack #7]. We will do this by re-creating natural phenomena in code.

The first time I went to Flash Forward (*http://www.flashforward2004.com*), Josh Davis talked about what made him tick. To paraphrase his 45-minute presentation into a single sentence, he said, "Look at nature, and see what it throws up at you, and then think what you can do with the result."

The Web is full of such experiments, and no hacks book would be complete without one or two such excursions.

Fractals

To get the following information on nature, I had a short conversation with my girlfriend Karen. We have a neat division of labor: she deals with the garden, and I deal with the computer.

Here's what I learned without having to set foot outside. Trees follow a very basic pattern, and this is usually regular. A branch will be straight for a certain length and will then split. The thickness of the parent branch is usually related to the branches that grow from it—normally the cross-section is conserved (the total thickness of the trunk is roughly the same as, or proportional to, the thickness of the branches that sprout from it). This means that a twig grows and splits in exactly the same way as a main branch: the relative dimensions are the same. You know that this self-same process between tree and twig is going on because, if you plant a twig (well, if Karen plants it; mine always dies), you end up with a tree.

With this in mind, I created a random tree generator. Two example results are shown in Figure 1-28.

Both trees (and many more) were created using the same code. Here is *tree-Gen.fla*, which is downloadable from the book's web site:

```
function counter( ) {
  if (branchCounter == undefined) {
    branchCounter = 0;
  }
  return (branchCounter++);
}

function grow( ) {
  // Grow this limb...
  this.lineStyle(trunkThickness, 0x0, 100);
  this.moveTo(0, 0);
  this.lineTo(0, trunkLength);
  // If this isn't the trunk, change the angle and branch size
  if (this._name != "trunk") {
```

Figure 1-28. I think that I will never see a screenshot as lovely as a tree

```
    this._rotation = (Math.random( )*angle) - angle/2;
    this._xscale *= branchSize;
    this._yscale *= branchSize;
}
// Grow buds...
var seed = Math.ceil(Math.random( )*branch);
for (var i = 0; i < seed; i++) {
    if (counter( ) < 3000) {
    var segment = this.createEmptyMovieClip("segment" + i, i);
    segment.onEnterFrame = grow;
    segment._y = trunkLength;      }
```

```
    }
  delete (this.onEnterFrame);
}

// Define the trunk position and set the onEnterFrame handler to grow( )
this.createEmptyMovieClip("trunk", 0);
trunk._x = 200;
trunk._y = 400;
trunk.onEnterFrame = grow;

// Tree parameters
var angle = 100;
var branch = 5;
var trunkThickness = 8;
var trunkLength = -100;
var branchSize = 0.7;
```

The basic tree shape is defined by the parameters in the last few lines of the listing:

angle
> The maximum angle a branch makes with its parent

branch
> The maximum number of buds (daughter branches) any branch can have

trunkThickness
> The thickness of the tree trunk

trunkLength
> The tree trunk's length

branchSize
> The ratio between the daughter branch and the parent branch (which makes branches get smaller as you move away from the trunk)

First, we create the trunk and set its position. We then attach *grow( )* as its *onEnterFrame* event handler. As its name suggests, *grow( )* makes our empty movie clip grow by doing two things. First, it creates our branch by drawing a vertical line of height trunkLength and thickness trunkThickness. If we are currently drawing the trunk, we leave it as-is, resulting in scene 1. If we are not drawing the trunk, we also rotate it by +/- angle, as seen in scene 2, and scale it by branchSize; as seen in scene 3; all are shown in Figure 1-29.

The code then creates between 1 and branch new buds. The hacky part is that these buds are given the same *onEnterFrame* event handler as the current one, namely *grow( )*, so in the next frame, the buds grow their own buds and so on. Here is the portion of *grow( )* that spawns a new movie clip for each bud and assigns the *onEnterFrame* event handler. Our tree could

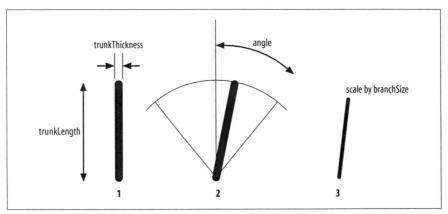

Figure 1-29. Grow, baby, grow

create new branches forever, but we need a limit; otherwise, Flash slows down and eventually crashes. To prevent this, the function *counter( )* is used to limit the total number of branches to 3,000.

```
var seed = Math.ceil(Math.random( )*branch);
for (var i = 0; i < seed; i++) {
  if (counter( ) < 3000) {
    var segment = this.createEmptyMovieClip("segment" + i, i);
    segment.onEnterFrame = grow;
    segment._y = trunkLength;  }
}
```

Finally, *grow( )* deletes itself, as it needs to run only once per branch.

So, we are using a self-calling function (or, rather, one that creates copies of branches that contain the same function attached to them) to create our fractal tree. Not only do we have a tree consisting of branches and sub-branches, but we also have the same hierarchy reflected in the movie clip timelines. You can see this by using the debugger (although you will have to set the maximum number of branches down from 3000; otherwise, you will be in for a long wait!).

The result is vaguely oriental in its simplicity. However, it doesn't involve motion graphics, and static Java tree generators are a dime a dozen. Therefore, we add movement to our tree in the next hack.

Blowin' in the Wind: Simulate Tree Movement
#7
Create forward kinematics with embedded movie clips.

We saw in the preceding hack how to generate a random tree. In this hack, we'll animate it. When trees move, they seem to follow the same tree-branch-twig hierarchy we used when generating the tree. It took me a while to work it out, although it's completely obvious once you grasp it:

- When the tree trunk moves, the whole tree moves.
- When a branch moves, all its daughter branches move.

The part that takes a bit of insight, though, is to figure out how much each part of the tree moves. I assumed that the trunk moves much less than the twigs at the fringes of the tree, but this isn't so. To see for yourself, plant a twig (cut up to its branch point) in the ground during a wind. You'll see it moves as much or as little as the trunk. The twig is weaker, but its surface area (assuming it has no leaves) is also less than the trunk, so the wind force is to the same scale.

A twig at the top of a tree moves more than the trunk simply because the motion of each branch in the hierarchy that supports it also moves, and all these movements are added cumulatively as you move up the tree. Wow! You learn something every day.

That tip for the day makes it easy to add a wind effect—you simply treat each branch the same as the trunk and all other branches!

Rather than delete each *onEnterFrame( )* handler as we did in our original tree-creation code [Hack #6], change this line that removed the *grow( )* function as the *onEnterFrame( )* handler:

```
delete (this.onEnterFrame);
```

and replace it with the *sway( )* function, once the branch is grown:

```
this.onEnterFrame = sway;
```

To create the wind effect, simply create a *sway( )* function that specifies a wind value that is added to each branch every frame using our new *sway( )* function:

```
function sway( ) {
  this._rotation += wind;
}
```

We need to vary the sway value, and here's one simple way to do it:

```
function sway( ) {
  wind += windEffect;
  if (wind > windStrength) {
    wind = -wind;
  }
  this._rotation += wind;
}
```

Of course, you need to provide initial values for the wind-related parameters. Here are the final values I plugged in for this example (new wind parameters are shown in bold):

```
// Tree parameters
var angle = 100;
var branch = 5;
var trunkThickness = 8;
var trunkLength = -100;
var branchSize = 0.7;
// Wind parameters
var windEffect = 0.05;
var windStrength = 1;
var wind = 0;
```

You can add some manual sliders to let the user control it interactively [Hack #61].

Figure 1-30 shows the tree bending in the wind. See *tree02.fla* from this book's web site for the motion graphics version in all its glory.

Figure 1-30. Tree in the wind

Final Thoughts

Although there's one or two bits of hacky code going on here, the real hack is the way of thinking. Copying from nature or whatever is around you is a time-tested way to get new inputs and insights into your Flash design.

One of the cool things about Flash that allows this form of exploration is that Flash is a graphic programming environment. You can create the code and get immediate graphical feedback. If you make more than one tree, experiment to see whether applying the same wind to all trees makes for a more realistic effect. I suspect a slight variation among trees would look more realistic, especially if the wind is coming from a direction where it would be blocked by other trees.

My personal muse is not nature but video games. I believe that all problems faced by motion graphics designers have already been faced and overcome by a video game production team, but that, as they say, is a different story.

CHAPTER TWO

Color Effects

Hacks 8–13

Although most Flash animators concentrate on animated movement and scaling when creating motion graphics, you can also animate color to create fades and transitions.

The compelling thing about animating color for the designer is that it can change both appearance and mood with little effort (and virtually no filesize increase). Changing the color scheme of a Flash animation allows you to create wide-ranging effects, such as shifting the animation from day to night. Changing the color of an image to sepia tones will give an old-time mood, whereas changing the colors to electric blues can be used to give a more techno feel.

You can apply color changes to anything that can be placed within a movie clip, including bitmaps, video, and vector graphics. In fact, anything that can be displayed on the Flash Stage can be color animated, and this animation can be controlled by tweens (performed at authoring time in the timeline) or ActionScript (performed at runtime).

This makes it easy to add runtime color effects, allowing you to make content appear more interesting with little or no bandwidth penalties. We will see how color effects can be applied to bitmaps to make them look more interesting, more in tune with a site design, or even to make your stationary bitmaps take on some of the features of video via video-like color transitions.

We will also look at applying color transitions to video, allowing you to make a short, repetitive video look like a much longer or more visually interesting one. Given that video is the most bandwidth-heavy asset, you can also optimize video content delivery by adding complex video transitions at runtime rather than applying them to the video source.

SWF files are one of the few web-based graphic assets in which color is "free"—there is no bandwidth penalty for adding lots of different colors to a Flash site. The downside is that you need to be more careful in managing this high level of choice. Therefore, we will look at several novel ways to manage color or to create sensible palettes quickly.

Finally, no review of Flash color is complete without looking at Action-Script. The options available for animating with color go up dramatically when you use scripting, and we will look at creating custom color effects that are written using ActionScript 2.0 object-oriented (OO) code.

HACK #8 Video Color Effects

Simulate a video transition using Flash color effects.

This hack alters video using the *Color* class to create a unique type of color transition. This is not an obvious technique and not one ordinarily applied to video transitions, but that's the whole point of a hack—to explore the nonobvious.

The Boy Can't Dance

You can always tell when videographers have to create a pop music video with a singer who can't move to the beat in a hip sort of way. In such a case, the videographer moves the camera or adds lots of video transitions and effects that are in sync with the music. That way, you get onscreen movement in time with the beat even if the band is standing hopelessly still and nodding their heads in a 70s prog-rock kinda way.

Flash video poses a similar challenge: video is bandwidth-heavy, and to keep compression ratios as high as possible, we have to create sequences in which not much changes between frames. Most codecs, including the Sorenson codec that Flash uses, perform both spatial and temporal compression. Spatial compression is performed by looking for similarities within the frame (for example, a solid colored background compresses very easily). Temporal compression is achieved by looking at consecutive frames and including only *deltas* (differences) between the frames. It therefore makes sense to reduce large-scale movement in our videos, allowing the *difference frames*, which contain only the deltas between frames, to be as bandwidth-light as possible. (For want of a better analogy, difference frames are akin to the tween frames used in animation within Flash's timeline. Video, like animation, has keyframes as well.) Video keyframes are used to maintain image quality and to handle situations in which the differences between frames are so large as to make difference frames inefficient. Therefore, more changes per frame requires either larger difference frames or more keyframes.

This leaves us stuck in the same situation as the pop music video; we can't have too much big movement in our visuals without a massive increase in the download size of the video.

The trick, as in pop music videos, is to add movement or effects somewhere else. We apply the effects programmatically at runtime (on the client side) so you don't affect the video compression (i.e., the bandwidth required) by adding big interframe discontinuities.

> The key to saving bandwidth without boring the viewer is to programmatically introduce variations that don't exist in the source video.

For example, you can also use runtime video effects to hide the fact that your video is looping, another popular way of conserving bandwidth. You can also make the video effects user-controllable, thus adding variation by making it an interactive element instead of a linear video.

Color Coding

You have probably applied colors to movie clips using the Advanced Effect dialog box shown in Figure 2-1. If you've never used color effects before, you can set up a color tween as follows:

1. Draw a black circle on stage in frame 1 and convert it to a movie clip symbol (F8).

2. Insert a keyframe in frame 10 by selecting frame 10 in the main timeline and choosing Insert → Timeline → Keyframe.

3. Click on the keyframe in frame 1, and apply a motion tween to the movie clip instance by setting the Tween option in the Properties panel to Motion.

4. Click on the keyframe in frame 10. Then use the Selection tool to click on the Stage to deselect the frame. Finally, click on the movie clip instance on stage to select it.

5. Set the Color option in the Properties panel to Advanced.

6. Click the Settings button in the Properties panel to open the Advanced Effect dialog box, and set the rb value, as indicated in Figure 2-1, to 200. Click OK to close the dialog box.

If you scrub the playhead across the first 10 frames of the timeline, you should see the movie clip change slowly from black to red, effectively creating a color transition. (If you didn't apply the motion tween properly, the clip remains black until frame 9 and then suddenly turns red in frame 10.)

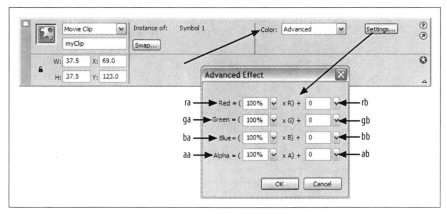

Figure 2-1. The Advanced Effect dialog box is used for applying color transformations

So far, so good. But how do you apply the color transition to a video at run-time? You can use the *Color* class to apply a similar transform to any movie clip, including a movie clip containing a video. The *Color.setTransform( )* method accepts one argument, a *transform object* with properties ra, ga, ba, aa, rb, gb, bb, and ab. So now you're thinking, "Whuh?"

A transform object (a.k.a. *transObject*) is just an instance of the *Object* class that contains properties used to perform the color transformation. The eight properties simply correspond to the values of the eight fields in the Advance Effect dialog box, as shown in Figure 2-1. To get a feel for what the properties do, play around with the Advanced Effect values manually.

Manually applying advanced color effects to a bitmap photograph image embedded inside a movie clip will give you the best indication of what can be done with color and a video instance. Experiment with one or more still images captured from the video for best results.

Color Video Transforms

This hack creates one typical transform type: an instantaneous effect, such as going quickly from normal color film to the photographic negative for a few frames, before returning back to normal. This looks really cool if you also sync sound to the same effect [Hack #59]. This technique can be extended to create another typical effect: fades and other gradual transitions [Hack #9].

Let's look at instantaneous effects first. Figure 2-2 shows the original image and Figure 2-3 and Figure 2-4 show two possible effects.

Figure 2-2 shows the original image, with a neutral transform of:

```
{ra:100, rb:0, ga:100, gb:0, ba:100, bb:0, aa:100, ab:0}
```

Figure 2-2. Original image (neutral transform)

Figure 2-3 shows the inverted image, with a transform of:

```
{ra:-100, rb:255, ga:-100, gb:255, ba:-100, bb:255, aa:100, ab:0}
```

Figure 2-3. Inverse image

You are not limited to the negative effect, though. Scripted transforms allow you to overdrive further than the UI will take you via the Advanced Effect dialog box. Figure 2-4 shows a high-contrast transform:

```
{ra:500, rb:-500, ga:500, gb:-500, ba:500, bb:-500, aa:100, ab:0}
```

Figure 2-4. High-contrast image

You can create lots of other effects, such as the "washout effect" in which the image appears overexposed, using the following transform to lighten the image:

```
{ra:100, rb:150, ga:100, gb:150, ba:100, bb:150, aa:100, ab:0}
```

You can boost the red tones with a transform of:

```
{ra:500, rb:-500, ga:100, gb:0, ba:100, bb:0, aa:100, ab:0}
```

You can darken an image with a transform of:

```
{ra:100, rb:-150, ga:100, gb:-150, ba:100, bb:-150, aa:100, ab:0}
```

For full appreciation of the effects, see the sample images or *colortransforms.fla* file downloadable from this book's web site.

The following code applies an instantaneous color spot transform to any content inside a movie clip:

```
function negativeFlick(targetClip, duration) {
  this.neutralizer = function() {
    negColor.setTransform(neutral);
    // Refresh the screen
    updateAfterEvent();
    // Clear the interval
    clearInterval(negInterval);
  };
  // Define a transform that reverses the current colors
  var negTrans = {ra:-100, rb:255, ga:-100, gb:255,
                  ba:-100, bb:255, aa:100,  ab:0};
  // Define and apply a neutral transform to cancel the effect
  var neutral = {ra:100, rb:0, ga:100, gb:0, ba:100, bb:0, aa:100, ab:0};
  // Target the specified clip and apply the transform
  var negColor = new Color(targetClip);
  negColor.setTransform(negTrans);
  // Set up a callback to reverse the effect some time later
  var negInterval = setInterval(this.neutralizer, duration);
}
```

Here we invoke the effect for one second on a clip named `bitmapClip`, which presumably is a clip we've created that contains a bitmap (make sure you give the clip an instance name of `bitmapClip` using the Properties panel):

```
negativeFlick(bitmapClip, 1000);
```

To apply the effect to a video, call *negativeFlick( )* with the name of the clip containing the video. Here is an example in which the effect is applied to a clip named `myVideo_mc` for two seconds (2000 milliseconds). Again, you should set the instance name of the clip, which presumably contains a video, using the Properties panel:

```
negativeFlick(myVideo_mc, 2000);
```

Typically, the script that defines the *negativeFlick( )* function and the call that invokes it are attached to a separate *actions* layer.

To invoke *negativeFlick( )* from the timeline of the myVideo_mc video clip, you would use:

```
negativeFlick(this, 2000);
```

The *negativeFlick( )* function creates a *Color* instance and uses it to apply our transformation to the target clip. The last line of *negativeFlick( )* also sets up an interval (i.e., a timer using *setInterval( )*) that invokes *neutralizer( )*. The *neutralizer( )* function negates our transformation by applying a neutral transform. The code clears the interval to prevent it from repeating, as it would periodically if we failed to clear it.

Note that *setInterval( )* is not tied directly to the frame rate, so the callback function, in this case *neutralizer( )*, will typically execute before other frame-based events (such as *onEnterFrame*). When using *setInterval( )* to produce graphic effects, the usefulness of having a non-frame-based event is lost if you have to wait for the next frame before you see the animated effect it creates. Therefore, the call to *updateAfterEvent( )* addresses the issue by forcing a screen refresh at the end of the callback function.

So, in this hack, we've seen several keys to applying color transforms to video:

- Use a color transform object to transform the video's color.
- Use an interval and a callback function to make the change temporary.
- Use a neutral color transform to restore the original colors.

These techniques aren't limited to videos. You can target any movie clip or even the main timeline. Furthermore, you need not reset the color scheme using a neutral transform. You could apply a random color transform periodically, for example. In that case, you would want to randomize the values of the color transform object's properties (instead of using a neutral transform in the callback function), and you wouldn't want to clear the interval in the callback function. See the *ActionScript Cookbook* by Joey Lott (O'Reilly) for more examples of using color transformations and generating random numbers.

HACK #9 Video Fade to Black and Fade to White

Create fade to black and fade to white video transitions.

Transitions can be applied to both still images and videos. For example, you can apply a color transformation to a video [Hack #8] to create instantaneous color effects. This hack applies a color transformation over time to create fade effects.

Transitions Over Time

For a time-based transition, we need a code structure that allows us to apply incremental changes to the color values over a number of frames. Two common transitions are "fade to black" and "fade to white." The color transform objects you need to end up with an all-black or all-white image are as follows:

```
transToBlack ={ra:100, rb:-255, ga:100, gb:-255,
               ba:100, bb:-255, aa:100, ab:0};
transToWhite ={ra:100, rb:255, ga:100, gb:255,
               ba:100, bb:255, aa:100, ab:0};
```

You will notice that these transforms change only the offset values (to either +255 or -255). The result is that the RGB value R:255, G:255, B:255 is added to each pixel to create a fade to white, or subtracted from each pixel to create a fade to black. Given that the three color channels have a range of 0 to 255 (0x00 to 0xFF in hex), this fades each pixel to either 255 (white) or 0 (black), regardless of the pixel's original color.

The following code gives us a way of spreading this color change over a number of frames to produce a fade over time:

```
function trans(targetClip, frames, targetTrans) {
  var transCol = new Color(targetClip);
  // Get the current color transform applied to the clip, if any
  var getTrans = transCol.getTransform( );
  var diffTrans = new Object( );
  // Calculate the differences for each of the 8 properties
  // and store them in the diffTrans color object.
  for (var i in targetTrans) {
    diffTrans[i] = (targetTrans[i]-getTrans[i])/frames;
  }
  targetClip.onEnterFrame = function( ) {
    var getTrans = transCol.getTransform( );
    for (var i in diffTrans) {
      getTrans[i] += diffTrans[i];
    }
    transCol.setTransform(getTrans);
    frames--;
    if (frames == 0) {
      // Explicitly set the target transform just in case the
      // target numbers were not exactly divisible by the
      // number of frames, then clean up.
      transCol.setTransform(targetTrans);
      delete this.onEnterFrame;
      delete transCol;
    }
  };
}
```

We need to know three things to animate a color video transition: the target clip (inside which the video is embedded), the number of frames we want the transition to occur for, and the transition type, such as fade to black or fade to white (or more correctly, the associated color transform object).

This is all covered by the arguments to our *trans( )* function: `targetClip`, `frames`, and `targetTrans`. For example, here we use it to set a fade to white transition on a video within the `myVideo_mc` clip, over a duration of 24 frames:

```
transToWhite = {ra:100, rb:255, ga:100, gb:255, ba:100, bb:255, aa:100, ab:
0};
trans(myVideo_mc, 24, transToWhite);
```

The *trans( )* function does three things.

First, it extracts the current color transform object applied to the target clip, using *Color.getTransform( )*, and stores it in `getTrans`. Then, it sets up an object, `diffTrans`, which tells us how much we need to add to `getTrans` every frame to end up at the final transform, `targetTrans`, within the specified number of frames. Assuming that no other transforms have been applied in the authoring tool, `getTrans` is always:

```
{ra:100, rb:0, ga:100, gb:0, ba:100, bb:0, aa:100, ab:0}
```

Why? If no transform has been applied, `getTrans` is a neutral transform object—the same one you will see in the Advanced Effects panel, shown in Figure 2-1, when no color changes are applied.

And `targetTrans` is whatever was specified in the *trans( )* function invocation. For fade to white, `targetTrans` is:

```
{ra:100, rb:255, ga:100, gb:255, ba:100, bb:255, aa:100, ab:0}
```

Subtracting `targetTrans` from `getTrans` and dividing by the number of frames gives us the difference to be applied during each frame iteration. We store these values in the `diffTrans` object:

```
diffTrans[i] = (targetTrans[i]-getTrans[i])/frames;
```

Following through with our preceding example, including a 24-frame transition, `diffTrans` would be:

```
{ra: 0 rb:10.625, ga:0, gb:10.625, ba:0, bb:10.625, aa:0, ab:0}
```

Finally, the *trans( )* function needs to set up an *onEnterFrame( )* handler to animate our color transition from `getTrans` to `targetTrans` over time. This is accomplished by defining a function and assigning it to the `onEnterFrame` property, as shown in the preceding code example.

In all honesty, applying a transition over a set number of frames doesn't make the most sense. Videos are time-based media, so we should rightly perform the color transformation over multiple steps using a time-based interval (created with *setInterval( )*). Time-based intervals make it easier to use the effect with a video and make the transition duration independent of the timeline's frame rate.

So the frame-based technique really is more useful for applying color transformations to movie clips that don't contain videos. We demonstrated the time-based method earlier [Hack #8], so let's examine the frame-based technique more closely here.

The *onEnterFrame( )* handler defined within *trans( )* adds diffTrans to the current transform object each frame until the effect is completed:

```
for (var i in diffTrans) {
  getTrans[i] += diffTrans[i];
}
transCol.setTransform(getTrans);
```

At the end of the transition, the transform may not have reached its target due to rounding errors, so we need to explicitly set it just to make sure. After we have done that, all we need to do to finish is clean up.

```
frames--;
if (frames == 0) {
  // Explicitly set the target transform just in case the
  // target numbers were not exactly divisible by the
  // number of frames, then clean up.
  transCol.setTransform(targetTrans);
  delete this.onEnterFrame;
  delete transCol;
}
```

Try running the script with other transformations, such as those earlier in this hack and the preceding hack.

Final Thoughts

The cool thing about the preceding two hacks is that they can target any movie clip, not just those containing video. For example, targeting _root allows you to apply transitions to the entire SWF file at runtime (although this might be too processor-intensive to be practical in some situations). As well as producing some cool effects, color transforms also have practical uses: inverting the color of all content on the Stage for 100 milliseconds might signify an incorrect response (Windows changes the screen color briefly to alert users of errors if you enable accessibility options, because a beep noise isn't audible to hearing-impaired users).

Adding video-like color transitions to something that is static (such as a bitmap) also has a big advantage: it can fool users into thinking that they are watching a video, particularly if you are really sly and have actual video portions mixed into the sequence. This technique works wonders for hiding your video preloads!

The more observant among you may have noticed that I haven't altered the alpha channel in the color transformation examples presented. However, to adjust the alpha channel, simply specify a transform object in which the ra, ga, ba, or aa properties are not equal to 100. By adjusting the alpha channel, you can start doing some really cool things such as cross-fades, in which you fade from one video clip into another (or even better, cross-fade seamlessly between video and Flash vector content). Alpha transitions are processor-intensive, but lucky for us, Flash Player 7 has a much faster video playback engine, so even that is not a big problem anymore.

The same principles apply to sound transforms. You can use sound transform objects supported by the *Sound* class to add scripted volume effects and cross-speaker fades [Hack #60].

A Custom Color Transform Class
#10   Create a custom class to perform color transformations.

We saw in the preceding two hacks that there are several common color transformations [Hack #8] you may want to perform on a target clip. Furthermore, we saw that this requires a bit of housekeeping, including setting up timers and callbacks [Hack #9]. The nature of the task suggests that it is a great candidate to be implemented as a custom class. The class can take care of all the grunt work, allowing us to perform a color transformation or fade using a few simple calls to the custom class's methods. In this hack, we implement a custom color transform class in ActionScript 2.0 using object-oriented programming (OOP) instead of the procedural timeline-based code seen in the preceding hacks.

An Object-Oriented Transformation

Using ActionScript 2.0 requires Flash MX 2004 or Flash MX Professional 2004. You must set the ActionScript Version to ActionScript 2.0 under the Flash tab in the File → Publish Settings dialog box. Furthermore, the custom *Transform* class we'll develop must be placed in an external plain-text file named *Transform.as* (both the capitalization of the name and the *.as* extension are mandatory). You can create and edit such a file in Flash MX Professional 2004 if you select File → New → ActionScript File. If using Flash MX

2004, you'll need an external text editor [Hack #74]. The *.as* file should be placed in the same folder as the *.fla* file that makes use of the *Transform* class. For many more details on ActionScript 2.0 classes and object-oriented development, see *Essential ActionScript 2.0* by Colin Moock (O'Reilly).

Although we can't give a full course on OOP and ActionScript 2.0 here, this custom color transform class can be used even if you don't understand OOP. And we'll examine several aspects of the code after the code listing.

Here is our object-oriented version, implemented as a custom *Transform* class, which must be stored in an external *Transform.as* file:

```
// This ActionScript 2.0 code must go in an external Transform.as file
class Transform {
  // NEG_TRANS inverts the color values.
  // NEUTRAL_TRANS resets the color values.
  // BLACK_TRANS sets the color values to black.
  // WHITE_TRANS sets the color values to white.
  // RATE sets the rate the effects will run at in ms.
  private static var NEG_TRANS:Object = {ra:-100, rb:255,
                          ga:-100, gb:255, ba:-100, bb:255, aa:100, ab:0};
  private static var NEUTRAL_TRANS:Object = {ra:100, rb:0,
                          ga:100, gb:0, ba:100, bb:0, aa:100, ab:0};
  private static var BLACK_TRANS:Object = {ra:100, rb:-255,
                          ga:100, gb:-255, ba:100, bb:-255, aa:100, ab:0};
  private static var WHITE_TRANS:Object = {ra:100, rb:255,
                          ga:100, gb:255, ba:100, bb:255, aa:100, ab:0};
  private static var RATE:Number = 50;

  private var interval:Number;
  private var startTime:Number;
  private var colorObj:Color;
  // Constructor accepts target clip to which to apply transforms
  public function Transform(targetClip:MovieClip) {
    colorObj = new Color(targetClip);
  }
  // Inverts the color values
  public function invert(duration:Number):Void {
    applyTransform(NEG_TRANS, duration);
  }

  // Resets the color to the default values set in the authoring tool
  public function reset(duration:Number):Void {
    applyTransform(NEUTRAL_TRANS, duration);
  }

  // Performs a fade to black over specified duration in ms
  public function fadeToBlack(duration:Number):Void {
    applyTransform(BLACK_TRANS, duration);
  }
```

```
// Performs a fade to white over specified duration in ms
public function fadeToWhite(duration:Number):Void {
  applyTransform(WHITE_TRANS, duration);
}

// Function to initiate a fade and set up an interval to
// complete it over time.
private function applyTransform(transObject:Object,
                               duration:Number):Void {
  var getTrans:Object = colorObj.getTransform( );
  var diffTrans:Object = new Object( );
  startTime = getTimer( );
  for (var i in transObject) {
    diffTrans[i] = (transObject[i] - getTrans[i]) / (duration / RATE);
  }
  // Use the form of setInterval( ) that invokes a method of an object,
  // so that instance properties are in scope (the object is this).
  // First parameter is the object (this) on which to invoke the
  // method specified by the second parameter (in this case
  // "transition", which must be passed as a string).
  // Third parameter is interval duration in ms.
  // Fourth, fifth, and sixth parameters get passed to transition( )
  interval = setInterval(this, "transition", RATE, transObject, diffTrans,
                         duration);
}

// This method applies each step of the color transformation.
private function transition(transObject:Object, diffTrans:Object,
duration:Number):Void {
  var getTrans:Object = colorObj.getTransform( );
  for (var i in diffTrans) {
    getTrans[i] += diffTrans[i];
  }
  colorObj.setTransform(getTrans);
  if (getTimer( ) - startTime > duration) {
    // Complete the final step in the transition
    colorObj.setTransform(transObject);
    // Clear the interval to stop the effect
    clearInterval(interval);
  }
  // Force the screen to refresh between frames
  updateAfterEvent( );
}

public function die( ):Void {
  // Perform any cleanup code here
}
}
```

There's a lot of code there, so let's take a closer look. But first, you may wonder why we didn't add the methods of our custom *Transform* class to the *MovieClip* or *Color* class. In ActionScript 1.0, doing so would have been common and even recommended. But in ActionScript 2.0, the preferred approach in most cases is to create a custom class rather than enhancing existing classes.

If you are not familiar with ActionScript 2.0 syntax, notice the class keyword used to define the class. Several variables are declared for the class and its instances, outside of any of the methods within the class. The *static properties* or *class properties*, defined with the keyword static, are defined once for the class (here, we've initialized various common transformation types and the refresh rate at which we want our transitions to work, RATE, is set to 50 milliseconds).

The remaining variables declared without the keyword static are *instance properties* (i.e., each instance of the class maintains its own value for the property). The private keyword identifies class properties and instance properties that are not to be accessed from outside the class. Variables declared within a method, such as getTrans, which is declared within *applyTransform( )*, are local variables. The datatypes for all variables, properties, parameters, and method return types are specified using a colon followed by the datatype, such as :Number.

It is good practice to use a standardized variable-naming convention in all code, but because of the precise structuring and datatyping of OOP code, it is perhaps more important here than in other coding styles. Constant variable names (i.e., our static datatypes) have been defined in UPPERCASE, and non-constants have been defined in so-called "camelCase" (a mixture of upper- and lowercase).

Next, notice the constructor function, *Transform( )*, optional in Action-Script 2.0, which is used to initialize instances of the class. Our constructor accepts the target clip to be used later by other methods of the class. The class then defines several public methods that can be invoked on instances of the class, such as *invert( )* and *fadeToWhite( )*, and private methods that are for internal use only.

Notice in particular the form of the *setInterval( )* invocation. In this case, the first parameter passed is an object. We invoke *setInterval( )* with the keyword this, which represents the current object (i.e., the instance of the *Transform* class on which *applyTransform( )* was invoked). The second parameter is the name of the method to invoke on this, namely "transition" (which must be specified as a string). Thus, at the appropriate time, the *Transform.transition( )* method is invoked on the current instance, this. Invoking a method on the current instance ensures that instance properties, such as interval and colorObj, are in scope within *transition( )*. The fourth and fifth parameters passed to *setInterval( )*, diffTrans and duration, are passed as parameters to *transition( )*, when it is invoked. The *transition( )* method performs the specified transform over the specified duration and clears the interval when complete.

To use the code, first instantiate an instance of the *Transform* class, as follows (where myVideo_mc is an existing movie clip whose instance name has been set in the Properties panel):

```
var transformer:Transform = new Transform(myVideo_mc);
```

Then, invoke any methods of the class on the object:

```
transformer.invert(3000);      // Invert the colors for 3 seconds
transformer.fadeToWhite(2000);  // Fade to white over 2 seconds
```

To clean up when you are done, use:

```
transformer.die( );
delete transformer;
```

Consider enhancing this custom class to implement additional features, such as:

- Making the RATE value user-definable.

- Adding controls to repeat the transitions. This would allow blinking or other repetitive effects.

- Adding more complex methods that involve more than one movie clip, allowing cross-fades between two movie clips. This would introduce some powerful effects useful with video.

The use of ActionScript 2.0 allows you to create new features that can be accessed via methods of new classes. This is the preferred way of building up libraries of commonly used features not native to ActionScript.

For many designers, the ActionScript 2.0 OOP coding style may initially seem a little long-winded because more lines of code seem to be concerned with building up the code structure than actually solving the problem at hand, especially for modest classes. This extra structure is, however, a real advantage in the long term. It gives you a structured way to make your code flexible enough to reuse in several different applications and also makes your code easier to transfer to other users (which is particularly useful in a design environment consisting of an ActionScript coder and several non-scripting designers).

Finally, although OOP code may appear longer than other styles of code, the compiled bytecode can be more efficient [Hack #100]. Flash Player 7 is optimized for OOP code. Benchmarking of well-written OOP code against procedural ActionScript shows that OOP can increase performance through the greater use of local variables and passing of data as arguments, both of which tend to create more optimized bytecode.

Create and Organize Custom Swatches

#11   Save and organize your color swatches without having to use the Color Swatches panel.

One of the most important factors in setting the mood and graphic impact of your Flash site is the color scheme. You can save the current palette from the Color Swatches panel as a Flash color set (CLR file). However, incorporating the colors in the Color Swatches panel into your workflow, such as arranging your colors into meaningful groups, isn't easy.

Of course, there's nothing stopping you from creating your own swatches. Simply create a layer called *swatches*, turn it into a guide layer (using Modify → Timeline → Layer Properties → Type → Guide), and add a few rectangles in which to store your colors. Just as oil painters keep a separate painting area on which to test colors before committing them to the final work, you can create as many ordered swatches as you want. To change or read the color of a particular swatch, use the paint bucket and eyedropper, respectively.

Figure 2-5 depicts storing skin tone and lip colors as a series of swatches outside the Stage area in the FLA document. Because the swatches are on a guide layer, they will not be exported as part of the final SWF.

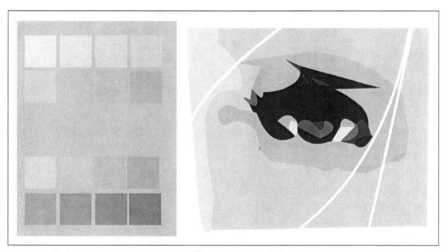

Figure 2-5. Storing custom swatches off stage in a guide layer

Of course, there is still the problem of getting your colors into Flash in the first place.

Importing Colors

The Color Swatches panel contains that aging dinosaur of a bygone era, the web-safe palette. For the most part, the web-safe palette is no longer relevant. If a computer cannot display more than 256 colors, chances are it doesn't support the Flash Player (the exception might be handheld devices).

Furthermore, the web-safe palette is designed to work on hardware that can display a palette based on standard memory sizes (8, 16, or 32 bits). Web-safe colors do not display accurately on computers set to display 24-bit color.

If you use a gradient in Flash, you are no longer using web-safe colors, even if the colors controlling your gradients are taken from the web-safe palette.

You can use Photoshop to create your color palettes (you could also use Fireworks). The Swatches tab in Photoshop, shown in Figure 2-6, has the ability to display many more palettes than just web-based ones; it also includes many print-based presets.

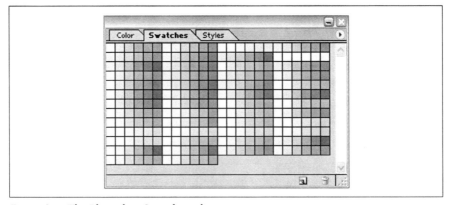

Figure 2-6. The Photoshop Swatches tab

Unfortunately, Flash does not allow you to import a native ACO (Adobe Color palette) Photoshop swatch file. Not to worry; both Flash and Photoshop understand another (rather well-hidden) palette format, the ACT (Adobe Color Table) file.

An ACT file can be created only from an image that uses indexed color, typically a GIF or PNG-8.

To create such a palette in Photoshop:

1. Create your image.
2. Select File → Save for Web.

3. Select either GIF or PNG-8 in the Settings section of the Save for Web dialog box that appears.

4. Set the Colors drop-down list to the number of colors you want in your palette.

5. Finally, to save the palette, click on the little triangle at the top right-hand corner of the Color Table (the Color Palette Menu), as shown in Figure 2-7, and choose Save Color Table.

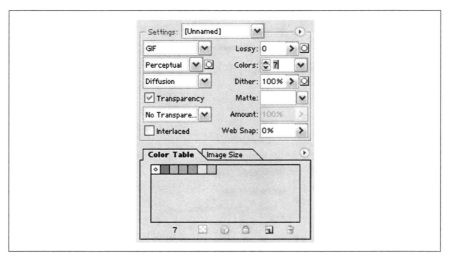

Figure 2-7. Saving a color palette file from Photoshop

Back in Flash, to load the color table, select Add Colors from the Color Swatches panel's Options menu. The colors are appended to the end of the current swatches.

A far easier way of importing colors from Photoshop is to draw a set of swatches in Photoshop using a solid brush or airbrush, as shown in Figure 2-8, then import the bitmap in a lossless format (PNG-32 of TIFF) into Flash.

Figure 2-8. An image used to move a color palette from Photoshop to Flash

The color picker will recognize the individual pixels in the bitmap. Using the bitmap in much the same way as the off-stage vector color blocks, you have a very efficient way of passing color to Flash from Photoshop.

Final Thoughts

Despite the fact that color is an important way of setting the mood and look-and-feel of your web sites, the color-based features of the Flash interface can be somewhat confounding; you cannot sort the colors of a swatch into related groups of your choosing, for example. Creating your own swatches in the workspace outside the visible Stage is a good workaround to this limitation.

Additionally, Flash's interface is not as suited to choosing and designing color schemes as is Photoshop's, so it is important to be able to export color information from Photoshop and import it into Flash.

Borrow Color Schemes from Nature
HACK #12   Sample real-world color to capture natural color combinations and schemes.

Using the Color Mixer panel is a rather artificial way of creating new color palettes [Hack #11]. The human eye is relatively poor at discerning color. A dark red set against other dark reds will appear darker if it is viewed around whites and may even appear black. This is to be expected because the human eye has evolved to discern relative differences between currently visible colors and not absolute color.

With this in mind, it is sometimes far easier to choose your color palettes by taking colors from images of real life. For example, Figure 2-9 shows the colors available in a knife blade and flower petals.

Both these images were sampled using an inexpensive flatbed scanner, which is far faster than looking up web-safe color swatches on the Web and less expensive than buying a color process swatch book!

You immediately see the trouble in trying to pick colors from either of these images, though. Adjacent pixel colors are highly variable, so if you try to pick a color from a yellow flower petal, you shouldn't be surprised if you actually sample a light green. To make selecting colors easier, we are better off making the images more friendly to the color picker. We can do this by using some Photoshop filters.

To reduce noise in the sampled image using Photoshop, select Filter → Noise → Despeckle. This reduces the problem somewhat, but still leaves us with the problem of accurately selecting colors while maintaining the image as a natural palette. Luckily, we can get to this via a single filter. Select Filter →

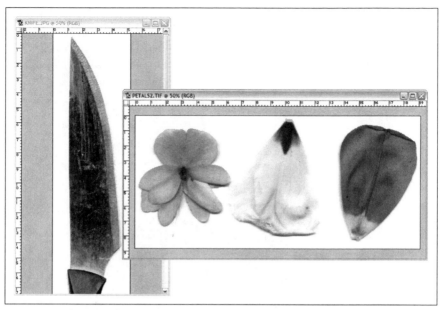

Figure 2-9. The scan of a knife blade contains a number of grays in a real-life context, and the flower scans provide real-life vivid colors

Pixelate → Pointillize. Your image will break up into a series of swatchlike daubs, looking much like an oil painter's paint swatch, as shown in Figure 2-10.

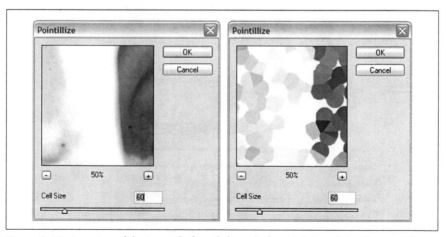

Figure 2-10. A section of the image before (left) and after (right) applying the pointillize filter

Save the image in a lossless format supported by Flash (such as PNG-32 or TIFF) and import the image into Flash.

In Flash, place the image off stage in a guide layer so that it doesn't get exported to the final SWF. Now you have an instant natural palette with colors adjacent to other colors with which it would appear in real life. To select a color from your naturally created swatch, simply use the Eyedropper tool, as shown in Figure 2-11.

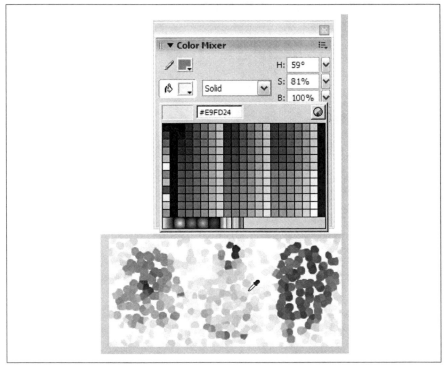

Figure 2-11. Picking a color from the swatch bitmap using the Color Mixer and Eyedropper tool

Final Thoughts

Designing color schemes in Flash (and many other applications) can be a little hit and miss, because colors that you choose in isolation look substantially different when placed with other colors. By scanning in an image of a naturally occurring object or scene that already contains your proposed color scheme and then turning it into a swatch, you can make more accurate color selections because you are viewing the colors in context. The Gliftic utility can extract color schemes from an image automatically (*http://www.ransen.com/Gliftic/Gallery/NaturalColors/Natural-Color-Schemes.htm*).

—Inspired by the work of Joshua Davis and others

Simulate Sepia Effects

HACK #13

Simulate hue/saturation effects in Flash to create sepia tone images.

Most graphics editing packages, including Photoshop and Fireworks, can change the hue and saturation of an image to create change-of-color effects, such as sepia tone effects. Flash also has this ability, although it is not immediately apparent. This hack shows how to create a sepia effect manually in Photoshop and then convert the workflow to Flash.

Creating a Sepia Effect in Photoshop

Sepia tones imitate the look of so-called sepia prints (a.k.a. albumen prints) produced in the latter half of the nineteenth century using a process invented by Louis-Desiré Blanquart-Evrard in 1850. The dark brown tones commonly associated with an antique look are not due to aging but rather caused by the original photographic development process. See the Royal Photographic Society (*http://www.rps.org/book/terms/albumen.html*) for more details on albumen prints.

If you are using a graphics editor with built-in support for sepia tone effects, the process is straightforward. For example, you can open the image in Fireworks and choose Commands → Creative → Convert to Sepia Tone.

Here we cover the more general process in Photoshop, so you can create variations beyond sepia tones. With an image open in Photoshop, select Image → Adjustments → Hue/Saturation. The Hue/Saturation window, as shown in Figure 2-12, appears. Check both the Colorize and Preview options.

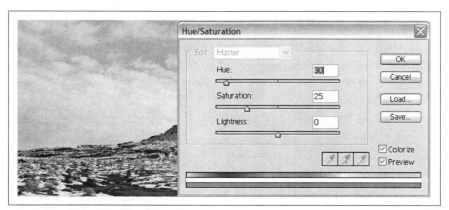

Figure 2-12. The Hue/Saturation window in Photoshop

Creating a sepia tone image consists of two steps:

1. Desaturating the image so you are left with a black-and-white image
2. Colorizing the image with a particular hue (sepia is a deep brown)

You can desaturate the image by setting the Saturation slider all the way to the left, but that's further than we want—we need some color information to remain so we can colorize. Set it to 25.

To colorize the image, set the Hue slider to a dark red/brown (0 to 30).

Note the final Hue value. You will need it when you reproduce the effect in Flash.

The original sepia photographs sometimes had a pinkish pigment, so hue values around 330 to 350 are also valid.

Reworking the Effect in Flash

Flash color effects allow you to colorize, but they do not allow desaturation because the *Color* class uses the RGB model and cannot therefore easily separate color from brightness. The only way to remove all color is to drastically increase or decrease brightness, which has the unfortunate side effect of also making your image fade to either white or black!

So, we have to start with a desaturated image. To desaturate an image in Photoshop, select Image → Adjustments → Desaturate.

Import the desaturated image into Flash and place it on the Stage. Select it and convert it into a movie clip symbol (F8). This allows us to apply color effects to the image or allows us to target the image with a *Color* instance.

Next, we need to find the color that we want. In the Color Mixer panel (Window → Design Panels → Color Mixer), select HSB mode from the panel's pop-up Options menu, then enter the Hue value you used in Photoshop (30 in our example), adding 50% and 75% for the Saturation and Brightness values, respectively, as shown in Figure 2-13. Leave the Color Mixer open.

With the movie clip containing your image selected, use the Properties panel to set the Color option to Tint. Change the Tint Amount (to the right of the color swatch) to 25%. Select the color swatch and click on the color you just created in the Color Mixer. Your image should now change color from black and white to the colorized sepia effect.

Although the Flash version of the sepia effect will have the same basic colorization, it will not maintain the bright areas as well as the Photoshop version. This is because Photoshop is performing a much more complex color

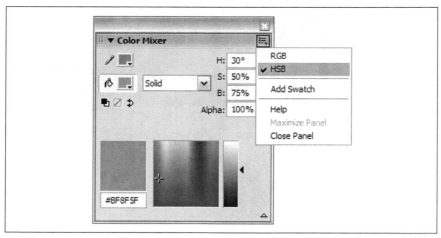

Figure 2-13. The Color Mixer panel

change (it is preserving brightness), whereas the Flash version is also coloriz-ing the highlights. This is the downside of real-time effects versus offline effects: Flash has to do things quickly so it cannot be expected to perform color changes as accurately as Photoshop.

Finally, if you want to re-create this effect in ActionScript, change the Color option to Advanced, click the Settings button, and note the color values, which can be used to specify color transforms at runtime [Hack #10].

Using the Sepia Effect in Static Graphics

Using sepia and other colorization effects at runtime allows you to add inter-est to an image without significantly adding to the filesize of the SWF. Com-bined with other effects, you can make the images look significantly different. For example, framing the image via a circular border, as shown in Figure 2-14, will hide the rectangular nature of the original image, as shown in Figure 2-15, as well as avoid the artifacts you would encounter if you faded the image directly and exported it at low image qualities consistent with web use.

As well as sepia effects, you can of course colorize images to other base col-ors. In particular, applying blue colorization and adding techno-style lines and shapes over an image creates a more modern feel, as shown in Figure 2-16. Not only does this allow your images to fit in with a techno site design, overlaying vectors over the image allows you to add movement and hide any pixelation in the image.

Replacing the film grain bitmap with a techno overlay consisting of graph lines and meaningless text (instead of film scratches and dirt) allows you to

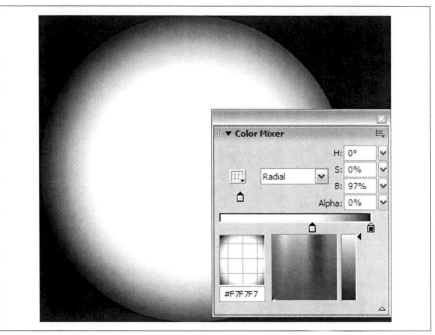

Figure 2-14. Creating a frame containing an inner hole with alpha faded edges

Figure 2-15. Displaying our sepia-colorized image through the frame

Figure 2-16. A techno style image created with blue tones and overlain text

change the old film grain [Hack #3] into something decidedly more modern. Just the thing for a client who wants a modern and edgy site or for a retailer selling hand cams to Cyborgs.

Dynamic Sepia Effects with the Color Class

You can animate the sepia effect in much the same way we add colorization effects to video [Hack #10]. Combining this hack with old film grain effect [Hack #3] gives you an image that no longer looks static, but rather like a themed video clip. Adding sepia and other colorization effects allows you to perform runtime image manipulation.

Colorization is not limited to a single bitmap. If you apply it to an entire SWF by applying it to the _root timeline, you have a quick way of changing the site color scheme. Couple this with changing between sepia and techno image overlays, and you get to change the site theme. You can also use colorization to denote different states—for example, tinting parts of the UI that are not available or tinting thumbnails in an online portfolio with slightly different color tones depending on whether the full-size image is loaded and available to be viewed.

CHAPTER THREE

Drawing and Masking
Hacks 14–25

When we say "drawing" in Flash, we can be talking about two different things. The more traditional form of drawing is freehand vector drawing as used by animators who create Flash cartoons. The other type uses scripts to do the drawing for you, something I like to call "kinetic drawing." In kinetic drawing, not only do the graphics themselves move, but you can also create the graphics in real time, and you might display the interim steps to the user for effect. To draw at runtime, we use the so-called Drawing API, which is just a collection of methods of the *MovieClip* class including *lineStyle( )*, *moveTo( )*, *lineTo( )*, and *beginFill( )*, which can be used to create strokes and fills.

For the traditional animator, this chapter includes a number of hacks to address common problems, such as reducing the pixelation around the edges of bitmaps [Hack #23] (which allows you to effectively mix bitmaps with vector content, as well as reducing the appearance of jaggies).

The scripter will find a number of fixes to common Flash problems, such as alpha property inaccuracy [Hack #19] and the bitmap "shifting pixel" problem [Hack #24]. We have also included hacky shortcuts to creating common building blocks when you are creating graphic content dynamically with scripts, such as drawing a circle with just a single straight line [Hack #14].

Drawing in Flash is a crucial ability whether you are a scripter or an artist, so the hacks presented should be some of the most accessible for all Flash users. It should come as no surprise to experienced Flashers that several hacks presented here rely on masks. If you are unfamiliar with masks, refer to the introduction to Chapter 1 for a quick primer.

Create Filled Circles Quickly at Runtime

Creating filled circles at runtime can be processor-intensive. Draw circles using a single straight line for performance and greater flexibility than author-time drawing allows.

Drawing filled rectangles with the Drawing API is relatively easy—you define four corner points and fill the area enclosed by them. Circles are more problematic. You either have to approximate the circle's curvature with multiple straight lines or use the *MovieClip.curveTo( )* method to create a series of arcs. In either case, the trigonometry slows down your code and makes it impenetrable to those of us put off by sines and cosines. Not to worry, there's a far easier way to draw filled circles in Flash—draw a single straight line.

Whenever you draw a straight line, you will notice that the ends of the line are rounded, as shown in Figure 3-1.

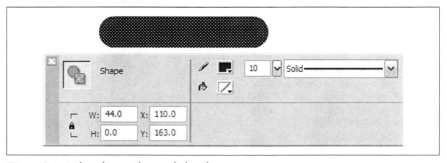

Figure 3-1. A short line with rounded ends

So you may be thinking, "Hey, I see what he's getting at. If I draw a line short enough that the two rounded ends touch, I end up with a circle, right?" Sort of. The Pencil and Line tools don't allow you to draw a line short enough, and they limit the line thickness to 10, which doesn't allow you to create large circles. And the whole idea is to draw circles at runtime, so the hack relies on ActionScript to draw very short, very thick lines. Try this:

```
var clip:MovieClip = this.createEmptyMovieClip("circle_mc",
                     this.getNextHighestDepth( ));
circle_mc._x = circle_mc._y = 150;
circle_mc.lineStyle(200, 0x0, 100);
circle_mc.moveTo(0, 0);
circle_mc.lineTo(0.2, 0);
```

The preceding code draws a circle as shown in Figure 3-2.

The circle consists of a single line 0.2 units long but of thickness 200 units. Because the line is so short, Flash draws the two curved endpoints very close together, resulting in a nearly perfect filled circle of diameter 200.

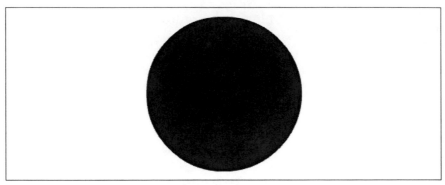

Figure 3-2. A line so short that the rounded ends form a circle

You can use this trick in all sorts of applications when you want to draw circles dynamically.

The Code

The following code (available as *dynaButton.fla* on this book's web site) creates a menu consisting of our hacky circles used as buttons. The lines in bold create our hacky circles within a movie clip:

```
function createButton(dynaButton, dynaLabel, depth, x, y) {
  var clip = this.createEmptyMovieClip(dynaButton, depth);
  clip.lineStyle(15, 0x0, 100);
  clip.moveTo(0, 0);
  clip.lineTo(0.2, 0);
  clip._x = x;
  clip._y = y;

  var txt_fmt:TextFormat = new TextFormat( );
  txt_fmt.font = "_sans";
  txt_fmt.size = 12;

  this.createTextField(dynaButton + "_txt", depth + 1,
                       x + 10, y - 10, 100, 20);
  var textLabel = this[dynaButton + "_txt"];
  textLabel.text = dynaLabel;
  textLabel.setTextFormat(txt_fmt);
}
createButton("home_btn", "home", 1, 100, 10);
createButton("products_btn", "products", 3, 100, 30);
createButton("about_btn", "about us", 5, 100, 50);
createButton("links_btn", "links we like", 7, 100, 70);

home_btn.onRelease = function( ) {
  // Do stuff
};
products_btn.onRelease = function( ) {
  // Do stuff
```

```
};
about_btn.onRelease = function( ) {
  // Do stuff
};
links_btn.onRelease = function( ) {
  // Do stuff
};
```

When you run the code, you will see the dynamically generated menu shown in Figure 3-3.

● home
● products
● about us
● links we like

Figure 3-3. A menu using hacky circles as bullet points

Hacking the Hack

To make the code much more flexible, we could extend the idea by creating an ActionScript 2.0 button-making class as follows:

```
// This ActionScript 2.0 code must go in an external CreateButton.as file
class CreateButton {
  // Variable target is the timeline that the
  // CreateButton instance will create buttons on.
  private var target:MovieClip;

  // Constructor.
  public function CreateButton(targetTimeline:MovieClip) {
    target = targetTimeline;
  }
  // Define createBtn( ) method
  // Arguments:
  //    buttonName - The instance name of the created button.
  //    dynaLabel  - The label text of the created button.
  //    depth      - The depth of the created button.
  //    x, y       - The position of the created button.
  // Returns:
  //    A button movie clip with instance name buttonName.
  public function createBtn(buttonName:String, dynaLabel:String,
                    depth:Number, x:Number, y:Number):MovieClip {
    // Initialize.
    var clip:MovieClip;
    var clipMask:MovieClip;
    var txt_fmt:TextFormat;
    var clipText:TextField;

    // Create button clip.
    clip = target.createEmptyMovieClip(buttonName, depth);
```

```
            drawPip(clip);
            clip._x = x;
            clip._y = y;

            // Create button hit area.
            clipMask = clip.createEmptyMovieClip("mask", 0);
            clipMask._visible = false;
            drawPip(clipMask);
            clip.hitArea = clipMask;

            // Create TextFormat object for applying formatting.
            txt_fmt = new TextFormat();
            txt_fmt.font = "_sans";
            txt_fmt.size = 12;

            // Create textField (i.e., the button label).
            clip.createTextField(buttonName + "_txt", 1, 10, -10, 100, 20);
            clipText = clip[buttonName+ "_txt"];
            clipText.text = dynaLabel;
            clipText.setTextFormat(txt_fmt);
            return clip;
        }
    private function drawPip(clip):Void {
        clip.lineStyle(15, 0x0, 100);
        clip.moveTo(0, 0);
        clip.lineTo(0.2, 0);
    }
}
```

To use the *CreateButton* class, place the preceding code in a file named *CreateButton.as*. Then create a new *.fla* file in the same directory as *Create-Button.as*. From this *.fla* file, create a new instance of the *CreateButton* class as follows:

```
    var buttonGen:CreateButton = new CreateButton(this);
```

The *CreateButton* class takes one argument, the timeline (i.e., main timeline or movie clip) on which we want to create buttons. Once we have created our *CreateButton* instance, we can use the *CreateButton.createBtn( )* method to create buttons on our target timeline:

```
    var home:MovieClip = buttonGen.createBtn("home", "home",
            this.getNextHighestDepth( ), 100, 10);
    var products:MovieClip = buttonGen.createBtn("products", "products",
            this.getNextHighestDepth( ), 100, 30);
    var about:MovieClip = buttonGen.createBtn("about", "about us",
            this.getNextHighestDepth( ), 100, 50);
    var links:MovieClip = buttonGen.createBtn("links", "links we like",
            this.getNextHighestDepth( ), 100, 70);

    home.onRelease = function( ) {
      trace("You clicked the home button");
    };
```

```
products.onRelease = function( ) {
  trace("You clicked the products button");
};
about.onRelease = function( ) {
  trace("You clicked the about button");
};
links.onRelease = function( ) {
  trace("You clicked the links button");
};
```

This code creates the same buttons as the previous listing, but it has a number of advantages:

- It creates more structured buttons. This time, the text label is inside the button clip. To ensure that only the button is clickable (and not the label text), the *createBtn( )* method also creates a hit area clip, mask, inside each button to define the circle as the clickable area.

- It allows you to define where the buttons are created. Simply instantiate a new *CreateButton* instance targeting the timeline on which you want to create buttons.

There have been a lot of complaints that Flash MX 2004 components are too bloated [Hack #73] if all you want are simple buttons and scrollbars [Hack #64] (the most typical UI components required). The preceding code presents a simple solution—create a component-making class of your own! Not only is this more bandwidth efficient than the Flash MX 2004 v2 components, it is also more bandwidth efficient than the older Flash MX v1 components.

Of course, knowing a hacky and quick way to generate a circle graphic makes runtime generation of the component, and also the component graphics, much easier.

> Our button-making class is less than 1 KB when compiled because it consists of code only, so it compresses very well. This makes it very useful for sites that need to be bandwidth-light, such as sites for mobile devices or the "see what you can create in 5 KB" competitions!

The circles can also be used in a Flash drawing application or 3D wire-frame toy to represent draggable points, as implemented in the following listing (available as *dynaPoint.fla* on this book's web site):

```
function createPoint(dynaPoint, depth, x, y) {
  clip = this.createEmptyMovieClip(dynaPoint, depth);
  clip.lineStyle(20, 0x0, 100);
  clip.moveTo(0, 0);
  clip.lineTo(0.2, 0);
```

```
      clip._x = x;
      clip._y = y;
    }
    function drag( ) {
      this.startDrag(true);
      paper.onMouseMove = drawLine;
      this.onPress = drop;
    }
    function drop( ) {
      this.stopDrag( );
      delete (paper.onMouseMove);
      this.onPress = drag;
    }
    function drawLine( ) {
      this.clear( );
      this.lineStyle(2, 0x0, 100);
      this.moveTo(point1._x, point1._y);
      this.lineTo(point2._x, point2._y);
      updateAfterEvent( );
    }
    // Example usage:
    createPoint("point1", 1, 100, 100);
    createPoint("point2", 2, 120, 100);
    point1.onPress = drag;
    point2.onPress = drag;
    this.createEmptyMovieClip("paper", 0);
```

To test the example, click on a point to drag it, as shown in Figure 3-4; click again to stop dragging.

Figure 3-4. Clicking and dragging a dynamic circle

As you can see from the previous two code examples, being able to create filled circles very quickly has more uses than you might realize. A single filled circle is the most commonly used shape for a button or clickable area.

HACK #15   Create Synthetic Art

Instead of downloading large bitmaps or creating predetermined layouts, make Flash generate artwork on the fly.

Just as computers can be made to create songs based on a small set of musical rules, you can make them generate simple images based on a few graphical layout or positioning rules.

As with all creative output coming from a computer though, most of the artistic skill resides within the programmer rather than the machine. In generative art, the trick is to create substantially complete (but interchangeable) sections of a piece and then allow the computer to perform the final placing of the sections to create the complete work.

This hack presents a typical example of this trick by Anthony "Ant" Eden (a.k.a. arseiam): a pop art pattern. It works by creating a grid of randomly nested clips, each of which contains a number of simple shape sections.

The Code

Our image is created out of several different shape sections, each of which exists on a keyframe of the movie clip node. Some of our shapes are shown in Figure 3-5. The source file is available as *antart.fla* on this book's web site.

Figure 3-5. Shapes for our generated art

The following code generates a 12×8 grid of our node clips whenever the user clicks on the Stage and makes each copy go to and stop at a random frame number:

```
this.onMouseDown = function( ) {
  var depth = 0;
  for (var i = 0; i < 12; i++) {
    for (var j = 0; j < 8; j++) {
      var me = "n" + i + j;
      this.attachMovie("node", me, depth++);
      this[me]._x = 50 * i;
      this[me]._y = 50 * j;
      this[me].gotoAndStop(random(100) + 1);
    }
  }
};
```

The code creates a random grid of our shapes, which results in patterns such as the one shown in Figure 3-6.

Figure 3-6. A random pattern generated from our basic shapes

To make our pattern appear more complex, we can nest further copies of node into the pattern. Each copy of node contains the following code:

```
if (Math.ceil(Math.random( ) < 0.80)) {
  this.attachMovie("node", "n", 0);
  this["n"]._x = 50*i;
  this["n"]._y = 50*j;
  this["n"]._xscale = n._yscale = _parent._xscale / 1.5;
  this["n"].gotoAndStop(Math.ceil((Math.random( )*10)));
}
```

When the conditional is true (80% of the time), the *if* clause creates a smaller copy of node over the top of the current node instance. This creates a smaller embedded shape and adds complexity to the appearance of the current node.

The embedded copy will itself contain the same code and also has an 80% chance of creating a smaller, nested version of node within itself, thus adding further complexity.

The pattern is thus random on two counts—the code varies the shape at each grid position and it randomizes the number of nested shapes each grid position contains. Figure 3-7 shows one possible result.

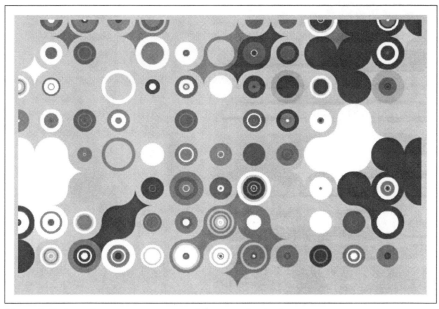

Figure 3-7. A random pattern generated from our basic shapes

Final Thoughts

The examples shown use two common ways of creating generative art: *recursion* (drawing smaller copies of the same clip inside the current node) and random placement. By creating shapes that will interlock well whatever the placement and nesting, Ant Eden has created a pattern that always looks as if it "fits," and therefore appears to have been created with some forethought.

Of course, the forethought is coming completely from Ant—the fact that the shapes have been designed to interlock is the key!

This is always the case with generative art—the trick is to create a series of phrases or visual sequences that fit together (or create rules for generating open-ended random sequences that will always fit), and then let the code churn out sequences!

—Thanks to Ant Eden for use of his graphics and inspiration

Create Seamless Tiles

#16   Create tiles that mesh seamlessly more easily than you might think. Even nonartists can create repeating tiles using very basic techniques.

Throughout this book, I try to emphasize that you don't need to be an art expert or a music major to create compelling content. Here is a hack that artists and mathematicians alike can appreciate. It shows you how to create graphics that can be used in creating synthetic art [Hack #15].

Negative Space

The principle for creating tiles that mesh seamlessly is surprisingly simple. Start with a uniform grid of rectangles, squares, triangles, or hexagons, as shown in Figure 3-8, and modify each tile into something more interesting.

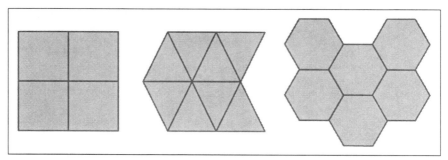

Figure 3-8. Dividing a plane into uniform shapes

Let's start with a grid of squares because it is easiest to work with.

To create a more interesting pattern, we can create some negative space by simply cutting out or darkening a given area. To start with a grid of squares, akin to graph paper, you can use Flash's gridlines feature (View → Grid → Show Grid and View → Snapping → Snap to Grid). Now draw a dark circle on the Stage so that it fills one cell of the grid, and duplicate it a few times to fill in all the squares in, say, a 2×2 box area, as shown in Figure 3-9.

You're left with negative and positive space within the 2×2 grid, and you can make either of them into a pattern using the various drawing tools to select and alter fills and strokes, as shown in Figure 3-10.

In Figure 3-11, we've created a simple circular and curved diamond shape, like those used in our synthetic art hack [Hack #15].

By creating more diamond shapes, we can make the 2×2 tile into a repeating pattern, as shown in Figure 3-12.

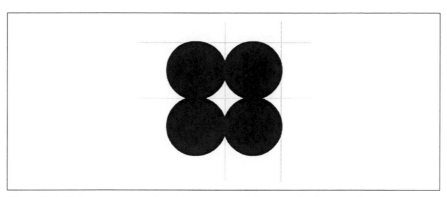

Figure 3-9. Using negative and positive space to define seamlessly repeating tiles

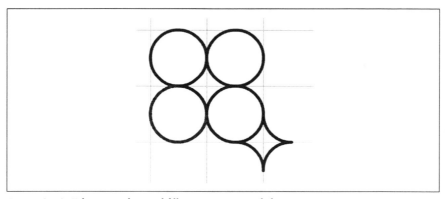

Figure 3-10. Editing strokes and fills to create varied shapes

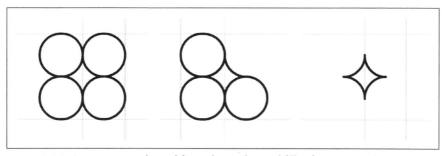

Figure 3-11. Some patterns derived from the strokes and fills of negative and positive space

We can then slice up that pattern to create a single tile, as shown in Figure 3-13, that we'll use to efficiently re-create the pattern at a later time, as shown in Figure 3-14.

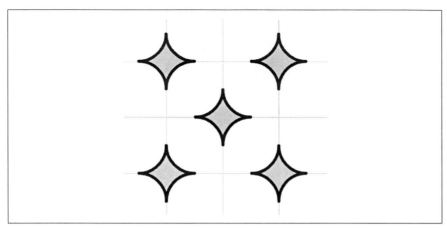

Figure 3-12. A repeating diamond pattern

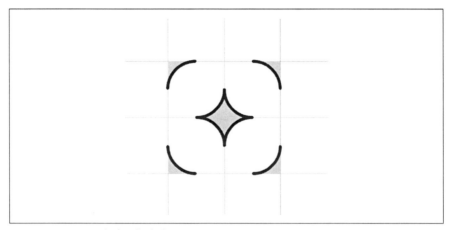

Figure 3-13. A single finished tile

Final Thoughts

Of course, tiling manually isn't really the ideal way to do it, and the tiles are pretty useless unless we can use them to fill shapes and areas of our choosing. So let's get busy tiling [Hack #17].

Before we go on, however, try to create some designs yourself by drawing, say, triangles instead of circles within the square cells. Or start with rectangular cells, or some other tiled shape from Figure 3-8.

Figure 3-14. Manually tiling to create a repeating pattern

HACK #17 Fill Areas with Patterns

Flash can't fill a nonrectangular area with a custom tile pattern at runtime. But you can fill any shape with a pattern of custom tiles by using masking.

Like most graphics applications, Flash has a Paint Bucket tool that can fill an arbitrary area with a solid color or a gradient. Flash treats the fill as a separate entity from the shape's border (stroke). The Paint Bucket tool uses the fill color specified using the Fill Color swatch in the Colors section of the Tools palette (Window → Tools). For example, you can select a gradient fill by clicking on the Fill Color swatch and selecting one of the gradient chips from the pop-up palette.

Furthermore, you can use the Color Mixer panel to customize the gradient for a fill. Simply select a fill using the Selection tool and then choose Window → Design Panels → Color Mixer. In the Color Mixer panel, you can set the fill type to a Linear gradient or Radial gradient using the pop-up menu in the center of the panel. You can even choose a Bitmap fill, in which case Flash prompts you to select an image to use as a tile to fill the specified area.

Therefore, filling an area during authoring is relatively trivial. Furthermore, you can customize (scale, skew, rotate, and translate) a gradient or bitmap fill using the Tools palette's Fill Transform tool. However, the built-in ActionScript options for specifying fills are more limited. The *MovieClip* class's *fill( )* and *beginGradientFill( )* methods, part of the Drawing API, allow you to create solid, linear gradient, and radial gradient fills, but not patterned tile fills at runtime.

Earlier we learned how to create a tile that could be repeated to form a fill pattern [Hack #16]. Let's use our tile to fill different shapes with our custom pattern.

Filling a Rectangular Area

Assuming you have given your tileable movie clip symbol a linkage ID of tilePattern in the Symbol Linkage properties dialog box, the following code generates a rectangular pattern from it:

```
function tiler(linkageID:String, target:MovieClip, clipName:String,
               depth:Number, x:Number, y:Number,
               row:Number, column:Number):MovieClip {
  var pattern:MovieClip = target.createEmptyMovieClip(clipName, depth);
  var depthCount:Number = 0;
  for (var j:Number = 0; j < column; j++) {
    for (var i:Number = 0; i < row; i++) {
      var tile:MovieClip = pattern.attachMovie(linkageID,
                           "tile" + i + "_" + j, depthCount);
      tile._x = x + (tile._width * i);
      tile._y = y + (tile._height * j);
      depthCount++;
    }
  }
  return pattern;
}
var patternClip:MovieClip = tiler("tilePattern", this,
                            "patternClip", 1, 50, 50, 15, 5);
```

The preceding code creates a movie clip named patternClip and fills it with a pattern consisting of 15×5 tiles, with the top-left tile positioned at (50, 50), as shown in Figure 3-15.

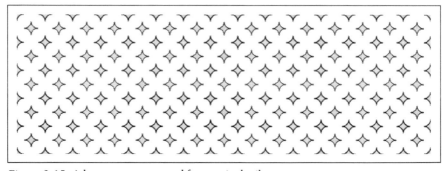

Figure 3-15. A large pattern created from a single tile

The *tiler( )* function shown in the previous listing accepts eight arguments:

linkageID
: The linkage name of the tileable movie clip symbol

target
: The path to the timeline that you want to create the pattern on

clipName
: The movie clip that will contain the pattern

depth
: The depth at which you want to create clipName

x, y
: The position of the first (top-left corner) tile

row, column
: The number of rows and columns of tiles you want in the pattern

Our *tiler( )* function offers a useful way to add a vector-based pattern around your SWF when your Stage size is smaller than the browser window and you want to fill the unused border area [Hack #92]. You could also use a pattern fill, such as an area of diagonal lines, atop content to signify something about that content (such as "this is not selectable" or "this part of the UI is currently disabled").

Filling a Nonrectangular Area

Although it is easy to fill a rectangular area, filling an irregular area is more challenging. For example, if you are creating a Flash-based online drawing application, it would be nice for the user to be able to create pattern-filled shapes. Flash allows you to create vector shapes with solid or gradient fills at runtime, but not with pattern fills. Masking offers a way around this limitation.

The following code uses our rectangular pattern tiling routine to create a filled circle. It works by making a dynamically created circle a mask for the tiled pattern.

Let's see how it works. First, the code creates an empty clip named myCircle. Inside myCircle, it creates two further movie clips. One is named mask and consists of a circle. The other is named pattern and contains a tiled area with enough rows and columns to ensure there are enough tiles to fill the circle (plus some overlap to make sure we always have complete tiles inside the circle). Figure 3-16 shows the rectangular fill overlain with a circular mask.

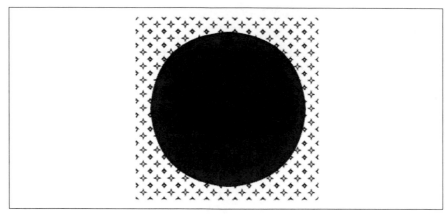

Figure 3-16. The rectangular fill overlain with a mask shape

Figure 3-17 shows the mask used to hide everything outside the circle, giving us a pattern-filled circle.

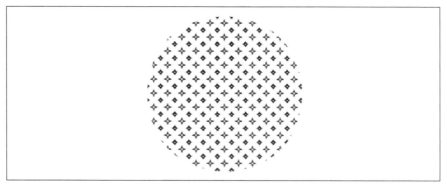

Figure 3-17. Using the mask to hide everything outside the circle yields a pattern-filled circle

The following code uses our earlier function, *tiler( )*, to create the pattern fill. Apart from the following points, it is pretty straightforward:

- The *patternCircle( )* function creates an extra movie clip named dummy, which contains only one tile. The function does this to find the dimensions of the tile. This dummy clip is overwritten by the pattern because they share the same depth.

- The circle shape is created using four curves drawn with *curveTo( )*. Although this creates a circle that is far from mathematically correct, the approximation improves speed. In any case, Flash never creates mathematically perfect circles (they are always an approximation to gain performance), so we are in good company in this decision!

Here's the code. The *tiler( )* function is the same as in the previous listing and therefore not repeated here:

```
function patternCircle(linkageID:String, target:MovieClip,
            clipName:String, depth:Number,
            x:Number, y:Number, r:Number):MovieClip {
    var r2:Number = r*0.93;
    var mc:MovieClip = target.createEmptyMovieClip(clipName, depth);
    mc._x = x;
    mc._y = y;
    // Capture required pattern size
    var dummy:MovieClip = tiler("tilePattern", mc, "dummy", 0, 0, 0, 1, 1);
    var size:Number = Math.ceil( (2*r) / dummy._height) + 1;
    // Draw pattern
    var pattern:MovieClip = tiler("tilePattern", mc, "pattern",
                                    0, -r, -r, size, size);
    // Draw a circle
    var circle:MovieClip = mc.createEmptyMovieClip("mask", 1);
    circle.lineStyle(undefined, 0x0, 100);
    circle.moveTo(-r, 0);
    circle.beginFill(0x0, 100);
    circle.curveTo(-r2, -r2, 0, -r);
    circle.curveTo(r2, -r2, r, 0);
    circle.curveTo(r2, r2, 0, r);
    circle.curveTo(-r2, r2, -r, 0);
    circle.endFill( );
    // Make circle a mask for the pattern
    pattern.setMask(circle);
    // Return created clip
    return mc;
}
myCircle = patternCircle("tilePattern", this, "myCircle", 1, 270, 200, 100);
```

Final Thoughts

Flash does not support arbitrary vector pattern fills (it supports bitmap fills, but only at authoring time) but that shouldn't stop us from trying to hack a way around the limitation.

Using negative space is a really easy way to create interlocking tiles that can fill rectangular areas [Hack #16], which in turn can be used to fill any shaped area via masking.

HACK #18 Imitate Escher

Create repeating tiles reminiscent of M.C. Escher's artwork.

Repeating tiles need not be limited to simple geometric grids. This hack explores the principles of the divided plane to create complex interlocking tiles.

Even if you're not familiar with M.C. Escher by name, you'll undoubtedly recognize many of the Dutch artist's famous works. We didn't license them for reproduction, but you can find them all over the Web, such as at *http:// www.mcescher.com*. Some of his most popular works make use of *divided planes*, in which one or more repeated shapes interlock seamlessly. Some of Escher's most famous examples include interlocking birds, fish, and reptiles.

You can Google for "tessellation" or "divided plane" to find many such examples on the Web. ("Tessellation" is just a fancy word for seamless tiling, such as in a checkerboard or mosaic pattern.)

The Divided Plane

With the negative-space trick [Hack #16] behind us, you may be feeling pretty confident. That technique used a single tile with negative and positive space to simulate a geometric pattern, but the tiles were all square, and the design consisted of simple geometric shapes. What if you want to create an Escher-like repeating pattern that uses complex interlocking shapes? How do we make tiles more interesting than squares and hexagons yet ensure they interlock seamlessly?

The trick to making seamless tiles is to start with a regular shape and modify it into something more interesting. Let's again start with a square because it is easiest to work with.

Draw a square. Convert it a movie clip symbol using F8. Next, tile other square movie clips around it (i.e., arrange multiple instances of the movie clip symbol on stage) so that you end up with a 3×3 grid as shown in Figure 3-18. Double-click the middle clip in the grid to edit it in place.

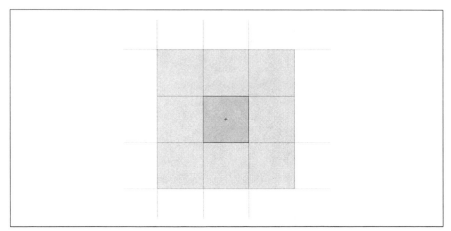

Figure 3-18. A grid of squares forms the basis for our interlocking tiles

Now modify, say, the left side of the square by curving the side using the Selection tool. All nine movie clip instances change to reflect this, as shown in Figure 3-19, so you can see what a 3×3 grid of your new tile will look like. However, you'll notice that some of the tiles obscure the curved part of tiles below, so the pattern isn't seamless.

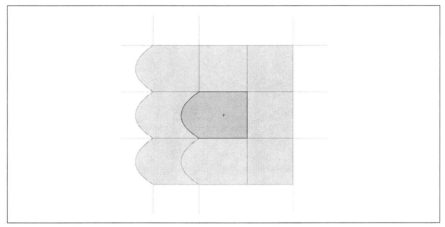

Figure 3-19. Adding a curved side to make the tile more interesting

So let's modify the righthand side of our clip so that it still tiles seamlessly with the left edge of the adjacent tile. How do you make a perfect fit? Simply copy the stroke from the left edge of the clip and use it to replace the right edge of what was formerly a square. You can, of course, use the Zoom tool to get the placement right. You will see the other instances again give you real-time feedback of the finished pattern. Figure 3-20 restores our seamlessly tiled pattern in a slightly more interesting design than the original square tiles.

Without much effort, you've created a new shape that can be tiled.

 The trick to maintaining seamless tiles is to always add to one side of the shape what you've removed from the opposite side.

Of course, this is a long way from the work of Escher, or is it? You can create a tile with an arbitrary outline by "cutting" pieces from one side of the shape and pasting the piece on the other side of the shape. Then you can look at the outline of the shape and decide what it looks like. Draw in an eye and some feathers, and perhaps it looks like a bird. Draw in scales and fins, and perhaps it looks like a fish instead.

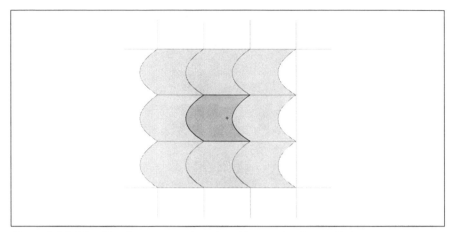

Figure 3-20. Matching the curve on the other side to maintain tessellation

A repeating tile doesn't necessarily have to cover the entire area seamlessly to interlock. So far, we have just changed the shape outline, but you can also increase the whitespace between tiles simply by scaling the movie clip you are editing. The 3×3 grid will automatically update to reflect the additional areas between tiles created by this change, as shown in Figure 3-21. You can now create more complex tile patterns because the tiles must interlock only where they touch. We are effectively assuming the whitespace is actually part of the tile and using it as our "positive space."

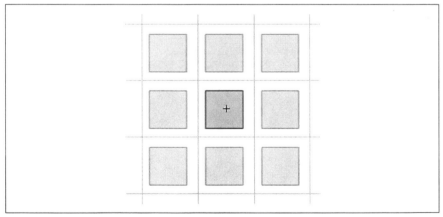

Figure 3-21. If you scale the middle movie clip while in Edit in Place mode, the other instances will reflect the change and also scale down

As soon as you realize that the tiles don't necessarily have to completely fill the tiled area (but do have to interlock), you can create a new set of shapes similar to the ones shown in Figure 3-22.

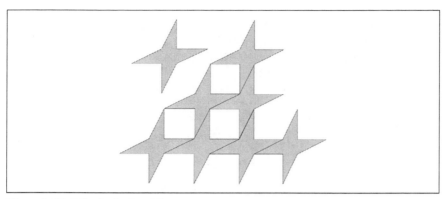

Figure 3-22. A flock of spiky things...

The shape at the top left of Figure 3-22 doesn't look as if it will tile, but it does, as you can see by the pattern created beneath it. The trick is to scale your shape as well as change its basic outline. You can also rotate it: the symmetry of the grid will reflect anything you do as long as you do not exit out of Edit in Place mode. We are effectively using the fact that the 3×3 matrix will remain symmetrical around any line that passes through the center of the matrix.

Of course, a flock of spiky things is not of much use, but that was just my starting point. After creating a 3×3 grid of spiky things, I turned them into something much more in keeping with Escher, as shown in Figure 3-23. Here, I made sure that the curves of the bird's wings and neck fit into each other even when offset. I started by adding lots of positive space (i.e., I scaled the squares down to create lots of whitespace between them), then filled it with the bird's wings, tail, and neck. I also rotated the whole 3×3 matrix slightly to get the diagonal effect of the tessellated flock (note that this is different from rotating the central square in Edit-in-place mode, which causes each tile to remain where it is but rotate on its own axis). And if you draw in the ears and a nose, the negative space in Figure 3-23 looks like a sleeping bunny rabbit!

The only difference between our regular, rectangular-shaped tiles and these more complicated tiles is that you cannot easily get the offset values for each tile just by looking at the clip _height and _width. Instead, you have to work the offsets out manually by looking at the (x, y) positions between tiles when they have been placed in an interlocking pattern. The same code we used previously [Hack #17] will then work with our "flock of birds" tiled pattern.

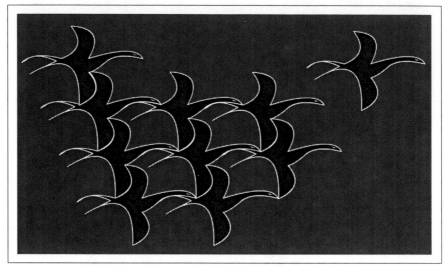

Figure 3-23. ...Becomes a flock of Escher-esque birds in flight

Final Thoughts

As with most design, it's always a good idea to try emulating the style of well-known artists, just to see where it takes you and what new ideas you can bring to your designs. In this case, we've just scratched the surface of the prints created by M.C. Escher. Emulating some of his works will certainly create some striking Flash animations and sites!

Fix Alpha Property Inaccuracies

The movie clip alpha property can return inaccurate results. Work around the problem by storing a custom internal alpha-like property, resulting in smoother and more accurate fades.

The `MovieClip._alpha` property is used to set and retrieve a movie clip's transparency. But Flash rounds the value internally, so you may get a different value when retrieving it than the last value set. In this hack, we store a custom alpha property to avoid problems caused by the rounding discrepancy in Flash's built-in _alpha property.

The `MovieClip._alpha` property is stored internally as an integer between 0 and 255. ActionScript is feeding us a lie when it claims to be working with alpha values on a 0% to 100% scale. You can demonstrate the potential cumulative error by running the following code:

```
var clip:MovieClip = this.createEmptyMovieClip(
                "clip", this.getNextHighestDepth( ));
clip._alpha = 0;
```

```
for(var i = 1; i <= 100; i++){
  clip._alpha++;
  trace(i+"% =   " + clip._alpha + "% alpha");
}
```

This code creates an empty movie clip and then changes the movie clip's _alpha property from 1 to 100 in steps of 1, or so we thought. In fact, Flash converts each of the values from 0% to 100% to the nearest approximation on the 0 to 255 scale. The last few values generated by this code look like:

```
95%  =  74.21875% alpha
96%  =  75% alpha
97%  =  75.78125% alpha
98%  =  76.5625% alpha
99%  =  77.34375% alpha
100% =  78.125% alpha
```

So, by the time we expect 100% alpha, Flash has messed with our values so much that the actual alpha value being displayed is 78.125%, an error of more than 20%! How is this possible? Well, every time we set the _alpha property, it is rounded to the nearest value in the range 0 to 255. But when we requery the _alpha property, the value is rounded down, resulting in each increment increasing the value by less than 1%.

The way to avoid the rounding error is to either use alpha percent values that aren't rounded or to write code that uses a custom property to store the current alpha value you want set.

The Five Alpha Values that Result in No Error

The _alpha property rounding error is caused by attempting to convert a 0% to 100% range to a 0 to 255 integer range. Although most percentage values have no corresponding exact value in the 0–255 range, five of them do: 0%, 25%, 50%, 75%, and 100%.

For example, suppose you want to change the alpha of a movie clip to "nearly transparent." The best value to pick here is 25% transparency, because 25% will give you a movie clip that is exactly 25% transparent. This is because 25% on the 0% to 100% scale gives you a whole number in the 0–255 range, namely 64. You can prove this is the case with the following code:

```
var clip:MovieClip = this.createEmptyMovieClip("clip",
                        this.getNextHighestDepth( ));
clip._alpha = 25;
trace(clip._alpha);  // Gives 25
clip._alpha = 20;
trace(clip._alpha);  // Gives 19.921875
```

Setting the alpha to 25% and then reading it back returns the same, unadulterated 25%. Using other values, such as 20% (for example), returns a value that is nearly, but not exactly, the value you set.

Mirroring the _alpha Property

Using the five alpha values that result in no error is cool when you want to set your movie clip to an alpha value and leave it there, but they are not as useful when you want to create an animated transition from one alpha value to another. In this case, you should write code that doesn't rely on _alpha being accurate.

For example, the following code creates a transition from 0% to 100% alpha and forces Flash to do it properly:

```
function fader(mc, startAlpha, endAlpha) {
  mc.fade1 = startAlpha;
  mc.fade2 = endAlpha;
  mc.onEnterFrame = fade;
}
function fade() {
  this._alpha = this.fade1++;
  if (this.fade1 >= this.fade2) {
    this._alpha = this.fade2;
    delete this.fade1;
    delete this.fade2;
    delete this.onEnterFrame;
  }
}
var clip:MovieClip = this.createEmptyMovieClip("clip",
                          this.getNextHighestDepth());
var size:Number = 100;
clip._x = 275;
clip._y = 200;
clip.lineStyle(0, 0x0, 100);
clip.beginFill(0x0000FF, 100);
clip.moveTo(-size/2, -size/2);
clip.lineTo(size/2, -size/2);
clip.lineTo(size/2, size/2);
clip.lineTo(-size/2, size/2);
clip.endFill();
clip._alpha = 0;
fader(clip, 0, 100);
```

The preceding code assumes that the value returned by querying the _alpha property may be incorrect (rounded from the value to which it was previously set). So it doesn't rely on the accuracy of the retrieved value. Rather than increase the value of _alpha directly, the code increases the value of a separate property, fade1, and equates _alpha to it. This technique prevents errors from building up over time. Rather than examining the _alpha value to see if it has reached 100%, we examine fade1 instead, because it doesn't suffer from any inaccuracy. When we have reached the required value (100% in this case), we explicitly set the _alpha value to the required value.

Alpha transparencies make Flash render more slowly because it has to draw both the foreground and background pixels. If rounding errors result in an alpha value that is a fraction below 100%, Flash may run sluggishly. When a fade transition completes, set _alpha explicitly to 100 to avoid performance degradation.

Avoiding Alpha Errors via Classes/Prototypes

If you are creating something that makes heavy use of alpha effects, the extra code to address inherent inaccuracies in the _alpha property might make your code more difficult to read or maintain. In that case, consider creating a custom class that fixes the problem. The following example creates a new class named *AlphaClip*, which must be stored in an external file named *AlphaClip.as*. This class defines getter and setter functions that read (get) or write (set) its own property (alphaInternal) that does not suffer from the MovieClip._alpha rounding error. Notice that *AlphaClip* is not a subclass of *MovieClip*, but it does store a reference to a movie clip as one of its properties.

```
// This ActionScript 2.0 code must go in an external AlphaClip.as file
class AlphaClip {
  private var alphaInternal:Number;
  private var target:MovieClip;

  public function AlphaClip(mc:MovieClip) {
    target = mc;
    alphaInternal = mc._alpha;
  }
  public function get _alpha( ):Number {
    return alphaInternal;
  }
  public function set _alpha(alphaIn:Number):Void {
    target._alpha = alphaIn;
    alphaInternal = alphaIn;
  }
}
```

Assuming there is a movie clip named myClip on the Stage, reading and writing the MovieClip._alpha property directly can create discrepancies between the value we set and the value we get back on reading. If we use the _alpha property of our custom *AlphaClip* class instead, we see that the value returned is the same as the value we set, because it uses the more accurate AlphaClip.alphaInternal property behind the scenes. Using this intermediate value prevents errors getting larger over time. We use getter and setter methods so that the developer can refer to the familiar _alpha property instead of referring directly to the alphaInternal property.

```
var myAlpha:AlphaClip = new AlphaClip(myClip);

// Change movie clip _alpha directly (old way)
myClip._alpha = 20;
trace(myClip._alpha); // Displays: 19.921875
// Change movie clip myClip._alpha indirectly via myAlpha._alpha
myAlpha._alpha = 20;
trace(myAlpha._alpha); // Displays: 20
```

The preceding approach solves the problem, but it is somewhat cumbersome to use because developers must remember to create an *AlphaClip* instance in addition to the target movie clip whenever they want to avoid the potential inaccuracies of MovieClip._alpha. A more formal ActionScript 2.0 OOP approach would be to make *AlphaClip* a subclass that extends (inherits from) the built-in *MovieClip* class. The inheritance approach has the marginal benefit that the developer doesn't have to create separate *AlphaClip* and *MovieClip* instances to deal with a single clip, but he still has to remember to create an *AlphaClip* instead of a *MovieClip* instance when the alpha property inaccuracy is an issue.

In the preceding example, we opted for the simpler *object composition* approach rather than formal inheritance. That is, rather than extending the *MovieClip* class via the extends keyword, our *AlphaClip* class refers to a particular *MovieClip* instance using the target property.

(*MovieClip* subclasses and object composition are both covered extensively in Chapter 13 of *Essential ActionScript 2.0* by Colin Moock.)

However, for the convenience of the developer, we'd prefer a direct replacement for MovieClip._alpha without the need to instantiate a separate class or subclass. So here we opt to use the ActionScript 1.0 style of modifying the *MovieClip* class by attaching properties or methods to its prototype. This code also works in ActionScript 2.0:

```
// Define getter and setter functions
getAlpha = function () {
  return this.alphaInternal;
};
setAlpha = function (alphaIn) {
  this._alpha = alphaIn;
  this.alphaInternal = alphaIn;
};
initAlpha = function () {
  return 100;
};
// Add the new property MovieClip.alpha (no underscore)
MovieClip.prototype.addProperty("alpha", getAlpha, setAlpha);
MovieClip.prototype.alphaInternal = initAlpha();
```

This time, I have used *addProperty( )* to create a new *MovieClip* property named alpha (without the underscore) that uses getter and setter methods. This property does exactly the same thing as MovieClip._alpha, except that it doesn't suffer from the same rounding error problems (it uses the more accurate intermediate variable alphaInternal).

Here we perform a fade in the *onEnterFrame( )* handler, which stops when the custom alpha property is zero:

```
myClip.onEnterFrame = function( ) {
  this.alpha--;
  if (this.alpha == 0) {
    delete this.onEnterFrame;
    trace("done")
  }
};
```

If you use the built-in _alpha property (with an underscore) instead of the custom alpha property (no underscore), the *onEnterFrame( )* handler will never be "done" because _alpha is never set exactly equal to zero:

```
myClip.onEnterFrame = function( ) {
  this._alpha--;
  if (this._alpha == 0) {
    delete this.onEnterFrame;
    trace("done")
  }
};
```

Final Thoughts

Animated alpha effects are some of the most processor-intensive graphic effects you can create in Flash, so the potential inaccuracy in the _alpha property can really sap performance. A clip whose alpha is set to 99.6078% looks just like one whose alpha is set to 100% (opaque, not transparent) but it renders much more slowly! Writing efficient animation code for alpha effects depends on knowing about and hacking around the _alpha property inaccuracy.

Although some OOP purists will wrinkle their noses at the prototype-based ActionScript 1.0-style solution, this syntax is still supported in ActionScript 2.0. Bear in mind that ActionScript 2.0 subclasses compile down to the same bytecode as the prototype-based approach. You can use whichever approach you are most comfortable with (prototype-based inheritance, object composition, or formal class-based inheritance).

Use Complex Shapes as Masks

#20   Flash doesn't support masks with cutouts (such as doughnuts). Create
complex shapes that conform to Flash's masking limitations, while allowing
cutouts for see-through effects.

Masking is one of those features that seems to have few applications, but
experienced Flashers know that whenever a clever Flash graphical trick
appears, masking is usually at play. As explained in the introduction to
Chapter 1, masks can be added either during authoring time or at runtime.

Flash MX was the first version to support the ability to create a scripted
mask, which is a mask applied dynamically at runtime with the *MovieClip.
setMask( )* method. Naturally, developers must be aware of how using
scripted masks affects runtime performance.

During the Flash MX beta, Macromedia released a version of the application that allowed any shape, however complex, to act as the mask but later
had to withdraw this feature because of performance issues. One of the biggest dissidents over the "you can't use complex masks" limitation was Erik
Natzke (*http://www.natzke.com*). Erik creates loads of head-turning (as well
as page-turning) tricks that initially dumbfound everyone **[Hack #25]**. It comes
as no surprise that Erik uses a lot of masking in his work.

This hack shows you how to get back the functionality of complex masks
without compromising performance. It is loosely based on discussions
between Macromedia engineers and beta testers during the Flash MX beta
period.

Using Complex Masks

A Flash mask must be a solid shape. If Flash sees a complex shape such as a
doughnut used as a mask, it will simplify the shape. You can see the problem by setting up this simple FLA.

In a new movie, change the name of the first layer to *background*, and add
two layers above it called *maskLayer* and *actions*, as shown in Figure 3-24.

Figure 3-24. Setting up layers in a masking movie

On the *background* layer, create a filled rectangle that covers the Stage. Give this rectangle a linear gradient fill, as shown in Figure 3-25. Press F8 to convert it to a movie clip symbol. Give it the symbol name *back* in the Symbol Properties dialog box. Give it an instance name of backClip in the Properties panel. Lock the layer.

Figure 3-25. A gradient

In the *maskLayer* layer, create a doughnut shape, as shown in Figure 3-26. Press F8 to convert it to a movie clip symbol. Name the symbol *mask*, and give the clip an instance name of maskClip.

Finally, attach the following script to frame 1 of the *actions* layer:

```
function dragDrop(mc:MovieClip){
  mc.onPress = function( ) {
    this.startDrag(true);
    this.onMouseMove = function( ) {
      updateAfterEvent( );
    };
  };
  mc.onMouseUp = function ( ) {
    delete this.onMouseMove;
    this.stopDrag( );
  };
}
dragDrop(maskClip)
backClip.setMask(maskClip);
```

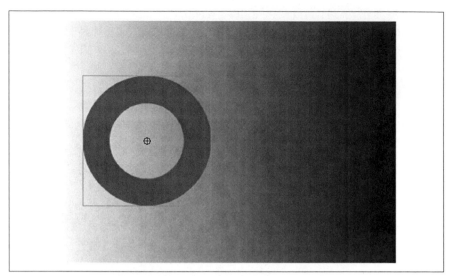

Figure 3-26. A doughnut shape atop the gradient

As an aside, smoothly dragging and dropping a clip is such a common task that you might also consider making it a class. Here's an example of a class that performs smooth dragging:

```
// This ActionScript 2.0 code must go in an external SmoothDrag.as file
class SmoothDrag {
  public function SmoothDrag(targetClip:MovieClip) {
    dragDrop(targetClip);
  }
  private function dragDrop(mc:MovieClip):Void {
    mc.onPress = function() {
      mc.startDrag(true);
      mc.onMouseMove = function() {
        updateAfterEvent();
      };
    };
    mc.onMouseUp = function() {
      delete mc.onMouseMove;
      mc.stopDrag();
    };
  }
}
```

The availability of such a class would reduce our code to only a couple of lines:

```
var myClipDragger:SmoothDrag = new SmoothDrag(maskClip);
backClip.setMask(maskClip);
```

We will, however, continue with the original, non-class-based version.

Function *dragDrop( )* allows you to click and drag maskClip; it drops the clip
when you release the mouse button. By making maskClip the masking clip
for backClip, we should see only that portion of backClip that is underneath
maskClip.

However, we actually see all portions of backClip that are inside the perimeter of maskClip. Flash treats our complex doughnut mask as a simple circular mask, as shown in Figure 3-27.

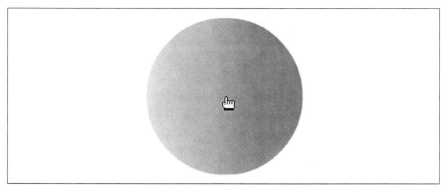

Figure 3-27. A doughnut is treated as a circular mask

Flash masks are limited by the need to have a continuous perimeter. By
making a small gap in the doughnut, we can make our doughnut have one
perimeter. The trouble is that cutting a gap will make our "O"-shaped
doughnut look more like a "C." We need to make the gap so small that
Flash ignores it when drawing the shape but large enough for Flash to treat
the entire shape as if it possesses a single perimeter. The trick is to make the
gap a hairline.

Select the maskClip instance and double-click it to edit it in place. Using the
Line tool, draw a hairline across the doughnut wall, as shown in Figure 3-28.

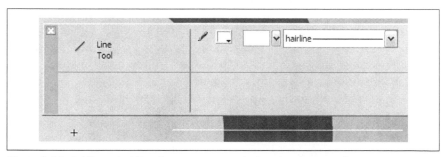

Figure 3-28. Adding a hairline fracture to our priceless doughnut mask

Select the entire hairline. Use Modify → Shape → Convert Lines to Fills to turn the hairline into a shape. Notice that the thickness of the shape created is less than 1 pixel (it is 0.3 pixels on my machine). Delete the hairline shape. When Flash removes the shape, it leaves the doughnut with a 0.3-pixel gap. Zoomed in and viewed against the pixel grid, as shown in Figure 3-29, you can see that the gap is still less than 1 pixel.

Figure 3-29. A gap of less than 1 pixel

This small gap means that, although Flash thinks we have now created a "C" with a single continuous perimeter, the vector renderer draws this shape as on "O" with no gap at all. Test the movie using Control → Test Movie.

You will see one of two things. If you are lucky, you will see a doughnut-shaped mask without any gap, as seen in Figure 3-31. If you are not so lucky, you may see the hairline gap in the doughnut, shown on the left side of Figure 3-30 and greatly magnified on the right side of Figure 3-30.

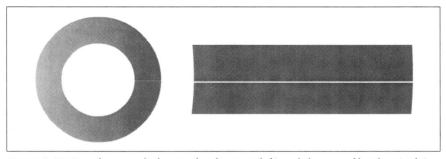

Figure 3-30. Doughnut mask showing hairline gap (left) and close up of hairline (right)

If you encounter the problem depicted in Figure 3-30, use the Subselection tool to make the gap a little smaller. Using Snap to Pixel sometimes helps; move the edge of the gap that is furthest away from a pixel snap line up to the snap. You should see a perfect doughnut mask, as shown in Figure 3-31. Zooming in might show the gap, but the renderer ignores the gap during redraws at normal magnification.

In [Hack #21], we'll see some interesting effects that can be achieved with the seemingly innocuous mask feature.

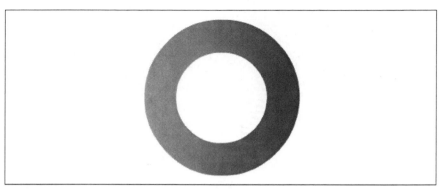

Figure 3-31. The desired doughnut mask

Interference Patterns and Ripple Effects

#21 Create moiré interference patterns and ripple effects using complex masks.

Masks are one of those weird features that seem useless until you start learning what they can do and seeing tricks that use them. Here are a few applications of doughnut-shaped scripted masks [Hack #20], and these are just the tip of the iceberg.

A series of circles interfering with themselves can create some really cool pattern effects, as shown in Figure 3-32. The effect is symmetrical in that either shape can be the mask.

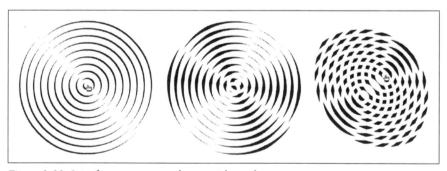

Figure 3-32. Interference patterns drawn with masks

This effect in Figure 3-32 is created via two sets of rings that use a hairline gap [Hack #20] so there are no enclosed spaces in the masks, despite initial appearances. When placed over one another, they create a solid circle, but when one shape is displaced and masks the other, you get the patterns shown in Figure 3-32. Make the circles really thin and close together and it starts getting really psychedelic, as shown in Figure 3-33!

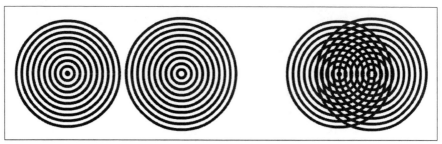

Figure 3-33. Interference patterns with masks with concentric circles

These circular patterns, when used to mask images or other content, can be used as interesting transition effects. Without knowledge of this hack, nobody will be able to re-create them either, which is a bonus for the Flash trendsetters looking for the next cheesy mouse-follower-type effect (go on, admit it!).

Using complex masks, you can also create lots of separately masked parts of an image and create scripted wave/ripple or rotation effects. The visual effect in Figure 3-34 is created by two masked leaves, one of which is rotating.

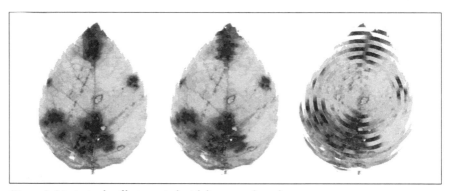

Figure 3-34. A ripple effect created with leaves and masks

Final Thoughts

Masking is one of the most underused secrets in Flash. Although the Flash documentation tells us masking is used to hide content, that doesn't really do justice to what masks can be used for. Masking is used in everything from freaky way-out transition effects to the totally utilitarian v2 UI components. Scripted masking was an absolute godsend for the more tuned-in designers when it first appeared, until everyone realized the limitation of simple mask shapes. Well, now that you know this hack, there is no excuse!

I uncover a particularly clever use of masking when I deconstruct the ideas behind the page-turning trick [Hack #25].

Feather Bitmap Edges

Vectors are great for their smooth edges at any resolution, but sometimes you need to use bitmap art. Improve the apparent quality of a bitmap's edge by cleaning up jaggies via alpha channels or vector edges.

Bitmaps are sometimes preferable to vectors, especially when you are trying to represent anything with texture (as opposed to areas of solid or near-solid colors, which are better represented with vector shapes only). A number of recent animations—desiderata at *http://www.centrifuga.net/desiderata.html* and paper sky at *http://www.centrifuga.net/gab.html* being good examples—have tended to use bitmaps for this reason.

The big disadvantage with bitmaps is that they can appear pixelated. This hack shows two ways to reduce the aliased edges of bitmaps. Pixelation is usually most evident at a bitmap's edges where there is the greatest color change between an image and its background (subtle gradations of hues tend to hide the pixelation elsewhere within an image). The technical term for jaggies (also called "staircasing") is *aliasing error*. Aliasing is seen in any digital data in which you *undersampled* the original data. Undersampling generates artifacts caused by the sampling frequency or process (i.e., you see *aliases* of the sample rate). In the case of a bitmaps image, this undersampling shows itself as obvious pixels. Aliasing occurs in other digital data, particularly sound [Hack #58]. Addressing the aliasing problem is known as *antialiasing*. One way to address it is using alpha transparencies, which tend to soften the edges around bitmaps so they blend better with the background, avoiding the halo effect (in which an image has light pixels around its perimeter).

Feathering Bitmaps

Suppose we want to import the bitmap shown in Figure 3-35 into Flash.

Very pretty from a distance. A closer look at the wing edges, as shown in Figure 3-36, reveals the dreaded bitmap jaggies.

To fix the jaggies, you can feather the edges in Photoshop before importing the image into Flash.

Load the image in Photoshop. Flatten the image if required, so that you have all the pixels on a single Photoshop layer. This layer is called *Background*, and Photoshop does not easily allow you to add alpha to the pixels on this layer. To fix this, right-click (Windows) or ⌘-click (Mac) on this layer in the Layers panel and select Duplicate Layer. Accept the default name (*Background copy*).

Figure 3-35. A butterfly bitmap

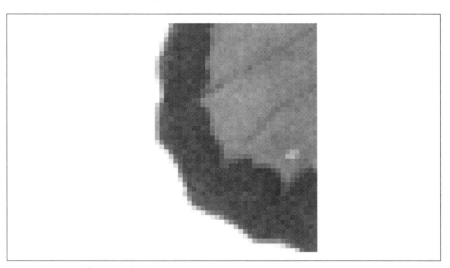

Figure 3-36. A close-up showing jaggies

Next, select the background areas around your image with Photoshop's Magic Wand tool. To avoid a halo effect, choose Select → Modify → Expand, and expand the selection by about 1 pixel. Press the Delete key to remove the background, as shown in Figure 3-37.

We've lost the butterfly's antennae, but we can replace them with two vector curves once we are in Flash.

Next, we add the feathering—graduated edges to hide the pixelation at the edges.

Figure 3-37. The butterfly image without a background

With the selection still in place—you can get it back by clicking the Magic Wand tool anywhere in the no-pixel (checkerboard) area of the image if you have inadvertently unselected it—choose Select → Feather and set the Feather option to 2 pixels. Using the Eraser tool (100% opacity), erase around the perimeter of the selection. Figure 3-38 shows the before and after views of the edges of the bitmap.

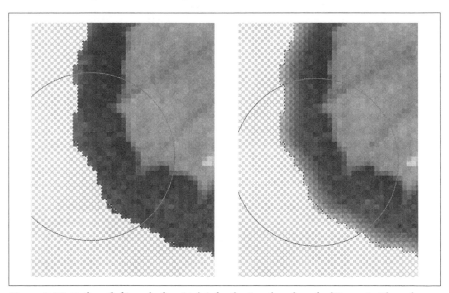

Figure 3-38. Before (left) and after (right) feathering the edge of a bitmap in Photoshop

Feather again if required, this time using a 1-pixel feather range.

Finally, save your image as a PNG with File → Save As. You will be given the choice of saving the file as Interlaced or Non-interlaced. Choose Non-interlaced. Import it into Flash using File → Import → Import to Stage. Alternatively, you can choose File → Import → Import to Library and then drag the asset from the Library to the Stage to use it in the timeline.

You can see in Figure 3-39 that the feathered butterfly wing is much less blocky than the same bitmap without feathering.

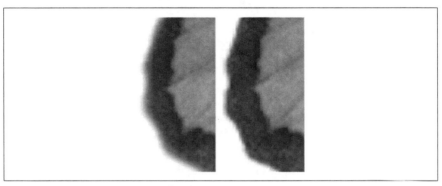

Figure 3-39. Close-up of feathered (left) and unfeathered (right) bitmap edges

The edge is an alpha blend and not a color blend; if you put the butterfly over any background, it would still blend into its surroundings. Although this makes the image more versatile, in some cases you may not need alpha, particularly when the image will be seen in Flash against a solid colored background.

HACK #23 Add a Vector Edge to a Bitmap

When you need a graphic that contains textures and a sharp edge, you are stuck. A vector shape will give you the sharp edge but is not able to show complex textures. A bitmap can show complex textures but will have no sharp edge. Create the best of both vectors and bitmaps in Flash—a bitmap with a vector edge.

For some images (particularly logos or other graphics that contain text or a "spiky" edge rather than the smoothly curving butterfly wing), the feathering technique [Hack #22] loses the sharp edges of the original. In such cases, we can do the opposite—create a sharp vector edge.

In this hack, we hide the jaggies by covering them with a vector stroke or by masking them out with a vector mask.

We perform the bitmap manipulation in Photoshop, but you can achieve similar results in other programs, including Fireworks.

Select the image created in the preceding hack [Hack #22] and export it as a PNG using File → Save As. You also need to export a second image in which you have turned all the nonzero pixels to black, as shown in Figure 3-40. You can do this in Photoshop by selecting Image → Adjustments → Brightness/Contrast. Set both the brightness and contrast sliders in the Brightness/Contrast window all the way to the left to turn all pixels to black.

Figure 3-40. The black silhouette (left) of the original butterfly image (right)

Import both of the images into Flash using File → Import → Import to Stage. Select the black silhouette and convert it to a vector using Modify → Bitmap → Trace Bitmap. This leaves you with a black vector shape. You can add a stroke around the shape to create an outline of your bitmap.

You can either use the stroke outline, as seen in Figure 3-41, as a cookie cutter or use the shape as a standard vector mask. The latter method is immediately obvious, but the former is more efficient computationally because it doesn't require Flash to constantly apply the mask (which is helpful if you need to animate the bitmap later).

When you convert the PNG into a vector, you do not end up with the black shape encased in a white shape (which would happen if you imported a bitmap consisting of a shape on a white background). Because there is no background in our PNG (and because Flash can correctly convert zero alpha pixels into "no vector"), your vector conversion is faster, with less cleanup afterward.

So let's move forward with the cookie-cutter method, given that it is by far the more hacky and nonobvious.

Place the outline in a layer above the bitmap and align it over the bitmap, as shown in Figure 3-42. If necessary, use the Subselection tool to make the stroke follow the edges of the bitmap better. Aim to get the stroke to outline

Figure 3-41. A cookie-cutter outline

the bitmap with a slight overlap. When you do this, it may be a good idea to view the layer containing the vector as Outlines (you can do this by clicking on the colored square to the left of the layer title).

Figure 3-42. An outline used as a cookie cutter

Break apart the bitmap using Modify → Break Apart. This allows you to edit it with the vector tools.

Move the vector outline from its current layer to the same one as the bitmap. The easiest way to move the vector outline between the layers is via the clipboard:

1. Lock all layers except the one the vector outline is in.

2. Press Ctrl-A (Windows) or ⌘-A (Mac) to select the outline; then press Ctrl-X (Windows) or ⌘-X (Mac) to cut it to the clipboard.

3. Unlock the layer the bitmap is in. Lock all other layers. With nothing selected, right-click (Windows) or ⌘-click (Mac) and select Edit → Paste in Place.

Select all pixels outside the outline and press Delete.

Finally, carefully delete the stroke, as shown in Figure 3-43, to reveal a perfectly sharp vector edge around your bitmap!

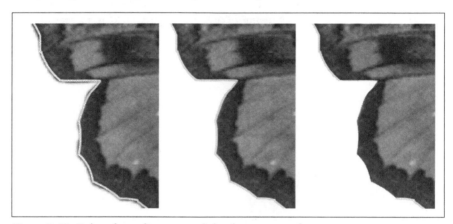

Figure 3-43. Delete the outline to reveal the sharp vector edge

Your bitmap has become a hybrid shape with the advantages of both vectors (sharp edge) and bitmaps (complex textures). Cooler still, the vector edge remains editable. You guessed it—you can even animate the vector edge, as shown in Figure 3-44, should the urge arise.

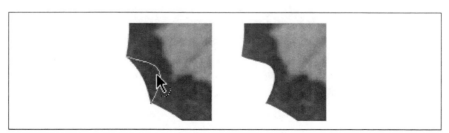

Figure 3-44. Animating the vector edge of a bitmap

Final Thoughts

As you can see from this hack, there is an awful lot you can do to merge bitmaps into the clean, vector-sharp world of Flash. Not only can you hide your jaggies using a PNG image and its associated alpha mask, you can also create a Flash-only "pseudo vector shape" consisting of a bitmap with a vector outline. It's actually a vector with a bitmap as a fill. The shape is sized exactly the same as the bitmap, so the bitmap is tiled exactly once.

Solve the Bitmap-Shift Bug

In Flash Player 6 and below, bitmap images are displaced and distorted. Place the bitmap at the right location and correct for the distortion in those versions of the Flash Player.

As with most extensive tools, you must learn a few tricks to overcome Flash Player's drawbacks. Bitmap shifting is one such drawback; it's a bug dating back to the earliest Flash Players and was corrected only recently—in Flash Player 7.

Even if you're creating movies with Flash MX 2004, you still have to deal with this problem if you're exporting your movies for Flash Player 6 or below. And considering Flash Player 7 is not yet ubiquitous, this problem will face Flash developers for some time.

Flash has a primarily vector-based renderer, and the bitmap-rendering routines in the Flash Player have a few calculation problems that end up distorting the bitmap display. As a result, a compiled Flash movie running in a browser won't always look the same as it did when being tested in authoring: bitmap images may have their content shifted or appear to jump or shake even though there's no movement on the image at all. Macromedia technote 14256 "Bitmaps shift in Macromedia Flash" (*http://www. macromedia.com/support/flash/ts/documents/bitmaps_shift.htm*) discusses the so-called image-shift bug.

In practical terms, when you use an image in Flash, some content of the image is shifted 1 pixel down and to the right. The entire image is not shifted, just some pixels within it. Not only is most of the image shifted, it's also distorted; you may notice some pixel rows/columns disappearing or getting duplicated. If you use the image inside a movie clip, depending on your registration point (the movie clip origin), you'll notice different portions of the image getting distorted.

It's easier to understand with a visual example. Consider the sample image on the left of Figure 3-45, When you import this image into the Flash authoring tool (including Flash MX 2004), position it properly (on whole

pixels, with no decimal places in the X and Y values), and export it as a
Flash Player 6 movie, the result is the distorted image on the right of
Figure 3-45.

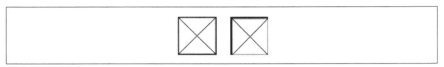

Figure 3-45. A sample image (left) showing the image-shift bug (right)

The content was shifted down and to the right. While the left column and
the top row of pixels were unaltered, because of the shift on the rest of the
content, the top and left outlines became stronger while the bottom and
right outlines almost disappeared. Depending on the bitmap's registration
point, you'll notice different areas of the image shifting.

How Not to Fix It

This bug is widely known in the Flash community, although getting around
it is still black magic for most people. Unfortunately, several solutions are
floating around, most of which are ineffective or have more drawbacks than
they're worth. For clarification's sake, avoid or otherwise be careful if you're
trying to fix this bug by any of these techniques:

Using 99% alpha on your image
> This fixes the flickering problem on a tweened animation, but it modi-
> fies your image colors (albeit imperceptibly) and slows movie playback
> if you have any animation on top of your image. And it doesn't fix the
> content-shift problem.

Using a 2-pixel transparent border
> This is hard to do (you have to create all images with a transparent bor-
> der) and will not fix the content-displacement problem, but rather just
> hide it from the user.

Toggling the Allow Smoothing option in the bitmap properties in the Library
> While this will fix image flickering if you're shifting from a moving
> image to a still image, this has nothing to do with the image-shift bug
> and also doesn't fix it.

Breaking apart the image and moving parts of it
> This simply divides the problem and moves it to other parts of the
> image.

Resizing the image by a fraction
> While resizing does work in avoiding unsolicited pixel displacements, it
> will modify your image anyway.

While these so-called "solutions" are effective to some extent, they fail to really fix the problem, so it's hard to recommend any of them, save for image resizing (which is useful in one special case—read further).

How to Fix It (the Good Way)

On careful examination, you'll notice this bug occurs only when your image's X and Y positions within the clip or on the Stage are positive. An easy solution then, is to move your image to the area of a movie clip in which the Flash Player has to deal with negative numbers to calculate each pixel position. Doing this is easy: after placing your image on the Stage in the desired position, convert it to a movie clip symbol by pressing F8. In the Convert to Symbol dialog box, shown in Figure 3-46, give it a name, and, more importantly, select the bottom-right box as being the position for the registration point. This positions the movie clip contents—your image—on the top-left side of the middle axis (i.e., in the quadrant for which X and Y positions are negative).

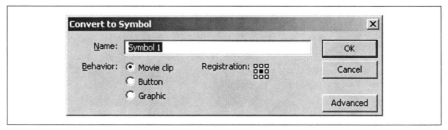

Figure 3-46. Setting the registration point in the Convert to Symbol dialog box

Moving the registration point is enough to fix the image bug when using images in the Flash authoring environment; you won't have any more image shifting or flickering bugs.

One slight problem though—Macromedia "fixed" the bug in Flash Player 7 by reversing the problem! In Flash Player 7, the bug occurs when your image's X and Y positions are negative rather than positive. The rationale there was that almost everyone will place their images in the positive portion of the clip coordinates.

 This means that the fix for the bug in Flash Player 6 actually causes a problem in Flash Player 7. If you are exporting in Flash Player 7 format, you should not use this hack.

How to Fix It in Dynamically Loaded Files (the Effective Way)

While the previous solution is enough to get around the image-shift bug when working with bitmaps inside the Flash authoring tool, it does not apply when loading images into Flash with *loadMovie( )*. Unfortunately, you can't move a loaded image's registration point so that the graphic location is in the upper-left quadrant (negative X and Y coordinates); since the loaded image is a movie clip container itself, the image content will still be on the positive side of the axes. For example, the following code produces the same results as Figure 3-45; content is shifted down and to the right:

```
// Creates and loads the image into the Stage
this.createEmptyMovieClip("myImage", 1);
this.myImage.loadMovie("testImage.jpg");
```

However, there's a simple solution to this problem. By scaling the image by a very small fraction—so small it's unnoticeable—you can force the Flash Player to use precise values that'll make the end image seem correct when calculating pixel position. This has to be done *after* the image is loaded.

The image can be scaled slightly in several ways. The following code fires the resize commands as soon as the image is loaded, thus counteracting the bug:

```
// Creates and loads the image into the myImage clip
// and places it on stage
this.createEmptyMovieClip("myImage", 1);
this.myImage.loadMovie("testImage.jpg");

// Creates a "watcher" movie to fix the size as soon as it's loaded
this.createEmptyMovieClip("myImageLoader", 2);
this.myImageLoader.onEnterFrame = function() {
  if (this._parent.myImage._width > 1) {
    // Image has been loaded
    this._parent.myImage._xscale = 99.98;
    this._parent.myImage._yscale = 99.98;
    this.removeMovieClip();
  }
};
```

While resizing the image is usually not desirable, in this special case it's acceptable because it's the best way to avoid the image-shift bug. Usually, distortion, if any, caused by resizing isn't noticeable. In the preceding code, for example, resizing the test image solves the bitmap-shift problem, but it still maintains the same width and height; if you do a *trace( )* on the image _width after loading, you'll notice it displays the original image width.

—Zeh Fernando

A Page-Turn Effect (Exploit Symmetry and Masking)

Create a page-turn animation and other Flash effects with scripted drawing and masks, and by exploiting symmetry.

Many designers see clever Flash effects, and think, "Wow! I wonder how that works!" After reviewing the initial draft of this chapter, I couldn't help but think there was one important hack missing: how to think up drawing effects yourself or how to deconstruct drawing tricks created by other designers. To be able to see how to create an effect simply by looking at the SWF online may seem like a dark art, but it can be done as long as you are looking out for the most common structures (rather like being able to replay a piece of music on a guitar after hearing the music several times).

In this hack, I show how I deconstructed the effect du jour: the page turn. First though, let's look at the most common structure of all: symmetry. And our old friend masking comes in handy, too.

A Mathematical Hall of Mirrors

In mathematics, something on the left side of an equation is equated to something on the right:

```
3 = 1+2
e = mc²
```

Many designers I know start backing toward the door as soon as they see an equation because they don't like to think nonvisually. Of course, that ignores the fact that the preceding equations are simply a way to quickly express a *visual* concept: symmetry.

The equals sign is just a formalized way of representing a mirror. The left-hand side is the same as the righthand side. As soon as you know that, you have a powerful tool to plan drawing effects. (Don't confuse the equals sign in common mathematics with the ActionScript assignment operator, =. In ActionScript, the = operator is used to evaluate the expression on the right side and assign it to the variable or property on the left. This hack is talking about symmetry/equality in the mathematical sense, not the programming sense. For what it's worth, ActionScript uses the == and === operators to test whether two expressions are equal.)

Whenever you are planning an effect (or trying to deconstruct this month's popular Flash trick), look for symmetry and mark it up on a diagram. To show this in practice, let's look at an effect that, on the face of it, looks very complicated. Although it appears nonobvious, it's based on simple symmetry.

Page Turning

One of the classic recent Flash tricks is the page-turn effect (see *http:// welcome.hp.com/country/us/en/msg/corp/flashdreamworks.html* for one of the earliest examples of it). When discussing the initial ideas for this hacks book, my editor, Bruce Epstein, said, "It would be cool if we could get the page-turning effect in the book. I saw Erik Natzke outline the process briefly in his Flash Forward session. Do you know how it is done?" I did not have a clue how to do it, but while we were speaking, I was sketching (like many people, I'm always sketching when I'm on the phone; it helps me to think). Figure 3-47 shows what I drew.

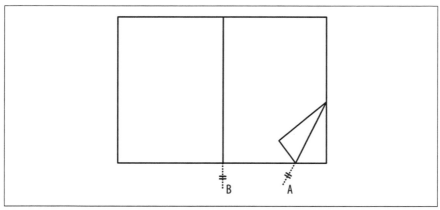

Figure 3-47. The solution to the page-turning effect

Figure 3-47 depicts my solution to the page-turning effect! It describes the single premise behind the whole effect, and as soon as I'd drawn it, I said to Bruce, "I think it won't take me long to figure out the page-turning effect, let's add it."

What does this sketch mean, and how did I come to draw it?

First, I knew the page-turning effect has something to do with page turning (duh), so I drew a turning page.

Next, I knew that most scripted drawing problems use symmetry some-where, so I kept looking at the diagram until I found a symmetrical struc-ture. In this case, it was staring me in the face. The triangle that represents the turning page is the mirror image of the triangle that is the revealed page below it. The two triangles are symmetrical about the dotted line A with an equals sign through it, shown in Figure 3-47. At the end of the page-turn-ing animation, we have two new pages, which are still symmetrical (about the book spine). All that has really happened is that symmetry line A has moved so it is now line B. The scripting for the page-turning animation is fundamentally concerned only with moving the line of symmetry during the animation!

Sometimes symmetry is seen in nature as related concepts, fractals (mirroring the same process at all levels) and particles (creating large effects with lots of little identical effects). Nature also tends to arrange symmetry into hierarchies, so that symmetry can be recursive as in the branching of a tree [Hack #6].

All these more complex effects are rooted in symmetry, and you will be hard pressed to find many Flash drawing effects that do not use symmetry (often combined with a slightly random behavior to prevent things from looking too symmetrical).

The sketch in Figure 3-47 is what I call a "visual equation." Like a math equation, it has an equals sign in it, but I am keeping the equation true to its original form—a visual representation of the problem—rather than moving over to the symbolic world of math equations. The sketch tells me that something is symmetrical (equal) about the dotted lines.

The center line with an equals sign through it is just my shorthand; it is not a standard symbol. In geometry, however, it is typical to draw hash marks through two line segments to indicate they are equal or proportional to each other.

Okay, so that's the premise. How does it actually work in practice? Well, we now need to work out the relationships that describe what happens over time.

The one thing that is changing over the course of the animation (shown here via the four pictures, left to right, in Figure 3-48) is the position of the line of symmetry. It starts off at 45 degrees at the righthand corner of the turning page and ends up at the lefthand corner of the same page and at 90 degrees (i.e., pointing straight up).

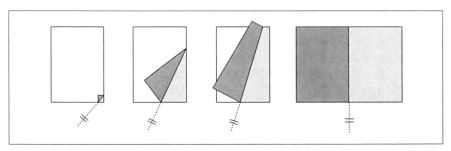

Figure 3-48. The line of symmetry moving over time

The line of symmetry is only the concept behind the effect, not the effect itself (an important point to remember when you generalize!). To create the effect, we need to break it down further into things that can be implemented. Figure 3-49 shows my route to this solution.

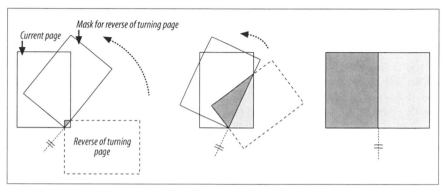

Figure 3-49. One of the two masks controlled by the line of symmetry

The effect animates by moving two movie clips around the symmetry line. One of these is the image for the reverse of the turning page (we will call this reverse_mc for clarity). It starts off rotated by 90 degrees, at the position of the dotted rectangle in Figure 3-49. The clip reverse_mc tries to make its right edge parallel to and at the same position as the symmetry line. The other clip is the mask for reverse_mc, which we will call maskReverse_mc. This clip starts off at 45 degrees but tries to get to the same end position as reverse_mc. This means that at the end of the animation, the reverse_mc clip is fully visible because none of it is masked out.

From symmetry, you can also see that the light gray area in Figure 3-49 (the visible area of the new page) is the symmetrical opposite of the area we just discussed. The revealed clip stays stationary, but its mask clip is very similar to maskReverse_mc. It moves in the same way but is mirrored around our symmetry line. Figure 3-50 shows this new mask as maskNew_mc.

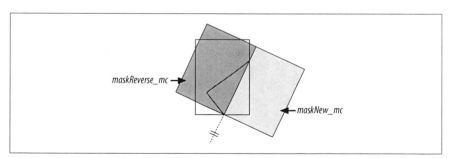

Figure 3-50. The mirrored mask

The fact that the two masks are placed symmetrically around the symmetry line is, of course, one big reason why the area of the turning page and revealed page underneath are symmetrical. There is a hierarchy of symmetry revealed here, and it should be obvious by now that the whole effect is just a series of fiendishly placed mirrors!

Final Thoughts

The page-turning effect was first created by Erik Natzke (*http://www.natzke. com*), a designer whose SWFs tend to be very visual. Looking at his work in particular, I can see that many of his drawing engines are based on symmetry or particle effects (and sometimes both). Taking on that same mindset does more than just reproduce Erik's work—it allows you to expand from it.

These hacks show the core trick behind the page-turning effect to illuminate a common way to deconstruct such effects:

- Look for and pick out basic structures (of which symmetry is the most common, but they may also appear as fractal or particle effects), and then sketch diagrams showing where in the effect they exist, using whatever visual shorthand you feel comfortable with.

- Expand the idea with further sketches that look to build from the basic idea and move it toward implementation in Flash. As a general rule, if you can't see what could create the effect, then it is probably a mask. Based on experience, I can say that masking combined with scripting usually creates the most nonobvious tricks.

- Don't worry about moving the concepts into written math straight away, because visually representing processes makes it easier to pick out patterns or useful high-level concepts. Despite their big advantages, math equations are actually very poor at giving you something that you can visualize immediately. Equations are more symbolic than visual (which is, I guess, the reason the more visual designers intuitively dislike them!).

This hack concentrates on finding the hack rather than implementing it. I hope you will agree that this is a more important ability. It's the key that will open up next year's big Flash drawing trick as well as the current king of the hill. That said, a sample implementation of this effect, *pageturn.fla*, can be downloaded from this book's web site.

CHAPTER FOUR

Animation

Hacks 26–34

This chapter covers a topic near and dear to Flash's heart: animation. The Flash interface is based on the techniques of traditional cel animation. The Flash timeline is the digital equivalent of a flip book, with each frame representing a slice of time and successive cels (frames) displayed over time to create the illusion of motion. Like traditional cel animation, Flash supports the concept of layers, which are used to build up an animation from the background to the foreground, with various elements at appropriate depths.

Keyframes and tween frames, in which the master artist creates the keyframes and underlings create the in-between (tween) frames, will also be familiar to traditional animators. In Flash's tween-based system, the artist creates the keyframes and Flash can generate the tween frames automatically. All changes created by the animator, such as moving a graphic to a new location, must occur on a keyframe. Frame 1 is always a keyframe and you can create additional keyframes using Insert → Timeline → Keyframe (F6). So you might create a graphic in frame 1 and position it at the left side of the Stage. Then you can create a keyframe in frame 19 and move the graphic to a new position at the right side of the Stage. You can apply a motion tween by selecting the animation's beginning and ending keyframes in the timeline and setting the Tween option in the Properties panel to Motion (or by choosing Insert → Timeline → Create Motion Tween). Flash automatically tweens the animation, which makes the graphic appear to move across the Stage in 19 steps as you scrub the playhead across the first 19 frames.

When a graphic is placed in a layer, it appears on Stage until a blank keyframe is encountered in that layer. For example, if you want a graphic to be removed from the Stage after frame 19, you can insert a blank keyframe in frame 20 (using Insert → Timeline → Blank Keyframe or F5).

Even though Flash does a lot of the work for you, this chapter has a number of hacks that benefit the traditional animator and newcomer alike. Creating animation can require a lot of time and skill, so this chapter offers hacks that both reduce the time required and simplify the process. Unlike traditional animators, Flash animators must also be concerned with download times and runtime performance. This chapter looks at ways of reducing or automating common animation tasks by:

- Simplifying animations (for both the animator and Flash)
- Generating complex animation via third-party tools, particularly for character animation
- Showing how to make long nonrepetitive animations via short, repetitive animations

Flash also allows you to generate scripted motion. In scripted motion, the appearance of the next frame in the animation is calculated and drawn by ActionScript. This form of animation is the route best taken when you want to create interactive animation or when your animations are controlled by mathematical rules (such as physical equations of motion).

When using scripted animation, be aware that Flash uses print-based coordinates, not mathematical ones. A printed page takes the origin at the top-left corner, whereas the traditional Cartesian axes use the bottom-left corner as the origin. This means that the Flash origin is at the top-left corner of the Stage, and the positive Y direction is downward, as shown in Figure 4-1.

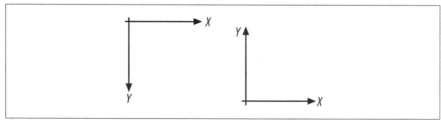

Figure 4-1. Flash coordinate axes (left) and traditional Cartesian coordinate axes (right)

For scripted motion, the limiting factor is performance, and we will look at ways of making your code create animations that are as smooth and responsive as possible. We will also look at several quick ways of creating common scripted animation effects.

Smooth Scripted Motion

Increasing the frame rate can cause Flash's rendering engine to hog processor time. Create visually smooth animations without simply increasing the frame rate.

One of Flash designers' worst habits is increasing the frame rate to absurdly high values to make animations appear smoother. Although this may work in a simple FLA performing a lone animation, when you are building a larger Flash movie or site, you shouldn't let screen drawing hog all the processor time. Setting the frame rate to 95 frames per second (fps) forces Flash to constantly render images to the screen. The resulting lack of idle time can make sounds pop and cause delays in event processing, which can make interactivity appear sluggish.

This hack looks at how beginning Flashers are often taught to animate and why it isn't always the best solution. Then we'll look at ways to create smooth animations without changing the frame rate.

User-Actuated Movement (Breaking the onEnterFrame Monopoly)

In the simplest case of animations created at authoring time, the Flash play-head progresses through the timeline and displays each frame in turn. This is so-called frame-based animation, like a digital flip book. In such a scenario, the obvious way to increase the speed of the animation is to increase the frame rate (you can set the frame rate in the Document Properties dialog box accessible via Modify → Document). When a traditional animator learns Flash, he feels right at home with these techniques.

But when that same Flasher learns scripted animation, he must change his mode of thinking. Most beginning scripters are taught to implement scripted motion using *onEnterFrame( )* handlers. In simple cases, in which the frame rate is not excessive and scripting animation should be tied to the frame rate, using *onEnterFrame( )* is a reasonable option. But when your animations become more sophisticated, so must your techniques. Otherwise, performance is likely to suffer or your creativity is apt to be limited.

Don't fall into the trap of thinking that all motion graphics should be controlled via *onEnterFrame( )* handlers. Because *onEnterFrame* events are tied to the frame rate, the easiest way to create smoother animations is to increase the frame rate, which increases the frequency of *onEnterFrame* events. However, if the user interacts with graphics and animation, *onMouseMove( )* is a far more efficient event handler to employ. A drag-and-drop feature is a good candidate to be implemented in an *onMouseMove( )* handler. Likewise, features in which the user controls animation or performs drawing with the mouse can both be controlled via *onMouseMove* events.

Rather than increase the frame rate to make a draggable movie clip move smoothly, use *updateAfterEvent( )* within an *onMouseMove( )* handler to redraw the Stage while the mouse is moving.

The following code performs a drag-and-drop operation smoothly, even if you set a low frame rate, such as 1 fps:

```
function pressHandler( ) {
  this.startDrag( );
  this.onMouseMove = function( ) {
    // Refresh the Stage while the item is being dragged
    updateAfterEvent( );
  };
  this.onRelease = function( ) {
    this.stopDrag( );
    delete this.onMouseMove;
  };
  this.onReleaseOutside = this.onRelease;
}
// Create a movie clip and make it draggable
var puck:MovieClip = this.createEmptyMovieClip("puck",
                 this.getNextHighestDepth( ));
puck.lineStyle(40, 0xCCCCCC, 100);
puck.moveTo(-1, 0);
puck.lineTo(1, 0);
puck._x = 275;
puck._y = 200;
puck.onPress = pressHandler;
```

Let's review key portions of the code. The main code (following the *pressHandler( )* definition) creates a small movie clip and makes *pressHandler( )* its *onPress* event handler. This triggers the action when the user clicks on the movie clip.

The function *pressHandler( )* attaches an *onMouseMove( )* event handler to the movie clip, which redraws the screen repeatedly as the mouse is dragged. This arrangement causes Flash to redraw the screen at a higher rate only when the item is being dragged, giving us smooth movement without having to increase the frame rate. This implementation is provided to allow ActionScript 1.0 scripters to focus on the techniques being taught. Similar drag-and-drop code can be implemented using OOP and ActionScript 2.0 [Hack #20].

The same principle can be seen in the following listing. Here, the *onMouseMove* event is used to create a simple Pencil tool. If the *onMouseMove* event was changed to *onEnterFrame*, the event handler would be running when it is not required (i.e., when the cursor has not moved).

```
function penDown( ) {
  this.moveTo(_xmouse, _ymouse);
  this.onMouseMove = function( ) {
```

```
    this.lineStyle(null, 0xCCCCCC, 100);
    this.lineTo(_xmouse, _ymouse);
    updateAfterEvent( );
  };
  this.onMouseUp = function( ) {
    delete this.onMouseMove;
  };
}
var drawClip:MovieClip = this.createEmptyMovieClip("drawClip",
                              this.getNextHighestDepth( ));
drawClip.onMouseDown = penDown;
```

Final Thoughts

Although the temptation to use *onEnterFrame( )* event handlers to animate everything always exists, it is not the only event that can be used to create animation in Flash. We just saw a case in which using the *onMouseMove* event produced both more efficient and smoother animation. It was more efficient because it uses less processing power (it refreshes the screen only when needed), and it is smoother because the frequency of *onMouseMove* events (unlike *onEnterFrame* events) is unrelated to the frame rate.

Although using the *onMouseMove* event applies only when the user action is related to mouse movement (such as for drag-and-drop or pen drawing operations), you can look for other events on which to trigger screen refreshes. For example, you might update the screen when data is received or when a sound completes.

However, in some cases you may want an animation to be performed over time. Luckily, *onEnterFrame* is not the only time-related event available. When you want to create several animations that will run at different rates, it is usually better to use *setInterval( )* to create a separate timed event for each [Hack #27] (rather than use *onEnterFrame* for all of them).

Time-Controlled Movement
#27

All scripted subanimations do not need to run at the frame rate. Make a subanimation run at a rate independent of the frame rate by using timed events.

You can change the rate of both scripted and unscripted time-based motion in several ways. To change the speed of an animation, you can tween it out over more (or fewer) frames or change the frame rate. You can insert additional frames in the timeline using F5. You can delete frames by right-clicking (Windows) or ⌘-clicking (Mac) in the timeline and choosing Remove Frames from the pop-up menu.

You can control scripted animations in a time-based manner by increasing the frame rate and performing screen updates in the *onEnterFrameFrame( )* event handler. You can rely on other event handlers, such as *onMouseMove( )* [Hack #26], to be more judicious in screen updating, which allows you to increase animation smoothness without hogging the processor.

But in some cases, we want the animation to be time based, not based on some event such as mouse movement. Rather than use very high frame rates when you require extremely smooth animation, it is better to use the *setInterval( )* function to create an *interval* (i.e., a timed event). The advantage of this is three-fold:

- Flash doesn't waste time by redrawing the entire screen at a high frame rate (as would happen if you simply increased the frame rate).
- Different portions of the animation can be run at different speeds.
- Animation speed can be timed relatively precisely, independent of the frame rate or length of the animation in the timeline.

A standard interval is created like this:

```
intervalID = setInterval(eventHandler, period, arguments);
```

where:

`intervalID`

Is the interval ID returned by the call to *setInterval( )*. You need to know this to remove (a.k.a. stop or clear) an existing interval.

eventHandler

Is the name of the function you want to use as the event handler (the function to trigger at each interval).

period

Specifies how often (in milliseconds) you want Flash to invoke the event handler.

arguments

Specify zero or more arguments to be passed to the event handler. If you want more than one argument, separate them by commas (*argument1*, *argument2*, ...*argumentn*).

An event handler invoked by *setInterval( )* is not the same as a normal instance event handler, such as *onMouseMove( )* or *onEnterFrame( )*, because when it is invoked, the scope is not that of an instance method. To invoke a method on an object (i.e., to invoke a method within the scope of an instance), you can use the alternative form of *setInterval( )*:

```
intervalID = setInterval(object, "method", period, arguments);
```

where:

object

Is the object, such as a *MovieClip* instance, on which to invoke the
method specified by *"method"*

"method"

Is the method name, as a string, to invoke on *object* at each interval

The remaining arguments are the same as in the previous form of *setInterval( )*.

If you pass this as the *object* parameter, then the method invocation will
have the scope of the current instance [Hack #10], meaning it can access the
current instance's properties.

You can also invoke a function within the scope of a clip by specifying a target instance as the first argument. The following *setInterval( )* call creates an
interval for a movie clip instance, myClip, that will attempt to invoke the
clip's *myEvent( )* method every millisecond (or as close as Flash can get to it):

```
intervalID = setInterval(myClip, "myEvent", 1);
```

The function is invoked repeatedly until the interval is cleared. To clear an
interval, use *clearInterval( )*:

```
clearInterval(intervalID)
```

You need to make sure that the intervalID variable is in scope from wher-
ever you clear the interval. Typically, the function invoked by *setInterval( )*
clears the interval after some condition is met (or the first time it is called, in
the case of a one-time event).

Another way to create a *setInterval( )* event is to make it invoke a method of
the movie clip instance. This ensures that the handler is scoped to the movie
clip being controlled. The next example defines *mover( )* as a method of
movie clip myClip. The *mover( )* function will run every 1 ms (or as close as
Flash can get to this) and will increase the myClip._x property to animate the
clip until the x position exceeds 300.

There is a problem though: the *mover( )* function has no way of knowing the
interval identifier (intervalID), which is needed to properly clear the interval. So we make the interval ID a property of the movie clip, in such a way
that it is available as this.intervalID within the interval handler, *mover( )*:

```
function mover( ) {
  this._x++;
  if (this._x > 300) {
    clearInterval(this.intervalID);
  }
  updateAfterEvent( );
}
```

```
// Store the interval ID as a property of the clip
myClip.intervalID = setInterval(myClip, "interval", 1);
myClip.interval = mover;
```

The Code

The following code demonstrates the differences between and benefits of using *setInterval( )* instead of an *onEnterFrame( )* handler to update the animation. The code creates two movie clips and makes them move across the Stage in 1-pixel steps. The puck1 clip appears to move much more quickly and smoothly because it is being animated as fast as the Flash Player can run. The puck2 clip moves at the current frame rate, which will be 12 fps by default.

```
mover = function( ) {
  this._x += speed;
  if (this._x > 550) {
    clearInterval(this.interval);
  }
  updateAfterEvent( );
};

function enterFrameMover( ):Void {
  this._x += speed;
  if (this._x > 550) {
    delete this.onEnterFrame;
  }
}
function drawBall(clip:MovieClip, x:Number, y:Number):MovieClip {
  var mc:MovieClip = this.createEmptyMovieClip(clip.toString( ),
                            this.getNextHighestDepth( ));
  mc.lineStyle(40, 0xCCCCCC, 100);
  mc.moveTo(-1, 0);
  mc.lineTo(1, 0);
  mc._x = x;
  mc._y = y;
  return mc;
}
var speed:Number = 1;
var puck1:MovieClip = drawBall(puck1, 20, 200);
var puck2:MovieClip = drawBall(puck2, 20, 300);
puck1.intervalMover = mover;
puck1.interval = setInterval(puck1, "intervalMover", 1);
puck2.onEnterFrame = enterFrameMover;
```

Note the way *setInterval( )* is created:

- The interval ID returned by *setInterval( )* is of type *Number*.
- The interval ID has to be known so that we can remove the interval to which it refers at the end of the animation. The interval ID could be passed as an argument, but in this case we add it as a timeline variable, interval, on the puck1 clip.

Of course, making the frame rate really high, such as 95 fps, would ensure that both movie clips moved quickly and smoothly, but that technique has two limitations. First, if all the animations are dependent on the frame rate, it is harder to vary the speed of different graphic elements. Second, if you try to make everything move too fast, the Flash Player won't be able to achieve the requested frame rate. The *setInterval( )* technique allows you to selectively target the critical areas of your motion graphics that must run quickly [Hack #71]. It is worth noting that if you make the whole SWF run faster, the maximum frame rate you can achieve is considerably less than if only portions run faster.

Final Thoughts

Despite complaints that the Flash Player isn't fast enough, you can do a lot to make your code more efficient. Choosing your event handling [Hack #26] so that you run code only when it is required improves animation smoothness and apparent performance. See Chapter 9 for more performance-related hacks.

Quick, Bandwidth-Efficient Character Animation

> Animating by hand can take ages. Skirt some of the hard work with a few insider tricks from a Disney animator.

Flash animation is all about doing the minimum to get across the story, because both bandwidth and Flash performance are at a premium. One trick used to minimize work and bandwidth requirements is the *walk cycle*. By creating a repeating animation of a left step and right step, which when repeated appears as a seamless and continuous walk, the number of frames you need can be reduced significantly versus animating a walking figure with lots of nonrepeating frames. The number of frames and the difficulty in creating them is still high, however, so you will most likely need to prune the frame count further.

This hack was created as part of web design work I am doing with Adam Philips, an award-winning Disney animator. His job with Disney involves working out how to produce optimized animations with the fewest number of frames, a skill he uses to the full in his web cartoons, as seen at *http://www.biteycastle.com*. This hack shows a number of ways he reduced the number of frames used in a cartoon character we're developing named Scribble.

Hacky Wacky Walking

There are two problems to overcome when creating a realistic walk cycle:

- We walk with more than just our legs—our head dips up and down, and our arms swing as our hips sway slightly. Unless you include all of these in an animation, it will look like someone walking while wearing clothes that met with a starch-related laundry accident.

- You have to make your character walk at the same speed he appears to be moving. Sounds simple, but you've probably seen video games or low-budget cartoons whose characters seem to glide along the floor, because they are walking at a different speed from the one at which they are moving across the screen.

To create a realistic walk cycle requires lots of frames and a good eye for movement.

The hacky way around this is to create a walk cycle in which breaking the preceding rules doesn't matter. Create a simplified animation (using far fewer frames) that can look a bit wacky and unlike a normal walk or one that spends at least some of the time totally off the ground, thus minimizing the glide effect. When done well, it has the advantage of giving your characters personality.

The Tasmanian Devil from the Warner Bros. cartoons is the most extreme example of this. He moves by twisting around so fast you can't see him, and the twister glides across the screen. This is a good example of building "ease of animation" into your cartoon subjects from the start.

The site Adam and I are creating has a novel interface—rather than navigating with your cursor, you move around the site by enticing a cartoon character named Scribble to follow you. Unless he is doing something else (such as sulking, interacting with something he has found, or generally up to his own thing), he will simply follow the mouse.

For example, if the mouse is to the right of him, as shown in Figure 4-2, he uses the walk cycle in Figure 4-3 to move to the current mouse position.

Figure 4-2. The stationary character with the mouse pointer to his right

Figure 4-3. An efficient walk cycle

Scribble moves very quickly in the final work, far too quickly for the viewer to notice the reduced number of frames in the animation. He also spends a lot of time in the air, thus minimizing the slide walk effect.

Of course, when two designers get together, easy options always go out the window. In our case, we chose to animate in three dimensions. Scribble and the mouse move in a faux 3D world. Sounds like a big deal animation-wise, right? A Swift 3D rotating text effect takes upwards of 20 frames to create a passably smooth animation. A 3D walk cycle would require many more frames because the rotating object (Scribble) is itself changing as is the direction/orientation.

Figure 4-4 shows how Adam did it.

Each radial line shows Scribble's walk cycle in a particular direction. Adam used three very subtle hacks to minimize the zillions of frames a 3D walk cycle would normally entail:

- The "run left" walk cycle is the mirror image of the "run right" walk cycle. We can do this because Scribble has no directional shading—he's all in black. So the three walk cycles to the left are simply mirror images of the three to the right. To reverse a graphic or symbol instance, bring up the Transform panel (Window → Design Panels → Transform), uncheck the constrain checkbox, then change the sign of either the horizontal or vertical percentage scaling value (depending on which axis you want to mirror across). For example, set the horizontal scaling to -100 to mirror the character across the Y axis.

- The "walk north" frames are the same as the "walk south" graphics, but with the eyes on the other side of the head (or rather, omitted).

Figure 4-4. A 3D walk cycle

- Each walk cycle contains lots of repetition. The frames with the left foot down are simply the same point on the right leg flipped over, so optimizations can occur between these frames.

- Scribble's movement is constrained to one of eight cardinal directions.

- We used an animation that looks good at various speeds (kind of a loping, jumping walk). In the real world, the gait for walking is different from the gait for jogging or running, so we used an imaginary gait that looks good at both speeds. You couldn't do that with a realistic horse animation, since walking, trotting, cantering, and galloping all have distinctive gaits.

With all this optimization, only 10–20 frames are needed for the full 3D walk cycle. Nothing bandwidth-heavy here!

Final Thoughts

Although the ideas behind this hack are obvious as soon as you have read this, you don't see them used often in Flash web animation. The same techniques can be used in any cyclical animation, such as a bird flying.

You don't always need smooth animation, and, in many cases, fewer frames give a bigger sense of motion and personality. Of course, the positive effects on workload and download time are also beneficial!

You can follow the development of my collaboration with Adam Phillips in a forthcoming book from O'Reilly (working title *Mastering Flash Animation and User Interface Design*) in which readers will learn animation from Adam and the associated scripting from me, as we slowly build up Scribble's world.

For those curious to see Scribble in action, look at one of our early works in progress, *scribbleWalk.fla*, downloadable from this book's web site. Also worth looking at is the associated code on frame 1 of the *actions* layer of the downloadable FLA. A few other approximations will become apparent when you look at the code, but we'll leave you to search them out!

alt-Flash: Motion Graphics Alternatives

As much as we love Flash, it isn't the only game in town. Create motion graphics with some of the alternatives to Flash.

Flash is the number one motion graphics and multimedia delivery platform for the Web, but it is not the only one available. Putting aside the mainstream applications, such as Toonboom (*http://www.toonboom.com*) and Macromedia Director (*http:///www.macromedia.com/software/director*), and specialized applications, such as text effect generators and Swift 3D (*http://www.swift3d.com*), there are a few notable stand-outs. Processing (*http://www.processing.org*) is interesting because it is geared toward scripted animation without the historical baggage of Flash's timeline-based approach.

KoolMoves *(http://www.koolmoves.com)* is a more specialized tool with character animation features not found in Flash. Both are possible alternatives to Flash for developers and animators interested in those more specialized areas.

Processing

Flash is moving in the same direction as the rest of the Web, with Macromedia pushing Rich Internet Application (RIA) development, Flash ubiquity, ease of deployment, and increasing usability. It wasn't always like that, of course—Flash used to be the underground web tool of choice, and I remember attending the first few Flash Forward conferences *(http://www. flashforward2004.com)* and coming away with all the cool, creative, and totally noncommercial stuff that was being shown.

It hurts to say it, but Flash is no longer the unchallenged underground digital media king. That crown may soon move over to Processing *(http://www. processing.org)*, a graphic programming API that is a cinch to learn for ActionScript programmers. Some example images created by Alessandro Capozzo *(http://www.ghostagency.net)* are shown in Figure 4-5.

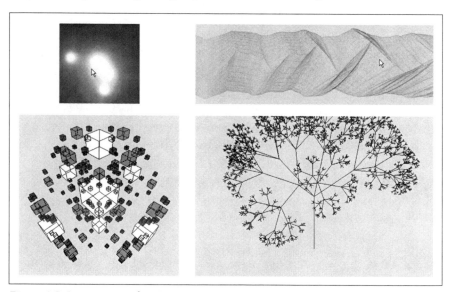

Figure 4-5. Images created in Processing

Based around Java, Processing is a programming language and environment designed with two purposes in mind:

- To teach programming fundamentals in a visual way to the electronic arts and visual design communities

- To serve as an electronic sketchbook that allows visual artists to create animation programmatically

The best thing about Processing is that it is fast, free, and runs in any Java-enabled browser. For noncommercial web art and math exploration pieces, it's looking to be a Flash-beater.

If you aren't convinced that this is going to be big, check out the notable names in the Flash world that are already into Processing:

Cinema Redux: Brendan Dawes (*http://www.brendandawes.com*)
Gallery of Computation: Jared Tarbell (*http://www.complexification.net*)
Point Man: Ant Eden (*http://www.arseiam.com/proce55ing/man*)
Sonic wire sculpture: Amit Pitaru (*http://www.pitaru.com*)
Keith Peters (*http://www.bit-101.com*)

As you can see, Processing is appearing on more than a few Flash radars in 2004.

KoolMoves

On the surface, KoolMoves (*http://www.koolmoves.com*) is a cut-down and low-cost Flash authoring tool with a feature set somewhere between Flash 3 and 4, except that it has a number of animation tools not available anywhere else.

Of particular interest is the *bones* feature, shown in Figure 4-6. This allows you to create advanced hierarchical soft-bodied animation, something that is very difficult in Flash. At only $49 and with a free trial version (which doesn't allow saves but is otherwise fully functional), it's worth a look, especially if you do a lot of scriptless tweens. It is not as highly recommended for script junkies (who have probably put down the book and are downloading Processing even as we speak).

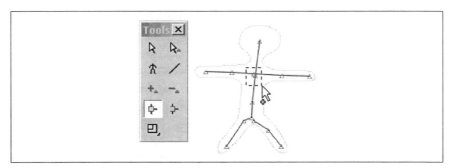

Figure 4-6. KoolMoves supports bones for soft-bodied animation

Final Thoughts

There are many alternatives to the Flash authoring tool, some of which use the SWF format (and require the Flash Player for playback) and others that don't. Adobe LiveMotion is no longer available and no longer supported. Other alternatives include:

Ming (http://ming.sourceforge.net)

Ming is a C library of routines that can be controlled via common server-side scripting languages—such as Perl, Python, PHP, and Ruby—to generate SWF files dynamically. These can then be loaded into the client SWF as a nested movie clip or used to replace the currently loaded SWF in the Flash Player. Note that Ming can only generate SWFs; it cannot alter existing SWFs.

SVG

Although Flash is the most common way to create web-based content, SWF isn't the only available distribution format. Like Flash, SVG (Scaleable Vector Graphics) is vector-based. SVG graphics are created via an XML text markup, which means that the contents of the file can be accessed by search engines more easily than the binary SWF format. SVG can be written in any text editor. Although various SVG authoring tools are available, none are as mature as the Flash MX 2004 authoring tool. However, most browsers aren't equipped to recognize SVG content (see *http://www.macromedia.com/software/player_census/flashplayer*), and the SVG plugin is larger and typically harder to install than Flash Player. Therefore, the greater ubiquity of the Flash Player makes SVG an interesting alternative for limited situations rather than a likely replacement for Flash and the SWF format. The SVG FAQ (*http://www.svgfaq. com*) and SVG Cafe (*http://www.svg-cafe.com*) are good starting points to learn more about SVG from the people who know it best. But be prepared to field questions or accusations about what Flash/SWF are all about (and ignore the rampant misinformation about Flash from people who don't know any better). For what it's worth, at the October 2003 MAX conference in Salt Lake City, Utah, Macromedia sneak-peeked a version of the Flash Player that had limited SVG-rendering capabilities. So the Flash Player will likely render SVG content in the future, although not support the full SVG specification.

Flex (http://www.macromedia.com/software/flex)

Flex is Macromedia's so-called *presentation server* product that dynamically generates SWF files via an XML-like language (called MXML). Flex also uses ActionScript 2.0 to add scripting control beyond standard timeline effects. Flex is aimed at enterprise Java developers. It seeks to address complaints server-side developers had regarding the Flash authoring tool—namely, you can author in text rather than visually, and you can use the editor and source code control system of your choice. Thus, it combines many of the strengths of both SVG and Flash.

Deja New Animations

Repeating animations are efficient but get dull fast. Create nonrepeating animation cycles to add variety without excessive overhead or resorting to ActionScript.

Tweens are the animation method of choice for the non-code-savvy animator, but they suffer from a number of limitations. The most obvious is that they are less conducive to interactivity than scripted motion. That's fine for many applications of Flash, particularly animated cartoons.

Animations require another common feature that cannot normally be performed without using scripted animation: random or nonrepeating movement. Tweens are fixed animations, so they are never random and simply repeat.

For example, assume we had two tweens contained within two separate movie clips, one of 10 frames and one of 20 frames. If we played both tweens continuously as part of the same overall animation, that animation would repeat every 20 frames. The user experience suffers because the animation appears repetitive.

If we were animating clouds across the Stage for a 30-second shot, we could create 30 seconds of animation, but that would be time consuming. We should instead animate a single cloud or several clouds and combine them to fill the sky and create variation. But if that 30-second looping animation was used as a background for a 5-minute cartoon, it would get repetitive. Ideally, our sky would consist of many individual animated clips that rarely repeat.

The standard way around this is to lock yourself in a room for a week and learn ActionScript and the joys of *Math.random( )*. The hacky way is to use prime numbers in your tween animations.

A prime number is any number that is evenly divisible only by itself and 1. The prime numbers between 1 and 100 are 2, 3, 5, 7, 11, 13, 17, 19, 23, 29, 31, 37, 41, 43, 47, 53, 59, 61, 67, 71, 73, 79, 83, 89, and 97. You can quickly look up additional prime numbers by searching for "prime number" or "prime series" on the Web.

The big deal about prime numbers is their indivisibility. A mathematical consequence of this is that the lowest common multiple of two primes is the product of the primes themselves (i.e., the prime numbers multiplied together).

Applying this to our situation, if you have two animations of lengths *n* and *m*, where *n* an *m* are prime numbers, a third animation combining the first two won't repeat for *n* times *m* frames. So, if you change your two animation tweens so that both have frame lengths that are prime numbers (say, 11 and 19), an animation combining the two movie clips will not repeat for the longest time possible—the product of the two frame lengths. That's only once every 209 frames (every 20.9 seconds at a frame rate of 10 fps), rather than the original of every 20 frames (once every 2 seconds). Not bad considering our longest animation is only 19 frames. So, making sure that each looping tween animation has a frame length that is a prime number (a different prime number from other animations), you can create an animation that takes a long time to repeat.

A good example of the use of prime numbers is a FLA I have had for so long that it may be the first Flash file I ever created. I wanted to create an animated study of a butterfly at rest. Like most real moving things, the motion of a butterfly is random and nonrepeating:

- The wings occasionally open and close, even if the butterfly has no intention of taking off.
- The antennae move.
- The whole insect constantly jitters around slightly.

Figure 4-7 shows a few frames from the animation, my first real attempt at animation all those years ago.

Figure 4-7. The butterfly animation

But I had no idea how to make the butterfly animation appear random and lifelike, as opposed to an obvious and mechanical-looking, repeating tween loop. I had been working with Flash for only a morning and did not know much about Flash ActionScript (which at the time wasn't that much anyway—I had learned the 15–20 or so actions available by the same afternoon!).

The way I did it was to use separate tweens for the three animating parts:

- The tween for the wings is 97 frames long.
- The tween for the antennae is 31 frames long.
- The whole butterfly moved in the final "jitter" animation, which is 41 frames long.

Thus, the whole butterfly animation is 97×31×41 frames long, or approximately three hours between repeats (at 12 fps). Nobody would wait that long to see the repeat, but given that it was the first Flash content I had ever pulled off, I came pretty close.

To see a finished example of the butterfly animation, download *butterfly.fla* from this book's web site.

Final Thoughts

Although creating nonrepeating animations with ActionScript is often easier, some animations just work better as tweens. The problem with tweening is, of course, that the animation is then fixed and repeating. The use of a little math and a bit of lateral thinking can easily address this problem.

Hacking The Matrix

Quickly re-create the famous falling green text effect from *The Matrix*.

Suppose we want to make a quick, nonscripted version of the green letter waterfall effect from *The Matrix* film trilogy. This effect consists of lots of randomly falling, reversed Katakana characters (see *http://japanese.about.com/library/weekly/aa052103a.htm* for details on Katakana).

The first symbol, named *text*, is a simple three-keyframe timeline, as shown in Figure 4-8.

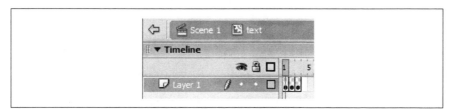

Figure 4-8. A three-keyframe timeline for our text symbol

The three keyframes display the three static text fields shown in Figure 4-9. Although this is a very repetitive animation cycle, nobody will notice because it happens so fast.

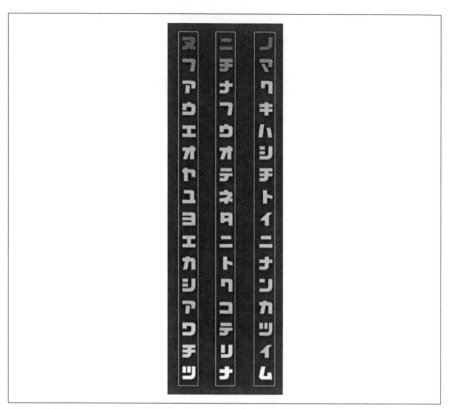

Figure 4-9. Three static text fields to be used as the basis for our animation

The Matrix waterfall effect consists of lots of these text streams falling randomly down the screen over time. To create truly random falling text, we have to do the whole thing with scripts (and judging by a quick look at the online Flash community: (a) not everyone knows how to do this, and (b) a lot of people want to create a Matrix waterfall effect but assume you need to know scripting to do it).

Well, we can't create a truly random animation with just prewritten tweens, but the one presented here repeats only once every 14,535,931 frames (about every two weeks assuming 12 fps), which might as well be random.

The way I did it was to create five tween animations, each within its own movie clip. Each movie clip consists of the text clip falling downward, as shown in Figure 4-10.

The difference between the five tweens is that each is a different number of frames long. Movie clip waterfall19 lasts 19 frames, and waterfall37 is a similar animation lasting 37 frames. The five tweens' names are shown in the Library in Figure 4-11.

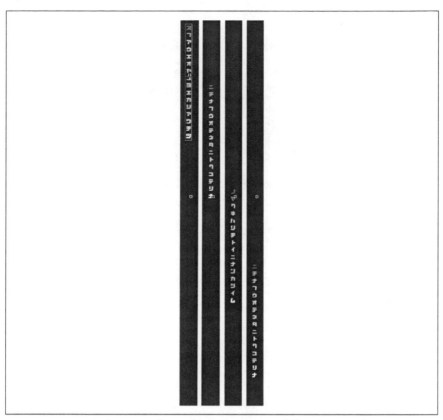

Figure 4-10. Movie clip tweened animation showing text falling downward

Figure 4-12 shows three successive shots of the final effect running. Each line in the waterfall is one of our five movie clips, all of which were started at the same time. Each repeats, so the overall animation will eventually repeat itself. Because the five animation tweens have frame lengths that are prime numbers [Hack #30], $19 \times 23 \times 29 \times 31 \times 37$ frames must elapse before the effect repeats (a rather long period of time).

You'll have to wait a considerable time before the animation repeats if you enjoy a distinct déjà vu feeling. If you are a fan of the first film in the series, you know that déjà vu is a very bad thing and is best avoided, but you'll probably want to add "waterfall" audio to more closely re-create the effect from *The Matrix*.

Final Thoughts

It's common to watch even a commercially successful animated feature film and see repetitive animation cycles. The main character could be driving down a road, and you will notice that the same combination of scrolling

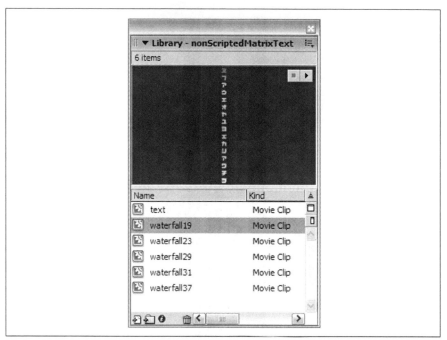

Figure 4-11. *The Library showing movie clip symbols with prime-numbered frame lengths*

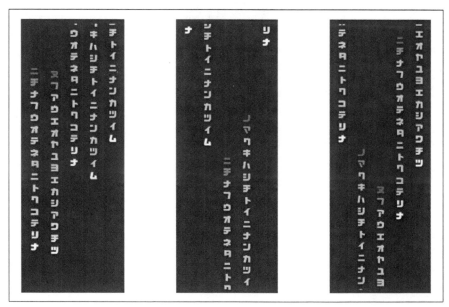

Figure 4-12. *A three-frame sequence of the final Matrix animation*

treeline, suburban houses, and parked cars seems to crop up suspiciously regularly. The fact that the same kids are playing in the front garden of every 56th house kinda gives the game away. The reason this has to happen, even in big-budget productions, is that animation is costly, and any time saving that can be made will be made. You don't want to give the game away easily though, and the prime number hack allows you to hide individual animation cycle repetitions by combining them in a way that they do not produce an overall animation that is also extremely repetitive. With increasingly realistic computer-generated effects, even real-life scenes repeat themselves. For example, the crowd in the Washington, D.C. scene in *Forrest Gump* was really a small tile of people repeated many times. In the movie, *The Truman Show*, the occupants of the fake town even repeat their movements regularly (cars circle the block, etc.), something which the title character (played by Jim Carrey) comments on.

Back in math class you probably thought prime numbers were only for rocket scientists. Now you know even Tom and Jerry have to use them.

Funny how things work out.

HACK #32 Computer-Generated Character Animation

If you don't have the time or skill to create character animations by hand, use Curious Labs' Poser application for Flash character animation.

Old hands will remember the buzz created during Flash 4's heyday when faux 3D first appeared in Flash sites. Early users of the technique such as Manuel Clement (*http://www.mano1.com*) did the whole thing by hand, but the introduction of a number of dedicated 3D-to-Flash exporters and stand-alone applications (most notably Swift 3D, *http://www.swift3d.com*) made it possible to automate the whole process.

Applications like Swift 3D are cool for creating 3D interfaces and other regular objects. Sure, it's good to have around, but it's not something mainstream motion graphics designers will use every day. Another form of 3D that is used every day by some Flash designers is character animation. Many Flash cartoons feature faux 3D characters, and almost all of them are done the old way—hand drawn.

Automating Character Animation with Poser

Curious Labs' Poser 5 application (*http://www.curiouslabs.com*), formerly from MetaCreations, is specifically designed to make 3D figures. Unlike other 3D character animation applications (such as 3D Studio Max's associated character animation suite, Character Studio), it doesn't have a steep learning curve; anyone familiar with Swift 3D can quickly pick up Poser 5. Also, unlike most other 3D applications supporting dedicated character animation, Poser is relatively cheap.

Like all 3D applications, Poser takes some time to master, but it saves you having to hand draw all your character animations. A typical Flash hand-animated feature takes months to develop, so taking the time to learn Poser should quickly pay off.

Don't be put off by the bad reviews of Poser you may find on the Web. Those refer primarily to the "dot oh" release of Poser 5, which had a number of issues. When used with the available patches installed, Poser becomes a stable and reliable tool.

Poser can be used in two ways with Flash:

- To create realistic animated figures that you can use as guides for your own animations. This is the original purpose for which Poser was created—as a digital version of the wooden mannequins used by traditional artists.

- To create final animations directly and export the animations into Flash as SWFs (in much the same way as 3D animations are exported into Flash from Swift 3D).

We will look at the latter way as an introduction to Poser and Flash, since it is the route that includes features specifically built into Poser to allow Poser-to-Flash export.

Using Poser to Create Animation Directly

Although Poser allows you to design your own characters and animation sequences, I will show what Poser can do by running through the export of an animation consisting of a preset model and preset animation.

On Poser 5's startup screen, you are presented with the default model in the default pose, as shown in Figure 4-13.

Select any part of the default figure and press the Delete key to delete it (you will get an Are You Sure? dialog box. Click yes).

From the Poser Library (select Window → Libraries if you don't see it on the far right), select Figures → Additional Figures → Cartoons to display the characters shown in Figure 4-14. Double-click on Minnie.

Minnie should appear in the main window in the standard 3D character model's default "T" pose (standing upright with arms outstretched to the sides). We need to add an animation to Minnie. Still in the Library, select

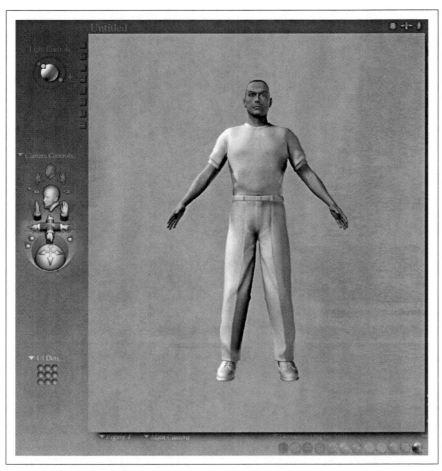

Figure 4-13. The Poser 5 startup screen

Pose → Cartoon Poses → Minnie. Select the Point pose, as shown in the middle left of Figure 4-15. This is a 28-frame animation (as stated by the number in the top right of the pose thumbnail).

Minnie will change to reflect the start of this pose in the main window, as shown in Figure 4-15.

You may have to move Minnie back a little on Poser's Stage so that all parts of her will appear on the Flash Stage when she is animated as a SWF (this is because the Poser Stage area is square, whereas the Flash Stage is typically rectangular, causing the top and bottom of the figure to be cropped when seen in Flash). To do this, find the Editing Tools icons (select Window → Editing Tools if you don't see them). Click and hold on the Translate In/Out (Z-index) icon, shown in Figure 4-16, and drag the mouse up or down to move Minnie backward or forward.

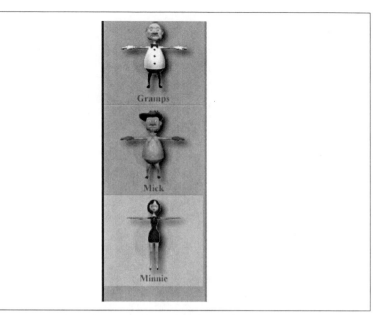

Figure 4-14. Gramps, Mick, and Minnie, three of Poser's built-in characters

Figure 4-15. The Point pose thumbnail in the Library (left); the Minnie 3D model shows
the first frame of this pose in the main window (right)

Figure 4-16. The Translate In/Out (Z-index) icon in Poser

To export the animation as a Flash SWF, select Animation → Make Movie, which opens the Make Movie dialog box shown in Figure 4-17. For the Sequence Type, select Macromedia Flash (.swf). In the Frame Rate section, select the Use This Frame Rate radio button, and select the frame rate of your target SWF. The Poser default frame rate is 30 fps. Setting a frame rate that is much lower than 30 fps may result in a jerky animation caused by too few frames, so it is best to set your SWF's frame rate at or near 30 fps.

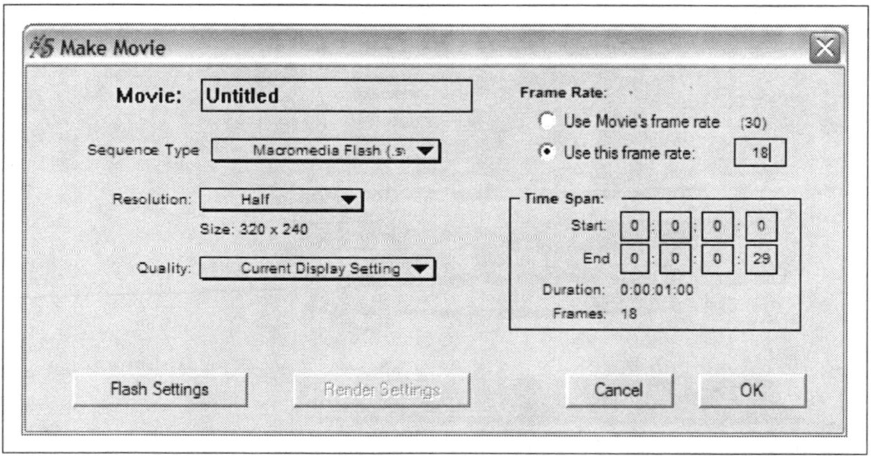

Figure 4-17. Poser's Make Movie dialog box

Select the Flash Settings button in the Make Movie dialog box. The options in the Flash Export dialog box, shown in Figure 4-18, allow you to define how you want the images that Poser renders converted into vectors. The settings for the most optimizable SWF are shown in Figure 4-18 (namely, 4 colors with Quantization set to All Frames and other options unchecked).

The optimal number of colors to use depends on the character being created. Minnie has a reduced palette and can be exported as a vector with very few colors. Remember though—the more colors you select, the more vectors will be created.

Click OK to accept your Flash Export settings, and click OK again to create the SWF.

To import the generated SWF into Flash, open a new or existing FLA and select File → Import → Import to Stage.

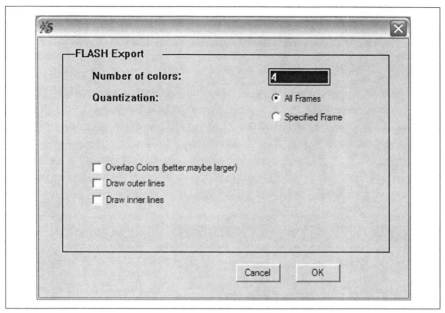

Figure 4-18. Poser's Flash Export settings dialog box

The animation appears as a series of keyframes on a single layer. Graphic shapes are grouped. As with all exports, the next step is optimizing the animation. Optimizing Poser output is very similar to optimizing Swift 3D output. If you are good at the former, you should have no problems with the latter.

The following tips should help:

- Ungroup every frame's content and then optimize (Modify → Shape → Optimize) and/or smooth it (Modify → Shape → Smooth).

- As with Swift 3D, Poser doesn't intelligently turn often-used shapes into symbols and reuse them. It's up to you to seek them out and fix the problem. For example, Minnie's legs and skirt look as if they could be replaced with a small number of symbols that could be reused between frames.

Figure 4-19 depicts the process of optimizing frames using onion-skinning outlines and the standard Flash optimization and drawing tools.

More experienced Flash designers may want to consider importing the Poser images as guide bitmaps and tracing them to create the vector shapes from scratch, as shown in Figure 4-20. This is my preferred route; although it is less automatic, it retains the hand-drawn feel of traditional animation while still speeding up the process. It also results in more optimized graphics.

Figure 4-19. Optimizing Poser animations imported into Flash

Figure 4-20. Output from Poser that can be imported into Flash and used as character animation guides

Final Thoughts

Poser is a tool that is often used with Photoshop for any work that would otherwise require source material consisting of images of human models and stand-ins, but it is currently rarely used with Flash.

Although creating your own custom 3D characters and animations in Poser, then hand-optimizing each frame in Flash, is still a long task, it may shorten at least some of the months of hard work required to do the whole thing by hand, particularly if you already have some 3D experience through Swift 3D.

For the traditional animator who prefers to hand draw his characters, Poser offers a quick and easy way to create accurate animation guide images.

Particle Effects

#33
Add realism to any animation using effects with small particles, such as explosions, sparks, rain, or snow.

When animating using timelines, one of the hardest things to achieve is common particle effects such as snow, star fields, or moving water. Flash doesn't have native support for particle effects, and animating thousands of tiny movie clips in different directions is time consuming. But it is easier than you may think to create varied effects.

The simplest particle is one that moves in only one direction—straight down. So let's start with a simple "dropping particle," created using a nested movie clip. This clip can be rotated to create a number of different effects without too much effort on your part.

```
function mover( ):Void {
  this._y += this.speed;
  if (this._y > 400) {
    this._y = 0;
    this.speed = Math.random( )*10+5;
  }
}
var path:MovieClip = this.createEmptyMovieClip("path", 0);
var dot:MovieClip = this.path.createEmptyMovieClip("dot", 0);
dot.lineStyle(0, 0x0, 100);
dot.moveTo(0, 10);
dot.lineTo(0, 15);
dot.speed = Math.random( ) * 10 + 5;
dot.onEnterFrame = mover;
```

The preceding code creates a movie clip, path, inside which another clip, dot, is created. The dot clip is then made to move from the top of the screen downward. You're probably thinking, "What's the point of path?" Well, that's the hacky part—by rotating path, we can change the direction in which dot moves. Try adding this to the end of the previous listing to see how it works:

```
// Move the clip to (100, 100) so it is visible even if rotated.
path._x = path._y = 100;
path._rotation = 50;
```

By rotating path, we rotate the direction in which dot falls. Further, by scaling path as dot moves, we can create complex acceleration without doing too much work.

Star Field

The following listing shows a modified version of the preceding code. Note the scaling and rotation effects highlighted in bold. Also, note that the code assumes you have turned the Stage color to black (choose Modify → Document, then click on the color swatch and select black).

```
function mover( ) {
  // Move the particle over time
  this._y += this.speed;
  this._yscale += 10;
  this.speed++;
  if (this._y > 500) {
    this._y = 0;
    this.speed = Math.random( ) * 10;
    this._yscale = 100;
  }
}
function starField(x, y, n) {
  // Generate a starfield of specified dimensions with n stars
  for (var i = 0; i < n; i++) {
    var star = this.createEmptyMovieClip("star" + i, i);
    var dot = star.createEmptyMovieClip("dot", 0);
    star._rotation = Math.random( ) * 360;
    star._x = x;
    star._y = y;
    dot.lineStyle(0, 0xFFFFFF, 100);
    dot.moveTo(0, 10);
    dot.lineTo(0, 15);
    dot.onEnterFrame = mover;
    dot.speed = Math.random( )*10;
  }
}
starField(275, 200, 100);
```

In the preceding code, we create multiple star clips, each of which takes the role of the path clip in the earlier example. Each star clip is rotated at a random angle, as shown in Figure 4-21.

We also scale the star clips; elongating the path (the star clip) while the dot is moving along creates acceleration, simulating the way things appear to get faster as they get closer to us.

Figure 4-21. A star field created with particle effects

Using the "scale the path clip as the dot clip moves" trick, you can create gravity effects [Hack #38]. This code listing employs the same techniques to simulate moving water:

```
function mover( ):Void {
  this._y += this.speed;
  this._yscale += 10;
  this.speed++;
  if (this._y > 500) {
    this._y = 0;
    this.speed = Math.random( ) * 10;
    this._yscale = 100;
  }
}
function waterfall(x1, x2, n) {
  for (var i = 0; i < n; i++) {
    var star:MovieClip = this.createEmptyMovieClip("star" + i, i);
    star._x = Math.random( ) * x2 + x1;
    star._y = 0;
    var dot = star.createEmptyMovieClip("dot", 0);
    dot.lineStyle(0, 0xFFFFFF, 100);
    dot.moveTo(0, 10);
    dot.lineTo(0, 15);
    dot.onEnterFrame = mover;
    dot.speed = Math.random( )*10;
  }
}
waterfall(200, 300, 800);
```

The final effect shown here is snow. By varying the angle of the particle paths randomly, we get a flurry of moving particles that look a lot like snow:

```
function mover( ) {
  this._y += this.speed;
  if (this._y > 500) {
    this._y = 0;
    this.speed = Math.random( )*10+5;
  }
}
function snow(a,  n) {
  for (var i = 0; i < n; i++) {
    var star:MovieClip = this.createEmptyMovieClip("star" + i, i);
    star._x = Math.random( ) * 550;
    star._rotation = (Math.random( ) * 2 * a) - a
    star._y = 0;
    var dot:MovieClip = star.createEmptyMovieClip("dot", 0);
    dot.lineStyle(0, 0xFFFFFF, 100);
    dot.moveTo(0, 10);
    dot.lineTo(0, 15);
    dot.onEnterFrame = mover;
    dot.speed = Math.random( ) * 10 + 5;
  }
}
snow(30,  800);
```

Final Thoughts

Although it is normal to attempt to create particle effects using (x, y) coordinates, you can sometimes get bogged down with the trigonometry or complex motion effects. By using an embedded clip to allow you to define a particle angle and speed (i.e., a polar coordinate description), many particle effects become much easier and require minimal calculations, which means you can have lots of them, and they become very easy to create.

Shape Tweening Complex Shapes

Shape tweening is underutilized due to the difficulty in getting predictable morphs. Create better shape tweens by simplifying your shapes into "single perimeters."

One of the easiest (and most used) applications of shape tweening is morphing text. To create such a shape tween, use the Text tool to type a letter, such as "e" in frame 1. Insert a keyframe (F6) in frame 10 and, in frame 10, delete the "e" and replace it with the letter "c". In each keyframe, select the letter and choose Modify → Break Apart to convert the text to a vector shape (if you have multi-letter text, you need to choose Modify → Break Apart twice). Then select one of the tween frames (frames 2–9) and choose Shape from the Tween pop-up menu in the Properties panel. Scrub the playhead across the timeline to see Flash perform the shape tween.

Although a shape tween between an "e" and a "c" seems as if it should be easy, Flash gets totally confused and adds odd intermediate swirls, as shown in Figure 4-22.

Figure 4-22. A really bad shape tween from an "e" to a "c" caused by shapes with different numbers of perimeters

Flash's shape tweening algorithm doesn't like it if one of your shapes has enclosed areas (such as the eye of the lowercase letter "e") and the other (such as the letter "c") does not. The problem cannot be fixed even if you add shape hints, because one shape (the "e") has one more continuous perimeter than the other (the "c").

You can see what Flash is trying to do here if you think in terms of perimeters. Flash correctly tries to tween the outer perimeter in the "e" to the outer perimeter in the "c." But Flash doesn't know what to do with the inner perimeter (the one around the eye of the "e") because the "c" doesn't have a second perimeter. So Flash does nothing much with this extra set of lines.

Earlier we looked at how to cut gaps in shapes [Hack #20] to fool Flash into thinking that a complex shape (one with one or more enclosed spaces) is a simpler shape. You can use the same trick to force dissimilar shapes to look more similar, which is required for smooth shape tweening.

Applying the same technique here, we simply add a hairline gap in the eye of the "e" to ensure that both letters have a single perimeter. Pick the location for the hairline gap (break) that makes it easiest for Flash to morph one shape into the other. This may take experimentation, but you'll develop an intuitive feel with practice. In this case, the best location is anywhere along the horizontal line that forms the lower edge of the eye of the "e." Using a hairline stroke (by setting the hairline option for the Line tool using the Properties panel), draw a line at the required point. Then, convert the stroke to a fill using Modify → Shape → Convert Lines to Fills and delete it, which opens up the enclosed area and results in a single perimeter.

If you test the shape tween again, you will see much better results, as shown in Figure 4-23. The swirls immediately disappear and Flash makes more sensible decisions in controlling the tween transition. Flash can now correctly map the outlines between the "e" and the "c" because they both have one perimeter.

Figure 4-23. An improved shape tween from an "e" to a "c" enabled by having two shapes with the same number of perimeters

The mismatched perimeters problem explains why Flash doesn't like to tween letters with disconnected areas (like "i" and "j") to contiguous letters (such as a "t"). The problem is depicted in Figure 4-24.

Figure 4-24. A bad tween from an "i" to a "t"

One hacky way around this is to remove the dot over the "i" just before you perform the shape tween, as shown in Figure 4-25.

Figure 4-25. An improved tween from an "i" to a "t" enabled by removing the dot before performing the tween

However, if you are tweening from a "t" to an "i," you'll need to either use the hairline trick to break the "t" into two perimeters or wait until the tween finishes before adding the dot over the "i."

Final Thoughts

Vectors are cool for low-bandwidth delivery, but because they are computationally expensive, Flash has a number of limitations in their use, such as assuming that the start and end of a shape tween have the same number of perimeters. As we have seen, understanding these limitations is the key to overcoming them. As soon as you realize that Flash is looking at not only matching points between the start and end of a shape tween but also the perimeters, you can set about finding ways to fix the problem.

3D and Physics
Hacks 35–41

The Flash Player is somewhat underpowered in terms of computational and animation speed. Therefore, processor-intensive applications, such as 3D, are problematic in Flash. Flash doesn't include any native 3D ActionScript commands or 3D hardware support, unlike Macromedia Director (which supports the Shockwave 3D format).

However, good design is all about knowing the system, working within its limits, and hacking around the obstacles with a bit of lateral thinking or by simplifying the problem. Regardless, while being able to rotate and zoom a 3D model of a wristwatch before you buy it is cool, most customers are more impressed by good 2D photography and proper graphic design in the product presentation.

You can best use 3D as a part of other applications, rather than as the entire application. For example, you can mix 3D animation with traditional animation that relies on the drawing ability of the animator to imply 3D. For a good example of mixing 3D and 2D animation, see the Flash cartoon "HitchHiker Part Two" at Bitey Castle (*http://www.oohbitey.com/hh2Window.html*). The car animation was authored with Swift 3D (*http://www.swift3d.com*), then superimposed on the 2D background animation.

Most modern operating systems include faux 3D effects in their GUIs, and you can create faux 3D windows and buttons in Flash. Sites like layerbit (*http://www.layerbit.com*) take 3D effects to the extreme. The Volkswagen UK site promoting The Phaeton (*http://www.thephaeton.co.uk/universe*), however, is a more subdued example of scripted 3D that pushes the limits of what Flash can produce in real time without exceeding them.

Simulate 3D

Flash doesn't support true 3D, but you can fake it by arranging 2D image slices as if they are filling a 3D space.

Although Flash doesn't support 3D assets, you can simulate 3D in various ways using 2D assets. One simple approach is to arrange slices of 2D imagery but offset them to create the illusion of 3D. That is, a stack of flat 2D slices is used to create the illusion of a 3D object with volume.

This hack is inspired by a number of sites including the 3D head at sofake (go to *http://www.sofake.com*, click the 10th white square at the bottom of the home page, and click the link for *haircut.swf*) and Andy Foulds's "Leader of the Free World" (go to *http://www.foulds2000.freeserve.co.uk/index_v2.html* and click on the 8th square above the Amusements heading). However, I first saw this trick used back in Flash 4 by Rouien Zarin (*http://www.zarinmedia.com*) and Ant Eden (*http://www.arseiam.com*). Ant Eden also designed a wonderful 3D slice engine, which extends the concept by rotating and scaling the slices (click on the 3D icon at *http://www.arseiam.com/index2.htm*). This allows his slices to move in 3D space, rather than in just two dimensions as per this hack.

We learned earlier how to create a Flash animation by stripping a GIF, importing it into Flash, and then rebuilding it with a richer set of animation options [Hack #4]. This hack introduces the O'Reilly mascot (a tarsier from the cover of *Learning the vi Editor*) to the world of 3D. Although he doesn't look very 3D in Figure 5-1, see the *critter02.fla* on this book's web site to fully appreciate the effect.

Slice 2D to Create an Extra Dimension

Suppose you are slicing an apple parallel to the core. If the slices are cut really thin, you end up with many 2D cross sections. By stacking them in the order they existed in the original apple, you can re-create a 3D apple.

This hack works on the same principle: create a lot of 2D slices of an object, then move them as if they were stacked together in the original object. If done properly, the result looks like it is a 3D shape that has volume.

Cut Up the Tarsier

We create our slices using the all-purpose "you'll never think of this" solution: masking. Think about what the tarsier would look like if we sliced him into cross sections (from front to back) and put him back together. Instead of seeing his internal organs, all you see is his outer pelt. Taking that into account, the slices we need would look something like those shown in Figure 5-2.

Figure 5-1. A 3D tarsier

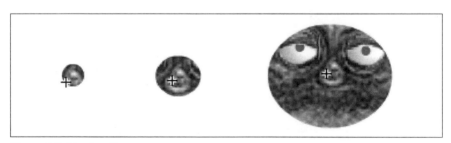

Figure 5-2. Tarsier slices

Get the picture? It's simply an expanding circular mask centered on the tarsier's snout (the closest point to us in 3D space). However, if we stack these slices on a flat screen, they don't appear to have any depth; all we see is the original tarsier. We add depth by emulating what happens when the tarsier turns his body. If the tarsier turns to his right (our left), in reality, the slices must rotate to display his left side (on our right). But if we keep the rotation small, we can approximate the 3D movement by simply sliding the slices around. The topmost slice (the one in the foreground) moves slightly to the left, and the bottommost slice (furthest away from the viewer) moves slightly to the right.

That's the whole premise of the hack, and once you know it, the rest is relatively simple.

To create the slices, we tween an expanding circle and use it to mask the original tarsier clip. The mask tween stops at frame 19 so that at frame 20 we can see our full, unmasked critter as the last slice. To see the slices, load up *critter02.fla* from this book's site, edit symbol *critter in 3D* in the Library, and scrub the playhead along the symbol's timeline, as shown in Figure 5-3.

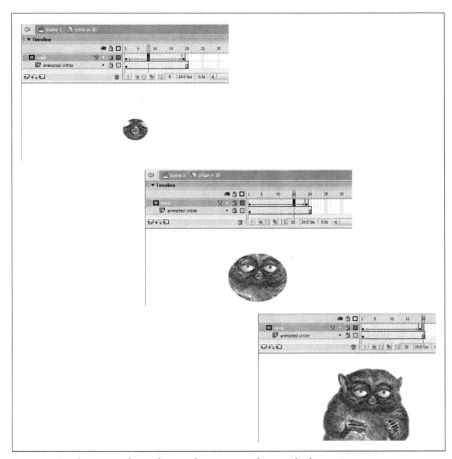

Figure 5-3. The tweened circular mask progressively reveals the tarsier

To display 20 slices of the tarsier on the Stage, attach 20 instances of the *critter in 3D* clip to the main timeline. Each slice's timeline is stopped at one of the 20 frames in our animation.

```
this.attachMovie("menu", "menu_mc", 1000);
// Place the O'Reilly bar on the Stage
menu_mc._x = 200;
menu_mc._y = 270;
```

```
// Create an initialization object for the
// movie clips we are placing on stage.
var init:Object = new Object();
init._x = 200;
init._y = 200;
var sliceDepth:Number = 20;
// Attach 20 critter movie clips to the Stage, each
// stopped at a different frame to create the slices.
for (var i:Number = 1; i < sliceDepth + 1; i++) {
  var critterName:String = "critter" + (sliceDepth - i);
  var critter:MovieClip = this.attachMovie("critter",
                          critterName, sliceDepth - i, init);
  critter.gotoAndStop(i);
  critter.offset = ((sliceDepth - i) - (sliceDepth / 2)) * 0.05;
  critter.onEnterFrame = initClip;
}
```

Attach the preceding code to frame 1 of the main timeline. The 20 slices (named critter20 through critter1) are placed at depths from 20 down to 1 at position (200, 200). All standard stuff. This line is the important one:

```
critter.gotoAndStop(i);
```

It stops each instance at one of the 20 frames in the masking animation, giving us 20 unique slices.

Another important line is this one:

```
critter.offset = ((sliceDepth - i) - (sliceDepth / 2)) * 0.05;
```

It adds a property named offset, whose value varies between -0.5 and 0.5, to each clip. The offset controls how much our slices move to the left and right in response to mouse movement (our pet tarsier is trained to turn toward the mouse position).

The event handlers that control the movement per slice are shown next. The *initClip( )* function is used as the *onEnterFrame( )* event handler for each slice; it's a simple initialization script that deletes itself after running once.

```
initClip = function () {
  // Initialize this slice
  this.startX = this._x;
  this.startY = this._y;
  delete (this.onEnterFrame);
  this.onMouseMove = mover;
};
mover = function () {
  // Move this slice according to its position in the slice stack.
  var distX = this.offset * (_xmouse - this._x) / 50;
  var distY = this.offset * (_ymouse - this._y) / 50;
  this._x = this.startX + distX;
  this._y = this.startY + distY;
  updateAfterEvent();
};
```

Following initialization, the *mover( )* function runs whenever the mouse moves. This *onMouseMove( )* event handler is almost identical to the earlier eye movement code implemented within an *onEnterFrame( )* handler [Hack #4]. The major difference is that in this slice animation, the offset property gives a slightly different range of movement for each slice.

That's all there is to the effect. It's a surprisingly simple concept and simple code.

Why did we choose a different event than the one used in earlier eye movement animation? Flash issues *onMouseMove* events as frequently as it can while the mouse is moving. The *onEnterFrame* event runs at the frame rate. When the mouse is stationary, *onEnterFrame* events are still issued, but during mouse movement, *onEnterFrame* events occur less often than *onMouseMove* events. You can confirm this by running both event handlers at the same time with the *onMouseMove( )* handler incrementing a counter variable each time it is called, and the *onEnterFrame( )* handler decrementing the same counter. You will find that the counter climbs when the mouse is moving because, during that time, *onMouseMove( )* is invoked more often than *onEnterFrame( )*.

So we choose an event to supply responsiveness in the user's area of focus: we concentrate more processing power [Hack #71] on the 3D animation because we expect the user to look at it more intently. The earlier eye movement animation is too subtle to look any better if we throw more processing resources at it, so we use the less-processor-intensive *onEnterFrame* event instead.

You can also vary the width and height of the slices as they move. As an object rotates left or right, each slice's width should change when viewed from the front. Likewise, when an object rotates up or down, each slice's height should change. Adding the following lines (shown in bold) to the main animation script sometimes (but not always) helps the effect look more realistic:

```
mover = function () {
    // Move this slice according to its position in the slice stack.
    var distX = this.offset * (_xmouse - this._x) / 50;
    var distY = this.offset * (_ymouse - this._y) / 50;
    this._x = this.startX + distX;
    this._y = this.startY + distY;
    this._width = 100 - Math.abs(distX)
    this._height = 100 - Math.abs(distY)
    updateAfterEvent();
};
```

Final Thoughts

Our 2D-to-3D bitmap effect could use further refinement now that you grasp the basic technique. The basic technique effectively maps the image slices onto a cone. If you move the mouse cursor a great distance from the tarsier, the cone shape reveals itself, as seen in Figure 5-4.

Figure 5-4. Slices are subject to distortion because they are mapped to a cone

Because the mask consists of a simple circle that gets bigger, the slices' perimeters mark out a cone. By hand drawing each slice mask using perimeters that map to the true 3D object more closely, you can create an effect that holds up at severe angles, allowing rotation to almost 180 degrees. (You can't rotate to a full 180 degrees because the thickness of the slices tends toward zero at that extreme. You'd have to switch to another set of slices created with the object viewed at a different angle.)

The more slices you use, the better the effect, which comes at the expense of performance. You can make your slices more numerous where the contour of the 3D shape curves the most. You must then vary the offset in a nonlinear way to emulate the fact that the slices are no longer equally spaced in depth.

HACK Panoramic Images
#36
Use a little ingenuity to create 3D panoramas for playback in Flash, simulating immersion in an environment.

Panoramic imaging is a rendering technique in which the viewer appears to be standing in the center of a 3D-like environment. The image can be rotated, and the technique uses a texture image with distortions to simulate the depth of the surroundings. This technique was popularized with technologies like QuickTime VR (*http://www.apple.com/quicktime/qtvr/authoringstudio*) from Apple.

Panoramic content abounds, especially on travel and tourist web sites. However, most solutions require Java or a third-party plugin, reducing the likelihood users will view them, and some require licenses for development or deployment tools. Although several techniques are used for panoramic imaging—spherical, cubic, and so on—cylindrical panoramas, in which the texture is projected on the walls of a round "room," are the most common. Cylindrical panoramas are both the easiest to create and fastest to render, allowing the Flash Player to display them with adequate performance.

Although the Flash Player lacks the features and speed of some panoramic viewing tools, it doesn't require the user to install more software beyond the Flash Player (which is more ubiquitous than Java or any other third-party plugin). It also allows panoramic views to be controlled from inside a Flash movie where you can add interactivity or integrate it with other content. Moreover, there's no licensing fee for development or distribution.

Creating Panoramic Images

A panoramic image (a.k.a. a *panorama*, or simply *pano*) is a long horizontal image representing a 360-degree view of the surroundings, as shown in Figure 5-5.

Figure 5-5. A panoramic image

This type of image is usually created by taking multiple shots from a given point with a rotating camera mounted on a tripod. Multiple images are often *stitched* together to create a flat cylindrical view. Various solutions can create and edit panoramas, from cameras that automatically create panoramic photos to stitching software designed to work with various image types.

Although creating panoramic images is beyond the scope of this book, it's simpler than it sounds. Sites such as Panoguide.com (*http://www.panoguide.com*) cover this topic in detail; you can find a guide to panorama editing software (*http://www.panoguide.com/software/recommendations.html*) and a gallery of downloadable panos (*http://www.panoguide.com/gallery*) on the same site.

To create our panorama-like view in Flash, we'll start with the *pano.jpg* panoramic image downloadable from the book's web site (the final Flash movie is also downloadable as *pano.fla*).

Using Flash for Image Manipulation

To emulate a 3D panorama, we'll cut our flat panoramic image into multiple strips, as shown in Figure 5-6. Each strip will have a different size and scale, to simulate a different depth. We'll achieve this simulated 3D using multiple instances and masks [Hack #35].

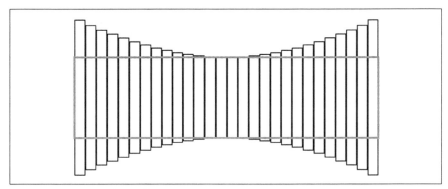

Figure 5-6. Vertical slices of a panorama

Although only the area indicated by the green outline in Figure 5-6 is shown at runtime, each image strip is seamlessly scaled to match the arrangement shown in the figure. When the images are cropped at the top and bottom, and the area outside the viewer's field of vision is hidden, the impression of depth is complete. The scaling provides the illusion of a 3D view—enlarging the strips on the periphery relative to those in the center approximates mapping the panoramic image on the inside surface of a cylindrical wall, with the viewpoint being at the center of the circle.

JPEG format is the typical image format used for panoramas. Once you've created a pano (or downloaded the sample *pano.jpg* from this book's web site or a sample from Panoguide.com's gallery), import the file into Flash (using File → Import → Import to Library).

Let's start the code by setting some simple data that will be used by our image movie clip:

```
var viewWidth:Number = 450;
var viewHeight:Number = 400;
var precision:Number = 8;
var viewFOV:Number = 60;
```

where:

viewWidth
    The width of the source panorama image.

viewHeight
    The height of the source panorama image.

precision

The precision specifies the width of each strip of image. Setting this to 1 ensures maximum fidelity but requires more processing power than Flash can muster. The optimal value is determined manually by testing, but starting with a reasonably high quality value (lower number), such as 8, is recommended. You should increase the width of the strips only if the effect seems too slow. You can also get a better impression of how the effect works if you set this value high (such as to 50), because then the strips in the effect become obvious.

viewFOV

The field of vision (a.k.a. field of view) in degrees. It controls how much the image will appear distorted (i.e., it controls the curvature effect of the distortion caused by scaling the strips as you get further away from the center of the image). This value depends directly on the size and aspect ratio of the image and that's why it must be set manually. Typical useful values are 60 to 80 degrees. A value of 1 yields a flat image (no 3D effect) in which the image is effectively mapped onto a plane rather than a curved surface. A value of 180 yields an abnormally high curvature (i.e., a "fish-eye" effect).

After our values have been set, we need to cut the image into strips. First, we'll need a function to create strips to be used as masks:

```
this.createBox = function (name:String, x:Number, y:Number,
    w:Number, h:Number, target:MovieClip):MovieClip {
  // This function creates the rectangles that are used as masks
  if (target == undefined) {
    target = this;
  }
  var box:MovieClip = target.createEmptyMovieClip(name,
                        this.currentDepth++);
  box._x = x;
  box._y = y;
  // Use the Drawing API to draw a rectangle.
  box.lineStyle(undefined);
  box.moveTo (0, 0);
  box.beginFill(0x000000, 30);
  box.lineTo (w, 0);
  box.lineTo (w, h);
  box.lineTo (0, h);
  box.lineTo (0, 0);
  box.endFill();
  return (box);
};
```

Then we can create the new images, each in its position, according to the view settings (viewWidth, viewHeight, precision, and viewFOV). We duplicate the original image (presumed to be previously imported into the Library) and create a strip mask for it. The *pano.fla* file on this book's web site contains a fully commented version of this code (reduced here for brevity):

```
var xpos:Number = 0;
var currentDepth:Number = 100;
var photoList:Array = [];
while (viewWidth%precision != 0) {
  viewWidth++;
}
var boxCount:Number = 0;
var stripMask:MovieClip;
var stripPhoto:MovieClip;
var posX:Number;
var ang:Number;
var h:Number;
var viewTotal:Number = (viewHeight * 180) / viewFOV;
for (var i = 0; i < viewWidth; i += precision) {
  // Find the correct height and scale for this strip
  posX = ((viewWidth / 2) - ( i + (precision / 2)));
  ang = Math.asin(Math.abs(posX / (viewTotal / 2)));
  h = (Math.cos(ang) * (viewTotal / 2) - viewTotal / 2) * -1;
  // Create mask box
  stripMask = this.createBox("box_" + boxCount,
                              i, s, precision, viewHeight);
  // Duplicate photo
  stripPhoto = this.photo.duplicateMovieClip("photo_" + boxCount,
                                              1000 + boxCount);
  stripPhoto._y = -h;
  stripPhoto._xscale = ((viewHeight + h * 2) / photo._height) * 100;
  stripPhoto._yscale = stripPhoto._xscale;
  stripPhoto.setMask(stripMask);
  photoList.push({photo:stripPhoto, mask:stripMask,
                  scale:stripPhoto._xscale / 100});
  boxCount++;
}
photo._visible = false;
```

Now, our strips are done; each strip is masked by a mask clip and the strips are correctly scaled. The Stage thus contains a large number of individual photo clips, each of which can be seen through the "slot" of the mask clip as it moves from left to right (i.e., each mask clip stays still as the image that it masks moves).

References to each clip have been added to the `photoList` array to make them easily accessible. We now need code to place all images at their correct positions to form the arrangement seen in Figure 5-6:

```
this.redrawStrips = function() {
  // Redraw (reposition) all photos.
  // Masks remain where they are.
  var tpos:Number;
  var cpos:Number = 0;
```

```
// Create local variables to handle the
// properties of each strip, photoList[i]:
//    mx: mask clip _x location
//    mw: mask clip _width property
//    pw: photo clip _width property
//    s:  strip scaling factor
var mx:Number;
var mw:Number;
var pw:Number;
var s:Number;
for (var i = 0; i < this.photoList.length; i++) {
  mx = photoList[i].mask._x;
  mw = photoList[i].mask._width;
  pw = photoList[i].photo._width;
  s = photoList[i].scale;
  tpos = mx - ((cpos + xpos) * s);
  // Update the photo x scroll position,
  // looping it back to the start if required.
  while (tpos > mx + mw) {
    tpos -= pw;
  }
  while (tpos + pw < mx) {
    tpos += pw;
  }
  // Fill in the gap between the start and end
  // of the pano to make it appear continuous.
  if ( (tpos > mx) && (tpos < mx + mw) ) {
    // Duplicate for filling, left
    var alt:MovieClip = photoList[i].photo.duplicateMovieClip(
                   "alternatePhoto", 998);
    alt._x = tpos - pw;
    var altM:MovieClip = photoList[i].mask.duplicateMovieClip(
                   "alternateMask", 997);
    alt.setMask(altM);
  } else if ( (tpos + pw > mx) && (tpos + pw < mx + mw) ) {
    // Duplicate for filling, right
    var alt:MovieClip = photoList[i].photo.duplicateMovieClip(
                   "alternatePhoto", 998);
    alt._x = tpos+pw;
    var altM:MovieClip = photoList[i].mask.duplicateMovieClip(
                   "alternateMask", 997);
    alt.setMask(altM);
  }
  // Move the current photo clip
  photoList[i].photo._x = tpos;
  cpos += mw / s;
  }
};
```

This code takes a position offset variable, xpos, and moves all the images up
or down based on the value of each strip's scale. At the end of this process,
each strip is moved up or down so that the strips take up the vertical positions shown in Figure 5-6.

Finally, we set our initial position and make sure the images are moved to their correct places:

```
this.xpos = 0;
this.redrawStrips( );
```

The code so far renders a static panoramic view in Flash, but we need code to let the user rotate the view so she feels the sensation of depth and can explore the panorama. Several possible user interfaces can give the viewer the ability to scroll the panorama. Allowing the user to click and drag to scroll the image is a good choice (another option would be using buttons for left and right scrolling). In this example, we will scroll the panorama based on the mouse cursor position. If the cursor is to the left of the screen's center and the user clicks and holds the mouse down, the panorama scrolls to the left. Scrolling to the right operates similarly. The scrolling speed is controlled by how far to the left or right of the image center the mouse pointer is. The final FLA also replaces the mouse pointer with a simple arrow clip, arrow, which shows the scrolling direction.

The preceding code set our offset variable xpos before calling our *redrawStrips( )* method (which controls the position of each photo under the strip, and therefore the scrolling). Since our replacement cursor, the arrow movie clip, is already in the Flash movie, we just need to add the following code to make it respond to mouse movement:

```
arrow.onMouseMove = function( ) {
  this.isInside = this._parent._xmouse > 0 &&
                  this._parent._xmouse < this._parent.viewWidth &&
                  this._parent._ymouse > 0 &&
                  this._parent._ymouse < this._parent.viewHeight;
  if (this.isInside) {
    // Arrow is over the pano, so show the custom
    // arrow cursor instead of the standard mouse pointer.
    if (!this._visible) {
      Mouse.hide( );
      this._visible = true;
    }
    if (this._visible) {
      // Show the left arrow or right arrow frame depending on whether
      // it is to the left or right, and make the custom cursor mouse.
      this.gotoAndStop((this._parent._xmouse < this._parent.viewWidth / 2) ?
            "left" : "right");
    }
  } else {
    // Arrow is not over the pano, so show the standard mouse
    // pointer instead of our custom cursor.
    if (this._visible) {
      Mouse.show( );
      this._visible = false;
    }
```

```
    }
  };
  arrow.onMouseDown = function( ) {
    // If mouse is down, change xpos to create the scroll effect
    // when redrawStrips( ) is called.
    this.onEnterFrame = function( ) {
      if (this.isInside) {
        this._parent.xpos -= ((this._parent.viewWidth / 2) - this._x) / 10;
        // Max moving speed.
        this._parent.redrawStrips( );
      }
    };
  };
  arrow.onMouseUp = function( ) {
    this.onEnterFrame = undefined;
  };
```

While this movement code creates only a left-right scrolling panorama (as opposed to being able to look up and down as well), it's reasonably simple code that can be easily modified.

For those feeling adventurous, you might try to simulate a panorama mapped onto the inside of a sphere rather than a cylinder. This would allow the user to look up and down as well as left and right. (Hint: you can mask the image a second time with vertical strips to create the vertical warping or use a series of square masks that get larger as you get further from the center of the image.)

Final Thoughts

While Flash is no match for other panorama viewer software in quality or speed, having in-movie panoramas that can be controlled by ActionScript is a big plus. Basic panoramic rendering is just the beginning; you could add hotspots or links using ActionScript. Many Flash sites use sliding images as a substitute for panoramic viewing. This cylindrical pano-rendering hack offers a more immersive experience without requiring the user to download other plugins.

—*Zeh Fernando*

An Optimized 3D Plotter
#37   Create a compact and fast 3D engine to plot 3D objects on Flash's 2D Stage.

True 3D requires presenting two different images to the viewer's eyes. The viewer's brain uses the differences in the two images to calculate the depth of each object in space (so-called stereo vision). For example, 3D movie glasses use red and blue filters (or vertical and horizontal polarizing filters) to ensure that each eye sees a slightly different image (the theater screen displays two offset images), and your brain constructs a single image with depth. However, so-called 3D computer displays don't present different images to each eye. Instead, they merely project a 3D image onto a 2D plane. The image looks the same even if you close one eye, and your brain makes reasonable guesses about depth based on scale and shading. Creating a basic 3D engine isn't as hard as you might imagine. This hack shows the math behind a simple 3D point plotter, which projects a 3D (x, y, z) coordinate into the 2D (x, y) space of Flash's Stage.

Like most graphics programs, Flash uses the coordinate system shown in Figure 5-7, in which the Y values increase as you move down the screen (the opposite of the Cartesian coordinate system). The X axis increases to the right, as you'd expect.

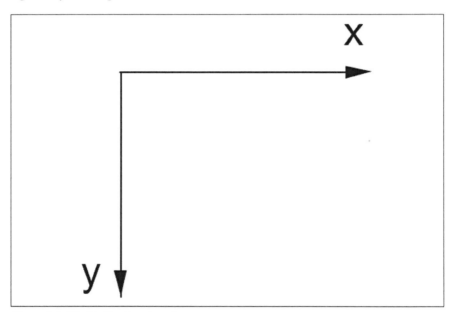

Figure 5-7. Flash's Y axis points down

Flash supports only 2D (X and Y axes). To simulate the Z axis, we use scaling to approximate the depth into the screen. In Figure 5-8, our cube becomes smaller as it moves further away along the Z axis. Depending on the perspective angle, we may also see the X and Y positions of the cube change as it moves along the Z axis.

The scaling of the x and y coordinates at a distance z, when viewed through a camera of focal length f_o is $f_o/(f_o+z)$.

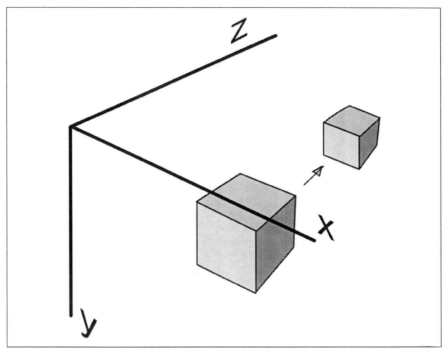

Figure 5-8. A cube moving along the Z axis

To plot a 3D point (x, y, z) in two dimensions, (x, y), with scaling s, we can use the following approximations:

```
scale = f₀ / (f₀ + z)
xLoc = x * scale
yLoc = y * scale
s = 100 * scale
```

Although the scaling of a true 3D object varies across its dimensions (faces closer to us appear bigger than faces further away), we treat a given object as existing at a single point for simplicity (unless the object is very large or very close to the camera, the approximation is sufficiently accurate).

The preceding approximation is very easy to implement in code as a basic 3D plotter. Create a new FLA with default Stage dimensions (550×400) and set its frame rate to 24 fps. Attach the following code to frame 1 of the main timeline:

```
function moveSpheres( ) {
    // This function moves the spheres
    for (var i:Number = 0; i < n; i++) {
        pX[i] += pXS[i];
        if (Math.abs(pX[i]) > wSize) {
            pXS[i] = -pXS[i];
```

```
    }
    pY[i] += pYS[i];
    if (Math.abs(pY[i]) > wSize) {
      pYS[i] = -pYS[i];
    }
    pZ[i] += pZS[i] * scale;
    if (Math.abs(pZ[i]) > wSize) {
      pZS[i] = -pZS[i];
    }
    threeDPlotter(i);
  }
}
function threeDPlotter(i) {
  scale = fLength/(fLength + pZ[i]);
  world["p"+i]._x = (pX[i] * scale);
  world["p"+i]._y = (pY[i] * scale);
  world["p"+i]._xscale = world["p"+i]._yscale = 100 * scale;
}
// MAIN CODE
var fLength:Number = 150;
var wSize:Number = 100;
var centerX:Number = 275;
var centerY:Number = 200;
var n:Number = 30;
var pX:Array = new Array();
var pY:Array = new Array();
var pZ:Array = new Array();
var pXS:Array = new Array();
var pYS:Array = new Array();
var pZS:Array = new Array();
// Create the 3D world
this.createEmptyMovieClip("world", 0);
world._x = centerX;
world._y = centerY;
// Initialize each sphere
for (var i:Number = 0; i < n; i++) {
  world.createEmptyMovieClip("p" + i, i);
  world["p"+i].lineStyle(10, 0x0, 100)
  world["p"+i].moveTo(0, 0)
  world["p"+i].lineTo(1, 0)
  pX[i] = pY[i] = pZ[i] = 0;
  pXS[i] = Math.random() * 5;
  pYS[i] = Math.random() * 5;
  pZS[i] = Math.random() * 5;
  threeDPlotter(i);
}
// Set up the animation's onEnterFrame event handler.
this.onEnterFrame = moveSpheres;
```

Executing the preceding code causes 30 spheres to bounce around a 3D world as shown in Figure 5-9. We'll see shortly why we drew the spheres as 2D black dots instead of true spheres with specular highlights.

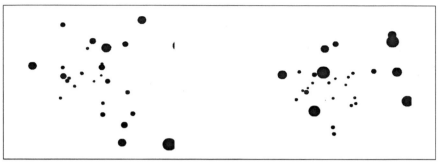

Figure 5-9. Dots in a 3D world shown at two different points

Let's review some portions of the main code. First it defines variables:

fLength
>   The focal length.

centerX, centerY
>   The position (relative to the Flash Stage) of the origin of our 3D world.

n
>   The number of dots in the animation.

wSize
>   The distance from the origin to each face of the 3D cube that forms the boundaries of our world. Because the origin is in the center of the cube, the size of the cube sides are 2*wSize.

The 3D world is shown in Figure 5-10.

Within the 3D world, we define the location and velocity of a point as follows (and as shown in Figure 5-11):

pX, pY, pZ
>   The (x, y, z) coordinates of each point in the animation

pXS, pYS, pZS
>   The (x, y, z) speed and direction (i.e., velocity vector) of each point

We then create a movie clip named world. Inside it, we create the clips for each sphere, p0 to p*n*.

The *moveSpheres( )* function constantly updates the positions of each sphere and makes them bounce off the walls of the world cube. This function also calls the *threeDPlotter( )* function, which transforms the (x, y, z) coordinates into the (x, y) position and scaling factor needed to generate a 2D projection of the 3D view.

By using black dots (i.e., all with the same solid color), we avoid the need to arrange our dots in distance order (z-buffering), because the viewer can't tell

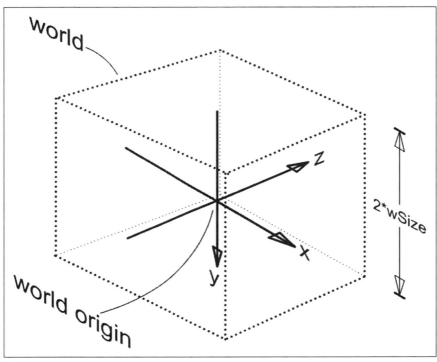

Figure 5-10. The 3D world

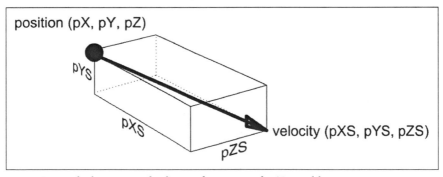

Figure 5-11. The location and velocity of a point in the 3D world

which sphere is in front of the others. This reduces the number of calculations needed to generate a moving 3D scene.

We create our 3D scene inside a clip, world, which allows us to move the origin by moving the world clip (and avoids having to use offsets in every frame in our calculations, which would slow down rendering).

Final Thoughts

Although basic, our engine is a good base upon which to build a number of more advanced 3D engines:

- By joining up our points via lines, we can build a 3D vector engine or wireframe viewer [Hack #85].

- By adding z-buffering, we can create a more compelling effect that more fully represents 3D depth (and allows us to, say, use spheres with specular highlights instead of black dots).

Real-time 3D is one of the most processor-intensive things you can do with the Flash Player. As seen here, keeping it simple can produce fast effects.

HACK #38 Use Acceleration to Simulate Gravity and Friction

Many real-world phenomena, such as gravity and friction, affect the velocity of objects over time. Model such changes by a simple acceleration equation to create realistic motion under simulated physical conditions.

Some physical effects are hard to get right in scripted animation unless you know the underlying math. Acceleration calculations are easier than they might appear. Like all forces acting on masses, gravity and friction cause acceleration (or deceleration). When you are performing iterative calculations (which you are always doing when you are animating sprites over time), the math works out to be surprisingly easy.

When modeling real-world movement, you often have an accelerating force and a decelerating force acting on the same body (such as gravity and air friction acting on a falling body). If the forces are balanced (such as when the thrust of an airplane counteracts the air resistance), the velocity of the object is constant (acceleration is zero). The trick is simply adding the forces together to determine the overall force on the object.

A force such as gravity provides constant acceleration, meaning that the velocity of the object changes over time (just as your car speeds up if you provide enough gas to accelerate). The velocity of an object at any time is equal to its existing velocity, plus the effect of acceleration over the time interval, such as:

```
newV = oldV + (acceleration * time)
```

Likewise, the position of an object at any time is equal to its old position, plus the effect of its velocity over the time interval, such as:

```
newPos = oldPos + (newV * time)
```

If we recalculate the position and velocity often enough that the speed doesn't change *during* each iteration, and we use 1 as the time interval so the units drop out, we can simplify the position equation as:

```
newPos = oldPos + newV
```

In words, this means, "To calculate the new position, take the old position and add the current velocity." For example, if I drive at 60 miles per hour (mph) for one hour, I've traveled 60 miles from my original position. Therefore, in each frame of the animation, we add a small amount to the position in the direction of the velocity vector.

At the end of an interval, we recalculate the velocity to account for acceleration. The velocity calculation can likewise be simplified as:

```
newV = oldV + acceleration
```

In words, this means, "To calculate the current velocity, take the old velocity and add the acceleration." For example, if I'm driving at 60 mph and I accelerate by 10 mph per second for one second, I'm now traveling at 70 mph. Therefore, in each frame of the animation, we add a small amount to the velocity in the direction of the acceleration vector (usually pointing down in the case of gravity).

Acceleration due to Earth's gravity is approximately 32 feet per second squared (or 9.8 meters per second squared), but if you aren't providing an accurate physics calculation, you can use any constant value for the acceleration that makes your animation run at the rate you'd like.

Resting friction (the friction acting on a body at rest) tends to be greater than rolling friction (the friction acting on, say, a rolling ball). Air friction generally increases in proportion to the object's speed, so we use a simple *coefficient of friction* to approximate the resulting force as a fraction of the current velocity.

The following code generates a number of particles [Hack #33] and animates them falling under the acceleration of gravity and being resisted by air friction:

```
function fall( ) {
  // Add acceleration due to gravity
  this.speedY += GRAVITY;
  // Reduce the speed due to friction
  this.speedY *= FRICTION;
  // Assume both forces work exclusively in the Y direction
  this._y += this.speedY;
  // Make the clip bounce up when it hits the "floor" (a line)
  if (this._y > 400) {
    this._y = 400;
    this.speedY = -this.speedY * ELASTICITY;
  }
}
```

```
function drag( ) {
  // When the user clicks on a clip, make it draggable
  // and stop animating it via onEnterFrame.
  this.startDrag( );
  delete this.onEnterFrame;
  // We could save a function call by using the following:
  //    this.onMouseMove = updateAfterEvent;
  // because the onMouseMove( ) handler calls only one function.
  // However, we use the following function definition in case
  // you want to add extra features, such as range checking
  // to prevent clips from being dragged off stage.
  this.onMouseMove = function( ) {
    updateAfterEvent( );
  };
}
function drop( ) {
  // Initialize the drop animation and
  // stop the clip being draggable.
  // The initial y velocity is zero.
  this.speed.y = 0;
  this.stopDrag( );
  this.onEnterFrame = fall;
}
// MAIN CODE
// Create 20 ball clips
for (var i = 0; i < 20; i++) {
  var ball:MovieClip = this.createEmptyMovieClip("ball" + i, i);
  ball.lineStyle(6, 0x0, 100);
  ball.moveTo(0, -3);
  ball.lineTo(1, -3);
  ball._x = Math.random( ) * 550;
  ball._y = Math.random( ) * 200;
  ball.speedY = 0;
  ball.onEnterFrame = fall;
  ball.onPress = drag;
  ball.onRelease = ball.onReleaseOutside = drop;
}
//Initialize physical constants
var GRAVITY:Number = 0.5;
var FRICTION:Number = 0.995;
var ELASTICITY:Number = 0.85;
// Draw the ground line
this.lineStyle(0, 0xDDDDDD, 100);
this.moveTo(0, 400);
this.lineTo(550, 400);
```

Gravity is simulated by applying the following line every frame. It changes the speed in the Y direction over time:

```
this.speedY += GRAVITY;
```

If the ball is falling, gravity increases the velocity and speeds the fall. If the ball is climbing, gravity decreases the velocity and slows the ascent, just as a bouncing ball would act.

The effect of air friction is simulated via the line:

```
this.speedY *= FRICTION;
```

If FRICTION is less than 1, it slows the ball down regardless of the direction it is moving, just like real friction. If set equal to 1, there is no frictional effect. If set greater than 1, it creates thrust, like that of a rocket (it speeds up the clip rather than slowing it down).

When the ball hits the floor and bounces, we want to simulate the loss of energy typical in such collisions. The elasticity coefficient is applied via the line:

```
this.speedY *= ELASTICITY;
```

If ELASTICITY is less than 1, the ball bounces with less energy each time it hits the floor, just like in the real world. If set equal to 1, the bouncing ball is perfectly elastic (it would bounce forever to the same height if not slowed by friction). If elasticity is set greater than 1, the ball bounces higher with each successive bounce (neat trick!).

Final Thoughts

Because animation works on a per-frame basis, equations involving motion are easier to code up than the equations of motion you learned in physics class. If you consider motion per frame, such motion always results in fundamentally linear equations, making your scripts short and efficient. See if you can simulate motion in the X direction as well as the Y direction (hint: gravity has no effect in the X direction, and you should give your ball an initial horizontal velocity).

You can add all sorts of variations to an animation by setting the gravity to a different value (or even a negative value to make things float). You can set gravity to 0 to achieve a 2D effect in which the camera appears overhead (such as balls on a billiard table, so you better add bumpers all around). Throw sliders on stage [Hack #61] to control the gravity, friction, and elasticity settings, and go wild! You can also add sounds or make the ball squish when it bounces.

Simulate a Throw
#39

To add a nice touch of realism to your interface, script a throw effect in which an object continues to move in the direction it was released.

As we saw previously, acceleration [Hack #38] due to gravity and friction (including air resistance) are far easier to emulate on a per-frame basis than by using the real-world equations from which they're derived.

This hack looks at a simple way to simulate an object being thrown.

When you throw a ball, you define an imaginary *force vector*. The direction of this vector defines the initial direction in which the ball moves, and the length of the vector is proportional to how hard the ball is thrown (and how far it will travel).

Although we don't know how hard anything is being thrown in Flash (given that forces and mass don't exist in Flash's virtual world), we can simulate motion in a way that appears realistic. As with all physics simulation in Flash, our math just has to be close enough to pass the motion off as authentic. In practice, we don't generate the precisely correct movement, but something that is proportional to it.

Consider Figure 5-12, which depicts a ball being thrown. The user can click and drag the ball to "throw" it around the Stage (it travels in the direction the mouse is moving when the user releases the mouse button).

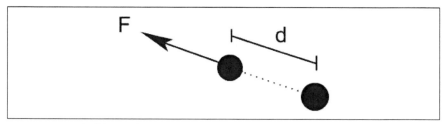

Figure 5-12. A ball being thrown

If we measure the distance our ball moves per frame, the force *F* with which the ball is thrown is proportional to the distance *d* between the last two known positions of the ball (assuming we are measuring the ball position at regular intervals, such as at the frame rate). The distance between the two positions is proportional to how fast you are dragging the ball. When you release the mouse button, the ball travels in the direction you "threw" it.

The following code (shown with line numbers for reference) implements the throw effect. Function *drawPip( )* draws our ball, and function *throwClip( )* defines the event handlers that control the throw initialization. The *onMouseMove( )* event handler tracks the difference between the last known and current ball positions and stores it as a vector (dirX, dirY). This vector defines our force in direction and magnitude.

You can see the force vector visually if you uncomment all the commented lines between the two sets of **Diagnostic** comments (lines 24–26 and 50–52). This makes the effect of the code much easier to see.

The animation cycle starts via the *onPress* event (line 15), when you click on the ball clip, whereupon the ball becomes draggable.

The point from which the ball is thrown is detected by the *onRelease* event if you click, drag, and release (i.e., "throw") the ball or via the *onReleaseOutside* event, which occurs if your mouse goes outside the Stage (whereupon the code forces you to drop, rather than throw, the ball). The *onRelease( )* and *onReleaseOutside( )* event handlers start at line 31 and set up an interval that invokes *mover( )* to control the ball animation after it has been thrown.

The *mover( )* function uses the dirX and dirY variables to control the motion of the ball. The vertical position is increased in the downward direction (i.e., dirY) over time via the GRAVITY constant, and both dirX and dirY are reduced over time via the FRICTION coefficient. The inertial mass of the ball is indirectly modeled by the MOMENTUM constant. The larger the value for MOMENTUM, the greater the amplitude of the force vector.

The interval is cleared (line 17) within the *onPress( )* function (starting at line 15) when the ball is clicked, at which point the throw cycle starts again.

```
1   // ActionScript 2.0 code
2   function drawPip(clip:MovieClip, clipName:String, clipDepth:Number,
3                     x:Number, y:Number):MovieClip {
4     var pip:MovieClip = clip.createEmptyMovieClip(clipName, clipDepth);
5     pip.lineStyle(20, 0x0, 100);
6     pip.moveTo(0, 0);
7     pip.lineTo(1, 0);
8     pip._x = x;
9     pip._y = y;
10    return pip;
11  }
12  function throwClip(clip:MovieClip):Void {
13    clip.oldX = clip._x;
14    clip.oldY = clip._y;
15    clip.onPress = function( ) {
16      clip.startDrag(true, -265, 190, 265, -200);
17      clearInterval(clipMove);
18      clip.onMouseMove = function( ) {
19        clip.dirX = MOMENTUM * (clip._x - clip.oldX);
20        clip.dirY = MOMENTUM * (clip._y - clip.oldY);
21        clip.oldX = clip._x;
22        clip.oldY = clip._y;
23        // **Diagnostic**
24        // clip.line = clip.createEmptyMovieClip("line", 0);
25        // clip.line.lineStyle(4, 0x0, 100);
26        // clip.line.lineTo(5 * clip.dirX, 5 * clip.dirY);
27        // **Diagnostic**
28        updateAfterEvent( );
29      };
30    };
```

```
31    clip.onRelease = clip.onReleaseOutside = function ( ) {
32      clip.stopDrag( );
33      delete clip.onMouseMove;
34      clipMove = setInterval(mover, 1, clip);
35    };
36  }
37  function mover(clip):Void {
38    if (Math.abs(clip._x) > 265) {
39      clip.dirX = -clip.dirX;
40    }
41    if (clip._y > 190) {
42      clip.dirY = -clip.dirY;
43      clip._y = 190;
44    }
45    clip.dirX = clip.dirX * FRICTION;
46    clip.dirY = (clip.dirY * FRICTION) + GRAVITY;
47    clip._x += clip.dirX;
48    clip._y += clip.dirY;
49    // **Diagnostic**
50    // clip.line = clip.createEmptyMovieClip("line", 0);
51    // clip.line.lineStyle(4, 0x0, 100);
52    // clip.line.lineTo(5 * clip.dirX, 5 * clip.dirY);
53    // **Diagnostic**
54    updateAfterEvent( );
55  }
56  var MOMENTUM:Number = 0.8;
57  var GRAVITY:Number = 0.5;
58  var FRICTION:Number = 0.99;
59  this._x = 275;
60  this._y = 200;
61  this.lineStyle(0, 0x0, 200);
62  this.moveTo(-275, -200);
63  this.lineTo(-275, 200);
64  this.lineTo(275, 200);
65  this.lineTo(275, -200);
66  var ball:MovieClip = drawPip(this, "ball", this.getNextDepth( ), 0, 190);
67  throwClip(ball);
```

Final Thoughts

Something to note for the Flash MX-style coders is the way that the current object, this, is never used in the event handlers. Instead, the code uses function arguments to pass the target clip name. This is much more efficient, and you can see the difference if you substitute clip with this in the most frequently executed event code (the *onMouseMove( )* handler, lines 18–30).

Flash Player 7 is optimized to handle data fastest when it is passed as an argument [Hack #100], which is the preferred coding style for ActionScript 2.0 code. This optimization occurs because the Flash Player saves arguments to several hardware registers rather than looking at the variables that source them.

If you use this in place of movie clip references passed as arguments, the Flash Player does not use the register optimizations and your code runs more slowly.

Detect Multiple Collisions

Collision detection is used in games and simulations. Optimize Flash collision detection to allow advanced motion graphics.

Flash allows you to perform collision detections between two movie clips with the *MovieClip.hitTest( )* method. The method will return true if a collision is detected and false if no collision is detected.

The definition of what constitutes a collision can also be varied. You can detect a collision between a point and a movie clip edge or between the bounding boxes of the two movie clips (i.e., the rectangles that you see around movie clips when you select them in the authoring environment). We look at both situations next.

Assuming you have two movie clips, clipA and clipB, on the Stage, the following code makes clipA draggable and displays the value true for every frame in which the bounding boxes of clipA and clipB overlap. Otherwise, it displays false.

```
clipA.onEnterFrame = function( ) {
  hit = clipA.hitTest(clipB);
  trace(hit);
};
clipA.startDrag(true);
```

The trouble with this type of collision detection is that it indicates a collision when the bounding boxes overlap, even if the pixels within the movie clips do not overlap. In Figure 5-13, the two circular movie clips do not overlap but the *hitTest( )* method in the preceding listing returns true because the bounding boxes overlap.

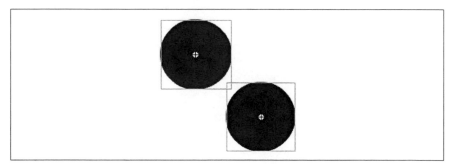

Figure 5-13. The hitTest( ) method returns true if the bounding boxes overlap

Detect Multiple Collisions

One solution is to perform manual collision detection. For circles, this happens to be easy. If the centers of the circles are closer than the sum of their radii, the circles overlap. Using the Pythagorean Theorem to calculate the distance between two points, the code to check for contact between two circles is:

```
function circleHitTest (circle1, circle2) {
  var a = circle1._x - circle2._x;
  var b = circle1._y - circle2._y;
  dist = Math.sqrt( Math.pow(a, 2) + Math.pow(b, 2));
  return dist < Math.abs(circle1._width/2 - circle2._width/2);
}
```

Another solution is to use near-rectangular graphics that fill or nearly fill the movie clip's bounding box. This idea is not as silly as it might seem, and this approach was routinely used in early video games (which is why the space invaders tended to be fairly rectangular).

You can also perform collision detection between a point and a movie clip. The following code checks for collisions between the mouse position and a movie clip named clipA:

```
this.onEnterFrame = function() {
  hit = clipA.hitTest(_xmouse, _ymouse, true);
  trace(hit);
};
```

That code returns true if the tip of the mouse pointer is over any occupied pixels within clipA (including pixels with zero alpha or even if the clip is hidden by setting clipA._visible = false).

ActionScript doesn't provide a native way of checking for collisions between individual pixels in two movie clips. You can test for collisions only between two clips' bounding boxes or between a point and the pixels within a clip.

Although in theory you can detect collisions between any two clips, in practice, the number of clips you can use is limited by Flash's ability to perform the calculations fast enough. The processor can't exhaustively check the thousands of possible combinations when numerous clips interact. Because there is no built-in event that notifies you of collisions, you have to test for collisions explicitly whenever you want to see if they occurred (known as *polling*). This can lead to very slow operation for any sizable number of clips.

However, there is a saving grace (it wouldn't be a hack without one, now would it?). Most developers don't realize that *MovieClip.hitTest( )* recognizes embedded movie clips when performing the collision test.

As long as you arrange your timelines in an appropriate "collision hierarchy" of embedded movie clips, you can test for a collision between a movie clip and a hundred others with a single hit test. Or you can create an optimized collision engine that runs only when certain collisions have already occurred (rather than having to poll for detailed collisions every frame). Let's see how.

A Collision Hierarchy

In most cases, you want to detect a collision between one thing and another group of objects. These other objects might be gas molecules in a physics simulation, a swarm of marauding aliens, or the walls in a maze. Let's assume you are checking collisions against a single graphic representing the player (the character controlled by the user).

The slow way of checking for collisions is to treat each movie clip as a separate entity. So if you have 20 aliens onscreen, you need to check for collisions between the player and each of the aliens.

The better way to do it is to place all the aliens inside a single movie clip, such as one named alienSwarm, so that you have a hierarchy, as shown in Figure 5-14.

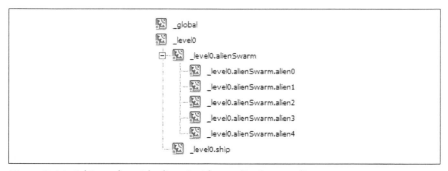

Figure 5-14. A hierarchy with aliens inside an alienSwarm clip

You can then detect collisions between the aliens and the player's ship by checking for collisions between alienSwarm and the ship clip, regardless of the number of aliens in the swarm. Better still, the detection process doesn't slow down significantly even if there are numerous aliens in the swarm!

To try this technique yourself, create a movie clip named ship, making sure its registration point is near the tip of the graphic, as shown in Figure 5-15. This represents the ubiquitous player's spaceship sprite.

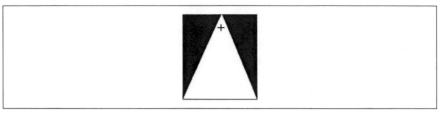

Figure 5-15. The player's ship with registration point near the tip

Create a second movie clip symbol named *asteroid*, as shown in Figure 5-16, and give it a linkage identifier of asteroid. The position of this movie clip's registration point is not important.

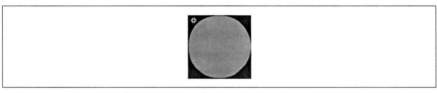

Figure 5-16. The asteroid movie clip symbol

Place the ship movie clip near the bottom of the Stage as per the typical Space Invaders player ship position.

Add the following code to the first (and only) frame in the timeline (like all timeline code, it is best placed in a layer named *actions* set aside for this purpose):

```
function shipMove( ) {
  // Detect keypresses and move ship accordingly
  if (Key.isDown(left)) {
    ship._x -= playerSpeed;
  }
  if (Key.isDown(right)) {
    ship._x += playerSpeed;
  }
  // Check for collisions
  if (asteroidBelt.hitTest(ship._x, ship._y, true)) {
    trace("collision");
  }
  updateAfterEvent( );
}

function asteroidMove( ) {
  // Move this asteroid
  this._y += this.asteroidSpeed;
  if (this._y > 400) {
    this._x = Math.random( ) * 550;
    this._y = 0;
  }
}
```

```
function createAsteroids( ) {
  // Create a movie clip named asteroidBelt. Inside it,
  // create 20 asteroids: asteroid0 to asteroid19.
  this.createEmptyMovieClip("asteroidBelt", 0);
  initAsteroid = new Object( );
  for (i = 0; i < 20; i++) {
    initAsteroid._x = Math.random( ) * 550;
    initAsteroid._y = Math.random( ) * 400;
    initAsteroid.asteroidSpeed = Math.round((Math.random( ) * 3) + 2);
    initAsteroid.onEnterFrame = asteroidMove;
    asteroidBelt.attachMovie("asteroid", "asteroid" + i, i, initAsteroid);
  }
}
// Setup
left = Key.LEFT;
right = Key.RIGHT;
playerSpeed = 10;
asteroidSpeed = 3;
shipInterval = setInterval(shipMove, 10);
createAsteroids( );
```

The *createAsteroids( )* function creates a movie clip named asteroidBelt and creates 20 asteroids (asteroid0 through asteroid19) within it. The asteroids travel down the screen over time.

The ship movie clip is controlled via the left and right arrow keys, and the goal is to dodge the asteroids.

The ship animation is given a much higher part of the Flash Player's performance budget [Hack #71] by controlling it via a *setInterval( )* event, whereas the asteroids are given *onEnterFrame( )* event handlers, which perform animation at a slower rate (the frame rate).

If the player collides with one or more asteroids, the Output panel displays the word "collision" for every frame in which the collision occurs. The key to maintaining performance is the single collision test used for the entire asteroid belt:

```
if (asteroidBelt.hitTest(ship._x, ship._y, true)) {
  trace("collision");
}
```

Collisions in the Reverse Hierarchy

Using a collision hierarchy offers a big performance enhancement, but it works in only one direction. We can detect collisions between the asteroid belt and the player, but we can't (for example) detect a collision between the ship's laser and individual asteroids, which we would need to do if we're going to make them explode when hit (as all well-behaved asteroids should).

Even in this reverse situation, a collision hierarchy still helps immensely by telling you when a collision has occurred. Using this information, you can optimize collision detection code because you know to run your laser-to-individual-asteroid collision detection routine only after a collision with the asteroid belt has already occurred.

Here is one possible scenario.

Test for a collision between the asteroid belt and the player's laser. If you detect a collision, you know the laser has hit an asteroid, you just don't know which one.

Look at either the _x or _y property of individual asteroids against the laser's position, and eliminate all asteroids that are too far away for a collision. This eliminates almost all the asteroids from the collision test.

Of those that are close enough, check using individual hit tests (i.e., using *MovieClip.hitTest( )*).

Your secondary collision detection routine (testing against individual asteroids) runs much less often than the primary *hitTest( )* (testing against the entire asteroid belt). When it does run, you know at least one collision has occurred, and you can optimize the code with this fact in mind.

Final Thoughts

Collision detection need not be a barrier to high-performance Flash simulations or motion graphics. By building your graphics in a hierarchy, you can substantially reduce the time needed to detect collisions.

In a typical shooting game, you have to make two frequent collision detections and one infrequent collision detection. The two frequent hit tests are between the alien swarm and the player, and between the player's laser and the alien swarm. If the second hit test gives a positive result, you have to make a less frequent (but more detailed) collision search between the laser and each alien instance within the swarm.

Turn Toward a Point

#41

Many games and simulations require the player's ship to rotate toward a point. Use angular motion to turn a sprite so it faces a target.

Computer animation is different from real life in a number of ways. A computer graphic can move in any direction, whereas, in real life, an object usually has to turn in a particular direction before it can move in that direction. Furthermore, if a real object is already moving, it cannot change direction instantaneously. Due to inertia, it turns in the new direction over time, thus traversing a curved path until it is facing the new direction.

You can make a computer graphic appear to be moving more realistically in several ways:

- Cheat by making your graphic look as if it is always facing in the right direction, such as by using a ball that is radially symmetrical and therefore "directionless" or a flying saucer that seems capable of moving in any direction without turning.

- Constantly move the target point your animated clip is trying to get to. If your movie clip is trying to get to a point on the screen that is moving in an intelligent or complex way, your movie clip will appear to be moving in the same way. The hack is to design your application in such a way that the code need not create the intelligence or complexity. In most games, the enemies chase the player's character. Because the player is (hopefully!) moving intelligently, the enemies' motion also seems intelligent.

- Create a graphic with a cardinal direction, but simulate turning in a way that merely approximates or implies the underlying physics. In real life, the rate at which an object can turn without skidding or tumbling depends on numerous attributes (velocity, friction, the object's mass and center of gravity, the terrain, etc.). In a real-time simulation (especially one in a weightless environment such as space), you can approximate all these effects by simply defining a *constant turn rate*, as discussed later.

Following a Moving Target

You can make a clip move to a point (in this case, toward the mouse cursor location) as follows:

```
// Create a ball clip
this.createEmptyMovieClip("ball", 0);
ball.lineStyle(50, 0x0, 100);
ball.moveTo(0, 0);
ball.lineTo(0, 1);
// Animate ball to follow the mouse
ball.onEnterFrame = function( ) {
  this._x -= (ball._x - _xmouse) / 4;
  this._y -= (ball._y - _ymouse) / 4;
};
```

This code creates the ubiquitous mouse follower with inertia (dividing the difference in the X and Y positions by 4 ensures that the ball doesn't jump right to the mouse cursor location). It moves the ball to the last mouse position in a straight line (or series of straight-line segments if the target is moving). This animation depends in part on the fact that the ball is radially symmetrical (i.e., as discussed earlier, it is directionless).

This hack shows the minimum code to create realistic motion that appears to take into account turning and arcing, although the code actually addresses neither of them.

This simple trick can be expanded by changing the direction that the clip appears to be facing without needing to model rotation, but instead switching between several predrawn graphics or animation sequences. For example, in cases in which a character lives in a 3D world, you'll need to use different animations for each direction of character movement [Hack #28].

Facing Toward a Point

Imagine a ship that turns toward a target before firing (assuming the ship always fires its weapons in the direction it is pointing). The following code creates a line pointer and keeps it facing the mouse position:

```
// Create tracker movie clip
var tracker:MovieClip = this.createEmptyMovieClip("tracker", 0);
// Draw a line within tracker
tracker.lineStyle(0, 0x0, 100);
tracker.moveTo(0, 0);
tracker.lineTo(100, 0);
tracker._x = Stage.width / 2;
tracker._y = Stage.height / 2;
// Set radian-to-degree conversion ratio
var RAD_DEG:Number = 180 / Math.PI;
tracker.onMouseMove = function() {
  // Rotate this movie clip in the
  // direction of the mouse pointer.
  var angle:Number = Math.atan2(_ymouse - this._y, _xmouse - this._x);
  this._rotation = angle * RAD_DEG;
  updateAfterEvent();
};
```

The code uses *Math.atan2( )*, a method that returns the angle to which the line must turn to face a point at the specified distance in X and Y (note that the method accepts the Y distance, not the X distance, as the first parameter). The geometry is summarized in Figure 5-17.

All Flash trigonometric functions return angles in radians, so we must convert the value to degrees, which are the units used by the MovieClip._rotation property.

The preceding code makes the clip turn instantaneously toward the mouse position. To slow down the turn, simply limit the turn rate (in this case, to +/- 5 degrees) by changing the *onMouseMove( )* event handler as follows:

```
tracker.onMouseMove = function() {
  // Rotate this movie clip in the
  // direction of the mouse pointer.
```

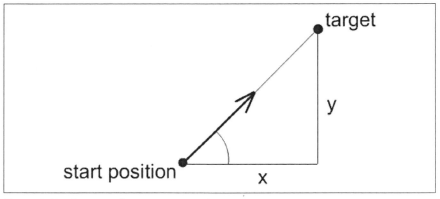

Figure 5-17. Geometry for turning toward a point

```
var targetAngle:Number = Math.atan2(_ymouse - this._y, _xmouse - this._x);
var errorAngle:Number = targetAngle * RAD_DEG - this._rotation;
if (Math.abs(errorAngle) > 5) {
  if ( ((errorAngle > 0) && (errorAngle < 180))
        || (errorAngle < -180) ) {
    this._rotation += 5;
  } else {
    this._rotation -= 5;
  }
}
};
```

The nested *if* statement in the preceding code checks errorAngle because the _rotation property is in the range -180 to +180, not 0 to 360. If you increment the _rotation property by 1 every frame, it changes, as follows, during a full rotation:

```
1, 2, 3, ... 179, 180, -179, -178, ... -2, -1, 0
```

Therefore, the *if* statement causes the tracker clip to rotate in the direction that traverses the shortest arc to reach to the desired direction. In other words, if the clip is pointing at 12 o'clock and needs to rotate to 9 o'clock, it turns 90 degrees counterclockwise rather than 270 degrees clockwise.

Adding Inertia

Now assume we want to add inertia so that the clip moves in an arc as it rotates. To make our pointing line move in an arc, add movement in the direction it is pointing at each instant. Try this:

```
function drawBlip(clip) {
  // Draw a small line graphic in a clip to indicate direction
  clip.lineStyle(0, 0x0, 100);
  clip.moveTo(0, 0);
  clip.lineTo(10, 0);
```

```
      clip._x = Math.random( ) * Stage.width;
      clip._y = Math.random( ) * Stage.height;
    }
    function realMove( ) {
      // Calculate the distance from this clip's current
      // position to the target position (the mouse pointer).
      this.xDist = _xmouse-this._x;
      this.yDist = _ymouse-this._y;
      // Calculate the angle from the clip's current position
      // to the target position and the difference between this
      // angle and the desired heading (errorAngle).
      var targetAngle:Number = Math.atan2(this.yDist, this.xDist);
      var errorAngle:Number = targetAngle * RAD_DEG - this._rotation;
      // Turn the clip based on errorAngle
      if (Math.abs(errorAngle) > 10) {
        if ( ((errorAngle > 0) && (errorAngle < 180))
           || (errorAngle < -180) ) {
          this._rotation += 10;
        } else {
          this._rotation -= 10;
        }
      }
      // Move the clip, taking into account the angle
      // at which it is currently pointing.
      this._x += Math.cos(this._rotation / RAD_DEG) * 20;
      this._y += Math.sin(this._rotation / RAD_DEG) * 20;
    }
    // Set radian-to-degree conversion ratio
    var RAD_DEG:Number = 180/Math.PI;
    // Create tracker clips
    for (var i:Number = 0; i < 100; i++) {
      var tracker:MovieClip = this.createEmptyMovieClip("tracker" + i, i);
      drawBlip(tracker);
      tracker.onEnterFrame = realMove;
    }
```

As long as you keep moving the mouse cursor, the movement appears
almost organic, like a flocking or group movement.

If you stick with one tracker clip, you get something that looks a lot like a
homing missile, especially if you give it a fading exhaust that is spewed out
in the direction opposite to the line of travel.

Final Thoughts

There's more than one way to simulate real motion. Turning toward the target point and simulating inertia in the direction of movement provides a
basis for animations with realistic motion.

Text

Hacks 42–51

Text in Flash need not be limited to static words whose only purpose in life is to remain still and be read. Flash can optionally treat your text as either vector shapes or as a series of movie clips, both of which have the advantage of enabling you to animate your text. You only have to look at film titles to see how striking animated text can become and how movement can amplify the meaning of the text, or even add subtexts in the same way body language is a subtext to the spoken word. The following Flash sites show some of the possibilities of text effects in Flash:

- Typorganism (*http://www.typorganism.com*) is dedicated to illustrating what it calls "kinetic typography"—effects that animate text to add meaning through motion.

- Overage4Design (*http://www.overage4design.com*) offers a modern design that uses text as a graphic rather than something that is simply there to be read.

- Yugo Nakamura's Mono-craft (*http://www.yugop.com*) was one of the first sites to use text in novel and interactive ways. Mono-craft Version 2.0 is considered one of the defining sites from the "golden age" of Flash 4 and 5 development, when the now-standard Flash design concepts were formulated by the first wave of Flash designers to use modern ActionScript techniques.

- Saul Bass on the Web (*http://www.saulbass.net*) is maintained by the well-known Flash designer Brendan Dawes. It pays homage to Saul Bass (1920–1996), who was one of the first people to use text as a moving graphic in film. Bass also used text as a graphic element in the associated film posters, as did the Soviet Modernist design movement (circa 1920) that predated him.

As well as its animation abilities, Flash text is much more configurable in terms of appearance than standard HTML. Vector-based Flash text can:

- Be displayed at any angle and at any size.
- Render characters with vectors and add antialiasing for all fonts.
- Use any font, including those not installed on the user's machine by embedding font outline information within the Flash *.swf* file.
- Allow the user to break up and edit the characters within a piece of text (using Modify → Break Apart), thus allowing the designer to quickly create logos or other text-based graphics quickly. You can even use a shape tween to morph one letter into another [Hack #34].
- Support more traditional CSS formatting and HTML text [Hack #46], even when content is displayed outside the browser (i.e., in the standalone Flash Player or if you export your Flash content as an executable).

Fonts

Flash supports both *system fonts* and *embedded fonts*. If you use one of the three default fonts—"_sans", "_serif", or "_typewriter"—the Flash Player finds the closest font on the user's system at runtime. The "_sans" font (equivalent to sans-serif in HTML/CSS) typically corresponds to Arial on Windows and Helvetica on the Mac. For the "_serif" and "_typewriter" default fonts (equivalent to serif and mono in HTML/CSS), Flash uses Times and Courier or other closely matched fonts.

Font outline information can be embedded in the SWF to allow you to perform text effects [Hack #48], such as rotating text. You don't have to embed default fonts in the SWF, but system fonts don't include vector information, so Flash cannot treat text formatted with a system font as graphics. Thus, text that uses system fonts typically disappears from the Stage if you rotate or scale the clip containing the text. If you try to embed one of the default fonts ("_sans", "_serif", or "_typewriter"), Flash embeds the closest font it finds on your development system at compile time. At runtime, the text can be rotated, scaled, and animated because Flash uses the embedded font information, not the system font from the end user's computer.

This chapter presents hacks for keeping text legible, implementing autocomplete text fields, importing text with complicated formatting, using CSS text, and using accessibility text as tool tips. Other text-related hacks, which discuss techniques such as transition effects created with text and masks [Hack #2], are sprinkled throughout the book.

Keep Text Legible
#42
Text legibility varies depending on the font, the point size, and the screen dimensions. Change the font metric on the fly to make the site legible on a variety of screen sizes.

Flash sites tend to use small graphics and text. That's cool, except that text legible on one machine may be illegible on another. For example 8-point text may be illegible on a Macintosh iBook. Likewise, text that looks good at a monitor resolution of 1024×768 may become unreadable at 1600×1200 resolution (the pixels are smaller at higher resolutions). And if I designed a site on my 1600×1200 desktop, the text may well look like the oversized font they use in early-reader books when viewed on a monitor set to 800×600. You could create a different site for each user, but we prefer a way of reading the user's screen size and changing the Flash presentation's text on the fly to suit the Stage dimensions.

Read the Screen Dimensions
Reading the user's screen resolution is simply a matter of reading the appropriate System.capabilities properties. The following code gives you the (x, y) screen resolution:

```
trace(System.capabilities.screenResolutionX);
trace(System.capabilities.screenResolutionY);
```

On my computer, I get 1600 and 1200 returned from this code, and, unsurprisingly, my screen resolution is set to 1600×1200. So what can we do with these values? One thing we can do is vary the size of our text based on the values. But first, we have to create our text.

The following code (available as *varyText.fla* on this book's web site) dynamically creates a text field containing some text:

```
1  var txtFmt:TextFormat = new TextFormat();
2  var myStr:String = "Hello and welcome to Flash Hacks, " +
3     "by Sham Bhangal and a host of co-contributors";
4  // Set up a font and font size for the text
5  txtFmt.font = "_sans";
6  txtFmt.size = 12;
7  var metrics:Object = txtFmt.getTextExtent(myStr, 200);
8  // Add text field
9  this.createTextField("my_txt", 1, 100, 100,
10        metrics.textFieldWidth, metrics.textFieldHeight);
11 my_txt.wordWrap = true;
12 my_txt.border = true;
13 my_txt.text = myStr;
14 my_txt.setTextFormat(txtFmt);
```

Lines 1 and 2 set up a *TextFormat* instance, txtFmt, that we use to display a string value, myStr. Line 4 sets the font to "_sans," one of three default fonts that Flash supports.

The *Object* instance metrics is then created (on line 7) using *TextFormat. getTextExtent( )*. This method returns an object with two properties—textFieldWidth and textFieldHeight—which define the width and height that a text field needs to display our string, myStr, given a text break after 200 pixels.

The second part of the code listing dynamically creates a text field named my_txt at depth 1 and position (100, 100) with width and height equal to the two properties of metrics discussed earlier.

The last four lines simply set up the text field's properties after it is created, including setting its value to our text, myStr, and applying the *TextFormat* object, txtFmt, which sets the point size and font.

The critical line is line 6:

```
txtFmt.size = 12;
```

Setting txtFmt.size to any other value (and applying it with *setTextFormat( )*) gives you a different size of text, plus a text field sized to fit (shown in Figure 6-1 for txtFmt.size equal to 8, 12, and 16 points, respectively).

Figure 6-1. Text fields scaled for three different point sizes of text

You're probably getting the game plan by now: if we set the size property based on the user's display resolution, we've cracked the legibility issue. Try replacing line 6 with:

```
if (System.capabilities.screenResolutionX > 800) {
  txtFmt.size = 12;
} else {
  txtFmt.size = 10;
}
```

Note that you don't have to check both the screen's X and Y resolution; you can usually get a good idea of the screen resolution by just looking at one dimension because screens usually have an aspect ratio of around 4:3.

A few designers are probably looking at this and thinking, "Um, okay, but won't all this resizing alter my carefully designed layouts?" Yep, but remember that you will usually make fairly small changes to the font size (+/- about 2 points, as we have done here), and that won't drastically change your layouts. In extreme cases, you can keep the text fields the same size but use scrollbars for large areas of text or reduce the line spacing as you increase the text size (smaller text usually requires relatively higher line spacing than larger text).

Final Thoughts

As the need to cater to a number of screen sizes increases (for cell phones, handhelds, PDAs, and other nonstandard devices), the requirement for your text to look good is paramount. The manual solution is to design a different presentation for each major device, but there are several classes of devices or even differences among devices of the same class. Some level of dynamic control is better.

You also have the ability to dynamically change the size of the Flash Stage and/or any text instances on it in response to the screen resolution (and the browser window size). Knowing the relationship between the Flash Stage size and the overall screen size gives you further options to rescale your Flash content dynamically. By incorporating dynamically resized text metrics and a dynamically resizable Stage [Hack #92], you gain a significant amount of control over how your SWFs adapt to differing runtime conditions.

Another useful application of the code listed for this hack is with pop-up help text. The code to create resizable and movable text on the fly can be easily modified to create help text [Hack #47] that always resizes and positions itself to appear near the mouse, but within the Stage area.

You might also want to change the font when changing the size of the text. For example, if you need to render text clearly at small sizes, you should use pixel fonts [Hack #67].

Autocomplete Text Fields

#43

Add autocomplete functionality to make Flash complete the data entry for your fill-in text forms.

Most of us don't want to type any more than we have to. For certain users—such as children, disabled users, or those using mobile devices with cumbersome keypads—saving keystrokes is a priority. One way to save time is to fill in commonly used words before the user finishes typing them (i.e., an autocomplete feature).

The 300 Most Common Words (*http://www.zingman.com/commonWords. html*) and alt-usage-english.org's *Commonest Words* (*http://alt-usage-english. org/excerpts/fxcommon.html*) purport to list the 300 most common words in written English. Other word lists include *The American Heritage Word Frequency Book* by John B. Carroll, Peter Davies, and Barry Richman (Houghton Mifflin).

When I first stumbled on those resources, I thought, "Hmm...that's a good start for creating an autocomplete text engine." After removing all words that are of two or fewer letters (and therefore don't save much time by being autocompleted) and sorting them alphabetically, Figure 6-2 shows the results.

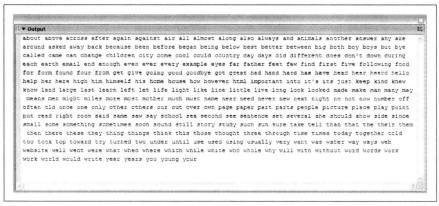

Figure 6-2. The most common words in written English with at least three letters

For those interested in stripping words from another word list they might encounter, here is the code I used:

```
function textLoader(data) {
    // Split the text file out based on any spaces
    dictionary = data.split(" ");
    // Sort the word list
    dictionary.sort();
    // Display the sorted word list, separated by spaces
    trace(dictionary.join(" "));
}
var myText:LoadVars = new LoadVars();
var dictionary:Array = new Array();
myText.load("commonWords.txt");
myText.onData = textLoader;
```

This assumes the words are in a file called *commonWords.txt* and that they are separated by spaces. You would change the filename and delimiter (such as a Return character) in accordance with the name and format of your word list.

My stripped-down word list takes up only 1.5 KB, and you can reduce that to 990 bytes—a bargain!—by copying the output from the preceding script into the ActionScript listing itself, like this (although the full version looks a bit messier, as shown shortly):

```
var myText:String = "about above across ... years you young your";
var dictionary:Array = new Array( );
dictionary = myText.split(" ");
dictionary.sort( );
delete (myText);
```

When you publish the SWF, Flash compresses the dictionary definition text.

To use the dictionary, I found a rather ingenious hack for adding the autocomplete text at the Stickman site (*http://www.the-stickman.com*).

It uses two text fields, one on top of the other. The top one is an input field, and the lower one is a dynamic field that displays our autocomplete suggestions. To create this arrangement, assuming you already have a layer named *actions* (to the first frame of which is attached the previous code listing), add two new layers named *entered text* and *completed text*, as shown in Figure 6-3.

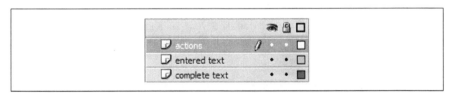

Figure 6-3. Setting up your layers for the autocomplete text hack

In the *entered text* layer, create a multiline, borderless input text field, named myText_txt, as shown in Figure 6-4.

Next, copy the text field, lock the *entered text* layer, and paste the text field in place into layer *completed text* (Ctrl-Shift-V on Windows or ⌘-Shift-V on Mac). Using the Properties panel, change the text field to a bordered dynamic text field, and change the text color to something other than the original text field's color (this will be the color of your autocomplete text). Change the instance name to complete_txt in the Properties panel, as shown in Figure 6-5.

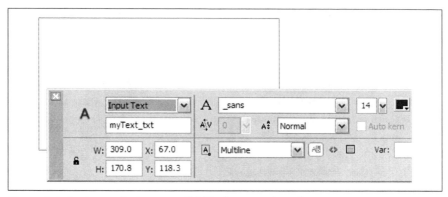

Figure 6-4. Setting up the input text field in the entered text layer

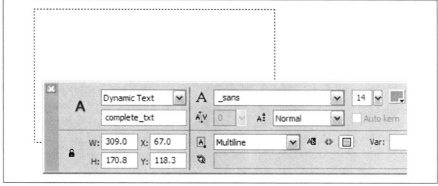

Figure 6-5. Changing the text properties in the Properties panel

The Code

Finally, change the script attached to the *actions* layer to the following, which contains both the code and the preinitialized dictionary of words:

```
function autoComplete( ) {
  // Function to accept the currently suggested autocomplete
  // text when the CONTROL key is pressed.
  if (Key.isDown(Key.CONTROL)) {
    myText_txt.text = complete_txt.text + " ";
    Selection.setSelection(myText_txt.text.length,
                          myText_txt.text.length);
  }
}
function fieldChange( ) {
  // Function to search for and display the
  // autocomplete text string.
  match = "";
  // Extract the last word in progress in the text input field
  startOfWord = this.text.lastIndexOf(" ") + 1;
  lastWord = this.text.substring(startOfWord, this.text.length);
```

```
    // Search for any matches in the dictionary to the last
    // word in progress.
    if (lastWord.length > 1) {
      for (var i = 0; i < dictionary.length; i++) {
        if (lastWord == (dictionary[i].substr(0, lastWord.length))) {
          // If match found, store the match string in variable match
          match = dictionary[i];
          search = i;
          break;
        }
      }
    } else {
      search = 0;
    }
    // Display the current match in the autocomplete text field
    complete_txt.text = this.text.substr(0, startOfWord) + match;
}

// Initialize
var myText:String = "about above across after again against air all almost
along also always and animals another answer any are around asked away
back because been before began being below best better between big both
boy boys but bye called came can change children city come cool could
country day days did different does don't down during each earth email end
enough even ever every example eyes far father feet few find first five
following food for form found four from get give going good goodbye got
great had hand hard has have head hear heard hello help her here high him
himself his home house how however html important into it's its just keep
kind knew know land large last learn left let life light like line little
live long look looked made make man many may means men might miles more
most mother much must name near need never new next night no not now
number off often old once one only other others our out over own page
paper part parts people picture place play point put read right room said
same saw say school sea second see sentence set several she should show
side since small some something sometimes soon sound still story study
such sun sure take tell than that the their them then there these they
thing things think this those thought three through time times today
together told too took top toward try turned two under until use used
using usually very want was water way ways web website well went were what
when where which while white who whole why will with without word words
work world would write year years you young your";

var dictionary:Array = new Array( );
var search:Number = 0;
var lastWord:String = "";
var startOfWord:String = "";
var control:Object = new Object( );
// Set up dictionary
dictionary = myText.split(" ");
dictionary.sort( );
// Set up events and listeners
myText_txt.onChanged = fieldChange;
control.onKeyDown = autoComplete;
Key.addListener(control);
```

The main part of this script is the *fieldChange( )* function, which runs whenever the user enters something in the text field.

First, it clears a variable, match, which holds our autocomplete guess. Next, it extracts the last complete word typed by the user. We do this by looking for the last incidence of a space and counting from the next character to the end of the text.

For example, in the sentence, "The cat sat," the last space is the one before "sat" (and its zero-relative index is 7). Adding 1 to it gives us the position of the first character of the word "sat." Using this information (startOfWord), we can extract the substring "sat" from the sentence, remembering that the last letter of "sat" corresponds to the end of our sentence so far. Here we repeat the relevant code:

```
function fieldChange( ) {
  match = "";
  startOfWord = this.text.lastIndexOf(" ") + 1;
  lastWord = this.text.substring(startOfWord, this.text.length);
```

It's not worth autocompleting until the current word is at least two letters long, so we use an *if* statement in the next section of code to avoid performing the check when only one letter has been entered. If the user has entered at least two characters, the *for* loop compares our word with each entry in the dictionary until it finds a match.

The variable search is used to optimize future searches. Because we know that the dictionary is sorted alphabetically, we know that any future matches for the current word will be after the currently found word in the dictionary. Therefore, remembering the position of the current word allows us to continue searching from the same position later:

```
if (lastWord.length > 1) {
  for (var i = 0; i < dictionary.length; i++) {
    if (lastWord == (dictionary[i].substr(0, lastWord.length))) {
      // Match found
      match = dictionary[i];
      search = i;
      break;
    }
  }
}
```

Finally, if we haven't yet attempted a search, it is because the current word is too short, so we reset the search position, because when the word is long enough, we want to start searching the dictionary from the beginning.

```
} else {
  search = 0;
}
```

The code is set up to allow the user to accept the current autocomplete suggestion by pressing the Ctrl key (we discuss alternatives later). When the user presses Ctrl, the *autoComplete( )* function is invoked via a listener event. The *autoComplete( )* function transfers the current contents of the autocomplete text into the input field, effectively completing the word for the user.

```
function autoComplete( ) {
  if (Key.isDown(Key.CONTROL)) {
    myText_txt.text = complete_txt.text + " ";
    Selection.setSelection(myText_txt.text.length,
      myText_txt.text.length);
  }
}
```

The last line of the preceding code moves the text cursor to the end of the current line. The trick is to set a zero-length selection to force the cursor to move to the end of the text field.

Figure 6-6 shows autocomplete in action. Entering "He sa" gives you an autocomplete suggestion of "He said." Pressing the Ctrl key adds the suggested text to the current input text. If desired, you can add static help text to inform the user that the Ctrl key initiates the autocomplete feature.

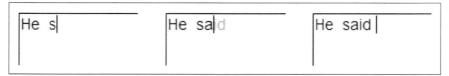

Figure 6-6. Autocomplete in action

Final Thoughts

This hack shows the basic code needed to create an autocomplete feature. Almost everyone will want to change it, the most likely candidate being to accept the autocomplete text by hitting another key such as the spacebar. You need a bit more code to do that, because although you can check for a spacebar press simply by looking for a " " at the end of the current input text, you need to be sure that the last pressed key was not a backspace. Another potential drawback is if you press the spacebar to go to the next word, already having a complete word, then the autocomplete adds more unwanted text. For example, if you enter "table" and then press the spacebar, the autocomplete feature might change it to "tablecloth." But this is unlikely because the common words in the word list tend to be shorter words.

The other thing that will probably irk some folks is the way I have added a blank space on the end of every autocompleted word. These are both minor details though; the basic principle remains the same even if you change the implementation details.

Using the most common words as the core autocomplete dictionary should also start you well on your way to adding a more useful list. Although the addition of a language dictionary sounds as if it should add a massive download to your SWF, the most common 300 words add less than 1 KB. The top 3,000 words (which approaches the number of words used in normal conversation, ignoring proper nouns and specializations) should consume no more than 10–15 KB! Not as much as you might think, which makes it feasible to teach a speech synthesizer [Hack #52] a vocabulary so that it can attempt reading plain text. You could have it kick out words it doesn't understand and add them to the dictionary [Hack #44] as you see fit.

Here is a list of other enhancements you might make:

- Trigger autocomplete on the Return or Enter key.
- Prevent the user from tabbing to the hidden field by setting the tabIndex property for myText_txt but not for complete_txt.
- Add logic so that autocomplete works even if you click in the middle of an existing text field.
- Deal with wrapping and scrolling as required by longer text input.
- Speed up the word search to accommodate longer dictionaries without degrading performance. For example, you can split the dictionary into multiple arrays stored in a hash table in which the key is the first two characters.

—Inspired by Stickman

Store a List of All Input Words

#44
Accumulate a list of popular words for the purposes of searching, indexing, or text autocomplete and store it in a local file.

We saw earlier how to autocomplete text [Hack #43] from a preinitialized word list (i.e., a limited dictionary). That works fine for common words, but in the real world, the definition of "common" can vary by situation. For example, the 300 or 3,000 most common words when talking about computers are not the same words used in common conversation (even if all your friends are geeks, they weren't the sample population used to determine the words in the preceding dictionary).

And the most common use for autocompleting text fields is when filling out online forms. These tend to be populated with uncommon words specific to the end user, such as her name and the name of her street and city.

So this hack shows how to dynamically build a list of words based on those that have been entered previously (which by definition means they're popular in your neck of the woods).

Add New Words to the Dictionary

We want to consider looking for new words only if the current text input has been completed by the user. On a form, this would occur when the user clicks a Submit button to indicate she has finished.

As part of the *onRelease( )* event handler of this Submit button, we can search the text entered in our text field(s) and add to our dictionary any words not already in it.

The Code

The following code achieves this (assuming the code in [Hack #43] is also present and that the Submit button's *onRelease( )* event handler invokes the function *entered( )*).

```
1  function entered( ) {
2    var newWords:Array = new Array( );
3    newWords = myText_txt.text.split(" ");
4    for (var i = 0; i < newWords.length; i++) {
5      if (myText.indexOf(newWords[i].toString( )) == -1) {
6        // New word not in dictionary,
7        // so add it and re-sort the dictionary.
8        myText += " " + newWords[i];
9        dictionary.push(newWords[i]);
10        dictionary.sort( );
11     }
12  }
```

Lines 2 and 3 of this function create a new array, newWords, consisting of all the words in the text field myText_text. If you had multiple text fields in your form, you could simply concatenate them all into one string with something like this instead of the current line 3:

```
newWords = (myTextField1_txt.text + " " +
            myTextField2_txt.text).split(" ");
```

The *for* loop's body (lines 4–11) searches the dictionary for every word in the text field (you could, of course, limit it to words with three or more letters). If the new word is not found, it is added to the dictionary, and the dictionary is re-sorted.

Although this code uses the text in the string myText for a fast search [Hack #79], it uses the dictionary array to store new words [Hack #43]. You can see this in action if you test the movie in Debug Movie mode (Control → Debug Movie) by looking at the array _root.dictionary as you enter "aardvark." When you click the Submit button, you will see that dictionary[0] now stores the word "aardvark." If you backspace until you have deleted "aardvark" and then start to retype it, Flash autocompletes the word once you enter "aa".

Save the Dictionary for Later Use

Storing the words in Flash variables is great, but the new words will be lost every time the user exits the form. We need to store the dictionary between sessions locally on the user's hard drive. The easiest way to do this is to save the variable myText, which is a string that holds the entire dictionary (including both default and new words).

The following listing shows the code needed to search for new words and store them locally (additions from earlier versions are shown in bold):

```
function entered( ) {
  var newWords:Array = new Array( );
  var needUpdate:Boolean = false;
  newWords = myText_txt.text.split(" ");
  for (var i = 0; i < newWords.length; i++) {
    if (myText.indexOf(newWords[i].toString( )) == -1) {
      // New word not in dictionary,
      // so add it and re-sort the dictionary.
      myText += " " + newWords[i];
      dictionary.push(newWords[i]);
      dictionary.sort( );
      needUpdate = true;
    }
  }
  if (needUpdate) {
    saveDictionary( );
  }
}
function saveDictionary( ) {
  var shared:SharedObject = SharedObject.getLocal("dictionary");
  shared.data.dictionary = myText;
  shared.flush( );
}
function loadDictionary( ) {
  var shared:SharedObject = SharedObject.getLocal("dictionary");
  if (shared.data.dictionary != undefined) {
    myText = shared.data.dictionary;
  }
}
```

```
function enterEvent( ) {
  entered( );
  // Do other Submit button stuff...
}
function autoComplete( ) {
  if (Key.isDown(Key.CONTROL)) {
    myText_txt.text = complete_txt.text+" ";
    Selection.setSelection(myText_txt.text.length,
                           myText_txt.text.length);
  }
}
function fieldChange( ) {
  match = "";
  startOfWord = this.text.lastIndexOf(" ") + 1;
  lastWord = this.text.substring(startOfWord, this.text.length);
  if (lastWord.length>1) {
    for (var i = 0; i < dictionary.length; i++) {
      if (lastWord == (dictionary[i].substr(0, lastWord.length))) {
        // match found
        match = dictionary[i];
        search = i;
        break;
      }
    }
  } else {
    search = 0;
  }
  complete_txt.text = this.text.substr(0, startOfWord) + match;
}
// Initialize
// Full list of words not shown
var myText:String = "about above... you young your";
var dictionary:Array = new Array( );
var search:Number = 0;
var lastWord:String = "";
var startOfWord:String = "";
var control:Object = new Object( );
// Load stored dictionary
loadDictionary( );
// Set up dictionary
dictionary = myText.split(" ");
dictionary.sort( );
// Set up events and listeners
myText_txt.onChanged = fieldChange;
control.onKeyDown = autoComplete;
Key.addListener(control);
enter_btn.onRelease = enterEvent;
```

The third line of the revised *entered( )* function defines a Boolean, needUpdate, that is set to true when new words are found that need to be added to the dictionary. The last line of *entered( )* calls *saveDictionary( )* if new words have been added to the dictionary. The *saveDictionary( )* function saves the text contained in the current full dictionary as a local shared object (LSO). An LSO is just a convenient way to store data between sessions akin to a browser cookie. We'll load the data back in when we need it.

When you attempt to store an LSO that exceeds the allowable size on a user's machine, the Flash Player requests the user's permission to store more data by displaying the Local Storage tab of the Settings dialog box. By default, the local storage limit is 100 KB per domain.

If you intend to store data locally, advise the user of its purpose and intended use. If he sees the dialog box appear unexpectedly, he may get very jittery, especially if it appears when filling out a form to purchase something online!

Loading the saved dictionary is accomplished by *loadDictionary( )*. This looks for a previously saved dictionary in the LSO and, if it exists, the new text is used to replace the default dictionary, myText.

You can test that new words are now persistent between separate sessions by testing the movie and entering "aardvark" in the text field, then closing the SWF file and running it again. The second time, you will see that "aardvark" autocompletes after the second letter.

Final Thoughts

Notice that the final listing searches the dictionary in two ways:

- When the user is typing words in the text field, we search alphabetically through the dictionary array for the purposes of autocompletion.
- When we want to see if any of the newly entered words are in the dictionary, we perform a search using the myText string.

Thus, we have two versions of the list of words, one that allows a structured alphabetical search and one that allows us to say if a newly input word is in our current dictionary. Both searches are optimized for speed.

Also, you may have noticed that we've assumed all words in the word list have equal popularity, or rather that their popularity matches their alphabetical order. That isn't necessarily true. For example, the word "said" is more popular than "sad" but if we arrange our dictionary alphabetically, "sad" will be suggested before "said." One solution is to list terms in order of popularity (either by using the popularity count provided by large statistical analyses or by simply counting their usage in relation to the current application). But this would slow down searching if the list isn't also (at least partially) alphabetical. If the word lists are small, searching should always be relatively fast. If the word lists are large, then the appropriate solution depends on the degree to which the alphabetical word order is counter-productive.

This technique of capturing popular words can be used for more than auto-completing text. It can be used to accumulate statistics to, say, track the most popular answer to a survey question or to suggest popular search terms when no matches can be found for the requested search term. Of course, those more sophisticated uses apply primarily when you are capturing data on the back end server. This hack captures data locally, assuming that each user's commonly entered words are specific to her (such as her name and street address). You could use Flash Remoting or other approaches to upload the data to a server and accumulate statistics across multiple users.

HACK #45 Import Complex Formatting in Flash

Reproduce complex text/graphic layouts such as mathematic notation in Flash using Microsoft Word as a capture buffer and cleanup tool.

As Flash becomes more ubiquitous, it is being used for applications other than pure web site design. Online learning sites require Flash to display complex text formatting, as seen in mathematical equations for science and engineering.

For example, the MathWorld site (*http://mathworld.wolfram.com*) exceeds the limitations of basic HTML fairly quickly; the equations at MathWorld are implemented as bitmap slices within HTML tables. Those pages must have taken ages to build! It is far easier to use Flash rather than HTML for nonstandard text layouts. Not only can Flash place text with pixel precision, but the text also remains editable.

Flash's formatting capabilities don't end with text layouts, however; you can reproduce other complex formatting in Flash beyond traditional web layouts. As we will see, you can copy an entire HTML page layout into Flash!

Create Math-Formatted Text

You can create math equations in Microsoft Word using the Equation Editor. This tool is not installed as part of the Microsoft Office default installation. To install it in Windows XP (using Office XP), go to the Windows Control Panel and click on the Add or Remove Programs icon. Find Microsoft Office XP and click the Change button. In the Microsoft XP Setup dialog box that appears, choose the Add or Remove Features radio button and click Next. You can now install the Equation Editor (you will find it under Office Tools), as shown in Figure 6-7.

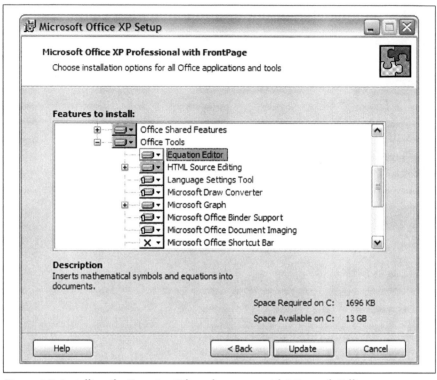

Figure 6-7. Installing the Equation Editor that comes with Microsoft Office

You can also install the Equation Editor on Mac OS X as part of the Microsoft Office Value Pack component that comes on the Microsoft Office for Mac OS X CD-ROM; however, this hack's techniques seem to work better on Windows than on the Mac.

After installing the Equation Editor, to use it from within Microsoft Word, select Insert → Object and choose Microsoft Equation. You can then create your equation using the Equation Editor toolbar that appears. The main Microsoft Word pull-down menus also change to facilitate adding further equation-specific formatting (particularly adding subscripts, superscripts, and Greek symbols).

You can upgrade the Equation Editor with MathType (*http://www.mathtype. com*), a third-party equation editor for Word. (Word may give you a pester dialog box to tell you about MathType when you first use the Equation Editor.) MathType objects are more complex than Equation Editor's standard output, and Flash doesn't seem to be able to import them. So decline the invitation if your goal is to use math equations in Flash.

Using Equation Editor, format your equation correctly in Word. To copy the equation into Flash, simply select the equation text so it all becomes highlighted, as shown in Figure 6-8, and press Ctrl-C (Windows) or ⌘-C (Mac) to copy it to the clipboard.

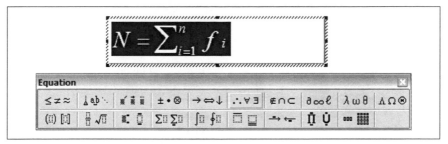

Figure 6-8. A math equation created with the Microsoft Office Equation Editor

You need to copy the live text *inside* the equation object and not the equation object itself. (You cannot copy the equation object while you are editing it in any case, so as long as you are able to highlight the text as shown in Figure 6-8, you should be okay.) If you copy the object, Flash will be able to import it as a bitmap only. To copy the equation text if you are not currently editing the equation object (i.e., if you cannot see the Equation Editor menu), double-click on the equation object, then highlight the text and press Ctrl-C (Windows) or ⌘-C (Mac). Once you've copied the text to the clipboard, switch to Flash. Once in Flash, click on the Stage and paste from the clipboard using Ctrl-V (Windows) or ⌘-V (Mac). The equation should appear as editable text embedded within a group, as shown in Figure 6-9.

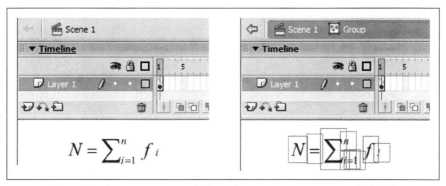

Figure 6-9. Pasting the equation into Flash makes it appear as a group of editable text

On Mac OS X, copying the equation from the Word document and pasting it into Flash may not display the correct characters. It works better if you copy the equation directly from the Equation Editor (before inserting the equation object into the Word document) and paste it directly into Flash.

If you are going to use the equation often, you should convert the group into a symbol (using F8).

That's a great technique for short equations, but it can be a long session for some of the bigger equations, particularly if you are creating a set of Flash slides on Wave Theory!

Import Formatted Text from Other Sources

You can import larger blocks of text equations as HTML or as PDF.

If you want to present standard equations, simply search the Web until you find a version of the equation formatted in HTML text, as shown in Figure 6-10. Highlight the equation and copy and paste it from the web page into Word. Then reselect and recopy it in Word and paste it into Flash. Word is much better at importing most things using copy and paste than Flash (and better than most other applications in this respect, for that matter).

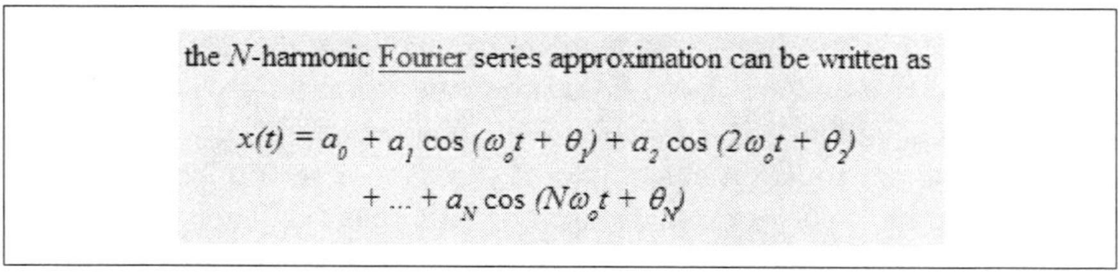

the N-harmonic Fourier series approximation can be written as

$$x(t) = a_0 + a_1 \cos (\omega_o t + \theta_1) + a_2 \cos (2\omega_o t + \theta_2)$$
$$+ \ldots + a_N \cos (N\omega_o t + \theta_N)$$

Figure 6-10. Formatted mathematical text on a web page

Figure 6-11 shows complex formatted text copied from an HTML table into Word.

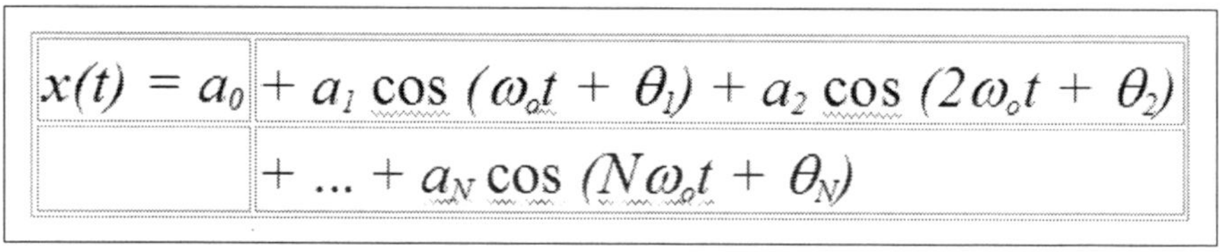

$$x(t) = a_0 + a_1 \cos (\omega_o t + \theta_1) + a_2 \cos (2\omega_o t + \theta_2)$$
$$+ \ldots + a_N \cos (N\omega_o t + \theta_N)$$

Figure 6-11. Complex text copied from HTML into Word may appear as a table

Complex text may appear as a table in Word, but copying it from Word and pasting it into Flash works just fine, as shown in Figure 6-12.

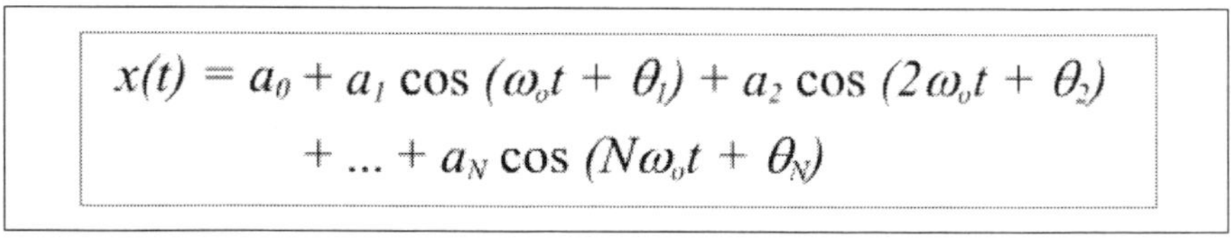

$$x(t) = a_0 + a_1 \cos (\omega_o t + \theta_1) + a_2 \cos (2\omega_o t + \theta_2)$$
$$+ \ldots + a_N \cos (N\omega_o t + \theta_N)$$

Figure 6-12. Table copied from Word into Flash MX 2004

Figure 6-13 shows the appearance of the group that Flash creates during the paste operation. Just think how long it would have taken if you did it by hand in Flash!

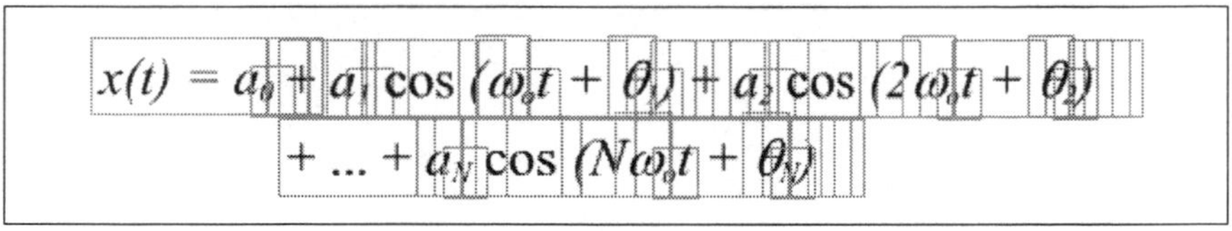

$$x(t) = a_0 + a_1 \cos(\omega_0 t + \theta_1) + a_2 \cos(2\omega_0 t + \theta_2)$$
$$+ \ldots + a_N \cos(N\omega_0 t + \theta_N)$$

Figure 6-13. A complex equation represented as a group of text elements in Flash

It doesn't matter where you copy your formatted text from, as long as you paste it into Word and then recopy and paste it into Flash. And the preceding trick is not just for equations; if you have any HTML that you want to use in Flash (for example, you may want to "Flashify" a static HTML menu and use the HTML version as a guide), simply copy it into Word from the HTML page, and then paste it into Flash. Amazingly, it works perfectly on Windows (although it might not work on a Macintosh).

 Copying and pasting is a great way to base the layout of a Flash form on an existing HTML/JavaScript form.

Figure 6-14 depicts highlighting the O'Reilly site mast and side menu and copying the HTML to the clipboard.

Paste the HTML content into Word, as shown in Figure 6-15, and then copy it from Word to the clipboard and from there to Flash.

Figure 6-16 shows the O'Reilly mast and side menu running in a SWF after being pasted into Flash and some minor cleanup being applied. All elements are static, but this layout could be used as a guide to rebuilding parts of the site in Flash.

If you want to import whole pages of a technical document (to create a Macromedia Breeze-style web tutorial on a technical subject, for example), the easiest way to do it is by distilling the Word document into a PDF (or getting the PDF from a third party) and then importing the PDF into Flash using File → Import.

Final Thoughts

Although you can use simple online PDF documents or formatted HTML to present technical discussions on the Web, Flash has an advantage over such methods—your technical diagrams can be animated. Illustrating physics concepts, for example, is difficult with static diagrams, but Flash SWFs with animations presenting the concepts will help immensely.

Import Complex Formatting in Flash

Figure 6-14. Highlighting the O'Reilly site mast and side menu

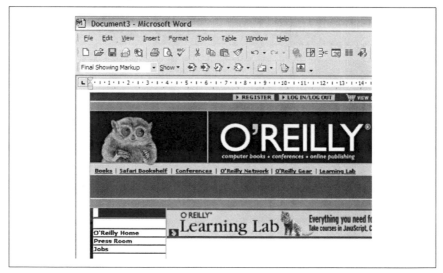

Figure 6-15. HTML pasted into Word, then reselected and copied back to the clipboard

If that doesn't convince you there is a need for presenting math formulas in Flash, take a look at a few of the animation engines being implemented in Flash (such as Robert Penner's scripted easing equations at *http://www. robertpenner.com*). Using Flash to explain them seems most appropriate!

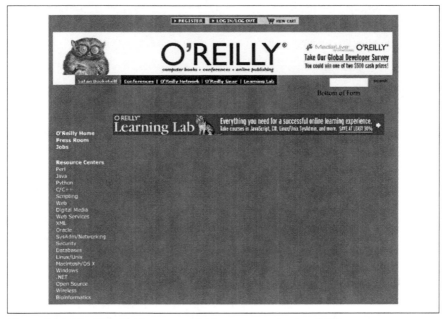

Figure 6-16. The O'Reilly site mast and side menu running in a SWF

Flash text-formatting facilities are not full-featured (even though Flash MX 2004's CSS support goes some way to addressing this). Microsoft Word has much better text handling, so it's just a matter of using Word and the clipboard to get the formatted text into Flash.

 Flash MX 2004 is the first version to offer spellchecking. If you are using earlier versions, you can spellcheck your text in Word and then copy it to Flash.

If you need to insert Flash elements into an existing HTML layout, you can import the full layout (including text and bitmaps) via the HTML-to-Word-to-Flash route. This technique even imports most JavaScript interface elements, such as fields, as bitmaps! (The techniques discussed work well on Windows, but Macintosh users may have mixed results.)

HACK #46   HTML and CSS in Flash

Flash MX 2004 offers increased HTML formatting support and adds CSS support. Use them together to create pages that look like Flash but load like traditional HTML pages.

Text in Flash can be formatted in numerous ways, such as using an instance of the *TextFormat* class to apply formatting to a *TextField* instance [Hack #42].

For those who prefer using HTML formatting tags, Flash MX and later support basic HTML formatting. Flash MX 2004 adds support for CSS formatting, which makes it easy to apply and change text styles across an entire Flash presentation.

Formatting text in Flash the way you can in HTML, however, doesn't make Flash behave entirely like HTML in a browser. One of the biggest problems with Flash sites is that you can't always see them load in the same way a simple HTML page does. An HTML page displays most of its assets as soon as they load, so you can see the page building up. There is no need for a preloader or any streaming or other bandwidth management.

Flash sites may be better than HTML for animation and interactivity, but the counterintuitive way that Flash sites tend to load is disconcerting to many users. In particular:

- Users cannot decide, within a second or two, whether a page is what they are looking for by scanning the first few loaded assets, as they can with a loading HTML web page.

- Flash content doesn't normally load in order of bandwidth weight. For example, most HTML web pages display text and empty tables almost immediately, then the images appear, and finally embedded media elements such as video appear. In Flash, if there is a 150 KB download for frame 1 of the timeline, followed by 3 KB of simple text on frame 2, you will not see that 3 KB of text until after the initial 150 KB loads.

Although both of these issues can be fixed by good Flash design, Flash MX 2004's HTML formatting support allows you to load a number of assets directly into text fields in the same way traditional HTML loads into the browser.

Formatting Text with HTML

Text fields typically render text literally. So, if you want to display verbatim text, you can use the TextField.text property. In this example, the HTML tags are ignored for formatting purposes and rendered as literal text:

```
myText.text = "Enter any <b>HTML formatted</b> text here";
trace(myText.text);
// Displays:
Enter any <b>HTML formatted</b> text here
```

However, to tell Flash to render the contents of a text field as HTML, set the html property to true and assign the HTML text to the htmlText property, as follows (note the bolded output):

```
myText.html = true;
myText.htmlText = "Enter any <b>HTML formatted</b> text here";
```

```
trace(myText.text);
// Displays:
Enter any HTML formatted text here
```

The string you equate to `myText.htmlText` can have any of the following HTML formatting tags within it: `<a>` (with attributes `href` and `target`), `<b>`, `<br>`, `<font>` (with attributes `face`, `color`, and `size`), `<i>`, `<li>`, `<p>`, `<span>`, and `<u>`.

The `class` attribute is also supported, allowing you to make CSS class definitions, and you can also make CSS style definitions, as we shall see in a moment.

There are a couple of differences between the Flash and HTML implementation of some of these tags.

First, if you surround a block of text with `<a>` and `</a>` (the hyperlink or anchor tag) in Flash, it will not change text style to imply a link (it doesn't automatically create underlined blue text). You have to set the formatting explicitly with other tags. For example, to make a link appear with underlining, use the `<u>` tag:

```
myText.html = true;
myText.htmlText = "This is a <u><a href = 'somelink'>link</a></u>";
```

This yields the text shown in Figure 6-17, with the word "link" acting as a link.

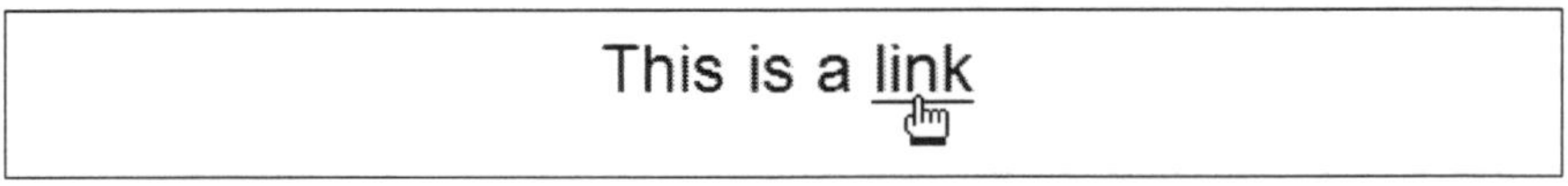

This is a link

Figure 6-17. Flash text using the anchor and underline tags together to create an HTML link

However, there is a better way to create HTML-like formatting using Flash MX 2004's support for CSS.

Formatting with CSS

Cascading Style Sheets (CSS) allow you to specify formatting using a stylesheet (stored either internally or externally in a .css file). Changing the stylesheet makes it easy to change the text styles throughout your entire presentation. Flash MX 2004 supports the HTML `class` attribute to define stylesheets, allowing you to add CSS formatting to your text. For example, you can define a stylesheet with a text style that makes hyperlinks blue [Hack #93]. You should also note that, when using external text files to define your CSS, you need to make sure that your CSS is fully loaded before using it, something browsers handle for you when loading stylesheets for HTML pages. The following code snippet correctly loads an external stylesheet named *myExternalCSS.css* and uses it to format some HTML text within a Flash text field:

```
// Define a new StyleSheet object
var myStyle = new TextField.StyleSheet( );
// When the stylesheet loads, use it to format the text
myStyle.onLoad = function( ) {
  myText.styleSheet = this;
  myText.html = true;
  myText.htmlText = myHTML;
};
myStyle.load("myExternalCSS.css");
myHTML = "<p class = 'title'>Creating an efficient walk cycle</p>"
myHTML+= "<br><p><span class = 'emphasis'>Scribble</span> moves very " +
    "quickly in the final work, far too quickly for the viewer to see " +
    "the lack of frames. He also spends a lot of time in the air, thus " +
    "minimizing the slide walk effect.</p>"
myHTML+= "<p>You can see an example of him moving <a href = " +
    "'someURL'>here</a>.<br><br>"
myHTML+= "<p>Of course, when two designers get together, easy options " +
    "always go out of the window...(etc).</p>"
```

The CSS file, *myExternalCSS.css*, is a simple text file defining our CSS classes and styles:

```
body {
  font-family: Verdana, Arial, Helvetica, sans-serif;
  font-size: 12px;
  font-weight: normal;
  text-decoration: none;
  color:#909090;
}
.emphasis {
  font-family: Verdana, Arial, Helvetica, sans-serif;
  font-size: 12px;
  font-weight: normal;
  text-decoration: none;
  color:#404080;
}
.title {
  font-family: Verdana, Arial, Helvetica, sans-serif;
  font-size: 16px;
  font-weight: bold;
  text-decoration: none;
  color:#8080A0;
}
a:link {
  font-family: Verdana, Arial, Helvetica, sans-serif;
  font-size: 10px;
  font-weight: none;
  text-decoration: underline;
  color:#8080A0;
}
```

```
a:visited {
  font-family: Verdana, Arial, Helvetica, sans-serif;
  font-size: 10px;
  font-weight: bold;
  text-decoration: underline;
  color:#333355;
}
a:active {
  font-family: Verdana, Arial, Helvetica, sans-serif;
  font-size: 10px;
  font-weight: bold;
  text-decoration: underline;
  color:#444444;
}
a:hover {
  font-family: Verdana, Arial, Helvetica, sans-serif;
  font-size: 10px;
  font-weight: bold;
  text-decoration: underline;
  color:#C08080;
}
```

There are a few things to notice here:

- Although Flash doesn't support HTML heading tags, such as <h1> and <h2>, we can overcome this limitation by defining our own CSS classes, such as .title in the preceding example.

- Flash treats the font measurements px (pixel) and pt (point) as the same thing. So it makes no difference which one you use in your stylesheet.

- Flash's CSS support allows you to define HTML links properly. The text representing the link will change between the link, visited, active, and hover states, as specified by our stylesheet.

- The color properties must be literal numbers, such as #444444. You cannot use color names commonly supported by browsers.

- Just as you can define the CSS file externally, you can define your HTML in a separate text file and load it via *LoadVars.load( )*. However, if you do load external HTML, make sure each text file is loaded before loading the next one: first load the CSS file, then load the HTML text file, then put the text data into the text field. Otherwise, the CSS definitions will not be defined, or the HTML text may not be loaded when you place it into the text field.

 If your HTML text is relatively short, define it within the SWF so that it is compressed. However, images within your HTML can be loaded at runtime using the <img> tag as discussed shortly.

Figure 6-18 shows the results of using the preceding code and CSS file, assuming the Stage contains a dynamic text field named myText.

> **Creating an efficient walk cycle**
>
> Scribble moves very quickly in the final work, far too quickly for the viewer to see the lack of frames. He also spends a lot of time in the air, thus minimizing the slide walk effect. You can see an example of him moving here.
>
> Of course, when two designers get together, easy options always go out of the window...(etc).

Figure 6-18. CSS formatted text in Flash

Embedding Images

The real beauty of Flash MX 2004's HTML support is using the <img> tag's src attribute to embed a JPEG image in a text field. For example, the following changes (shown in bold) to the preceding code specify an image within one of our <p> tags:

```
myHTML = "<p class = 'title'>Creating an efficient walk cycle</p>"
myHTML+= "<br><p><img src = 'walk.jpg' align = 'right'> " +
    "<span class = 'emphasis'>Scribble</span> moves very " +
    "quickly in the final work, far too quickly for the viewer to see " +
    "the lack of frames. He also spends a lot of time in the air, thus " +
    "minimizing the slide walk effect.</p>"
myHTML+= "<p>You can see an example of him moving <a href = 'someURL'>here</
a>.<br><br><br><br>"
myHTML+= "<p>Of course, when two designers get together, easy options always
go out of the window...(etc)</p>."
```

The preceding code yields the results shown in Figure 6-19.

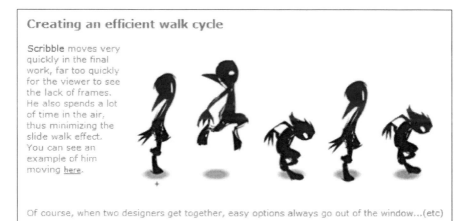

Figure 6-19. CSS-formatted HTML text, complete with embedded image, loaded at runtime

When the HTML text is parsed at runtime, the image is loaded. You will see the text appear first. Then, once the image has loaded, it too will appear, and the text will wrap to accommodate it. Just like browser-rendered HTML!

Note that the <p> and <img> tags can be a little nonstandard in their operation:

- The <p></p> blocks do not add whitespace between each other, so you have to resort to <br> tags, as per the preceding listing.

- The <img> tag can be temperamental and will not work if it is the only tag in a text field. You should place some HTML tags on either side of the <img> to fix this (usually paragraphs with a single blank space or a couple of <br> tags do the trick). Exactly which tags are required seems to vary and may be related to the size of the text field.

- Flash cannot load progressive JPEG images via <img>. If you use a progressive JPEG, the image will not appear.

- The <img> tag is supported only in dynamic and input text fields whose TextField.multiline and TextField.wordwrap are set to true.

- To embed a SWF, set the <img> tag's src attribute to the path of a SWF file. To embed a movie clip, set the src attribute to the linkage identifier of a movie clip symbol.

- Use the <img> tag's optional id attribute to specify a name that can be used to control the embedded content via ActionScript.

Final Thoughts

Flash MX 2004 includes much greater control of text via subsets of standard HTML and CSS definitions. To keep the Flash Player small, Macromedia has not provided a full implementation, and there are some differences from browser-based CSS. The subset of supported tags and CSS definitions has been carefully chosen. Tags such as headings are not supported, but you can easily define your own custom CSS classes or styles to take their place.

Although a number of designers have complained about the lack of support for any HTML-based tables or advanced CSS block and margin formatting, the HTML/CSS support allows you to quickly and easily load and position large amounts of text and images at runtime, something that was previously problematic.

More importantly, Flash MX 2004's support of CSS and HTML allows you to better separate your text and image content from the Flash site user interface (and even keep it separate from the SWF file), something that can make your content much more flexible for offline and online updates.

Use Accessibility Text as Help Text

#47   Accessibility text is normally used for screen readers for the sight impaired. However, you can also use it as help text for the sighted.

One of the big design issues that Flash MX addressed was making Flash content as accessible as other web content. The Accessibility panel was added to allow designers to define text strings that would be picked up by screen readers for the sight impaired. Flash MX 2004 carries this mission forward by building accessibility features, including better focus support, into the v2 components.

Of course, even the fully sighted sometimes want a little more help, and it may be useful to display the accessibility text to everyone, only in different forms. Here we use accessibility text as pop-up tool tips.

Adding Accessibility Properties

To add accessibility properties to a movie clip, button, or nonstatic text field (i.e., any graphical object), select the element on stage and add the appropriate information via the Accessibility panel. Figure 6-20 depicts adding accessibility text to the buttons in "Add Key Shortcuts to Your Site" [Hack #96].

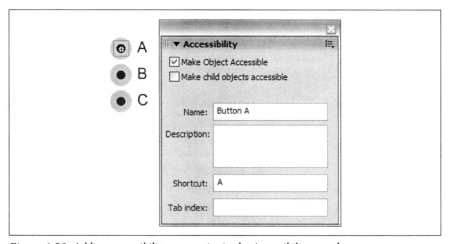

Figure 6-20. Adding accessibility properties in the Accessibility panel

If you test the movie, exported for Flash Player 6r65 or higher, you will find that the selected object has gained an _accProps property, as shown in Figure 6-21.

The Name, Description, and Shortcut fields of the Accessibility panel appear in the name, description, and shortcut subproperties of _accProps.

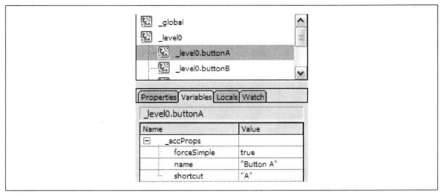

Figure 6-21. The _accProps property for buttonA

You can, of course, add _accProps to an element through ActionScript. This can be useful if you are, for example, attaching your content dynamically to the timeline or have included your accessibility text as a separate file that needs parsing at runtime. The following code adds an accessibility text description field to buttonA:

```
buttonA._accProps.description = "some text";
```

Knowing this, we can easily repurpose the accessibility properties for pretty much anything we want, including:

- Making Flash speak the accessibility text [Hack #52] for devices that have sound but are unlikely to have a screen reader, or when space is at a premium and you would rather provide verbal feedback than text on the screen.

- Displaying the accessibility text in a help text label.

In this hack we tackle the second task. When the user rolls over a button, we use the _accProps properties to create help text for sighted people, as shown in Figure 6-22.

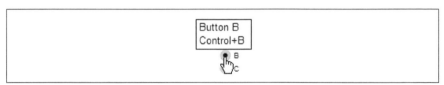

Figure 6-22. Pop-up help text

Using the code for keyboard shortcuts developed in [Hack #96], we need to add three new functions that:

- Set up the events to drive the help text. We will use the *onRollOver* and *onRollOut* events.

- Add help text boxes to the Stage.
- Remove the help text box when it is no longer needed.

First though, we need to create the help text either by creating the text field dynamically or by creating a new symbol that is attached to the Stage dynamically. I have chosen the second approach, and Figure 6-23 shows the movie clip symbol, helpText, containing a multiline dynamic text field with instance name helpText.

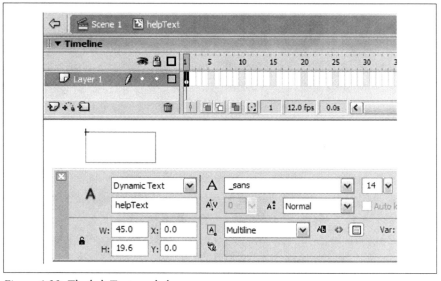

Figure 6-23. The helpText symbol

Give the text field a border and set it to 14-point _sans text.

The code to create a simple help text box derived from the _accProps properties is shown in the next section.

The function *addHelp( )* sets up the *onRollOver* event to call function *createHelpText( )* after 1.2 seconds and clears this timer and any currently showing help text (via the *onRollOut/onDragOut* events) if the user moves away from the symbol.

The function *createHelpText( )* attaches a new instance of the helpText movie clip symbol, populating it with _accProps information. Here are some things to note about this code:

- The function needs to know how big the helpText text field needs to be to contain the help text. It does this by setting up a *TextFormat* object that mirrors the text-formatting properties of our text field and uses

TexFormat.getTextExtent( ) to find out the sizing information. Unfortunately, the *getTextExtent( )* method returns sizing information that is usually too small, so to overcome this, I have specified a helpFormat. size value (font size) that is slightly larger than the actual font size used in the text field.

- We have to set the text field's background and backgroundColor properties via ActionScript, because there are no controls on the Properties panel to do this manually.

The Code

This code hijacks the accessibility text and uses it as help text. The code assumes there are three buttons with instance names buttonA, buttonB, and buttonC. The associated event handlers run when the user clicks on a button or presses the associated keyboard combo. The combos are:

Button A
> A

Button B
> Control+B

Button C
> Control+D

Note that the word "Control" must be spelled out in the Shortcut field despite this book's convention of using "Ctrl" as shorthand for the Control key. Additionally, each button should have accessibility properties defined. To do this, open the Accessibility panel (Window → Other Panels → Accessibility) and enter a name and shortcut for each button, as shown in Figure 6-24. In this example, we use only the Name and Shortcut fields, but you can modify the code later to also show the Description field.

The following code uses the accessibility properties defined per button to create our help text and the keyboard shortcut functionality. Comments are sprinkled throughout to explain it further.

```
function addHelp(target) {
  target.onRollOver = function( ) {
    // Delay the appearance of the help text by 1.2 seconds
    helpInterval = setInterval(createHelpText, 1200, target);
  };
  target.onRollOut = target.onDragOut=function ( ) {
    // Hide the help text when the user rolls off the clip
    clearInterval(helpInterval);
    removeHelpText( );
  };
}
```

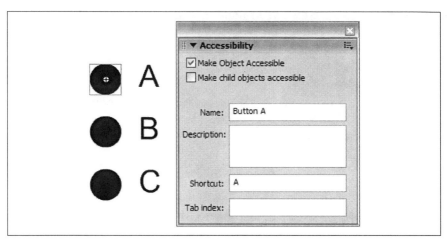

Figure 6-24. Adding accessibility properties to the buttons

```
function createHelpText(target) {
  // Create a clip to hold the help text
  var helpClip:MovieClip = attachMovie("helpText", "helpText",
                           this.getNextHighestDepth( ));
  clearInterval(helpInterval);
  // Set the attributes of the help text
  var helpText:TextField = helpClip.helpText;
  helpText.background = true;
  helpText.backgroundColor = 0xFFFFCC;
  // Format the help text
  var helpFormat:TextFormat = new TextFormat( );
  helpFormat.leftMargin = 2;
  helpFormat.rightMargin = 2;
  helpFormat.indent = 0;
  helpFormat.size = 15;
  helpFormat.font = "_sans";
  // If the target has an accessibility name,
  // display it in the help text box.
  if (target._accProps.name != undefined) {
    helpText.text = target._accProps.name;
  }
  if (target._accProps.shortcut != undefined) {
    // If the target has a keyboard shortcut,
    // add it to the help text box.
    helpText.text += "\n" + target._accProps.shortcut;
  }
  // Set the help text's dimensions
  var fieldSize:Object = helpFormat.getTextExtent(helpText.text);
  helpText._height = fieldSize.textFieldHeight;
  helpText._width = fieldSize.textFieldWidth;
  helpClip._x = _xmouse - helpClip._width / 2;
  helpClip._y = _ymouse - helpClip._height - 10;
}
```

```
function removeHelpText( ) {
  helpText.removeMovieClip( );
}
function aHandler( ) {
  // Event handler for button A
  trace("You clicked A");
}
function bHandler( ) {
  // Event handler for button B
  trace("You clicked B");
}
function cHandler( ) {
  // Event handler for button C
  trace("You clicked C");
}
function down( ) {
  // Function to detect a key combo and
  // run the associated button script.
  var allKeys;
  // Test to see if all the keys in the combo are down
  for (var j = 0; j < keys.length; j++) {
    allKeys = true;
    for (var i = 0; i < keys[j].combo.length; i++) {
      allKeys = allKeys && Key.isDown(keys[j].combo[i]);
    }
    if (allKeys) {
      // If all the keys in the combo are down, give the
      // associated button focus, and run the associated
      // button's event handler. Finally, disable further
      // events until the combo is released.
      Selection.setFocus(keys[j]);
      this.onKeyDown = undefined;
      this.onKeyUp = up;
      keys[j].btn.onRelease( );
      break;
    }
  }
}
function up( ) {
  // Function runs when a combo is released
  this.onKeyUp = undefined;
  this.onKeyDown = down;
}
//
var keys:Array = new Array( );
var keyListener:Object = new Object( );
keys[0] = {btn:buttonA, combo:[65]};
keys[1] = {btn:buttonB, combo:[Key.CONTROL, 66]};
keys[2] = {btn:buttonC, combo:[Key.CONTROL, 68]};
buttonA.onRelease = aHandler;
buttonB.onRelease = bHandler;
buttonC.onRelease = cHandler;
```

```
addHelp(buttonA);
addHelp(buttonB);
addHelp(buttonC);
keyListener.onKeyDown = down;
Key.addListener(keyListener);
```

Figure 6-25 shows an example of the code running. In this example, Button B has an accessibility name of "Button B," and the Shortcut field is Control+B; rolling over the button reveals this information. If the user presses Control+B, the button event handler *bHandler( )* runs.

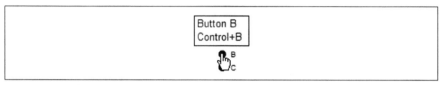

Figure 6-25. The help text for Button B

Note that the code doesn't check whether the help text is outside the Stage area, nor does it ensure that the text isn't obscured by the cursor (at the current mouse position). The preceding code shows the basic idea, and you can add other features fairly easily.

Final Thoughts

By developing this hack and adding keyboard shortcuts [Hack #96], you have a site that is not only more accessible to users who use screen readers but also a site that uses the same help information for the sighted. This allows you to free up screen real estate by placing information in your accessibility text, safe in the knowledge that everyone will see it, making for a cleaner and more pleasing overall design.

Text Effect Framework

HACK #48

Text effects allow you to animate or present text in interesting ways. Create a general text effect generator with surprising ease.

You may be familiar with text effects in presentation software such as Microsoft PowerPoint, in which text slides in or animates in a simple way. The range of possible animated text effects in Flash is as diverse as Flash is ubiquitous. Although text effects are often overused, they can also be an effective way to convey a message graphically or add subdued animation to buttons and banners.

There are a surprising number of third-party Flash text effects generators, including SWiSH (*http://www.swishzone.com*), Flax (*http://www.flaxfx.com*),

Magic Flare (*http://magicflare.com*), and Anim-FX (*http://www.flashtexteffects. com*). Better designers use text effects sparingly, so you may not want to pay for a text generator to create just an occasional effect. With this in mind, I developed the following code to create text effects quickly and easily.

The basic premises are:

- Our code animates each letter in the text separately.

- Our code animates the letters with a delay to simulate the text being "written." For example, if we want to animate the letters "c-a-t," we want the "c" to appear first, then the "a," and finally the "t." Alternative orders for the letter may make the text difficult to read, and this should be avoided unless it is part of the intended effect. If all the letters appear simultaneously and the text is large, it may slow down the effect.

- Our text effect ends with the text in its "normal" position and orientation. Although this is not always desirable (you may want your text to fade in, pause, then fade out, for example), it is a good premise from which to develop an initial general solution.

Create the Text

Although you can create empty text fields dynamically with *MovieClip. createTextField( )*, you need to create the text field inside an empty movie clip before you can animate it effectively (because the *TextField* class does not support an *onEnterFrame* event for frame-by-frame updates). You also have to make sure that the font your text field is using is correctly embedded in the final SWF. The easiest and least-error-prone approach is to create your text field within a movie clip and embed the font manually at authoring time. Then use ActionScript to place your manually created symbol onto the Stage at runtime.

Let's create a dynamic text field on the Stage using the Text tool. Inside it, enter the text "mm" to ensure that it is large enough to fit any one character in your chosen font. Using the Properties panel, as shown in Figure 6-26, make sure the text type is set to Dynamic Text, choose a plain sans-serif font (such as Arial or Helvetica), and set the point size to 24. Finally, give the text field an instance name of field.

Choosing a plain sans-serif font ensures that you are not using a complex font that contains many vectors. This ensures that your text will animate quickly in the final effect and the additional download caused by embedding the font is not large. Don't use a system font such as _sans because text effects don't work unless you embed the font.

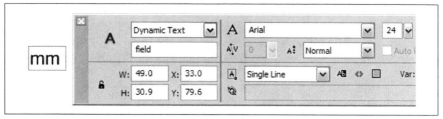

Figure 6-26. Setting the properties for the text field

Embed the Font

To embed the font in the SWF, with the text field still selected, click the Character button on the far right of the Properties panel (if the Character button isn't visible, you forgot to the change the text type to Dynamic Text). In the Character Options dialog box that appears (see Figure 6-27), select the Specify Ranges radio button and Shift-select the first four options (Uppercase [A..Z], Lowercase [a..z], Numerals [0..9], and Punctuation [!@#%...]) in the list.

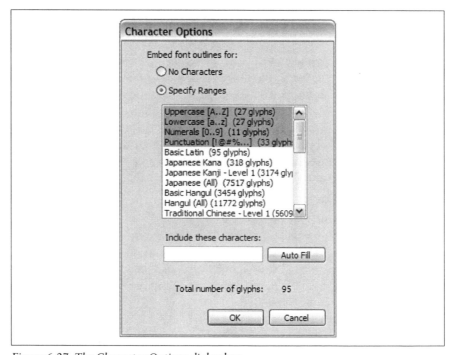

Figure 6-27. The Character Options dialog box

Wrap It in a Movie Clip

With the text field still selected, press F8 to make it a movie clip symbol (or rather, wrap the text field within a movie clip). Give the movie clip symbol the name letter. Double-click it to enter Edit mode, and move the text field (using the Selection tool) so that the bottom-left corner of the text field is at the registration point of the movie clip, as shown in Figure 6-28. Once you have done that, exit Edit mode by clicking Scene 1 in the Timeline panel's navigator area and delete the instance of letter on the Stage.

Figure 6-28. Aligning the bottom-left corner of the text field with the movie clip registration point

Finally, we need to give our movie clip a linkage symbol identifier so that ActionScript can place it on stage dynamically. Select the letter symbol in the Library and right-click (Windows) or ⌘-click (Mac) on it and select Linkage. Check the Export for ActionScript and Export in First Frame options. In the Identifier field, make sure the identifier name is letter and click OK.

Place the Text Dynamically

To place the text onto the Stage using proportional spacing, attach the following script on frame 1 of the timeline:

```
// ActionScript 2.0 code
function placeText(target:MovieClip, x:Number, y:Number,
                   banner:String, tFormat:TextFormat):Void {
  // For each character...
  for (var i = 0; i < banner.length; i++) {
    // Create a clip and place the current
    // character in the text field inside it.
    var char:MovieClip = target.attachMovie("letter", "char" + i,
                                  target.getNextHighestDepth( ));
    char.field.text = banner.substr(i, 1);
    char._x = x;
    char._y = y;
    // Add the width of the current text character
    // to the next letter's x position.
    x += tFormat.getTextExtent(char.field.text).width;  }
}
var format:TextFormat = new TextFormat( );
format.font = "Arial";
format.size = 24;
placeText(this, 100, 100, "This is a text effect", format);
```

The *placeText( )* function creates the text banner specified by the argument banner at position (x, y) on timeline target. It uses the character spacing defined by the *TextFormat* object tFormat. If you use a font other than Arial or a font size other than 24, change the two boldface lines in the preceding code accordingly. To accommodate a different font size, resize the text field by selecting it with the Text tool and dragging the bounding rectangle to the desired size.

Using the values specified in the last line of the code, you will see the correctly spaced text, as shown in Figure 6-29.

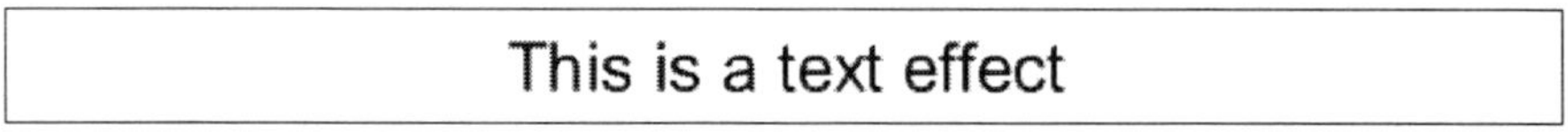

This is a text effect

Figure 6-29. Our text generator's output, proportionally spaced

If you do not use the *TextFormat* instance and instead place your text characters at fixed distances, you would instead see something like Figure 6-30.

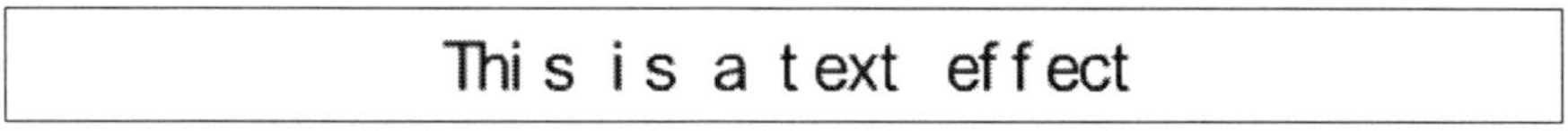

Thi s i s a t ext ef f ect

Figure 6-30. Text output without proportional spacing

The line in our code that makes this difference is:

```
x += tFormat.getTextExtent(char.field.text).width;
```

Changing this to a constant value, such as x += 12;, gives you the nonproportionally spaced text shown in Figure 6-30.

Although our banner looks like a normal line of Flash text, we have actually created a series of separate movie clips, each containing one character.

The best way to see how to create an animated effect from this starting point is to run through a few of them, including a typewriter effect [Hack #49].

Final Thoughts

Although there are a number of third-party text effect generators, the basic code to create text effects is always the same. Once you know the basic framework, you can easily roll your own. The writing of text transitions is limited only by your imagination.

Although famous movie text effects [Hack #31] can be created using various techniques, this all-purpose framework will help you generate your own text effects [Hack #50]. If you need a kick start in thinking up more effects, look at the opening titles for films such as *Star Wars*, *Seven*, or any Hitchcock film.

Typewriter Effect

#49

Create the classic typewriter text effect without any manual timeline animation.

The first experiment most Flashers want to try once they've developed a text effect framework is the classic typewriter effect. It is perfect for the opening credits to suspense thrillers, crime dramas, and movies about writers, such as *Adaptation*.

In this case, we implemented a typewriter effect complete with sound. The code assumes your Flash movie contains a sound with the linkage identifier typeClick (import the sound into Flash and set its linkage identifier in the Linkage Properties dialog box, accessible from the Library panel's pop-up Options menu). Naturally, we used the sound of a typewriter key in the example available as *typewriter.fla* on this book's web site.

The Code

Here is the code based on the earlier text effect framework [Hack #48]. Changes are shown in bold. The code assumes that a dynamic text field named letter is stored in a containing clip with the instance name field and that the sound typeClick exists in the Library.

```
function typewriter(target:MovieClip, delay:Number):Void {
  target.interval = function() {
    target._visible = true;
    keyHit.start(0,1)
    clearInterval(target.intervalID);
  };
  target.intervalID = setInterval(target, "interval", delay);
  target._visible = false;
}
function placeText(target:MovieClip, x:Number, y:Number,
                   banner:String, tFormat:TextFormat):Void {
  // For each character...
  for (var i = 0; i < banner.length; i++) {
    // Create a clip and place the current
    // character of the text field inside it.
    var char:MovieClip = target.attachMovie("letter", "char" + i,
                             target.getNextHighestDepth( ));
    char.field.text = banner.substr(i, 1);
    char._x = x;
    char._y = y;
    // Add the width of the current text character to the
    // next letter's x position.
    x += tFormat.getTextExtent(char.field.text).width;
    //
```

```
    // Here is the effect call.
    var timer = i*200 + Math.round(Math.random( )*200);
    typewriter(char, timer);
  }
}
var keyHit = new Sound(this);
keyHit.attachSound("typeClick");
var format:TextFormat = new TextFormat( );
format.font = "Arial";
format.size = 24;
placeText(this, 100, 100, "This is a text effect.", format);
```

At the end of *placeText( )*, we set up a delay, timer, of between 200 and 400 milliseconds per character. This time delay has to expire before the text is revealed (and the associated typewriter click sound is played) by function *typewriter( )*. This simulates the delay between keys as a user types text.

Any text effect always follows this same code pattern:

- Create a delay per letter, and change one or more properties of each letter.
- At the end of this delay, set each changed property to its final value to complete the transition.
- Go on to the next letter.

For the typewriter effect, the _visible property is set to false, making all letters initially invisible. When the delay time expires, the code in *typewriter( )* makes the text visible again. Figure 6-31 shows the typewriter effect in action. The delays reveal each character in sequence, left to right.

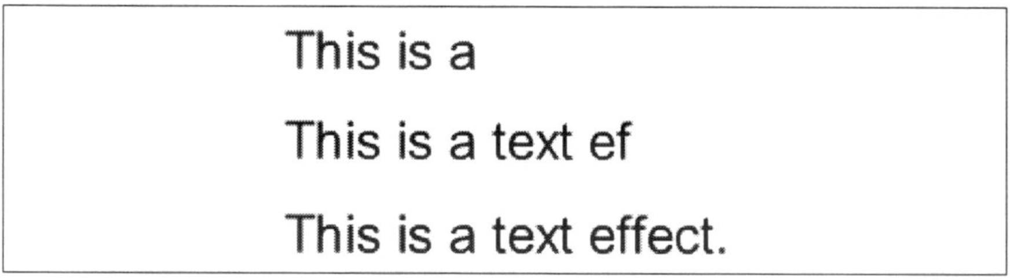

This is a

This is a text ef

This is a text effect.

Figure 6-31. The typewriter effect in action

Final Thoughts

The typewriter effect demonstrates that many possible effects follow a similar pattern. It also reveals that important aspects to any text effect include the time delay, the font face, and the accompanying sound. Without the accompanying sound or delay between letters, it wouldn't be nearly as convincing as a typewriter effect. Likewise, using a constant width (monospaced) font might make it even more effective.

Many text effects can be achieved using the right combination of timing, sounds, and fonts. For example, you might use the sound of chalk drawing on a chalkboard and an appropriate font to convey a handwritten, scholastic effect (in that case, each letter could be an animated movie clip that shows the letter being drawn using several strokes).

HACK #50 Time-Based Text Effects

Create various effects by varying the size and position of letters over time using the text effect framework.

We've seen how our text effect framework [Hack #48] could be used to create a typewriter text effect [Hack #49]. This hack presents three more text effects run atop a single code base to show you the various possibilities.

Stand-Up Effect

This text effect makes the text appear to "stand up" over time. As with other text effects, this is achieved by changing a clip property over time. In this case, the property being changed is _yscale (percent height). It is initially set to 0 so the text is invisible (it has no height). Notice that instead of changing the property immediately (as we do in the typewriter effect [Hack #49]), the transition is performed over time via an *onEnterFrame( )* handler. The *onEnterFrame( )* handler deletes itself when the _yscale property has reached its final value (100%).

The Code

The following code shows how to create a smooth effect by changing the letter properties gradually via an *onEnterFrame( )* handler. We've also modified *placeText( )* from the preceding hack [Hack #49] to accept the name of a function to execute and the time delay between characters. This makes it easier to reuse that function for different effects. The code assumes that a dynamic text field named letter is stored in a containing clip with the instance name field. The final version is available as *standup.fla* on this book's web site. Portions of interest are highlighted in bold.

```
function standUp(target:MovieClip, delay:Number):Void {
  target.interval = function( ) {
    clearInterval(target.intervalID);
    this.onEnterFrame = function( ) {
      target._yscale += 10;
      if (target._yscale > 95) {
        delete this.onEnterFrame;
      }
    };
```

```
    };
    target.intervalID = setInterval(target, "interval", delay);
    target._yscale = 0;
}
function placeText(target:MovieClip, x:Number, y:Number,
                   banner:String, tFormat:TextFormat,
                   effectFunction:Function, delay: Number):Void {
    // For each character...
    for (var i = 0; i < banner.length; i++) {
        // Create a clip and place the current
        // character in the text field inside it.
        var char:MovieClip = target.attachMovie("letter", "char" + i,
                                    target.getNextHighestDepth( ));
        char.field.text = banner.substr(i, 1);
        char._x = x;
        char._y = y;
        // Add the width of the current text character to the
        // next letter's x position.
        x += tFormat.getTextExtent(char.field.text).width;
        //
        // Here is the effect function call, passed in as a parameter
        effectFunction(char, i*delay);
    }
}
var format:TextFormat = new TextFormat( );
format.font = "Arial";
format.size = 24;
placeText(this, 100, 100, "This is a text effect", format, standUp, 100);
```

Figure 6-32 shows the stand-up effect in action. The effect changes the height of each character from 0% to 100% of the original size.

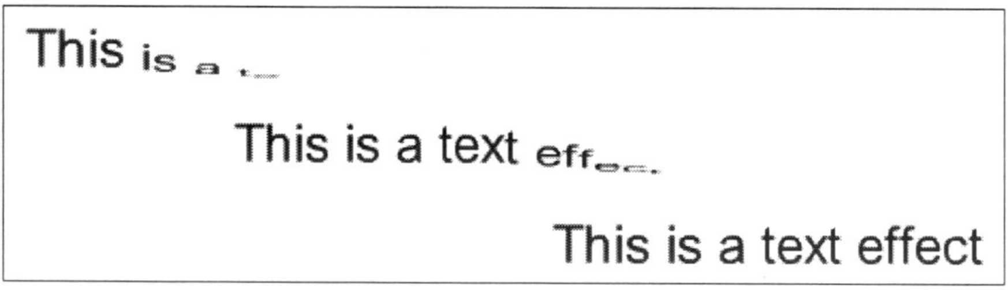

Figure 6-32. The stand-up effect in action

Drop Effect

By changing other properties and/or more than one property over time, we can create transitions that appear different while using similar code. To create a drop effect, we vary the _y property over time to make the letters appear to drop into place in sequence. We also set the _visible property to make each letter visible at the start of its drop sequence.

Also, note that a more gradual animation is created here by simulating inertia or easing via the code highlighted in bold. The *placeText( )* function (not
shown) is the same as in the preceding example, which again assumes that a
dynamic text field named letter is stored in a containing clip with the
instance name field. The final version is available as *drop.fla* on this book's
web site.

```
// ActionScript 2.0 code
function drop(target:MovieClip, delay:Number):Void {
  target.interval = function( ) {
  target._visible = true;
  clearInterval(target.intervalID);
    target.onEnterFrame = function( ) {
      target._y -= (target._y - target.startY) / 3;
      if (Math.abs(target._y - target.startY) < 1) {
        target._y = target.startY;
        delete target.onEnterFrame;
      }
    };
  };
  target.intervalID = setInterval(target, "interval", delay);
  target.startY = target._y;
  target._y = 0;
  target._visible = false;
}
var format:TextFormat = new TextFormat( );
format.font = "Arial";
format.size = 24;
placeText(this, 100, 100, "This is a text effect", format, drop, 100);
```

Figure 6-33 shows the drop effect in action. The delays cause each letter to
appear in sequence, followed by a drop animation.

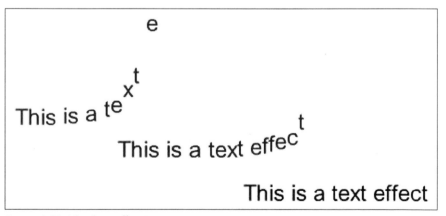

Figure 6-33. The drop effect in action

Time-Based Text Effects

Fade-in and Zoom Effect

Perhaps the best-known text effect is the fade-in and zoom, made famous by theVoid (*http://www.thevoid.co.uk*).

This effect changes the _xscale, _yscale, and _alpha properties over time, but the code is fundamentally the same as before. The transition is smoothed by using inertia for all of the property changes (as highlighted in bold in the listing). The *placeText( )* function (not shown) is the same as in the preceding examples and again assumes that a dynamic text field named letter is stored in a containing clip with the instance name field. The final version is available as *fadeIn.fla* on this book's web site.

```
function fadeZoom(target:MovieClip, delay:Number):Void {
  target.interval = function() {
    target._visible = true;
    clearInterval(target.intervalID);
    target.onEnterFrame = function() {
      target._xscale -= (target._xscale - 100) / 3;
      target._yscale -= (target._yscale - 100) / 3;
      target._alpha  -= (target._alpha  - 100) / 3;
      if (Math.abs(target._xscale - 100)<1) {
        target._xscale = 100
        target._yscale = 100
        target.alpha = 100
        delete target.onEnterFrame;
      }
    };
  };
  target.intervalID = setInterval(target, "interval", delay);
  target._xscale = 2000;
  target._yscale = 2000;
  target._alpha = 0;
}
var format:TextFormat = new TextFormat( );
format.font = "Arial";
format.size = 24;
placeText(this, 100, 200, "This is a text effect", format, fadeZoom, 100);
```

Figure 6-34 shows the fade-in and zoom effect in action. Although the effect looks more complex than the preceding examples, we are merely changing multiple properties over time.

To make the effect symmetrical, move the text field within the letter movie clip (using the Selection tool) so that the clip's registration point is at the center left of the text field, as shown in Figure 6-35.

Final Thoughts

Once you have the basic framework in place, you can create diverse text effects by changing various properties over time. You can either dream up a

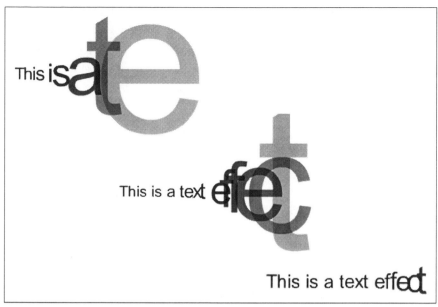

Figure 6-34. The fade-in and zoom effect in action

Figure 6-35. Moving the registration point to make the fade-in effect symmetrical

text effect and then try to implement it, or you can pick a property (or properties) to vary and see what visual effects they generate.

To create an interactive text effect generator, let your user specify the input text and vary parameters, such as the amplitude or speed of the effect, over time. You can create a library of more sedate text effects for business presentations or wacky ones for hipper web sites.

HACK #51 Timeline Text Effects

Some text effects can only be created using shape tweening. Create advanced timeline text effects with the rarely used but invaluable Envelope tool.

We've already looked at ways to create scripted text effects [Hack #50]. However, ActionScript-based text effects are limited to creating animations based on changing clip properties over time. Although property-based animation can change the position, transparency, color, orientation, and scaling of text, ActionScript cannot create complex animations that change the actual shape of your text. To do this, you have to instead convert your text into raw vectors and then treat the text as a primitive shape.

Having to edit a large number of shapes at such a low level can be daunting, but the Envelope tool is very useful in this situation. This tool is ignored by most designers, but it can quickly apply effects to multiple letters in a way that cannot be easily implemented via scripting.

Breaking Apart Text

Before you can edit text as vector shapes, you have to convert it to raw vector shapes, a process referred to as *breaking apart* in Flash. To do this, create your text using the Text tool, then, with the text still selected, choose Modify → Break Apart twice. The first Break Apart command splits your text field into several text fields (one per letter), and the second command splits each letter into a raw vector shape.

Once you convert a text field into a series of vector shapes, you can no longer edit the text directly, so check for spelling mistakes before breaking apart!

Using the Envelope Tool

Using the Selection tool, select all letters in your text. Then choose the Free Transform tool. In the Options for this tool (at the bottom of the Tools panel), select the Envelope icon. Your shapes will appear as shown in Figure 6-36, with the envelope bounding box enclosing them.

Figure 6-36. Text that has been broken apart and selected using the Envelope tool

The bounding envelope can be difficult to use because it has many points cluttering its perimeter. There are actually two types of points: the square points are control points, and the round points are the ends of bow-tie handles controlling the tension of the envelope as it passes through each control point. Just remember that there are two round points for each square point. You can see the control points better if you temporarily darken the background color, as shown in Figure 6-37. You can set the background color under Modify → Document (the envelope does not become deselected if you do this).

Figure 6-37. Darkening the background color makes it easier to distinguish the two types of points around the envelope

By moving the control points, you change the shape of the envelope, and the text inside it will conform to the new envelope shape, as shown in Figure 6-38.

Figure 6-38. Moving a control point

Changing the direction or length of the bow-tie handles associated with a control point affects the direction and tension of the envelope perimeter as it passes through the control point. Again, the text will conform to the envelope shape, as shown in Figure 6-39.

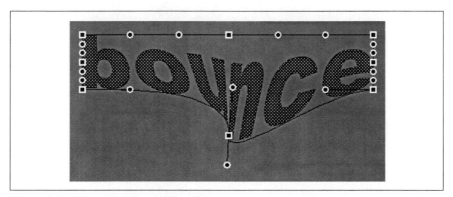

Figure 6-39. Changing a bow-tie handle

By varying the shape of the envelope, you can conform the text to new shapes. Although the text consists of many separate shapes, the envelope allows you to quickly modify them as a single entity while at the same time allowing you a large amount of control over the final shape to which the text will conform, as shown in Figure 6-40.

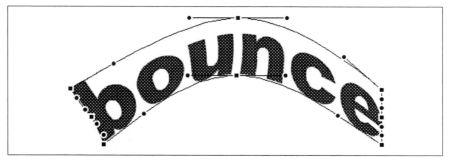

Figure 6-40. Changing the shape and/or orientation of the text shapes using the Envelope tool

There are a few issues to be aware of when using the Envelope tool:

- The envelope becomes deselected if you click on anything other than a control point or bow-tie handle. Don't miss when you attempt to click on either!

- The envelope is not remembered when you deselect. For example, if you deselect the envelope at the point shown in Figure 6-40, reselecting does not return you to the same curved envelope shape. Instead, the envelope appears as a rectangle bounding the "bounce" text. This can be very annoying, because even pressing undo (Ctrl-Z or ⌘-Z) does not bring back the envelope shape.

Notwithstanding these issues, the Envelope tool is a very quick way to create shape tweens using text shapes [Hack #34], as shown in the series of images in Figure 6-41. Here, a new envelope shape is defined per keyframe within a shape tween, quickly creating an organic "bounce" transition.

Final Thoughts

For animations that cannot be easily created using ActionScript, the best option is to edit your text at the vector level. This can be a very laborious task if you edit each letter's shape individually. The Envelope tool allows you to treat multiple letters as a single entity and can be a powerful (if unforgiving) tool. This hack shows how to transform text over time.

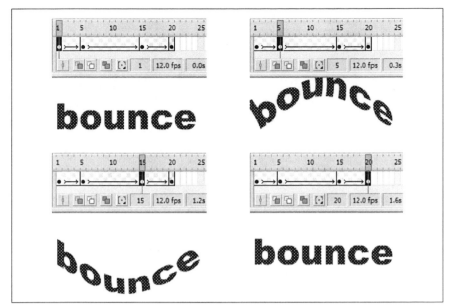

Figure 6-41. Creating a shape tween animation using the Envelope tool

For more complex shape tweens, you should consider editing your text in an external vector-based editing application such as Freehand or Illustrator (or even some of the latest versions of Photoshop), then importing the shapes into Flash using File → Import.

CHAPTER SEVEN

Sound

Hacks 52–60

Based on feedback from other work I have done, I know many web designers have a common misapprehension about sound, and it goes something like this:

> I am not a fine-art painter, but that does not stop me from being able to draw pictures or design graphically compelling web sites. I am not a musician, and that *does* stop me from creating sounds and making music files for my web sites.

That attitude is fine for an HTML site designer who doesn't have to do much with sound, but when it comes to web motion graphics, a lack of sound-authoring ability can be a big disadvantage. Sound is fundamental to animation and interactivity. Try navigating a few Flash sites with the sound turned down or playing Quake with the sound amp set at 2 instead of 10. It is just not the same!

The alternative to creating your own sounds is to buy a few sound source CD-ROMs, but the content from these are usually either of the "so overused that it will appear all over the Web in no time" or "so way-out wacky that nobody will want to use this" variety.

The problem is that sound is not well supported as a subject in its own right within web design. We all know how to optimize a bitmap for the Web without causing too many jaggies or stippling/banding/coloring noise, but sound optimization rarely extends beyond setting the MP3 export bit rate to give us a smaller filesize. In fact, sound optimization technology also has its own "jaggies" (aliasing frequencies) and noise effects (quantization noise), and you need to know about them to generate the best filesize-to-quality ratio.

 Sound is much more bandwidth-heavy than anything except video, so it is very important that sound is optimized as much as possible in any web content.

So, the main thrust of this chapter is to show hacks that allow you to create sounds for Flash without having to go to a (usually very costly) off-the-shelf sound source CD-ROM and without having to nurture any music talent. We also look at a number of issues that can stop Flash sound from working as advertised (and which have put off many Flash sound experimenters in the past).

A secondary aim is to present a few sound-related hacks that are not normally attempted. These techniques are hacks because they are sound applications that are not mainstream, such as Flash-based spoken word input and output.

Many of the routes to creating complex sound rely on recent additions to Flash (such as the *Microphone* class and more subtle enhancements like the ability to provide better timing and the overall stability of the Flash Player). This means that some of the sound hacks have really been viable only with recent revisions of Flash.

For the basics of using sound in Flash in the standard ways, refer to the *ActionScript Cookbook* by Joey Lott (O'Reilly). This chapter covers some of the nonstandard or lesser-known sound techniques, plus techniques for authoring raw sounds suitable for web use.

Create a Flash Speech Synthesizer
#52

Synthesize speech for added flexibility with reduced bandwidth—no need to record or download predetermined sounds.

This hack uses Flash sound events to splice sound samples seamlessly together to simulate one continuous sound effect, in this case digitized speech using *allophones* (phonetic speech sections from which the spoken word is built up).

The Trouble with Lasers

Some hacks rely on standard techniques or technologies used for an unexpected application. Science is filled with unexpected uses of technologies, such as lasers. Few envisioned that lasers could be used for everything from warfare to surgery, to listen to music, watch movies, and transmit international phone conversations.

In this hack, we'll see how the seemingly innocuous *onSoundComplete* event can be used to create a speech synthesizer in Flash.

Using Sound.onSoundComplete Event

As soon as the *Sound.onSoundComplete( )* method came out in Flash MX, I thought, "Cool! We can now easily synchronize sound accurately enough to create a sound mixing board," and sure enough, we can. The *onSoundComplete* event is accurate to a resolution of around 10 times the frame rate, so it's far more accurate than the keyframe/*onEnterFrame*-based sound controls common in Flash 5.

Like all event-driven code, *onSoundComplete* events might be delayed if there is a lot of other stuff going on at the same time, particularly processor-intensive animation. Overtaxing the Flash Player may result in slight hitches (delays) in playback, so go easy!

Have a look at the following code (or have a look at the file *groovyLoop.fla* from this book's web site):

```
function nextSound ( ) {
  myLoop.start( );
}
myLoop = new Sound(this);
myLoop.attachSound("groovy");
myLoop.start( );
myLoop.onSoundComplete = nextSound;
```

For this code to work, you need to have a sound file in the Library panel with the linkage identifier *groovy*. Although this is a standard requirement when using scripted sound, it is also the most likely cause of your sounds not playing if you get it wrong. Let's go through it:

1. After importing your sound file into Flash (with File → Import → Import to Library), right-click (Windows) or ⌘-click (Mac) on the sound file asset in the Library. Select Linkage from the contextual menu that appears.

2. In the Linkage Properties dialog box that appears, as shown in Figure 7-1, enter the linkage identifier **groovy** in the Identifier field. This can be any text string you want, but don't make it too complicated, long, or unmemorable, because you need to use exactly the same linkage identifier (surrounded by quotes) in your code.

3. Check the Export for ActionScript checkbox. The Export in First Frame checkbox will become selectable and checked when you do this. Leave Export in First Frame checked.

As part of the process of compiling a SWF, Flash searches through your timelines to see when all your symbols are attached. It orders content in the SWF based on this. Thus, when the SWF is streamed over the Web, the symbols are loaded into the Flash Player in the order they are required. For

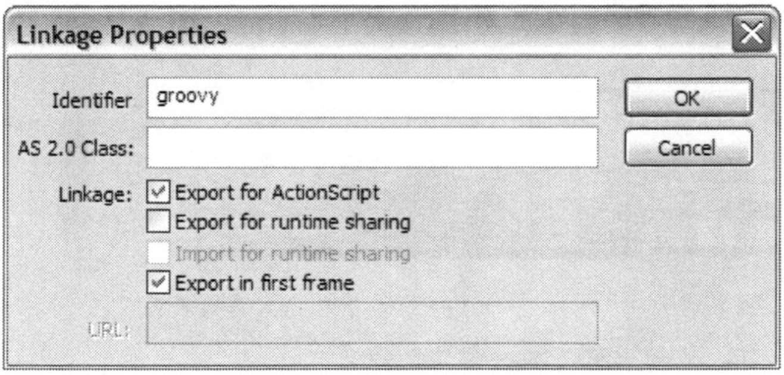

Figure 7-1. The Linkage Properties window, correctly filled in to define the groovy linkage identifier

symbols that are attached to timelines via scripting only, Flash will not see the symbols on the timeline during SWF compilation and does not add them to the SWF by default, in the assumption that they are unused. Checking the Export for ActionScript and Export in First Frame checkboxes overrides this default, and in doing so, you are telling Flash, "I will be using this symbol via scripting, so place the symbol in the SWF."

However, this forces the Flash Player to download the sound before frame 1 is even displayed. A better approach is to place your sound in a movie clip and use the *Sound.stop( )* command to prevent it from playing immediately [Hack #55]. Then place that movie clip on the frame of the main timeline in which you want the sound exported (i.e., the frame before you need the sound). But sound preloaders are not the subject of this hack, so let's return to our previous setup.

In the earlier *groovyLoop.fla* listing, a sound with the linkage identifier *groovy* is attached to the *Sound* instance myLoop. When the current sound completes playing, the *onSoundComplete* event invokes the *nextSound( )* function, which sets the sound going again. Well, so what? Surely something like the following can accomplish the same thing:

```
myLoop = new Sound(this);
myLoop.attachSound("groovy");
myLoop.start(0, 1000);
```

Here we are using the *Sound.start( )* method to cause our *groovy* sound to repeat 1000 times, more than long enough for most people to agree that our sound goes on forever.

The magic of *onSoundComplete* is that it is dynamic; you can change the sound on the fly to create things like sound mixing boards, because the call-back function (in this case *nextSound( )*) can choose a different sound to start at the end of the current one. You can thus create dynamic sound tracks on which the sound loops are changed interactively or based on other events. We won't look too deeply at that route here because it's a standard usage and not part of the hack. Instead, let's create a hack using a novel application that is fundamentally the same process.

Speech and Flash

When I first learned about *onSoundComplete,* I was also looking at accessibility and screen readers (plugins that the visually impaired use to convert web content into an audio speech stream). They are really cool, but they weigh in at more than 10 MB. Way back when we were all playing around with Commodore 64s and Atari consoles, speech could be created in about 32 KB. The trick was using a set of individual phonetic sounds called allophones, such as the "ou" in "you" and the "th" in "the." I got to thinking that the code that created speech in the old 64 KB computers must have spliced all these tiny allophones together using something like *onSoundComplete.* More to the point, I was pretty sure it shouldn't take 10 MB to do it, and that was the thing driving me to create this hack.

Although few people have the old 8-bit computer hardware lying around anymore, you can find numerous software emulators. Searching for "8-bit emulation" or "8-bit emulation allophone" in my search engine of choice (*http://vivisimo.com*) brings up a large number of emulator home pages. Many of these emulators are capable of emulating speech synthesizer hardware that was available for the emulated systems.

Fonetikally Speeking

Importing some allophones into Flash was a breeze. I used Adobe Audition (a sound-editing application) to:

- Remove any silent spaces at the beginning and end of each sample
- Reduce any clicks at the start and end of the samples (using fade in or fade out if necessary)
- Normalize the samples (so that all samples are at the same volume and power level)
- Optimize the samples for web use

I ended up with a library of synthesized voice samples, each of which I gave a name and linkage identifier that were both identical to the spoken allophone, as shown in Figure 7-2. For those not prepared to go through the same process, you can download *speech_final.fla*, complete with allophone sounds already imported, from this book's web site.

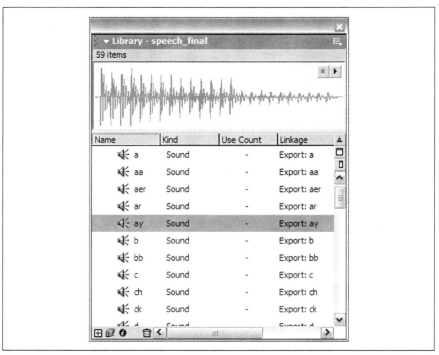

Figure 7-2. The Library, showing the sound files used for the allophones

The old 8-bit speech synthesizers did not convert conventional spelling to phonetic text. For example, to pronounce the word "knowledge," you had to ask the speech synthesizer to pronounce the phonetic equivalent, such as "nnolej" or something similar. To test my premise that Flash can be made to talk, I limited myself to writing a phonetic speech synthesizer. If you want to make a name for yourself, I'd welcome any code that converts from conventional spelling to phonetic spelling. (You might begin with technical linguistics papers you can find on the Web!)

So I tacked some string handling onto the simple sound code shown previously to create something that could take a raw allophone-based string and convert it to a simple sound queue serviced by an *onSoundComplete( )* callback function:

```
makePhrase = function () {
  if (soundCount < soundMax) {
    soundCount++;
    speech.attachSound(aPhones[soundCount]);
    speech.start();
  } else {
    delete speech.onSoundComplete;
  }
};
```

```
function say (phrase) {
  var i = j= 0;
  aPhones = new Array( );
  for (i = 0; i < phrase.length; i++) {
    if (phrase.charAt(i) != "|") {
      aPhones[j] += phrase.charAt(i);
      if (phrase.charAt(i) == " ") {
        aphones[j] = "space";
      }
    } else {
      j++;
    }
  }
  speech.attachSound(aPhones[0]);
  speech.start( );
  speech.onSoundComplete = makePhrase;
  soundCount = 0;
  soundMax = j-1;
}
function SoundInit ( ) {
  speech = new Sound(this);
}
soundInit( );
say("h|e|ll|oo| | | | | |h|ow| |ar| |y|ouu| | | | |tt|u|d|ay|");
stop( );
```

Unfortunately, some of the allophone sound names are too similar to differentiate between them easily. For example, "ooo" could be written as "o o o",
"o oo", or "oo o" and each variation would sound different. Instead, I used
the | character as an allophone separator. The pure programmer in me
would have renamed the allophones to "o1" and "o2" so the problem never
occurs, but the designer in me overturned this decision because it makes
manually creating the phonetic text string easier and more intuitive—"y|oo"
makes more sense than "y|o2."

Assuming we just wanted to say "hello," the code works as follows. The first
line sets the ball rolling. It sends our text to be spoken as a phonetically
spelled string argument to the *say( )* function:

```
say("h|e|ll|oo|");
```

The *say( )* function creates a new array, which overwrites any existing array
of the same name, so we don't need to clear data from previous function
calls. Following our example through, the array of allophones is:

```
aPhones[0] = "h"
aPhones[1] = "e"
aPhones[2]= "ll"
aPhones[3]= "oo"
```

We then attach the first sound, "h", to our *Sound* instance and use *onSoundComplete* events to sequentially attach "e", "ll", and "oo" in turn as each allophone completes. This is taken care of via the *makePhrase( )* function, which attaches the next sound file in our allophone sequence, aPhones, until all the entries in the array are sounded. Simple, eh? It works in a cool retro Speak & Spell digitized voice. Have a listen to *speech_final.fla*.

As a final hack-within-a-hack, note that I have used only one *Sound* instance, rather than one per sound file, which results in longer code full of too many *for* loops. Using one *Sound* instance is possible because you can use *Sound.attachSound( )* as many times as you like, and it is also fast, so you can do it on the fly. This has two very cool side effects for the advanced Flash sound programmer:

- You need to set up only one *onSoundComplete* callback rather than having to create one per *Sound* instance.

- Flash has eight sound channels, but you cannot normally access the separate channels. Flash assigns the channels behind the scenes, but this is not always desirable if you are creating complex scripted sound control. Instead, you can create eight *Sound* instances (channel0 to channel7), and then reassign the sounds to be played dynamically to each via *Sound.attachSound( )*. This gives you your eight *Sound* instances in a way that relates directly to the eight sound channels.

Final Thoughts

A Flash-based speech synthesizer is so cool because it carries its own speech engine in the SWF itself; no accessibility plugins are required. Although commercial screen readers such as GW Micro's Windows-Eyes (*http://www.gwmicro.com*) are available, they require the *Accessibility* class, which requires Windows ActiveX. The Flash speech code works happily on any system that supports the Flash Player's full sound capabilities.

You can build something that doesn't even require the user to look at the screen. (I picture someone carrying around a palmtop that says, "Reminder: your dental appointment is at 10 today.") You could also add speech to devices that have small displays so that things like help text don't clutter the valuable screen real estate.

Not just useful for sight-impaired users, it's also a new Flash-to-user info stream for everyone else. How many new applications does that put on the horizon?

Aren't lasers wonderful!

A Talking, Lip-Synched Avatar
#53
Synchronize an animated head to the speech synthesizer.

After completing the speech synthesizer [Hack #52], I showed it to Adam Phillips, and a few days later, he'd drawn a suitably robotic character named Charlie, shown in Figure 7-3.

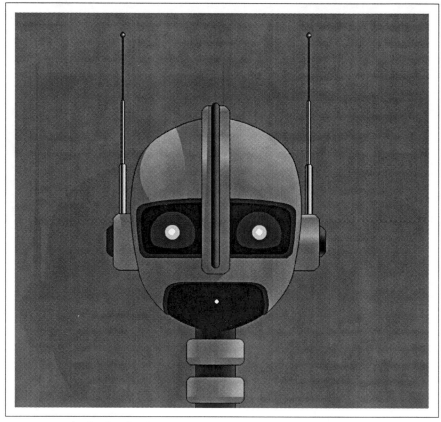

Figure 7-3. Charlie the 'droid

Adam also provided a complete set of mouth shapes for lip sync animations, as shown in Figure 7-4. Many of the mouth shapes are used for more than one allophone. For example, the symbol *JShCh* shows the mouth shape used for three different allophones: "j for jump," "sh for ship," and "ch for Charlie."

The next step was to map each of the 77 allophones to one of the 13 mouth shapes, in a way that allows a script to recognize when each allophone is spoken and display the appropriate mouth shape.

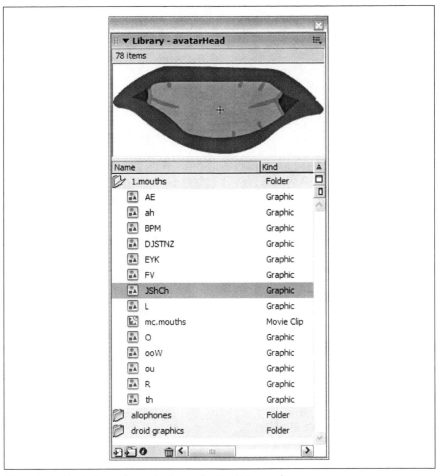

Figure 7-4. The full set of mouth shapes for English speech

First, I arranged the 13 mouth shapes as keyframes in a movie clip instance named mouth, as shown in Figure 7-5.

I then created an array to provide the link between the frame numbers in mouth with the allophone names. Rather than create a separate array element for each allophone, I created a separate array element for each voice shape. Why? Well, because there are far fewer mouth shapes than allophones (13 mouth shapes versus 77 allophones). I took advantage of a quick way of searching though an array [Hack #79].

Here's my solution.

First, I created an array of strings, one per mouth shape. Each string consists of all the allophones that are associated with that mouth shape. The

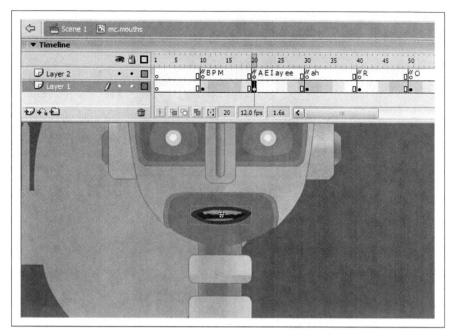

Figure 7-5. The mouth clip's timeline

allophones are padded on either side by spaces, making it possible to distinguish between "aer" and "r."

```
var shapes = new Array( );
// Define an array of mouth shapes with the corresponding allophones.
shapes[0]  = " space ";
shapes[1]  = " b bb m p ";
shapes[2]  = " a aer ay ee er err i ii ";
shapes[3]  = " aa ";
shapes[4]  = " r " ;
shapes[5]  = " o ";
shapes[6]  = " or ow oy ";
shapes[7]  = " oo ou ouu w wh ";
shapes[8]  = " ck d dd dth g gg h hh n ng nn s t tt z zh ";
shapes[9]  = " c e ear k y yy ";
shapes[10] = " f u uh ";
shapes[11] = " ch sh j ";
shapes[12] = " l ll ";
shapes[13] = " th ";
```

The *mouthAnim( )* function looks up an allophone string (such as "th") in the shapes array. It then uses the element number of the search result to jump to the frame in movie clip mouth that contains the most appropriate mouth shape. The first mouth shape is at frame 10, the second at frame 20, and so on. To better see how this works, uncomment the trace action (shown in bold) when you run the FLA.

```
function mouthAnim(phone) {
  for (var i = 0; i < shapes.length; i++) {
    if (shapes[i].indexOf(" " + phone + " ") != -1) {
      // trace(phone + " found in " + shapes[i]);
      mouth.gotoAndStop((i+1)*10);
      break;
    }
  }
}
```

The full changes to the code from the earlier speech synthesizer hack [Hack #52] are shown in bold:

```
makePhrase = function () {
  if (soundCount < soundMax) {
    soundCount++;
    speech.attachSound(aPhones[soundCount]);
    mouthAnim(aPhones[soundCount]);
    speech.start();
  } else {
    delete speech.onSoundComplete;
  }
};
function say(phrase) {
  var i = j = 0;
  aPhones = new Array();
  for (i = 0; i < phrase.length; i++) {
    if (phrase.charAt(i) != "|") {
      aPhones[j] += phrase.charAt(i);
      if (phrase.charAt(i) == " ") {
        aphones[j] = "space";
      }
    } else {
      j++;
    }
  }
  speech.attachSound(aPhones[0]);
  mouthAnim(aPhones[0])
  speech.start();
  speech.onSoundComplete = makePhrase;
  soundCount = 0;
  soundMax = j-1;
}
function mouthAnim(phone) {
  for (var i = 0; i < shapes.length; i++) {
    if (shapes[i].indexOf(" " + phone + " ") != -1) {
      // trace(phone + " found in "+ shapes[i]);
      mouth.gotoAndStop((i+1)*10);
      break;
    }
  }
}
var speech = new Sound(this);
```

```
var shapes = new Array( );
shapes[0]  = " space ";
shapes[1]  = " b bb m p ";
shapes[2]  = " a aer ay ee er err i ii ";
shapes[3]  = " aa ";
shapes[4]  = " r " ;
shapes[5]  = " o ";
shapes[6]  = " or ow oy ";
shapes[7]  = " oo ou ouu w wh ";
shapes[8]  = " ck d dd dth g gg h hh n ng nn s t tt z zh ";
shapes[9]  = " c e ear k y yy ";
shapes[10] = " f u uh ";
shapes[11] = " ch sh j ";
shapes[12] = " l ll ";
shapes[13] = " th ";
say("h|e|ll|oo| | | | | |h|ow| |ar| |y|ouu| | | | |tt|u|d|ay| |");
stop( );
```

The Poser application [Hack #32] can be made to lip sync to an animation
(although you may have to buy a separate application—Mimic by Daz, *http://
www.daz3d.com*—to do this). This allows you to either create animated
speaking characters/avatars or to create guide images to help you in creating
your animation keyframes. Oddcast (*http://www.oddcast.com*) is a good
example of a professional application using speaking avatars.

—*Art input and animation expertise from Adam Phillips*

H A C K   The Ubiquitous Sound-Kicker Hack
#54   Fix the Flash timeline sound-sync bug.

There is a problem in Flash with regard to the way it synchronizes sound to
keyframes—you can't do it.

If you use *event sounds* (that is, a sound that must be fully loaded before it
can be played, typically reserved for short sounds that are held in memory if
needed again), they will start at the keyframe you attach them to, but the
frame they end at is anyone's guess. If, for example, you start a 1-second
sound on a 12-fps timeline, there is almost no chance that the sound will
end exactly 12 frames later.

This "feature" causes real problems if you want to create a continuous
sound consisting of a sequence of sounds attached to keyframes. If the exact
frame when a sound will end is variable, you have no way of knowing when
to start the next sound. For example, suppose you had two sound files,
song01.wav and *song02.wav*, that create a continuous piece of music when
played one after the other.

To mesh seamlessly, your sounds' durations must be exact multiples of the frame rate. If they are not, you can change the sound duration [Hack #57] in a sound-processing application such as Sony's Acid, Adobe Audition, or Audacity. To make sounds mesh seamlessly, you must overcome the sound-sync bug, as well as make your sounds exact multiples of the frame rate.

If you attach the two sound files to your timeline so that when one stops the other starts, as shown in Figure 7-6, you might expect there to be a seamless transition between the sounds in Flash, but there isn't, because of the afore-mentioned bug.

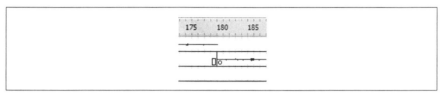

Figure 7-6. Attaching two sounds on the timeline doesn't guarantee that the second one starts when expected

Although the sound to the left finishes just before the one to the right starts, there will be a pause between the two because there is no real synchronization.

Flash guarantees synchronization only when using *stream sounds* (i.e., sounds that begin playing even before being downloaded in their entirety). But in some situations, stream sounds have disadvantages compared to event sounds. In particular, you have to reload a stream sound every time you want it to play, whereas event sounds stay in memory.

This hack gives you the synchronization you need by fooling the Flash Player into thinking that the timeline contains stream sounds when it actually contains event sounds.

To add a stream sound to fool Flash into synchronizing all sounds, create a keyframe in frame 5 of your timeline and attach a sound, as shown in Figure 7-7.

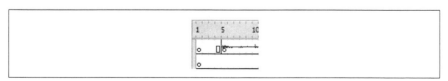

Figure 7-7. Attaching a stream sound to the timeline to force synchronization

Then Delete all frames in the same layer after frame 5. With the keyframe still selected, make this sound a stream sound using the Sync drop-down list in the Properties panel.

Finally, click the Edit button on the Properties panel, and use the Volume Envelope control points, as shown in Figure 7-8, to set the volume of your stream sound to zero.

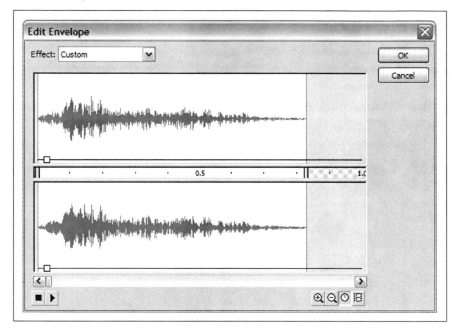

Figure 7-8. Volume Envelope control for a sound

This gives you a stream sound of duration 1 frame and zero volume. This sound "kicks" the Flash Player sound engine into treating the entire time-line as if it contains stream sounds, forcing it to sync all sounds (including event sounds) to the timeline. Testing will show that your previously unsynchronized event sounds play nearly seamlessly, allowing smoother and more reliable sound transitions.

Final Thoughts

Not being able to sync event sounds has put a lot of designers off trying anything complicated with Flash sound, especially in the pre-Flash MX days before *Sound.onSoundComplete( )*.

Creating a SWF containing kicker-synched sounds and loading it into a level using *loadMovieNum( )* is an easy way to create a downloaded sound track that contains the reusability of event sounds with the streaming ability of stream sounds. For more sound synchronization capabilities, use cue points [Hack #59].

Turn Low-Bandwidth Monaural Sounds into Stereo Sounds

Create stereo sounds without excessive bandwidth by splitting monaural sounds into two channels.

Flash will play any sound as a two-channel signal. It will play a monaural (mono) sound by sending the same signal to both speakers and play a stereo signal by sending the left channel to one speaker and the right channel to the other. You can change the volume of these two sound channels via a sound envelope (accessible via the Edit button in the Properties panel) or via ActionScript (using *Sound.setVolume( )*). You can also change the percentage of each channel sent to each speaker [Hack #60] using *Sound.setPan( )* or *Sound.setTransform( )*.

To turn a low-bandwidth mono sound into stereo using a sound envelope, start by importing the sound into Flash using File → Import → Import to Library. You can tell if the sound file you just imported is mono or stereo by the number of waveforms that appear for the sound file in the Library (one for mono, two for stereo).

In the Library, right-click (Windows) or ⌘-click (Mac) on the sound file you imported, and select Properties from the pop-up menu. The Sound Properties dialog box appears. Change the Compression option to MP3, as shown in Figure 7-9.

Compression:	MP3
Preprocessing:	☑ Convert stereo to mono
Bit rate:	16 kbps
Quality:	Best
	16 kbps Mono 2.7 kB, 1.1% of original

Figure 7-9. Sound export settings in the Sound Properties dialog box

You should almost always choose MP3 compression because it gives by far the best filesize versus sound fidelity trade-off. The main disadvantage of MP3 format is that it requires decompression at runtime, which can tax slower computers. If bandwidth is not an issue (i.e., for offline applications) and you're supporting slower computers, you might use RAW format because it requires no runtime decompression and therefore uses less processing power.

You can export the sound as either stereo or mono. When using MP3 compression above 20 Kbps, choose stereo because MP3 compresses stereo signal information well. If you drop the bit rate below 20 Kbps, the stereo option isn't supported. Low bit rates are suitable for most UI sounds and can reduce the total download size of your sound assets to nearly zero, but it would still be nice to have stereo while being able to select 16 Kbps.

You can obtain stereo at low bit rates by adding an envelope. Select a keyframe in the timeline. In the Properties panel, select a sound file from the Sound drop-down list. Make sure the Sync parameters are set to Event, Repeat, and 1, as shown in Figure 7-10.

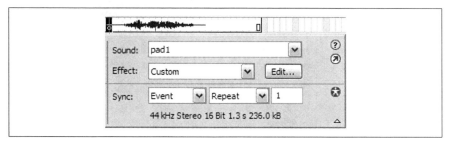

Figure 7-10. Sound sync settings

Click the Edit button to bring up the Edit Envelope window shown in Figure 7-11.

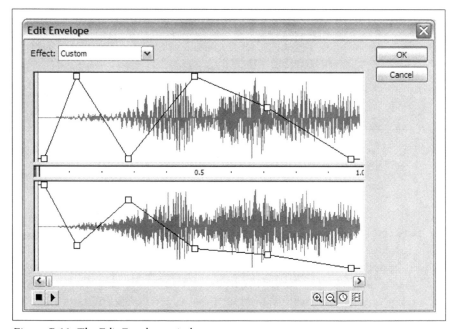

Figure 7-11. The Edit Envelope window

The two panels' waveforms in the window represent the two sound channels, and the graph lines represent volume. If the two channels have the same volume envelope shape (which is the default), a mono sound will be played through your speakers as the original mono sound. By making the two graphs dissimilar, the volume in each channel is different from the other channel. This creates a stereo output because the signal to each speaker is now unique.

The sound envelope supports up to eight control points (the draggable squares). To create a new control point, click on any part of the envelope that does not already have a control point. To delete a control point, drag it off the pane.

Many sites use ActionScript to control their sound rather than using time-line-attached sound. To use the previous technique with sounds attached at runtime with *MovieClip.attachSound( )*, create a sound-holder movie clip whose keyframes have the sounds attached to them. For each keyframe with sound attached to it, also place a *stop( )* action on the same frame. Also place a *stop( )* action on the first frame, as shown in Figure 7-12.

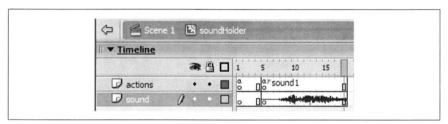

Figure 7-12. A sound-holder movie clip and stop( ) actions in the timeline

The ActionScript to control your sound should look something like this (assuming you've set the sound-holder clip's instance name to soundHolder using the Properties panel):

```
mySound = new Sound(soundHolder);  // Define the Sound object
soundHolder.gotoAndPlay("sound1"); // Start the sound
mySound.stop( );                   // Stop the sound
```

Using volume envelopes on a sound file allows you to turn a single mono sound into several stereo sounds. Rather than using several lower-quality UI sounds, you can use one high-quality UI sound but use volume envelopes to turn the sound into several different stereo sounds.

Real-Time Sound Effects

Save bandwidth by creating sound effects in real time on the client side. Add reverb and other effects to increase the variety of sounds available.

The *Sound* class allows you to play a sound with an offset via *Sound.start()*:

```
Sound.start(offset, loops);
```

Although that causes the sound to start playing *offset* seconds into the sound and repeat *loops* times, there is no direct way of playing a sample with a start and stop offset. The following code creates such a method, *Sound.startEnd(startTime, endTime)*:

```
Sound.prototype.startEnd = function(startTime, endTime) {
  var duration = (endTime-startTime)*1000;
  this.start(startTime, 1);
  this.endSound = setInterval(endTimer, duration, this);
};
endTimer = function (arg) {
  arg.stop();
  clearInterval(arg.endSound);
};
mySound = new Sound(this);
mySound.attachSound("UISound");
mySound.startEnd(0.5, 0.7);
```

The *Sound.startEnd()* method allows you to use small sections of any existing sound you already have in the Library as UI click sounds, saving you the need to create them separately.

Being able to cut sounds in this way is also useful when you want to create interactive soundboard mixing decks. It is also a good way to emulate the fast forward/rewind function seen on some CD players, whereby the CD player will play a 1-second sample for every 10 seconds of recorded sound, thus allowing you to search quickly through the CD material.

Another trick used to hide the fact that you are using the same basic sounds is to add real-time effects to them. The following code adds a reverb effect by playing two slightly time-displaced versions of the same sound:

```
mySound = new Sound(this);
mySoundEcho = new Sound(this);
mySound.attachSound("UISound");
mySoundEcho.attachSound("UISound");
mySound.start(0, 1);
mySound.start(0.1, 1);
```

Changing the last line to:

```
mySound.start(0.001, 1);
```

creates a phase-shift effect.

You can also overdrive the sound volume to more than 100% to create distortion effects:

```
mySound = new Sound(this);
mySoundEcho.attachSound("UISound");
mySound.start(0, 1);
mySound.setVolume(200);
```

Flash allows you to define negative volume levels. This produces a 180-degree-phase-shifted version of the original signal, which can be used to create phased effects (especially if you combine them with the reverb effect). This does, however, depend on the user having good audio equipment and well-set-up speakers (not as likely as you may think!).

As you can see, a number of avenues allow you to make the most of only one or two sounds in your SWF via real-time sound processing. This can be particularly important if you are asked to write Flash content (with sound) for extremely bandwidth-limited applications, especially banner ads, which are often limited to less than 12 KB.

HACK #57 Quickly Create UI Sounds

Create button clicks and UI sounds whether you are nonmusical, busy, lazy, or all three.

One of the core assets in any Flash movie is the sounds that your user interface makes when the user interacts with it. Traditional web designers don't worry much about UI sounds, given that the browser has its own default click sounds, but for Flash sites, sound design is more important. Survey the better Flash sites, and you'll see the major role that sound plays in the overall site feel.

Try watching the opening sequence of the Mondo site (*http://www.mondo.pl*) with and without the spot sound effects to see what a difference a little bit of audio makes to a UI.

Unlike most other core Flash assets though, not many people know how to create UI sounds from scratch. Many designers use the same predictable public domain sound effects, because it can be difficult to produce good ones unless you have professional sound equipment. Sometimes it gets so bad that I know the name of the web site from which the designer downloaded his sounds!

I guess most designers are not musically inclined or would rather use generic sounds from a royalty-free sound source or, worse yet, pick a few from little-known Windows themes. In all fairness, it is probably more a matter of priority than laziness. This hack presents the busy or lazy designer's guide to quick and dirty UI sounds.

One of the best starting points for web resources concerning sound is the site Sonify.org (*http://www.sonify.org*), which is dedicated to interactive audio for the Web and wireless. It has some up-to-date links for those wishing to find out more about Flash sound.

Unfortunately, many of the commercially available sounds tend to be a little overused; although large selections of sound files are available, the most usable ones are all over the Web already!

Here are two alternatives for the web designer who is not musically savvy enough to know a power chord from a power cord:

- Look in places where most other designers have not.
- Create UI sounds using a few simple filtering tricks.

Abandonware

Abandonware is the name given to software that is past its commercial life span and, although it may be under copyright, is not worth enforcing because the application has no paying customer base. You can find a number of sites that host downloads of abandonware simply by Googling for "abandonware" and looking for the *games* subsection on abandonware sites. We're talking really old games here—10- to 20-year-old games that run under DOS and don't use hardware acceleration. The cool thing about the abandonware games is that:

- They were developed before MP3 was around, and most of their sound assets are in much simpler formats, such as WAV files. WAV files tend to import very easily into Flash (unlike MP3s, where the variability of the format can often confuse the Flash import filter). Look in the game's *sound* folder for click sounds and other user interface sounds.

- Although game technology has advanced significantly since the time abandonware games were first published, a button click is still a button click, and the technology for creating sounds hasn't really advanced.

You can probably guess what I'm saying here—if the games are abandonware, then it's pretty likely that the sounds associated with their user interfaces are also dead in the commercial water, and nobody will mind your using them. There is, of course, always the chance that the sounds in some abandonware games were licensed from a still-current library despite the long passage of time. Regardless, copyrights don't lapse just because something isn't commercially viable, and copyright holders have the legal right to control their content. So there is one other option: create your own sounds.

Creating UI Sounds by Time Stretching

Modern desktop computers are capable of serious digital sound processing, but don't be surprised if manipulating a long sound file takes minutes rather than seconds.

Time stretching (or time compression) allows you to change the length of a sound while maintaining either pitch or tempo. It is used in sound recording to edit samples so that they fit in better with the overall composition. In our hack, we will use the fact that it is possible to turn a piece of music lasting several minutes into a sound a few tenths of a second long, while maintaining pitch.

Even simple freeware sound-editing applications can perform some pretty amazing feats. However, I tend to use Adobe Audition (currently Windows-only), formally known as CoolEdit, for general sound editing. Adobe offers a full-featured 30-day tryout version, which is more than long enough to create all the UI sounds you will need. Then you can reuse your own sounds for years.

A free alternative (which contains all of the features you will need) is Audacity (*http://audacity.sourceforge.net*), an open source product available for Windows, Mac OS 9/X, and Linux/Unix. It is no coincidence that the name "Audacity" is similar to "Audition"—the similarity extends somewhat to the feature set!

I include brief instructions for Audacity and Audition in the following steps. Many other sound editors are out there, of course, but these two are well-suited for editing sound destined for the Web.

To create your own collection of UI sounds, load any piece of music with sections that have little or no percussion. Figure 7-13 shows such a section of the sound waveform selected in Audition.

In either Audition or Audacity, find an interesting section of the music (about 10 seconds or longer) and delete the rest of the waveform by selecting it and pressing the Delete key.

If using Audition, in its Organizer window (the lefthand pane in Figure 7-13), select the Effects tab and find Real Time Effects → Time/Pitch → Stretch. (Use Alt-9 to open Audition's Organizer window if you can't see it.)

Double-click on the word Stretch to bring up the Constant Stretch tab of Audition's Stretch window, as shown in Figure 7-14.

For the Precision option, select High Precision. For the Stretching Mode option, select Time Stretch (Preserves Pitch). For Pitch and Time Settings, check the Choose Appropriate Defaults checkbox. To the right of the Stretch % slider, set Length to, say, 3 seconds. Click OK to perform the stretch.

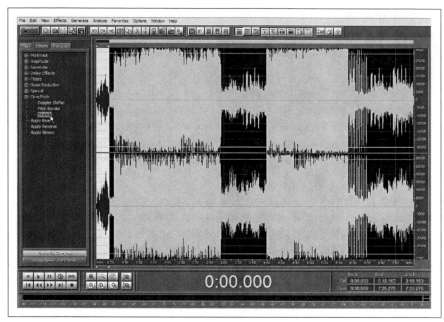

Figure 7-13. Editing sounds in the Organize window of Adobe Audition

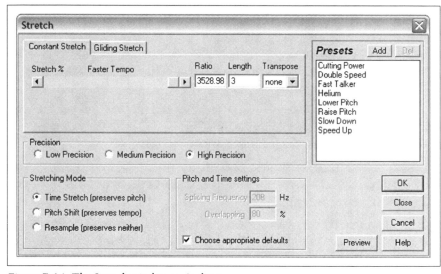

Figure 7-14. The Stretch window in Audition

If using Audacity, find an interesting 10-second section of the music, delete everything else, and select the remaining waveform. Select Effect → Change Tempo. The Change Tempo window, shown in Figure 7-15, appears. In the Length (seconds) part of Audacity's Change Tempo window, change the value to about 3 seconds. Click OK to perform the stretch.

Figure 7-15. The Change Tempo window in Audacity

Specifying a length shorter than the original duration effectively time-compresses the sound. Three things happen:

- The sound is no longer recognizable as belonging to the original piece, and enough information is lost via compression to make it impossible to return to the original.

- Because we have preserved pitch, the resulting sound remains as musically pleasing as the original. You have probably guessed why I insisted on a piece of music with no percussion—we are not preserving tempo in the time compression.

- The resulting audio "feels" as if it came from the original but does not sound like it.

You can now select all of (or a section of) the result and recompress it. By the time you have finished, you will end up with something that sounds as if it were created by a musician (because it was—the musician just wasn't you!). And if you repeat the trick with another section of the same original music, you will end up with a different sound but one that matches your earlier one. In this way, you can build up a set of UI sounds that follow the same musical theme.

Although stretching sounds (and the related effect—changing pitch or key, while keeping the sound duration the same) seems like a very specialized thing to do, its usefulness to the Flash sound designer is immense. You may even wonder how you got by with Flash sound without using it!

For example, if you are creating sounds longer than one Flash frame in duration ($1/12$th of a second by default) and you want to seamlessly start another sound as soon as the current one ends [Hack #54], stretch or compress the sound length to the nearest multiple of the Flash frame rate. Changing the sound length very slightly doesn't cause a perceptible change in the sound.

Other reasons to stretch/compress sound include:

- You want to combine a number of sounds from different sources. It makes sense for all your UI sounds to be about the same length, and stretching is better than simply chopping the sounds down, which may create obvious discontinuities.

- You want to create cartoon voices for an animation feature. You can either change the pitch and keep the voice duration the same or vice versa. In either case, the resulting sound remains more intelligible and sounds more professional than if you simply speed up the sound.

- You want to change a narration so that it fits the duration of an animation. If you have an animation that lasts for 12 seconds and a narration that lasts for 15 seconds, the temptation is to change the length of the animation, on the assumption that you cannot easily change the narration. Using time stretching to make the narration track fit the animation is much easier once you know about time stretching.

- You have a long animation that is synchronized to a sound track. You have added some new frames, but now the lip-synching is messed up. Simply select parts of the track and stretch them slightly. The animators will wonder how the sound track and animation sync so perfectly together, despite their deleting 5 frames from the beginning of the cartoon and 30 frames from the middle!

- You want to merge several sounds to form a new one, but they sound odd because they are in different keys or otherwise musically dissimilar. Pitch-shifting one sound to match the other fixes the problem. This is also a great help for web designers who fancy themselves as singers but can't hit the high notes.

Final Thoughts

Sound is perhaps the most underused asset when it comes to original content generation in Flash. Generic or commercially available sounds are of a high quality but they are costly and the chances of their matching your site design perfectly are low and the chances that you will find them also used on other sites is high. You wouldn't take that chance with graphics, so why do the same with sound?

Picking a piece of music that matches the mood of your site and then time-compressing sections of it to create a set of UI sounds is a quick and easy way to create unique sounds that enhance your site graphics with matching audio.

If you don't even want to do that, then there are always abandonware sound assets—maybe not totally free of copyright problems, but a much better way to go if the only other alternative is plundering the UI sounds from your OS again!

Optimize Sound

Optimize MP3 sound for Flash.

In Flash sites, sound is not only integral but can also be the largest bandwidth hog. It's easy to find information on optimizing bitmaps for web use, but there is very little on optimizing sound. This hack shows ways to edit sounds before importing them into Flash so that the maximum quality can be achieved for a given filesize (or the minimum filesize for a given quality).

Hacking Around Quantization Noise

The sampling process inherently introduces an error called *quantization error*, which produces *quantization noise*. Quantization is the technical term for the process of converting a continuous (analog) signal into a digital one that can be defined by a number of fixed levels (quantization levels). The more commonly used term for this process is *digitization*, and a signal consisting of a number of quantization levels is called a digital signal. Quantization noise causes the high-pitched edge you hear on low-quality sound samples. It is the effect that makes your telephone voice sound mechanical.

When you sample a continuous (analog) signal, you end up with an approximation that consists of discrete levels, creating a waveform that looks like a series of steps, as shown in Figure 7-16. These levels are the number of quantization levels. The quantization noise is the difference between the analog wave and its digital approximation (the digital signal is always an approximation of the original analog level).

There are two ways to reduce quantization noise. The standard way is to decrease the quantization step size by increasing the number of quantization levels. This is why using 16-bit sound samples (65,536 quantization levels) sounds much better than using 8-bit samples (256 quantization levels). It also doubles your filesize versus 8-bit samples.

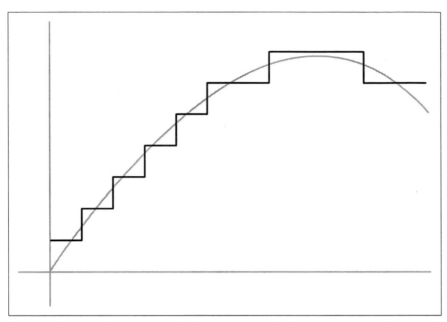

Figure 7-16. An analog waveform (light curve) and its digital approximation (dark steps)

The hacky way around is to use all the available quantization levels. Using as many of the quantization levels as possible increases the fidelity of the digitized signal. Also, unlike analog noise, which can increase as you increase the signal volume or power, quantization noise stays at the same level regardless of the signal volume (it depends on the spacing between available quantization levels rather than the signal amplitude). So increasing the signal level drastically reduces the signal-to-noise ratio (SNR).

Consider the two waves shown in Figure 7-17. The bottom one shows a wave that has been recorded at low volumes. The quantization levels are large compared to the signal, causing sampling resolution to be low and the SNR to be high. The top wave has a higher volume and uses more quantization levels; it will have a much better SNR and digitization fidelity.

The maximum benefit is achieved if you increase the volume of the sample so that it is just below the maximum quantization level (around 90–95%), as indicated by the dotted line at the top of Figure 7-17.

To increase the volume of a sample, you need to either increase its amplitude using a maximizer filter or normalize it. We will show how to normalize using Adobe Audition.

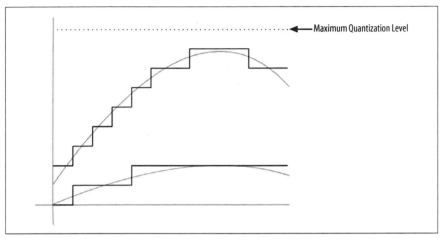

Figure 7-17. Improving the SNR by recording at 90–95% of the maximum quantization level

Maximizing a wave is performed via a special type of compression filter that dynamically pushes the power level of all frequencies toward saturation but prevents saturation actually occurring and was first used in the 1990s. Anyone with a record collection will know that recordings before this date are significantly less bassy and "quiet," with more recent music (especially dance music) being much more up-front, while maintaining a high level of clarity between individual instruments. Much of this more recent style is made possible by maximization.

The MP3 format loves maximized sound, and importing maximized audio into Flash results in the best possible quality-to-filesize trade-off. You will find that you can export maximized audio as much smaller MP3 assets than nonmaximized sounds, assuming the same sound fidelity. The downside is that maximizing sound software is expensive and not widely available outside software aimed at professional studio environments.

Normalizing a sound does not provide the same level of efficiency as maximizing, but it is a widely available filter in most sound-editing software.

Normalize the sound as follows.

Adobe Audition. If using Adobe Audition:

1. Open your sound file in Adobe Audition.

2. In the Organizer window (Alt-9), select the Effects tab.

3. Find and double-click on Off-line Effects → Amplitude → Normalize, as shown in Figure 7-18, to open the Normalize window, as shown in Figure 7-19.

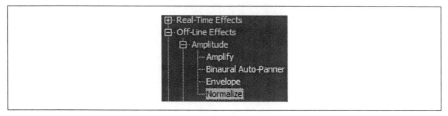

Figure 7-18. The Normalize option in Adobe Audition's Organizer window

4. In the Normalize window, select the Normalize To, Decibels Format, and Normalize L/R Equally checkboxes. In the text entry box next to Normalize To, enter 0 dB (the default).

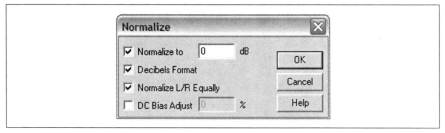

Figure 7-19. The Normalize window in Adobe Audition

Audacity. If using Audacity, select Effect Normalize. Make sure both checkboxes are checked and click OK.

The more confident among you may also want to add either bass boosting or compression, both of which will tend to hide quantization noise. In Audacity, the options to do this are easy to pick out from the Effect dropdown menu.

The before and after waveforms in Figure 7-20 and Figure 7-21 show the effects of normalization. The audio is rescaled so that it fills the full signal range. This ensures that more quantization levels are used and will reduce the effects of quantization noise.

Hacking Around Aliasing Noise

When you export a sound from Flash, you are reducing sound quality via compression. Usually, the results of this are much the same as if you *downsampled* (reduced the number of samples in) the sound file. Compressing or downsampling a sound generates *aliasing errors*, which may produce noticeable *aliasing noise*.

Aliasing is an effect caused by the sampling frequency that causes harmonics of the sampling frequency (the aliases) to be heard. This usually sounds

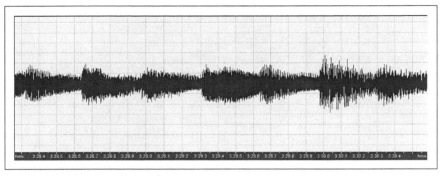

Figure 7-20. The original waveform

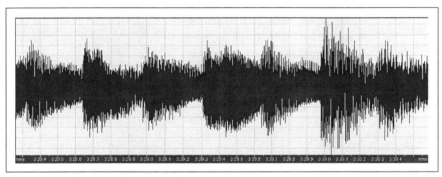

Figure 7-21. The normalized waveform

like a constant hum in the exported samples when you create your SWF. In extreme cases, it may appear as a screeching noise that makes the sample useless.

Aliasing is also a term used in bitmap errors, in which the effect can be reduced by antialiasing. In graphics, the sample rate corresponds to the pixel size, and the aliasing error appears as hard-edged "staircases" [Hack #22] when the original image had none. Although many designers are aware of the terms "aliasing" and "antialiasing," few realize that these terms originated in the audio- and signal-processing fields.

A digital sampling rule, known as Nyquist's Theorem, says you can reproduce a sound with perfect fidelity if you digitize at more than twice the maximum frequency in that sound. This is why the Redbook audio format (used for audio CDs) uses a 44.1 kHz sampling rate. The highest possible frequency that the human ear can sense is 22 kHz (and then only for a baby— your ears and my ears are probably down around 12–16 kHz). Doubling 22 kHz gives 44 kHz, and the 0.1 kHz gives us the "more than" in "more than twice the maximum frequency."

Thus, a listener cannot tell the difference between a CD recording and a live sound feed played through the same audio system.

When we undersample in Flash, we break this digital sampling rule, and aliasing frequencies spoil our samples. Most designers attempt to avoid aliasing noise by increasing the sampling rate, but that increases filesize. The hacky way to avoid aliasing noise is to delete higher frequencies that otherwise prevent us from staying within the "twice the maximum frequency" rule. This gives us a cutoff frequency for any audio that we want to use with a given export MP3 setting. If we can remove (filter out) any frequencies present in the original sample above this cutoff frequency, we eradicate the possibility of aliasing noise.

There is a problem, however; Flash doesn't specify the MP3 sampling frequencies but instead defines sampling in terms of data throughput per second (Kbps), as shown in Figure 7-22.

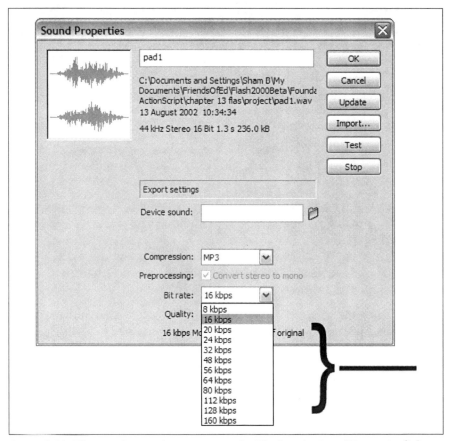

Figure 7-22. *The sound export bit rate settings (in Kbps) in the Sound Properties dialog box*

It's fairly easy to work out the cutoff frequencies corresponding to Flash Kbps export sound settings in Figure 7-22, and they are shown in Table 7-1. ("Fairly easy" is a relative term. I used an oscilloscope to look for the maximum frequency that each export setting could support without severe attenuation. Although it sounds a little complicated, it is all very easy in practice. You could probably also do it mathematically, but I'd rather not!)

Table 7-1. Cutoff frequencies corresponding to Flash's sound export bit rate settings

Bit rate (Kbps)	Cutoff frequency (kHz)
8	3.0
16	5.5
20	6.0
24	6.0
32	8.0
48	10.0
56	10.0
64	12.0
80	16.0
96	16.0

Assuming Adobe Audition is our sound-editing application and assuming that we want to export a sound at 20 Kbps, here are the steps we would need to take to ensure that the sound from Flash has no aliasing noise:

1. Load your sound in Adobe Audition.

2. In the Organizer window (Alt-9), select the Effects tab and double-click on Off-line Effects → Filters → FFT Filter, as shown in Figure 7-23.

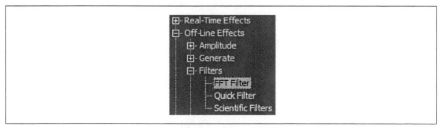

Figure 7-23. Selecting the FFT Filter option in Adobe Audition's Organizer window

3. In the FFT Filter window that appears, set up the checkboxes and radio buttons as shown in Figure 7-24, making sure that Lock to Constant Filter option is checked. Change Max to 0 dB and Min to -15 dB.

4. Create a curve in the upper part of the FFT Filter window as shown in Figure 7-24, with the step-down point of the curve at the frequency specified in Table 7-1 (for 20 Kbps, the cutoff frequency is 6.0 kHz). This creates a *low pass audio filter* that filters out all frequencies above our cutoff, 6.0 kHz (Audition uses Hz, so we set the cutoff at 6000 Hz).

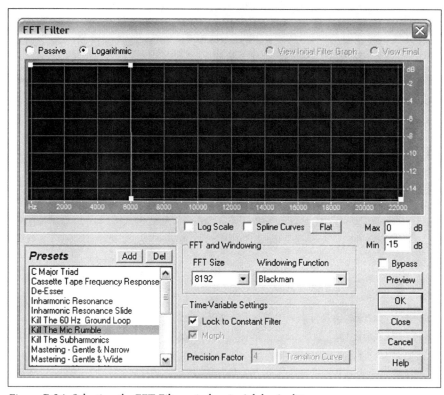

Figure 7-24. Selecting the FFT Filter window in Adobe Audition

5. Click OK to perform the filtering.

6. Save this file in MP3 format.

7. Import the sound file into Flash using File → Import → Import to Library.

You will find that the sound becomes deeper than the original because you have cut the high-frequency components. When you export the sound into the final SWF, you will find that there is no background hum associated with aliasing noise.

Final Thoughts

Normalizing a sound and filtering out any sound components above the cut-off frequency significantly increases the fidelity of the sound when you import the same sound into Flash for export into a SWF. This allows you to reduce SWF filesizes or gain better-quality sound at no additional bandwidth costs.

Although optimizing sound (rather than just compressing it in Flash and hoping for the best!) is a new technique for many Flash designers, it can pay real benefits to sound-heavy sites. You should at least give it a try. After all, you wouldn't dream of not optimizing bitmaps for an HTML page, and sounds can be significantly worse bandwidth hogs!

Sound Time Codes (Cue Points)

HACK #59

Associate timecode information with your sound files so Flash can react to your sounds as they play.

Although we can use Flash to play sounds, we cannot use Flash to access low-level information about the sounds. In particular, although we can set an overall volume for a sound object with *Sound.setVolume( )*, we cannot find out the instantaneous volume amplitudes of the sound file that is actually played. Instead, we can hack around the problem by adding this information to Flash separately.

In this example, we use Audacity (*http://audacity.sourceforge.net*) a free, open source sound editor for Windows, Max OS 9/X, and Unix/Linux. Although it doesn't have the precise controls of a commercial offering such as Adobe Audition, its presets are almost always what a typical web designer would require anyway, making it quick and easy to use. We will find beat-timing information about the sound and use this information every time the sound is played to allow Flash to act as if it can "read" and follow the sound.

You need a sound file containing percussion. If you don't have one lying around, you can always use mine, *groovyLoop.wav*, downloadable from this book's web site.

The file *groovyLoop.wav* has a useful property—it can be looped seamlessly. Creating such a sound from scratch unfortunately requires both musical ability and a fair amount of musical equipment, although you can cut sections of existing song files (using the features of Audacity and Audition) until you achieve a similar result. Doing this is not something I would recommend though, because there are copyright implications in sampling other works in such an obvious (and common) way.

Open the *groovyLoop.wav* sound in Audacity with File → Open. Select all of the wave (Edit → Select All).

Select Analyze → Beat Finder. We will use the Beat Finder, shown in Figure 7-25 to find the point of every new beat in our file. It's a bit of a trial and error process, but once you have the correct result, its very obvious. Looking at the waveform, choose a threshold value that would catch the peaks of the sound but miss the constant background levels. For *groovyLoop.wav*, this is about 75%.

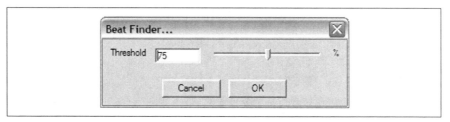

Figure 7-25. Setting the Beat Finder threshold level in Audacity

After the waveform has been processed, you should see a series of periodic (or nearly periodic) beat markers (labeled with "B") appear below the main waveform, as shown in Figure 7-26.

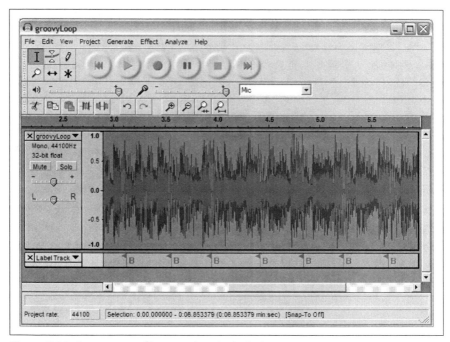

Figure 7-26. A correct set of beat markers in Audacity

If your beats do not look very periodic, as shown in Figure 7-27, you have set the Beat Finder threshold either too low or too high. In this case, you should delete the marker track (click the x above the track title at the start of the track) and retry the Beat Finder with a different value. The existing threshold is too low if the Beat Finder is finding too many beats. If you have the threshold set too high, you will see too few beat markers.

Figure 7-27. An incorrect set of beat markers

Finding the correct beat threshold is a bit like tuning a guitar by starting with a low value that you know is wrong and then working upward in value. That way, at least you know that the correct setting is in a particular direction (higher) from the current setting.

With Audacity still open, start Flash and import the sound using File → Import → Import to Library. Give it the linkage identifier [Hack #52] *groovyLoop*.

Attach the following code to frame 1 of the FLA:

```
beatHandler = function () {
  beatMarker++;
  clearInterval(beatID);
  beatID = setInterval(beatHandler, beatCode[beatMarker]);
  pulse();
};
repeatSound = function () {
  this.start(0, 1);
  clearInterval(beatID);
  beatMarker = 0;
  beatID = setInterval(beatHandler, beatCode[beatMarker]);
};
function pulse() {
  // Do something here...
}
beatCode = new Array();
beatMarker = 0;
beatCode = [];
for (var i = beatCode.length - 1; i > 0; i--) {
  beatCode[i] = beatCode[i] - beatCode[i-1];
  trace(beatCode[i]);
}
groovy = new Sound(this);
groovy.attachSound("groovyLoop");
groovy.start(0, 1);
groovy.onSoundComplete = repeatSound;
clearInterval(beatID);
beatID = setInterval(beatHandler, beatCode[0]);
```

We need to add values in the array beatCode corresponding to the markers. In Audacity, select the Selection tool (the first tool in the toolbox) and click on the waveform at the position of each marker in turn, starting with the first. Read the time for this marker (it will appear in minute:second:millisecond format at the bottom of the application window). Convert this to milliseconds. In Flash, add this value (in milliseconds) in the array beatCode.

Repeat this for all markers. You should end up with something like this for your beatCode array:

```
beatCode = [120, 556, 996, 1366, 1835, 2302, 2699, 3124,
            3559, 3938, 4414, 4827, 5232, 5661, 6091, 6512];
```

This array now contains the beat position information for our wave in milliseconds. It is in a form suitable to be used with *setInterval( )*, and that is exactly what the preceding code does—it executes *beatHandler( )* at the points defined by the beatCode array. To actually use the *setInterval( )* events, you need to make function *pulse( )* do something. This could be used to control a dancing figure or change an important parameter of a pattern effect. It could even be used to start another sound, so, for example, you could play another sample in time with the loop.

Music players such as WinAmp and iTunes allow you to create visualizations to accompany the currently playing track. These are pattern effects that rotate and pulse in time to the music. They work by detecting beats—exactly the same thing we used Audacity to do. Although the procedure stated here doesn't allow you to easily create beat tracks for entire songs, it does allow you to create beat tracks for loops, which are traditionally used in Flash web design as background tracks. You can also use the beats to drive a bar graph that will pulse in time to your music (many sites have one of these to signify the music on/off toggle but don't actually show a bar graph that moves in time to the music—with this code, it will!).

You can also fill the beatCode array with any timing values you like to synchronize to any point in the sound track, such as a crescendo or cymbal crash. That is, the beatCode array, along with the code presented, simulates what are called *cue points* in Director. That is, they create a way to trigger events at a particular time in a sound.

A Custom Sound Transform Class

#60   Create a custom class to perform sound fades and cross-fades.

You'll often want to perform sound fades or cross-fades (fading in one sound while fading out another). The common nature of the task suggests that it is a great candidate to be implemented as a custom class. The class

can take care of all the grunt work, allowing us to perform a sound fade
using a few simple calls to the custom class's methods.

Like the built-in *Color* class, the *Sound* class supports a *setTransform( )*
method. Earlier, we created a custom color transform class [Hack #10] and we
can apply the same concepts to create a similar custom class for sound.
We've chosen to implement the *SoundTrans* class as a subclass of the built-
in *Sound* class. The custom subclass contains two methods:

SoundTrans.fadeIn(duration, loop)
> Starts a sound and fades it in from 0% to 100% volume over *duration*
> milliseconds and plays it *loop* times

SoundTrans.fadeOut(duration)
> Fades a sound to zero volume over *duration* milliseconds

Here is our object-oriented version, implemented as a custom *SoundTrans*
class, which must be stored in an external *SoundTrans.as* file:

```
// This ActionScript 2.0 code must go in an external SoundTrans.as file
class SoundTrans extends Sound {
    // FADE_OUT fades out a sound.
    // FADE_IN fades in a sound.
    // RATE sets the rate the effects will run at, in ms.
    private static var FADE_OUT:Object = {ll:0, lr:0, rr:0, rl:0};
    private static var FADE_IN:Object = {ll:100, lr:0, rr:100, rl:0};
    private static var RATE:Number = 60;
    private var interval:Number;
    private var startTime:Number;

    // (Re)starts the sound and fades it in over duration ms
    // then loops the sound loop times.
    public function fadeIn(duration:Number, loop:Number):Void {
        // Invoke functions inherited from the Sound superclass.
        stop();
        start(0, loop);
        setTransform(FADE_OUT);
        // Invoke a custom method defined for the subclass.
        applyTransform(FADE_IN, duration);
    }
    // Fades out the sound over duration ms,
    // stopping the sound at the end.
    public function fadeOut(duration:Number):Void {
        applyTransform(FADE_OUT, duration);
    }
    // Initiate a fade and set up an interval to complete it over time.
    private function applyTransform(transObject:Object,
                                    duration:Number):Void {
        // Get the current sound transform object.
        var getTrans:Object = getTransform();
        var diffTrans:Object = new Object();
        if (duration < RATE) {
```

```
        duration = RATE;
      }
      startTime = getTimer( );
      for (var i in transObject) {
        diffTrans[i] = (transObject[i]-getTrans[i]) / (duration/RATE);
      }
      // First parameter is current object, this.
      // Second parameter is function to invoke (transition( )).
      // Third parameter is interval duration in ms.
      // Fourth, fifth, and sixth parameters get passed to transition( ).
      interval = setInterval(this, "transition", RATE, transObject, diffTrans,
      duration);
    }
    private function transition(transObject:Object, diffTrans:Object,
    duration:Number):Void {
        var getTrans:Object = getTransform( );
        for (var i in diffTrans) {
          getTrans[i] += diffTrans[i];
        }
        setTransform(getTrans);
        if (getTimer( ) - startTime > duration) {
          // Cleanup
          setTransform(transObject);
          clearInterval(interval);
        }
        updateAfterEvent( );
      }
  }
```

Note that our class doesn't add new methods directly to the *Sound* class (as
was typical when using prototype-based inheritance in ActionScript 1.0).
Instead, the *SoundTrans* class extends (i.e., subclasses) the built-in *Sound*
class. This has the advantage of keeping the new sound functionality (in our
SoundTrans class) separate from the existing *Sound* class, while at the same
time working seamlessly with the *Sound* class.

You can see this in the following code example, which demonstrates how to
use the *SoundTrans* class.

First, create an instance of the *SoundTrans* class. This code creates a
SoundTrans object that uses the *groovyLoop.wav* file (which is presumed to
be available in the Library with sound linkage identifier *groovyLoop*).

```
var groovy:SoundTrans = new SoundTrans(this);
groovy.attachSound("groovyLoop");
```

We can now use the methods of the *SoundTrans* class (or those of the *Sound*
superclass) with our *SoundTrans* instance. The following causes the sound
to start playing with the sound volume fading in from zero to 100% over
three seconds. The sound then loops twice:

```
groovyTrans.fadeIn(3000, 2);
```

The following fades out the sound over six seconds:

```
groovyTrans.fadeOut(6000);
```

Consider enhancing this custom class to implement additional features, such as:

- Making the RATE value user-definable.
- Adding a method that can accept an array of fade points, allowing you to create a scripted version of the sound envelope.

CHAPTER EIGHT

User Interface Elements
Hacks 61–64

Flash originally started as a low-bandwidth animation tool, but since then Macromedia has added many features that support building graphic user interfaces (GUIs).

In recent years, Macromedia has been promoting Flash as a platform for Rich Internet Application (RIA) development. To that end, Macromedia has enhanced Flash's event-driven language, ActionScript, making it easy to write application code that can respond to user interaction and thus act as "GUI glue"—the thing that holds your interface together and drives it.

The user interface (UI) and navigation can be implemented by using the Flash timeline as a nonlinear series of animation/content sections. In the final Flash site, the user navigates between the sections, each of which represents a different program state (such as different pages in a multipage form), via a simple point-and-click UI. The UI is also easy for the designer to set up with a minimum of scripting. Flash MX Professional 2004 supports new Slides and Forms features (collectively called Screens) to make visual development easier by hiding the timeline paradigm from the developer. Instead, it allows them to develop using a PowerPoint-like or Visual Basic-style authoring metaphor.

Flash MX and Flash MX 2004 provide numerous components [Hack #73], which are UI building blocks, such as combo boxes and radio buttons, that make it easy to build and customize (skin) the UI. Of course you can create your own UI elements, such as buttons [Hack #14] and sliders [Hack #61].

ActionScript also includes built-in methods to allow interactive control of multimedia streams, such as sound and video, using the *Sound*, *Microphone*, and *Camera* classes.

Regardless, the raison d'etre of Flash is to engage the user. Even when used to conduct business or provide education, your content must be engaging or you will lose existing viewers and fail to attract new ones.

Sometimes, your interface needs to be clear and clean, but in other cases, we need to create something that the user will enjoy using and that will fulfill the promise of over-the-Web rich content. In the end, it is up to you as the site designer or developer to make appropriate choices for your audience based on your business or artistic goals and to adjust your site based on user feedback.

However, this book is not about interface design but about stretching Flash in ways Macromedia might not have foreseen or intended. Therefore, the hacks in this chapter cover several nonobvious uses of UI elements within Flash. Some of them overcome apparent limitations in the UI facilities provided by Flash. But the first hack shows that UIs are not just for the end user, sometimes they can make development easier, too.

Speaking of author-time user interfaces, Flash MX 2004 and Flash MX Professional 2004 support *extensibility*—the ability to not only configure the Flash authoring environment, but also to modify existing features or add new ones.

The Flash authoring environment can be configured via the JavaScript API (JSAPI) using a dialect of JavaScript specific to the Flash authoring environment, JSFL (which stands for "Flash JavaScript"—yeah, I know the backward acronym is very unsatisfying).

As most web designers know, JavaScript allows access to the web browser's user interface and any open HTML documents using the Document Object Model (DOM). However, unlike the browser-based DOM, the JSFL DOM provides access to the Flash authoring environment user interface and any open FLA documents. Using JSFL and the associated DOM, you can:

- Access any part of the currently open Flash document (FLA) and programmatically edit it via JSFL. This allows you to create advanced commands (accessible via the Commands menu) that can automate workflows or create new tools.

- Access the Flash authoring environment user interface, allowing you to create (for example) new tools on the Tools palette. One such tool (the PolyStar tool) can be seen if you click-hold the Rectangle tool.

- Export a SWF from the Windows command line as described on moockblog (*http://moock.org/blog/archives/000058.html*).

As well as the power of the JSAPI, you can also create custom panels and requesters to allow user interaction between your JSFL scripts and the user, not only allowing you to run scripts that configure the Flash authoring interface, but also allowing users to customize the operation of the JSFL scripts themselves! This works via an XML-based language, XML to UI, which allows you to create custom UIs that appear in the Flash authoring environment and act as the interface between the user and your JSFL code. You can also communicate between standard ActionScript and JSFL, so that you can use a running SWF as part of your user interface. The *MMExecute( )* function allows a running SWF (typically embedded within your XML to UI interface) to execute JSFL scripts, thus allowing you to create large custom interfaces that can provide a variety of automated tasks and tools via a single custom panel.

In fact, Macromedia used the extensibility features within Flash MX 2004 to create new features such as Timeline Effects, Behaviors, and the ability to record macros via the History panel. It will be exciting when third parties begin to use JSAPI, XML to UI, and *MMExecute( )* to customize the Flash authoring environment and make those modifications available to other developers. (Note that JSAPI, JSFL, XML to UI, and *MMExecute( )* are relevant only to author-time customizations and additions. They are not designed for runtime use in the Flash Player.)

HACK #61 Amit's Dials (Interactive Testing)

User interface elements need not be limited to runtime use for the benefit of end users. Use UI elements during development to test various scenarios quickly.

Every time I go to a Flash conference, I learn something. Usually, it is something like how to use Flash MX 2004 components or the FlashCom server. Occasionally though, I learn a trick or hack that seems innocuous but really changes the way I work. This is one of those hacks.

During a talk by Amit Pitaru and James Paterson, James said something like, "Well, I do some freaky animations, and then Amit comes around and says 'hey, let's put a dial on this,' and so we kick it around with the dial for a bit to see what happens. Once we are happy with it, we make the dial setting permanent."

Around the same time, I attended a presentation by the guys who did the Banja site (*http://www.banja.com*). Banja is a full and complex adventure game, so I assumed they wrote some code to define the data for each location, but they didn't. They were using a more complex version of Amit's dials. Each location in the game requires data, which they input using lots of offscreen text fields and sliders. Rather than having to update a code section (or text file) whenever you add a new location, the whole thing is visual and contained in one file. Once you have drawn the location and filled in the offscreen text fields and sliders, you are done; no need to change any code.

Let's see how it works.

First of all, we'll create a dial, which is just Amit's name for any adjustable UI element such as a slider or knob. It need not use Flash's built-in UI components (in fact, we avoid them to keep the filesize small) and it need not be round like the dials on your oscilloscope (oh, we know you have one in the basement!).

For our "dial," we'll create a simple slider with a numeric readout. First, create a single hairline, 200 units in length, and convert it to a movie clip symbol; place the registration point halfway along the line, as shown in Figure 8-1. This will act as the line along which our slider's puck will travel. Name the symbol slider.

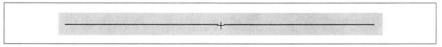

Figure 8-1. A hairline with its registration point in the middle

Next, inside the slider movie clip symbol, insert a new layer and name it *puck*. On the new *puck* layer, create a small 10 × 10 square and make it into a symbol named puck with a centered registration point. Then place it at (-5, -5) and give the on-stage clip the instance name puck_mc, as shown in Figure 8-2.

Figure 8-2. The puck_mc clip positioned along the slider

Finally, create a new layer named *actions* above the default layer, and attach the following code to frame 1 of the *actions* layer:

```
puck_mc.onPress = function( ) {
  this.startDrag(true, -100, 0, 100, 0);
  this.onMouseMove = _onMouseMove;
};
```

```
_onMouseMove = function( ) {
  _parent[_name + "_txt"].text = this._x;
  updateAfterEvent( );
};
_parent[_name + "_txt"].onChanged = function( ) {
  puck_mc._x = Number(this.text);
};
puck_mc.onRelease = puck_mc.onReleaseOutside = function ( ) {
  this.stopDrag( );
};
_parent[_name + "_txt"].onChanged( );
```

The preceding code makes puck_mc draggable along the hairline when you click on it. It also associates the puck_mc clip with a text field that is on the same timeline as the slider clip. The text field must have the same name as the slider clip, except with "_txt" at the end, such as slider_txt.

Using the Slider

When I was generating fractal trees [Hack #6], I worked out the "seed" values using sliders. There were two function values for which I didn't really have a feel for the suitable range. They were angle (which controls the angle of the branches) and branch (which controls how often the tree sprouts branches).

In the code where the values of these two variables were defined, I simply commented them out as follows:

```
// angle = 10;
// branch = 2;
```

Then, I quickly created my slider symbol and added a few slider instances and associated text fields off stage, as shown in Figure 8-3.

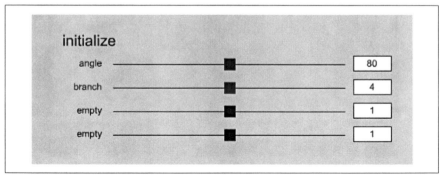

Figure 8-3. Sliders used to tweak my tree generator parameters

The first slider is labeled with the static text "angle" and has the instance name value01. The text field to its right (showing "80") is named value01_txt. When the SWF starts, this slider's puck moves to the position corresponding to 80 on its scale (the scale is from -100 to 100). When I click and drag the puck, it changes the value in value01_txt. If you make the text field an input field, you can enter a value directly into the text field and the puck position changes to reflect the new value. To make this text field control the value of the angle variable, commented out in the preceding code, select the value01_txt field on stage and specify **angle** in the Var field of the Properties panel.

The Var field, which is equivalent to setting the TextField.variable property, is provided for backward compatibility with the Flash 5 style of assigning a value directly to a text field. The recommended way to read/write the contents of a text field in Flash Player 6 and later is to use the TextField. text property. If you don't use the text property, some components that rely on it, such as scrollbars, may not react properly to changes in your text field. We are not using components in our slider and this is a hack, so we chose to use the Var field for simplicity.

Here's a version that uses the text property instead. The setup is a little different. It requires the text field to have the instance name angle_txt and the slider to have the instance name angle_mc in order to control a variable named angle. However, you no longer have to set the Var field in the Properties panel.

```
// Text field has the same name as the slider but with "_txt".
this.targetTextField = _parent[_name.split("_")[0] + "_txt"];

// The variable we're setting has the same name as the
// text field up to the "_".
this.targetTextField.targetVariable = _name.split("_")[0];

puck_mc.onPress = function() {
  this.startDrag(true, -100, 0, 100, 0);
  this.onMouseMove = _onMouseMove;
};
_onMouseMove = function() {
  this._parent.targetTextField.text = this._x;
  this._parent.targetTextField.onChanged();
  updateAfterEvent();
};
this.targetTextField.onChanged = function() {
  puck_mc._x = Number(this.text);
  this._parent[this.targetVariable] = Number(this.text);
};
puck_mc.onRelease = puck_mc.onReleaseOutside=function () {
  this.stopDrag();
};
this.targetTextField.onChanged();
```

Regardless of which technique you've used (Var or the text property), we have "sliderized" our input so that varying the slider value changes the value of our angle variable. Twiddle the slider to create different trees, as shown in Figure 8-4.

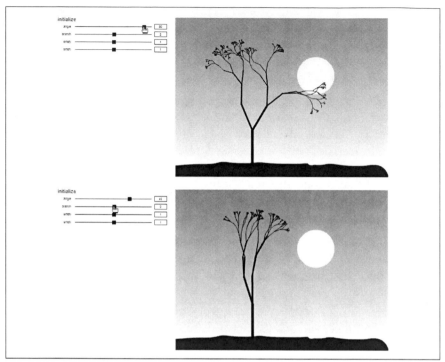

Figure 8-4. Two different trees generated by different inputs

Some of you will be saying, "I can do that in the debugger!" True, but this approach makes it easier to focus on the variables of interest and the slider value can be made permanent without having to change the code you are developing.

When you are happy with the results, note the value of each variable, stop the SWF, and enter the value directly in the text field, such as value01_txt or angle_txt, in the FLA. This makes your chosen value the default value when you publish the SWF. When you want to finalize the design so that the sliders are no longer able to change your values, simply delete the sliders from the Stage, leaving the text fields behind.

Final Thoughts

The longer you think about this technique, the cooler it is. Whenever you are unsure about the appropriate input values, simply wire the values up to sliders and fiddle around with them. This technique helps you work out initial values even if you have already finished the logic code. You don't need to go back into the code to change the values because the configurable variables have been abstracted from the code base. If you can't determine appropriate initial values using sliders, this fact might help you realize the limitation of your existing logic and the need to modify it.

The Banja site developers used a standard set of sliders to map out the island navigation visually, a big advantage on a team consisting of coders and designers. The coder writes the ActionScript and sets up the offscreen sliders. The designers can build the graphics and configure the navigation via the sliders. That is, even hard-core coders can benefit from this technique because it lets others tweak the inputs without touching the code. And you can even leave the sliders in the final user interface if you want to create a user-configurable experience or animation! If you don't like the idea of leaving the text fields in the movie permanently, you can hardcode the final variable values in ActionScript and delete the text fields, too.

 ## Right and Middle Mouse Buttons

Flash's documented mouse event handlers react to the primary mouse button only. Detect additional mouse buttons with the undocumented ActionScript.

Although Windows mice have two or more buttons, Flash detects mouse click events for the primary button only (usually the left mouse button, although the reader can change this in the Windows Mouse control panel).

Class of 800

There is no documented way to access the right and middle mouse buttons. Fortunately, the undocumented *ASnative( )* function can access additional internal ActionScript methods [Hack #83] using numeric indexes that roughly correlate to built-in classes.

Passing the index 800 as an argument to the *ASnative( )* function seems to access input/output methods of the *Key* and *Mouse* classes. It also includes some undocumented goodies. Try the following:

```
this.onEnterFrame = function() {
  if (ASnative(800, 2)(1)) {
    trace("Detected something...");
  }
};
```

If you run this code and click the left mouse button, the script displays "Detected something...". So ASnative(800, 2)(1) returns the left mouse button state: 1 (true) for down, or 0 (false) for up. Even though you can detect left mouse button clicks with the documented *Mouse.onMouseDown( )* event listener, the preceding code lets you detect the left mouse button's current state (for example, if you want to check whether the left mouse button is still down without setting a flag and waiting for the *Mouse.onMouseUp( )* event).

Changing the last argument in the *ASnative( )* call from 1 to 2 is even more interesting—it detects the right mouse button state:

```
this.onEnterFrame = function( ) {
  if (ASnative(800, 2)(2)) {
    trace("Right-click!");
  }
};
```

If the final argument is 4, the *ASnative( )* call returns a value that toggles every time you click or release the middle button in a three-button mouse. Most Windows mice with a wheel can also use the wheel as the third button; depressing the wheel is equivalent to "clicking button 3."

```
this.onEnterFrame = function( ) {
  if (ASnative(800, 2)(4)) {
    trace("Middle mouse button has changed state");
  }
};
```

So now we can detect the left, right, and middle button states! If your mouse has more than three buttons, use ASnative(800, 2)(5) and ASnative(800, 2)(6) to detect the states of additional buttons. The code ASnative(800, 2)(3) doesn't seem to do anything (at least, not when you use a mouse as your input device).

> *ASnative( )* is undocumented and therefore unsupported. The *ASnative( )* calls described here work in Flash Player 5, 6, and 7, but they aren't thoroughly tested and are not guaranteed to be supported in future versions.

These techniques detect the mouse button state using polling (checking in the *onEnterFrame( )* handler) because only the primary mouse button generates *onMouseDown* and *onMouseUp* events.

Of course, polling consumes CPU cycles so you should poll only when necessary. And you wouldn't want to add the polling code directly to a movie clip because multiple clip instances would all perform redundant polling for the mouse button state (which is the same regardless of which clip performs the polling). Instead, you could set up a centralized poller that broadcasts an event to any objects that have subscribed as a listener. The *rightMousePoller.fla* file, available on this book's web site, demonstrates the distinction. It has four "bad" pollers and three "good" pollers. When you right-click, all seven pollers respond by telling you how many times they polled to get that result. The good pollers always perform fewer pollings since there's only one polling for all three listeners, whereas the bad pollers each do their own polling.

Final Thoughts

Macintosh mice often have only one button, so these techniques apply primarily to Windows. However, if you want to detect the right mouse button, be aware that the right-click brings up the Flash Player menu when tested in a browser. The middle button is not assigned a function by default, but since most programs don't use the middle mouse button, many users configure it to do something special, such as minimize all desktop windows. Furthermore, many users don't have three-button mice, so you shouldn't rely on the middle mouse button for important functionality. The bottom line is that this hack remains primarily a curiosity unless you have a dedicated hardware setup, such as a kiosk, where you can control the mouse hardware and software configuration.

Flash Player 7 supports a new TextField.mouseWheelEnabled property to allow the mouse wheel to scroll text fields. Flash Player 7 for Windows also supports a new *Mouse.onMouseWheel( )* event listener, which is notified when the mouse wheel moves.

Button Movie Clips

#63 Create enhanced Flash buttons using instances of the MovieClip class instead of the Button class.

Flash buttons are traditionally made from instances of the *Button* class (not to be confused with the Flash MX Button component in the *mx.components* package). A Flash button has·three states—up, over, and down—plus a hit area. Flash displays the up state when the mouse is not over the button, the over state when the mouse cursor rolls over the button, and the down state when the user clicks the mouse on the button. The hit area is a graphic that defines the clickable area of the button (the portion that accepts mouse-clicks), which is often the same size as the graphics for the up, over, and down states. All four button states are represented by frames on the button symbol's timeline, as shown in Figure 8-5.

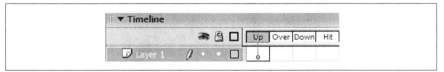

Figure 8-5. Button states represented by named frames in the timeline

A standard button is easy to create and easy to understand. For the beginner (or designer in a rush!), they are very useful. The *Button* class contains many of the properties and event handlers of the *MovieClip* class but none of its methods and no true timeline. Consequently, you cannot make a button instance act like a full-fledged movie clip. However, given that movie clips in Flash MX and Flash MX 2004 support all the methods of the *Button* class and more, you can create so-called *button movie clips*—movie clips that act as full-featured buttons.

With button movie clips, an ActionScript-savvy designer need never use standard buttons. Button movie clips have several features that simply cannot be created via standard buttons. Button movie clips can:

- Use the methods of the *MovieClip* class not supported by the *Button* class
- Add an *onEnterFrame( )* event handler to animate the button
- Be created dynamically at runtime

A button movie clip is not a new type of symbol. It is still a movie clip!

To create a button movie clip that acts exactly the same as a standard button, first create a movie clip symbol named hit. Within the hit symbol, rename the first layer to *actions* and create a second layer named *hit*, as shown in Figure 8-6.

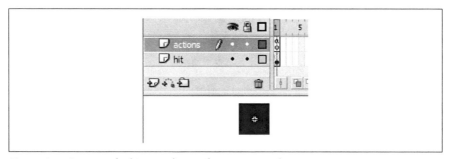

Figure 8-6. Creating the hit area for our button movie clip

The *hit* layer should contain a rectangle in the first frame (or a circle if you prefer); this shape will be your button's clickable area. On frame 1 of the *actions* layer, attach the following script:

```
this._visible = false;
_parent.hitArea = this;
```

Create a second movie clip symbol to act as the button movie clip, calling it clipButton. Rename the first layer to *actions*. Label the first frame of the *actions* layer as _up using the Properties panel. Add additional keyframes (Insert → Timeline → Keyframe or Insert → Timeline → Blank Keyframe) and label them _over and _down, as shown in Figure 8-7.

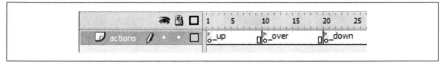

Figure 8-7. Simulating button states with labeled frames in a movie clip

> These three labels must be called _up, _over, and _down for the button movie clip to work. They correspond to the three button states: up, over, and down.

Attach a *stop( )* action to each keyframe (one for each button state) using the Actions panel.

Place your three button graphics in the three keyframes as you would with a normal button, using as many additional layers as you need. Place all of the new layers below the *actions* layer, as shown in Figure 8-8.

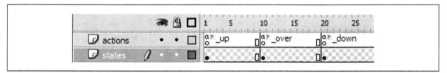

Figure 8-8. Button states in a button movie clip

Add a new layer named *hit*, as shown in Figure 8-9. On the first frame of this layer, place an instance of your hit movie clip symbol, resizing it as necessary to fit over your graphics in the other frames. Once you have done this, hide layer *hit*.

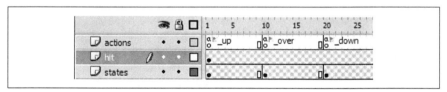

Figure 8-9. Adding the hit clip in the hit layer of the main button movie clip

If you now place an instance of your button movie clip onto the main Stage and attach a button script to it, it will act exactly like a standard button. That is, your movie clip will start to act like a button if you attach a button event handler to it. To do this, first give your button movie clip an instance name, such as cButton using the Properties panel. Then, add a new layer named *actions* to the main timeline (not the movie clip's timeline), and attach the following script to the first frame in the *actions* layer:

```
cButton.onRelease = function( ) {
  trace("you clicked me");
};
```

How does it work?

If you attach a button script to the movie clip (which we do indirectly via the preceding ActionScript on the main timeline rather than attaching the script to the clip's timeline), Flash sends the playhead to the frames labeled _up, _over, and _down whenever the corresponding events occur.

The script inside the hit movie clip symbol makes it into an invisible hit area for the parent clip (i.e., your button movie clip).

That's fine, but it doesn't really give us anything new or hack-worthy. All we have for our effort is a movie clip that operates like a standard button!

Well, there are a couple of things you can do with a button movie clip that you cannot do with a standard button.

You can use the methods of the *MovieClip* class, including those not supported by the *Button* class. For example, you can make your movie clip go to particular states without it being clicked. If you invoke cButton. gotoAndStop("_over") the button movie clip displays its over state. This can be useful when you want your button to change dynamically. For example, if you have a button used to load an image, you can specify the text "load image" as the up state and a "loading..." message as the down state. When the user clicks on the button, you would want it to remain at the down state until the image is loaded (even if the user releases the mouse button), and you can do this easily by using the *MovieClip.gotoAndStop( )* method.

You can also add *onEnterFrame( )* event handlers to a button movie clip, which, for example, allows you to make parts of your user interface animate after they've been clicked. In the following script, the button movie clip acts like a button until it is clicked. Within the *onRelease( )* handler, the button deletes its *onRelease( )* handler and defines an *onEnterFrame( )* handler. This turns it into an animated clip that slides off screen (to the right).

```
btn_mc.onRelease = function( ) {
  // Do some button type stuff here (not shown).
  // Now revert to an animated movie clip.
  delete this.onRelease;
  this.onEnterFrame = function( ) {
    if (this._x < 600) {
      this._x += 10;
    } else {
      delete this.onEnterFrame;
    }
  };
};
```

Perhaps most importantly, you can create button movie clips dynamically using *MovieClip.duplicateMovieclip( )* or *MovieClip.attachMovie( )* and place text inside them with *MovieClip.createTextField( )*. These techniques are impossible with the standard buttons because the *Button* class does not support these methods.

So, by emulating a button with a movie clip, we gain a fair bit of extra functionality over standard buttons. If we start editing the button movie clip so that it no longer apes a standard button but actively uses the more advanced features of the movie clip timeline, we can implement additional functionality.

Adding Button States

You can easily add new button states to a button movie clip. The easiest way to add the necessary code to all movie clips is via the `MovieClip.prototype` property (this approach is appropriate in both ActionScript 1.0 and 2.0):

```
MovieClip.prototype.disable = function( ) {
  this.enabled = false;
  this.gotoAndStop("_disable");
};
```

The preceding code adds a *disable( )* method to the *MovieClip* class. The method sends the button movie clip's timeline to the frame labeled _disable, effectively creating a new state that prevents the clip from responding to events.

To create the disabled state, add an appropriate graphic (typically a grayed-out version of the _up graphic) to a frame labeled _disable in the button movie clip's timeline, as shown in Figure 8-10.

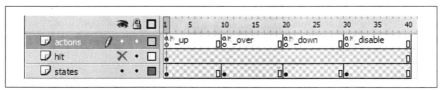

Figure 8-10. Defining the disabled state for our button movie clip

Of course, other states and features can be created, such as:

- A help state that displays help text one second after the *onRollOver* event occurs and displays it until the *onRollOut* event.

- An unclicked state to act as the default state. If you add an unclicked button graphic on frame 1 and move the up state later in the timeline, the unclicked state will be shown until the user clicks once on the button (after which the clip displays the up state when the mouse cursor is not over it).

- Animated button states (without the need for embedded clips). Rather than stop the timeline at each state, allow the timeline to run through an animation on the button movie clip timeline. Remember to stop the timeline on the last frame of the animation for that state before it jumps into the next state!

Final Thoughts

Although a button movie clip takes a little longer to create than a standard button, it is much more versatile because of its ability to run *onEnterFrame( )* scripts and because you can add additional button states as needed.

Dude, Where's My Scrollbar?

#64 Create a lightweight scrollbar component for Flash MX 2004.

The v2 components that ship with Flash MX 2004 are geared toward creating complex user interfaces and Rich Internet Applications. The v2 components offer several enhancements over the v1 components, including support for depth management, keyboard focus management, and accessibility. The v2 components are completely rewritten to work in ActionScript 2.0 (including strict datatyping and case sensitivity). The v2 components also share a new component framework designed to optimize filesizes when you use five or more components in a single SWF (as Macromedia's research found to be typical).

However, the Flash MX 2004 components can't be used as simple drop-in replacements for the Flash MX v1 components for several reasons:

- The first v2 component included in a SWF requires a 30 KB download to set up the initial classes for the component framework. To be fair, additional components cause only a small increase in download size, thanks to the common framework shared by all v2 components.

- The v2 components for Flash MX 2004 don't include a standalone scrollbar (although the 7.2 update is expected to include one).

And you can't simply use the old v1 components that ship with Flash MX if you export your SWF in Flash Player 7 format, because the old components don't conform to Flash Player 7's case-sensitivity requirements as discussed at *http://swfoo.com/archives/000034.html*. Even if you update a Flash MX (Flash Player 6) FLA file into Flash MX 2004 (Flash Player 7) format, including making your scripts case-sensitive, the code associated with the v1 components still may not work due to case and type casting inconsistencies within the components themselves and differences in the behavior of some built-in ActionScript functions in Flash Player 6 and 7. The workaround is to use the updated "Flash MX components for Flash MX 2004", as described next.

Although many third-party components, including scrollbars, are available, it would be nice to use Macromedia components to ensure compatibility with future versions of the Flash Player (Macromedia makes a serious effort to ensure that older SWFs run unmodified in newer versions of the Flash Player).

The v1 components from Flash MX included a standalone scrollbar and can be used in Flash MX 2004 when exporting your SWF in Flash Player 6 format (although you should avoid mixing v1 and v2 components in the same project). Flash Player 7–compatible versions of the v1 components, which are not as bandwidth-heavy as the v2 components, are available from the Flash Exchange (*http://www.macromedia.com/exchange/flash*), in the User Interface category, under the title "Flash MX Components for Flash MX 2004."

You can also access the Flash Exchange via Flash's Help → Flash Exchange option. The v1 components are distributed as an *.mxp* file. To install them, you must have installed the Macromedia Extension Manager, which is also available online at the Flash Exchange.

Once installed correctly, you will see the updated Flash MX components appear in the Flash MX 2004 Components panel, under Flash MX UI Components as shown in Figure 8-11. The Flash MX 2004 components are kept safely separate under UI Components in the Components panel.

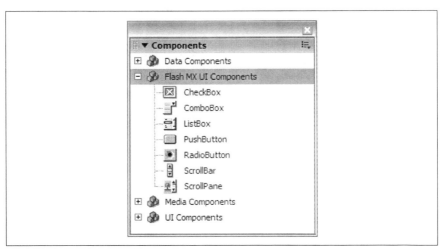

Figure 8-11. The Flash MX UI components in the Flash MX 2004 Components panel

The Flash MX components don't have all the sexy features of the Flash MX 2004 components. However, if the only component you need is a scrollbar for a text field or other slider control, as shown in Figure 8-12, you can simply drag the Flash MX UI scrollbar from the Components panel and drop it onto the Stage just as you did back in Flash MX. It will work even if you have the publishing options set to the Flash Player 7 and ActionScript 2.0. Best of all, the Flash MX scrollbar adds only 6 KB to the SWF filesize.

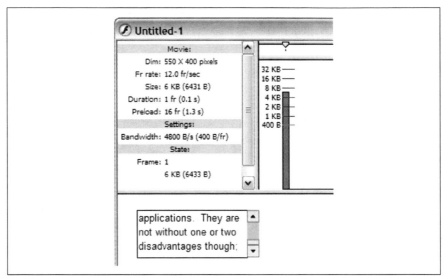

Figure 8-12. Using the Scrollbar component

Final Thoughts

Progress is great, and the Flash MX 2004 v2 components offer many advanced features such as focus management, depth management, and accessibility, but sometimes you just want one freakin' scrollbar!

If that's the case (and especially if 30 KB for one component is out of the question), you can use the solid and familiar Flash MX scrollbar from the v1 component set to meet your needs.

Performance and Optimization

Hacks 65–73

Flash's animation engine isn't the fastest one around because the Flash Player is optimized for a small download size, not for performance. Also, it is designed with web use in mind; therefore, it is optimized for small, low-bandwidth files rather than large, complex animation. In order to maintain its small footprint and ensure maximum compatibility, the Flash Player does not support hardware acceleration. Therefore, performance issues are often paramount for the Flash designer.

Three areas of possible optimization in Flash are as follows:

*   Reduce download time by creating efficiencies in content filesizes or changing the way content is downloaded [Hack #73]
*   Increase animation performance by optimizing graphics for fast redraw
*   Increase computing performance by writing code that executes quickly

Each point is considered in greater detail next.

Optimize Filesize and Download Time

Flash started off as a simple vector-based web animation plugin but is now routinely used for more bandwidth-heavy applications. Take care to ensure that the user is not kept waiting for content to load. The only way to ensure the lowest possible wait times is to test your site often during production.

Prior to the Flash MX 2004 Version 7.0.1 update, the built-in Bandwidth Profiler offered little help in modeling realistic web conditions for sites using multiple SWFs or other external assets. Although the latest version can test multiple SWFs and account for externally loaded assets, it still does not properly handle shared fonts, nor does it allow you to test your site from within a browser.

Third-party tools [Hack #66] help overcome the limitations of the Bandwidth Profiler and enable you to test the whole site (i.e., both Flash and non-Flash assets) under bandwidth-limited conditions using the browser.

Optimize Graphics

Flash's ubiquity is largely attributable to the small download size of the Flash Player and the ability to create low-bandwidth content. However, the filesize optimization comes at the cost of reduced performance as you increase complexity.

Vectors graphics are more compact than other image formats because vectors define the math (points, curves, and fills) required to draw the image at runtime rather than the raw graphic data. However, converting the vector data to the final image is time consuming and must be done whenever there is a change in appearance or position of a graphic. If your image contains complex shape outlines or large fill areas, and they also change every frame, your animations might run slowly.

In this chapter, we explore several ways of reducing the performance hit caused by using vectors, including how to design graphics [Hack #68] and when to substitute bitmaps for vector images [Hack #72].

Increase Code Performance

ActionScript is not compiled to native machine code like some languages (such as C++). Instead it is converted to *bytecode*, which is faster than an interpreted language but not as fast as native code. Although ActionScript can be slow, in most multimedia presentations, the assets such as graphics, audio, and video—and not the code—are often the limiting performance factor. Furthermore, the overall performance (or apparent performance from a user perspective) is also affected by download times and not just runtime execution. Of course, for a Rich Internet Application accessing a back-end database, performance might depend on the speed of database queries, data transmission, and text rendering.

Many hacks throughout this book cover ActionScript optimization. Furthermore:

- Flash Player 7 is already optimized for code that uses lots of function calls and local variables [Hack #100], and older performance tricks are no longer as necessary.

- Many optimization techniques are not specific to ActionScript but simply well-known techniques for writing code in any language without an optimizing compiler. For example, loops are faster if you remove items that don't change with every loop iteration and place them outside the loop instead.

- If your code runs slowly, it is often a sign that you need to reduce the scope of your application or look for a hack that solves the problem in a different way. You should identify and remove bottlenecks, for example, by optimizing your graphics.

- Often performance is about perception [Hack #71]. If you attempt to perform too much work in a single frame, Flash doesn't have time to render the Stage, and the user perceives a slowdown. If you break up the amount of work being performed into smaller chunks, Flash can refresh the Stage at the prescribed frame rate, and there is no perceived slowdown.

Although properly written ActionScript doesn't usually constitute a bottleneck, improvements can always be made. For those with an interest in ActionScript optimization, have a look at the following links:

- gotoAndPlay (*http://www.gotoandplay.it/_articles/2004/01/as_optimizations. php*) offers a tutorial on ActionScript optimization.

- Odd Hammer (*http://www.oddhammer.com/actionscriptperformance*) offers performance benchmarks of various ActionScript optimization techniques in different versions of the Flash Player.

Throughout this chapter, we'll explore ways to analyze and optimize performance in areas that are most likely to meaningfully affect runtime performance, download times, and the user experience. As with most topics, the optimal techniques depend on the situation, and there is often a trade-off between, say, performance versus convenience or download times versus runtime performance. The following hacks will help you make intelligent choices for your individual projects.

You can find numerous other optimization-related hacks throughout the book, such as how to optimize sound [Hack #58] and optimize character animations [Hack #28].

HACK #65 Beat Flash File Bloat

You may find that your FLA gets bigger every time you save it, even if you delete unused assets such as bitmaps and sounds. Beat the bloat with this hack.

When deploying Flash content online, filesize is the name of the game. The smaller the file you deploy, the faster it downloads. When compiling a FLA into a SWF, Flash omits unused assets in the Library [Hack #73]. However, the source FLA file contains not only unused Library assets, but even old assets that you have deleted from the Library! This is the cause of Flash FLA file bloat. It doesn't affect SWFs, but it is something to be aware of nonetheless.

In versions of Flash prior to Flash MX 2004, you will find that your files get larger each time you save them using File → Save, even after you delete unused content from them. Although Flash MX 2004's File → Save and Compact option reduces the FLA file's size, this option isn't available in prior versions of Flash. Furthermore, saving the FLA in Flash MX 2004 format prevents you from reopening the file in previous versions (although Flash MX 2004 and Flash MX Professional 2004 share the same file format).

Why the Big File?

You may wonder what causes the file bloat in the first place. In all versions of Flash, saving a FLA using File → Save adds only incremental changes to the FLA (known as an *incremental save* or *fast save*). Flash doesn't optimize the saved file by removing things you've deleted.

You can see this for yourself by creating a new Flash FLA file and importing a large media file (such as a bitmap or sound file). Then, save the file with File → Save or Ctrl-S (Windows) or ⌘-S (Mac) and note the file's size. Then delete the large media asset from both the Stage and the Library and resave the file with File → Save. You will see that the filesize remains constant even after deleting the large assets!

This is the root of the bloat problem; as you make changes to a FLA file, the deletions are never removed from the saved file. This can also be problematic if you delete some embarrassing or proprietary content and then inadvertently pass it onto a client (granted, the client would need to decompile the FLA [Hack #98] to get at it, but it is always a good idea to cover your tracks). Although you ordinarily would publish only SWF files, you should compact FLA files when, say, posting them as examples on the Web or transmitting them to clients or other developers.

The Fix

You can force Flash to compact a FLA file in two ways:

Save the file using File → Save and Compact (Flash MX 2004 and Flash MX Professional 2004 only)
>   This option forces Flash to remove unnecessary information during the save. Flash has to rewrite the entire file, so the operation may take longer, depending on the amount of content to save. You won't be able to reopen the file in previous versions of Flash, so be careful to retain backups of the legacy FLAs! It is a good idea to save a backup under another name in case the compact operation fails for some reason.

Save and rename the file using File → Save As (all versions of Flash)
This option does the same thing as File → Save and Compact but it assumes you will rename the file. Using another name is a good idea in case the file save operation fails, but you can save it using the original filename by clicking Yes when warned that a file of that name already exists.

So, why doesn't Macromedia change it so that the File → Save option performs a save and compact? Well, incremental saves can be considerably faster. Therefore, the optimal workflow is:

- Press Ctrl-S (or ⌘-S) to save the file every so often. This saves the file instantaneously so you can carry on without any pause.

- Make a backup of your file periodically to avoid losing any work or allowing you to go back to a previous version if you need to for some reason.

- Select File → Save As or File → Save and Compact on occasion (such as at the end of the day or before archiving files) to compact the file.

- Before permanently archiving a FLA file, save a backup copy. Then delete unused assets from the Library (bearing in mind that assets used via ActionScript should not be deleted). Then save and compact the file using one of the preceding techniques in order to minimize the FLA for archival purposes.

Final Thoughts

Although the bloat quirk is addressed in Flash MX 2004, you still need to know what's going on to manage it effectively within your workflow. Flash development often incorporates many design and asset changes, so files can get bloated very quickly. Minimizing the size of FLA files makes them load faster in the authoring tool and saves space when archiving or transmitting the FLA. Similar issues exist in many other commercial software products, including Macromedia Director and Microsoft Word.

Bandwidth Testing for Complex Sites
HACK #66
Use WebSpeed Simulator to sidestep the Bandwidth Profiler's inability to simulate bandwidth performance when testing through the browser (i.e., real-world conditions).

When creating a site, you want to know how long it will take to download at a particular connection speed. This helps you ensure the best experience for your target audience, most of whom will have slower connections than those common among developers. The Flash Bandwidth Profiler is useful for evaluating the download time for a simple SWF file when simulated in Test Movie mode. You can access it by using Control → Test Movie to enter Test Movie mode and then choosing View → Bandwidth Profiler to open the Bandwidth Profiler window. However, the Bandwidth Profiler assumes an ideal connection, so choose a target connection speed somewhat slower than the ideal speed of your lowest-bandwidth user. For example, choose 28.8 Kbps instead of 56 Kbps to simulate a typical 56-Kbps modem.

Regardless, the Bandwidth Profiler included with Flash MX 2004 Version 7.0 is too simplistic for more advanced sites. Most commercially produced Flash sites consist of far more than a single SWF. Additional assets—such as secondary SWFs, images, MP3 files, video files, remote data, and text files (CSS, XML, etc.)—are routinely loaded at runtime. Prior to the Flash MX 2004 Version 7.0.1 update, the Bandwidth Profiler did not include these assets as part of its simulation, so it understated the download times.

The third-party WebSpeed Simulator (*http://www.xat.com*) is a useful alternative to the Bandwidth Profiler. It works by creating a local bandwidth-limited HTTP server and allows you to:

- View the site loading in real time in a web browser on a simulated bandwidth-limited connection

- View a timestamped browser cache, allowing you to review the order in which files were loaded (plus what is left available in the cache after your site has been visited)

The WebSpeed simulator is extremely easy to use. However, because the simulator works as an HTTP server, it cannot emulate secure servers.

Assuming you want to test a site from your local hard drive, click the application Setup icon in WebSpeed Simulator's toolbar to bring up the Setup Web Server dialog box, as shown in Figure 9-1, and specify the location of the site (i.e., the location of the folder containing your home page, such as *index.html*). You may also have to clear the browser cache depending on your browser settings. (For example, to clear the cache in Windows Internet Explorer, use Tools → Internet Options → General → Delete Temporary Internet Files.)

Then, click the Restrict icon and specify your simulated connection in the Restrict Web Server dialog box, as shown in Figure 9-2. You can also specify whether you want to preserve the browser cache (i.e., if you visit the same site twice, content already in the browser cache will load immediately).

Finally, click the Browse icon. The simulator directs the browser to the folder you specified during setup and acts as a server, limiting bandwidth as specified in the Restrict Web Server dialog box. As each item is loaded in the

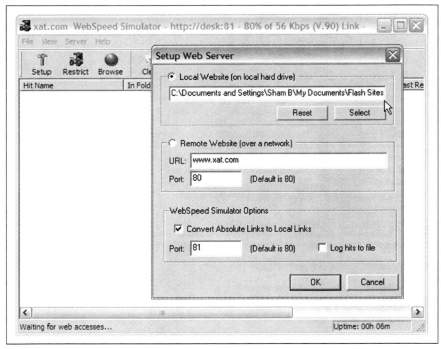

Figure 9-1. The Setup Web Server dialog box in WebSpeed Simulator

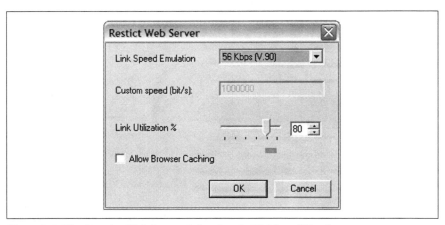

Figure 9-2. The Restrict Web Server dialog box in WebSpeed Simulator

browser, the WebSpeed Simulator displays the time each file takes to load, the order of loading, and the filesize, as shown in Figure 9-3.

I keep WebSpeed Simulator running whenever I am working in Flash. It addresses the failings of the Bandwidth Profiler and provides a clean interface for easily testing at various bandwidths. Setup is trivial and you don't

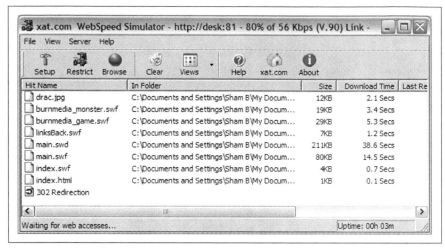

Figure 9-3. The WebSpeed Simulator results

need to change your browser settings or your physical connection to test at different speeds, so it is very easy to integrate into your normal workflow. It can even evaluate sites that mix HTML and Flash, whereas the Flash Bandwidth Profiler works with SWF files only. Experience with using WebSpeed Simulator confirms it is an accurate simulation—the times predicted by the simulator are very similar to the actual content download times.

Final Thoughts

Although WebSpeed Simulator isn't free (it costs $99, but a 30-day trial is available), it's by far the easiest environment I've found for testing bandwidth requirements on any web site design, particularly for multifile Flash sites.

Keeping it handy during the course of development will prevent surprises. The ease with which it can be set up allows you to even, say, demo a site under simulated web conditions to a client using your laptop. This comes in handy when helping your client understand bandwidth considerations when making design decisions. It even works for Flash applications that load a lot of dynamic data, so it is invaluable to RIA developers and motion graphics designers alike.

Hide Low-Quality Settings

#67   Increase performance and maintain visual appearance by hiding the effects
of a reduction in rendering quality.

There is an inherent trade-off between rendering quality and performance, and Flash offers several rendering modes. Understanding the issues at hand can help you to both make the appropriate choice and work around some of the limitations of the built-in rendering options.

The Flash rendering engine optionally uses antialiasing to smooth out vector edges and increase apparent quality by hiding aliasing errors (a.k.a. "staircasing" or "jaggies"). Antialiasing tends to hide sharp edges between contrasting areas by blending in pixels of intervening shades. In Figure 9-4, the curve on the left exhibits aliasing errors that show up as jagged edges caused by our pixels being too large to faithfully reproduce the curve. The one on the right is antialiased and looks smoother.

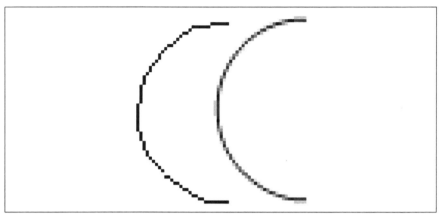

Figure 9-4. An aliased curve (left) and an antialiased curve (right)

Note that antialiasing doesn't fix aliasing errors but rather hides them from the human eye by using similar colors to smooth the transition between adjacent, contrasting colors.

Antialiasing can be processor-intensive, and you may prefer to turn it off to get the benefit of increased performance.

You can turn antialiasing off globally (i.e., for all content seen in the Flash Player) with the following line:

```
_quality = "LOW";
```

You can also set the rendering quality to Low under File → Publish Settings → HTML → Quality. Note that the MovieClip._quality, Button._quality, and TextField._quality properties are merely synonyms for the global _quality property and therefore affect antialiasing globally. Quality cannot be set on a per-instance basis.

In addition to "LOW", you can set the _quality property to "AUTOLOW", "MEDIUM", "AUTOHIGH", "HIGH", or "BEST". In the higher quality settings, text, bitmaps, and vectors are antialiased. At the lowest quality setting, none are antialiased. The exact details of each level of quality can be found in the Help panel (Help → Help or F1) if you search for "_quality." In practical terms, use the highest quality that your content and target audience's machines allow. This generally means using "BEST" for largely static sites, "HIGH" or "MEDIUM" for most general content, and "LOW" where speed is a priority, such as in games.

You can also make Flash selectively turn antialiasing off via the Auto High and Auto Low quality settings. At those settings, the Flash Player automatically switches between antialiased and aliased rendering depending on the playback performance of the machine on which it is running. The Auto High setting starts with antialiasing on and turns it off if overall performance suffers (i.e., the frame rate slows down unacceptably), whereas the Auto Low setting starts with antialiasing off but turns it on if the target frame rate is achieved.

The Auto quality settings are not often used because the change from high to low quality is usually very obvious and disconcerting to the user. For best performance, the trick is to permanently set the quality to Low and then try to hide, as far as possible, the resulting low-quality rendering.

Use Noncontrasting Colors

Given that antialiasing is needed most when contrasting colors are adjacent to each other, one solution is to use noncontrasting colors to begin with. In Figure 9-5, the aliased line (on the left) should look less blocky than in Figure 9-4 because the black curve is similar in color to the gray background (the difference is more apparent on screen than in print). Of course, by definition, reducing the contrast makes the curve harder to distinguish from the background, so don't make the background too similar in color. If necessary, you can improve contrast by making the line thicker or darker.

When attempting to improve apparent quality by using noncontrasting colors, you should avoid some color combinations:

- Black on white and black on yellow are the two most contrasting color combinations and should be avoided. Black and yellow is the most contrasting (which is why bees and hornets have black and yellow stripes as a warning coloration and why the phone company chose it for the yellow pages).

- The human eye is most sensitive to green and can differentiate between close shades of green better than shades of red or blue. Other things being equal, avoid greens when using low quality settings.

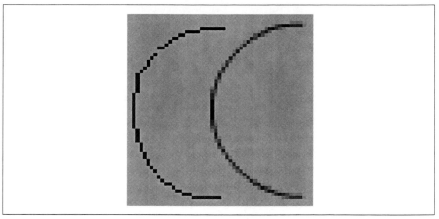

Figure 9-5. Aliased (left) and antialiased (right) curves on a low-contrast background

- There are several types of color blindness (and infinite variations along the spectrum), but the most common deficiency is an inability to perceive the difference between red and green. So avoid red-on-green or green-on-red color schemes. For more information on color schemes appropriate for color-blind users, see Toledo-Bend (*http://www.toledo-bend.com/colorblind*), which discusses various color perception deficiencies.

Use Horizontal/Vertical and Fast-Moving Shapes

Other ways to hide low-quality (aliased) vectors include making sure your Flash movie assets, whenever possible, use rectangular fills, are moving quickly, or consist of horizontal and vertical lines only.

Horizontal and vertical lines, including the edges of rectangles, do not need antialiasing, and you simply can't see the aliasing on something that is moving quickly. The latter point can be used in Flash video games. When you are at the title screen or game instructions, a quality setting of High or Best can be used without compromising performance, but once you get into the game, fast graphics become important, so you will be more likely to switch to Low quality. Additionally, if your game is moving fast enough (and you have only horizontal- and vertical-shaped static graphics, such as the Pacman maze), the user may not even notice the switch in quality.

Some caveats, however: if designing output for video, avoid 1-pixel horizontal lines. Because video for broadcast TV is interlaced, lines should be at least 2 pixels thick to avoid flickering. Even for online video playback, certain compression schemes have trouble with extremely thin lines. So perform tests before committing to your final design.

Also, even perfectly horizontal and vertical edges can benefit from aliasing to soften their edges. This is especially true for vibrant colors (particularly the primary colors when shown on a white background), which appear to bleed when given a hard edge.

Use Pixel Fonts

Turning on text antialiasing (which occurs to varying degrees when using any quality setting except Low), especially for large amounts of text or moving text, can really tax the processor. On the other hand, using aliased text in fonts designed for printing can result in poor onscreen appearance. Conversely, antialiasing can make text harder to read at small point sizes (below, say, 8-point text, depending on the font).

If using a lot of text or small text, you should use *pixel fonts*, which are fonts designed for onscreen that look better without antialiasing, as shown in Figure 9-6.

The quick brown fox jumps over the lazy dog.

Figure 9-6. Pixel fonts and small fonts look better without antialiasing

For general information on pixel fonts, see the Web Page Design for Designers site's pixel font FAQ (*http://www.wpdfd.com/pffaq.htm*) and primer on pixel font typography (*http://www.wpdfd.com/wpdtypo3a.htm*).

There are a number of free resources dedicated to Flash-specific pixel fonts, including:

- miniml (*http://www.miniml.com*) offers miniml fonts, a collection of vector-based pixel fonts.
- Fonts for Flash (*http://www.freepixelfonts.com/faqs.html*) has a Flash-specific FAQ on pixel fonts.
- Best Flash (*http://www.bestflashanimationsite.com/pixel-fonts*) offers links to Flash-related pixel font resources.

Final Thoughts

As you will realize when trying to create complex animations with Flash, there are limits to how fast Flash can render vectors. Reducing the image quality by turning off antialiasing (using a quality setting of Low) is one of the quickest ways to improve performance, but it seriously affects those crisp vector edges for which Flash is famous. As we have seen here, you have several options to minimize or hide the effects of this loss of quality. You might even incorporate the aliasing into your design to give it a retro feel. Of course, changing the rendering quality isn't your only option. The remaining hacks in this chapter present other ways to optimize performance.

Optimize Graphics for Performance

Graphics can be bandwidth hogs. Optimize graphics for large dividends in overall performance.

The Flash graphic-rendering engine is designed to minimize the filesize of your content by optimizing the drawing of vector graphics instead of bitmaps. Therefore, performance can be a problem when you want to move complex graphics around quickly. Once a graphic is downloaded, the biggest bottleneck is usually the time it takes Flash to render it to the Stage (by comparison, the time to execute most ActionScript is usually trivial). The larger the area of the Stage being updated per frame, the slower the performance. So large, low-bandwidth vector graphics can still take time to render.

The following tips are based on my experience and that of other designers in creating fast Flash sites.

Design with Speed in Mind

It sounds obvious, but most developers forget Flash can't do everything at once. Here are some potential performance killers:

Loading content
> Streaming in an animation at the same time as playing it will reduce the maximum achievable frame rate compared with loading the content first and then playing it after it is fully loaded. It is often better to have a preloader screen than try to play the animation before it is fully loaded (in which case you have to wait for the rest to download as the animation plays).

Playing MP3 files, especially long ones
> MP3 files are decompressed during playback, which requires lots of processor time. Although Flash can handle one or two short sounds easily, if you have long sounds and multiple sound channels, expect animation to slow down.

Updating text fields
> Updating a text field's content every frame is one of the biggest performance-sapping actions that can be easily avoided. Instead, you should change text field values only when their content actually changes or at the slowest rate you can get away with. For example, if you are updating a timer that displays seconds, you don't need to update it at a frame

rate of 30 fps. Instead, record the old value and reassign the value of the text field only when the new value is different from the previous value.

Using Flash MX 2004 v2 components

If you're using components, then you're usually creating an application with minimal animation, so animation performance is not the limiting factor. Flash MX 2004 v2 components are real performance killers. Not only are they bandwidth-heavy, but using more than a few onscreen slows runtime performance. If you want to run fast animations, use Flash MX's v1 components [Hack #73], use your own custom components, or create simplified user interfaces that don't require components.

Create and Test Optimized Graphics

Bitmaps can be larger than vectors to download, but the pixels required to render a bitmap don't need to be calculated at runtime. So once they are downloaded, they can be rendered relatively quickly. Vectors have the opposite characteristics. Because they are stored as a mathematical representation, vectors are very compact. However, unlike bitmaps, the pixels required to render the vector content must be calculated at runtime. You can sometimes improve performance by using bitmaps instead of vectors [Hack #72], but more often, you need to create vector graphics that Flash finds easier to draw.

The following tips will help you create vector graphics that render quickly:

- Avoid using transparency (alpha). Flash must check all pixels underneath a transparent shape, which slows rendering down considerably. To hide a clip, set its _visible property to false rather than setting the _alpha property to 0. That is, graphics render fastest when their _alpha is set to 100. Setting the movie clip's timeline to an empty keyframe (so that the movie clip has no content to show) is usually an even faster option. Sometimes Flash still tries to render invisible clips; move the clip off stage by setting its _x and _y properties to, say, (-1000, -1000), in addition to setting the _visible property to false, so Flash doesn't try to draw it at all.

- Avoid using vectors with gradient fills. Consider using a bitmapped gradient instead.

- Flash's drawing performance is tied to how many points are drawn per frame. Always optimize shapes after you have drawn them with the Modify → Shape submenu, then select either Smooth, Straighten, or Optimize (depending on your graphic) to reduce the number of points required to draw it. Changing strokes to hairlines (or not using strokes at all) can also significantly reduce the number of points needed. You can view the number of points contained in a stroke by clicking on it with the Subselection tool, and you can see the number of points in a shape by clicking on any of its edges.

- Flash's drawing performance is also tied to the number of pixels that have to change per frame, so avoid large changes. Make your animated content as small as you can get away with; for example, reducing the size of a graphic by 10% in each dimension reduces the area by 19%. The savings really add up when using multiple copies of the symbol, such as for a Space Invaders game.

- Use hollow (unfilled) shapes or other shapes that reduce the total number of pixels drawn if you can.

 Note that, unless you are using alpha effects, pixels that do not change between frames don't significantly affect performance.

Final Thoughts

Many aspects of a Flash movie contribute to its ultimate performance. Optimizing graphics is one of the areas likely to yield the biggest changes. Graphics can be optimized at any point in development; however, the earlier you optimize them in your design cycle, the greater the benefit you're likely to achieve. If you wait until the last minute, you won't have time to optimize everything, and certain design decisions that could have been adjusted earlier, such as whether to use transparency, will be much harder to change. The moral is to optimize early and optimize often.

Third-party vector optimization programs, such as Optimaze (*http://www. vecta3d.com*), reduce filesizes up to 60% and allow for faster rendering because the optimized vector calculations will be simpler.

 ## Benchmark Runtime Performance
#69
The Flash Bandwidth Profiler and third-party tools provide estimates of a Flash project's download time. Benchmark runtime performance to optimize playback as well.

The Flash Bandwidth Profiler and the third-party WebSpeed Simulator [Hack #66] calculate estimated download times, but they don't address runtime performance. Whereas the former varies with connection speed, the latter depends on the processing power of the playback machine. The user's overall experience is determined by a combination of the download times and runtime performance. It makes sense to make intelligent decisions about the trade-off between the two, as when substituting bitmaps for vectors [Hack #72].

Benchmark Runtime Performance

Runtime performance is inherently judged relative to the target frame rate, which is chosen by the Flash developer. If Flash can draw everything required by the time it is supposed to display the next frame, then it doesn't necessarily matter whether Flash had time to spare. However, this standard can overlook problems that might appear if you decide to increase the frame rate. You'd rather know which graphics are taking the longest to animate and which ActionScript is taking the longest to execute, so you can optimize each operation to reserve processor time for other things, like audio playback.

I use the following code to benchmark the effects of optimization. It uses a 1-millisecond interval, created with *setInterval( )* [Hack #27], rather than an *onEnterFrame* event, which is tied to the frame rate. This forces Flash to redraw the screen as fast as it can, but it won't run every millisecond (perhaps every three milliseconds) due to performance limitations.

```
function animate(target) {
  // Animation script to move target clip across the Stage.
  target._x = (target._x + 1) % 400;
  count++;
  updateAfterEvent( );
}
function controller( ) {
  clearInterval(animater);
  // Display average redraw time (in ms).
  trace(clip[clipPointer]+ " " + 20000/count);
  // Animate next clip for 20 seconds (if there
  // is another clip still to test).
  clipPointer++;
  if (clipPointer < clip.length) {
    count = 0;
    animater = setInterval(animate, 1, clip[clipPointer]);
  } else {
  // If there is no other clip to test, stop.
    clearInterval(timer);
  }
}
// Setup
var clip:Array = new Array( );
var clipPointer:Number = 0;
var count:Number = 0;
clip[0] = clip01;
clip[1] = clip02;
clip[2] = clip03;
var animater:Number = setInterval(animate, 1, clip[clipPointer]);
var timer:Number = setInterval(controller, 20000);
```

In the preceding code, if clip01, clip02, and clip03 are three instances of a movie clip (for example, three versions of the same shape with different levels of curve optimization applied via the Modify → Shape submenu), the code will animate each instance as fast as it can for 20 seconds. It returns the average time to redraw the movie clip in milliseconds, and this can be used to make a comparison between the clips.

> The preceding code is designed to benchmark reasonably complex shapes. It doesn't account for the time taken to run the code, but it does give you an idea of the relative rendering times.

By using such a testing scheme, you can get impartial data with regard to system performance. This is much more reliable than asking beta testers whether an animation was fast or slow. You can accumulate data on a variety of machines, especially the low end of your target machines, to evaluate the appropriate trade-offs between appearance and performance. You'll often find that minor differences in visual appearance (hardly apparent to users) result in measurable improvements in runtime performance.

Final Thoughts

The benchmark code offers a more realistic evaluation of performance than relying on the general optimization rules alone. It also helps you evaluate the trade-offs between techniques that conserve or consume processor power. For example, a complex shape containing many points may animate faster than a larger, simple circle. Furthermore, a solid shape moving in front of a bitmap may cause a bigger performance hit than a movie clip with transparency that is moving over a much simpler background.

Using code to benchmark your optimizations gives you the best idea of what has the most impact on performance for your particular animation. This type of benchmarking is best for comparing techniques to see which is relatively faster, not to see how fast an animation or application runs in real life [Hack #70], which depends heavily on the end user's computer and processing load.

HACK #70   Adjust the Animation Complexity Dynamically

> Measure the Flash Player's runtime performance in order to adjust the complexity of an effect or animation dynamically to run optimally on both low-end and high-end machines.

In the preceding hacks, we've seen ways to improve performance, regardless of the playback system, by optimizing a Flash movie's assets at authoring time. Optimization of that sort is essentially a lowest common denominator affair. This hack addresses the need to maximize animation and other effects for faster machines without creating a movie that bogs down on slower machines.

Although Flash Player 7 performs better than previous versions, it is still not a speed demon. The underlying goal of Flash is to optimize filesize (i.e., reduce download time) rather than provide breathtaking performance. Although we can improve performance by lowering the render quality [Hack #67], in many cases, turning off antialiasing can result in an unacceptably poor appearance for your site.

A better way to improve performance is to adjust the complexity (i.e., how much is happening per frame) of a graphical effect rather than its quality or frame rate. This approach can yield better results over a wider range of user systems with varying processing power than a one-size-fits-all optimization.

Adjusting the complexity is often an iterative process based on experimentation (with time it will become second nature and require fewer iterations):

- Start with a target frame rate, such as 18 fps.
- Measure the achieved frame rate, as covered shortly.
- If the desired frame rate is not achievable on the test machine, reduce the complexity of the effect.
- If the effect is rendered quickly enough, you have the leeway to increase the complexity of the effect.

Now that you understand the basics of the approach, let's automate it so that Flash decides dynamically whether to reduce or increase the complexity of the animation. This approach protects against sluggish performance on slower machines and (when done well) enhances the effect on faster machines.

We do not intend to change the frame rate, but rather change the complexity of the effect, in such a way that it always completes just before the next frame starts.

Calculate the Achieved Frame Rate

The following code creates an empty movie clip called perfMon (performance monitor) and attaches an *onEnterFrame( )* event handler to it. This event handler calculates the average frame duration (in milliseconds) using the last two timer measurements, creating a rolling average. This rolling average, time, is compared against the expected duration, FRAME_DUR, and a

Boolean flag, slow, is set to true or false based on whether the Flash Player is achieving the target frame rate.

```
function performanceMonitor( ) {
  this.createEmptyMovieClip("perfMon", 10000);
  perfMon.onEnterFrame = function( ) {
    time = (getTimer( ) - lastTime) / 2;
    lastTime = getTimer( );
    // Set slow to a Boolean based on whether the
    // elapsed time exceeds the allowed frame duration
    slow = time > FRAME_DUR;
  };
}
// Set FRAME_RATE to match the movie's target frame rate
var FRAME_RATE:Number = 18;
var FRAME_DUR:Number = (1 / FRAME_RATE) * 1000;
var time:Number = 0;
var lastTime:Number = getTimer( );
performanceMonitor( );
```

A slow value of false indicates that we can make the Flash Player do more without compromising performance because it is completing all its tasks before the start of the next frame. Ideally, we would want the Flash Player to finish all tasks for the current frame just as the next frame starts. We know this is happening when our rolling average, time, is equal to the expected frame duration, FRAME_DUR.

Adjust the Complexity Based on Performance

Let's see how to make Flash increase or decrease the animation's complexity based on the performance monitor's calculation. One simple approach is to draw more or fewer movie clips depending on the value of our slow flag. For the sake of example, let's use a star field particle effect [Hack #33]. The following code assumes a default Stage size of 550×400 pixels, with a dark background color. The effect works best with a frame rate of 18–24 fps. To set the background color and frame rate, select Modify → Document and adjust the properties as desired. The following code assumes a frame rate of 24 fps, and if you choose any other rate, you will need to change the following line to reflect this:

```
var FRAME_RATE:Number = 24;
```

Note that you have to do this manually because there is no property or method in Flash that returns the movie's target frame rate (strange but true!).

We've modified the *starfield( )* function from [Hack #33] to draw a single star at a time. Instead of setting the slow flag when the animation is running slowly, we use an *if* statement to adjust the animation's complexity. If the animation is running quickly enough, it draws additional stars by calling *starfield()*; otherwise, it deletes stars to maintain performance.

Again, it is important to realize that we are not varying the frame rate (and doing so would not be transparent to the rest of the SWF, in any case), but rather the complexity of the animation so that the time taken to render each frame in the animation is equal to all the available time per frame.

```
function performanceMonitor( ) {
  var perfMon:MovieClip = this.createEmptyMovieClip("perfMon", 10000);
  perfMon.onEnterFrame = function( ) {
    time = (getTimer( ) - lastTime) / 2;
    if (time < (FRAME_DUR)) {
      // Speed is okay
      stars++;
      starField( );
    } else if (time > (FRAME_DUR + 10)) {
      // Running too slowly
      _root["star" + stars].removeMovieClip( );
      stars--;
    }
    lastTime = getTimer( );
  };
}
function mover( ) {
  this._y += this.speed;
  this._yscale += this.speed;
  if (this._y > 275) {
    this._y = 0;
    this.spccd = Math.ceil(Math.random( ) * 10);
    this._yscale = 100;
  }
}
function starField( ) {
  var star:MovieClip = this.createEmptyMovieClip("star" + stars, stars);
  star._rotation = Math.random( )*360;
  star._x = 275;
  star._y = 200;
  var dot:MovieClip = star.createEmptyMovieClip("dot", 0);
  dot.speed = Math.ceil(Math.random( ) * 10);
  dot.lineStyle(1, 0xFFFFE0, 100);
  dot.moveTo(0, 2);
  dot.lineTo(0, 5);
  dot.onEnterFrame = mover;
}
// Set FRAME_RATE to match the movie's target frame rate
var FRAME_RATE:Number = 24;
var FRAME_DUR:Number = (1 / FRAME_RATE) * 1000;
var time:Number = 0;
var lastTime:Number = 0;
```

```
var stars:Number = 0;
performanceMonitor();
```

If you run the preceding code, you will see the star field build from no stars up to a maximum of several hundred stars, as shown in Figure 9-7. Use the Variables tab in the Debugger panel to view the variables on the main time-line, which displays results similar to those shown in Figure 9-7.

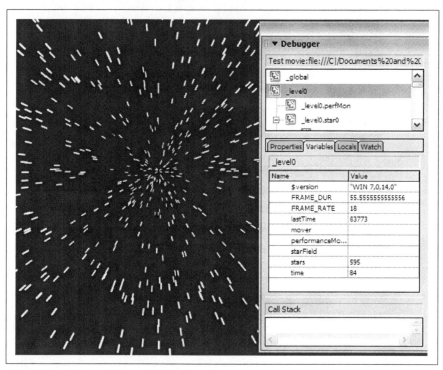

Figure 9-7. The star field and the performance monitor

The number of stars increases until time is close to FRAME_DUR, at which point the code adds or deletes stars to maintain equilibrium. If you do anything to change this equilibrium (such as run other code or resize the SWF), the change in performance causes a new equilibrium to be reached. Note that the Flash frame rate tends to change spuriously even when equilibrium is reached, so the effect will be almost constantly adding and deleting movie clips. You can build in a buffer if you prefer. For example, you might delete or add clips only if the actual time per frame is more than 15% above or below the target frame rate.

Final Thoughts

Graphical effects that work well on your development machine might bog down on user machines with lesser performance. To make your Flash content run appropriately on as many machines as possible (including mobile devices with significantly slower performance characteristics), you should strive for *scalability*. Your content should adapt to the user's machine. This hack shows one fairly simple approach: calculate how fast the user's machine is performing and adjust the graphical complexity accordingly. Measuring true performance at runtime is usually easier and more reliable than trying to estimate performance based on, say, the device type or screen resolution.

The many adjustments you can make at runtime to dynamically change the movie's complexity include:

- Limiting the number of items onscreen (stars in a star field, monsters in a game, users in an avatar-based chat room).

- Reducing the number of audio channels in use.

- Reducing the alpha effects (i.e., turn off transparency on slower machines).

- Limiting the amount or frequency of movements (such as using fewer frames in a walk cycle [Hack #28]). Digital and 3D artists unfamiliar with performance requirements usually create too many in-between positions. Often 3 or 5 will suffice instead of the typical 15 or 20 positions artists provide.

- Using smaller screen dimensions or reducing the active area of the screen. You can make the screen size appear larger by adding static graphics around your active area, such as a border to achieve a "picture frame" effect or static gauges to achieve a "dashboard" look.

- Using still bitmaps or videos with color effects [Hack #8].

You will find that some changes affect performance in more than one way and offer benefits on both low-end and high-end machines. For example, in a bartending game, you might reduce the number of patrons in the bar and the frequency with which they talk. This reduces the number of items to be rendered and the number of sound channels in use. Or you might reduce the size of the patrons so they take up less screen real estate. On higher-performance machines, this allows you to place more patrons at the bar. On lower-end machines, this ensures that the patrons displayed are rendered more quickly.

Runtime performance of the playback machine isn't the only reason to adjust your Flash content. You should also take into consideration the user's personal performance on interactive exercises. For example, you might display directions or play audio help if the user does something wrong or is taking too long to perform the desired operation. Or you might make a video game or educational game easier on the first level in response to the user failing repeatedly.

There are many other ways to affect the perceived performance or user experience. For example, implementing keyboard shortcuts [Hack #96] makes an application feel more responsive than requiring mouseclicks. Likewise, an animation that plays repeatedly becomes boring no matter how well it performs. Shorten the animation if it is played repeatedly, limit the number of times it is played, or allow the user to turn it off or skip it.

Performance Budget

A financial budget tells you where you are spending your money. Create a performance budget to understand and adjust where you are expending resources.

We saw earlier how to estimate download times [Hack #66], allowing you to cram the maximum presentation into the smallest filesize. Performance has a lower priority in the Flash Player design than does filesize optimization, which means that although Flash allows you to create compelling content in very few kilobytes, you have limited resources from which to extract performance. Although the total processor cycles available to the Flash Player are limited, you can control where Flash spends its time. A *performance budget* reflects a conscious effort to adjust the amount of time Flash doles out to each of the parts of your movie.

Areas of Focus

Like all budgets, your performance budget should include priorities. That is, not all aspects of your presentation are equally important. For example, users notice hiccups in audio tracks more than hiccups in videos or animation. Designers also tend to lavish attention on things the typical user won't ever notice or appreciate. The user generally looks closely only at the things she is currently interacting with; elements within the user's "area of focus" get the greatest attention from her and therefore should be given priority in your performance budget. Items in the user's peripheral vision may be ignored entirely or noticed only when they do something unexpected, such as shift by a pixel. Therefore, allocating your performance budget and designing an interface that serves the user's needs are complementary tasks.

If you can anticipate (or control) the user's area of focus, and make that perform well, the user gets the impression of greater overall performance even if peripheral items are static or perform less well.

For example, in video games (and intensive real-time graphics), items closest to the viewer in the 3D virtual world are rendered with the most detail. The detail can drop off significantly with distance; even if the player notices, it mirrors reality in which things further away are generally less visible/detailed. Likewise, the collision detection algorithm [Hack #40] used by distant parts of the game can be less precise for the same reason—they are not close enough to be in the user's area of focus. This allowance frees up some of the performance budget for real-time lighting, physics, and other trappings of virtual worlds.

Set Process Priorities

There are a number of ways to give your area of focus the lion's share of the performance budget. The easiest approach is to simply give the area of focus an "on-change" event handler and use a periodic event to update the rest of the movie. For example, if you are implementing a pong game, you can use an *onMouseMove( )* event handler to control the user's paddle and an *onEnterFrame( )* event handler to control the opponent's paddle and the ball. If the part of the game that the user controls is responsive, the entire application feels more responsive.

However, just setting two different priorities doesn't allow us detailed control over the performance budget. A better approach is to use several different priorities. Here we allocate our priorities based on the likelihood and directness of user interactivity:

High priority
    Processes with which the user will interact directly

Normal priority
    Processes with which the user will interact indirectly

Low priority
    Processes with which the user will rarely or never interact

In terms of a game (the most common high-performance Flash application), the high-priority process is the player's ship or character (a.k.a. token). Normal-priority processes include the enemy graphics; although the user expects them to move at an adequate speed, the slowdown won't be as noticeable as long as the high-priority stuff doesn't slow down as well. The user will just assume that the slow-moving enemy target is supposed to move slowly.

Low-priority processes are things like the score update or a scrolling background—the user notices if they break, but if they work adequately, the user pays little attention.

Low-priority processes can be hard for game designers to identify because developers are personally vested in every pixel and audio cue. You'll be more apt to let go of your rigidly held beliefs if you realize that everything you deprioritize allows you to lavish more attention (or performance) on things that matter more. And don't forget that the sound effect that was cute the first time might get really boring after the user hears it a thousand times. So the best option is to put your prototype version in front of beta testers. Ask them what they like, what seems too slow, what they find annoying, and so on. By definition, these are the people you are trying to entertain, attract, or serve, so listen to their feedback.

You can also trick your audience into thinking you are doing more than you actually are. For example, you can have a scrolling star field with many stars when the game is displaying the static high score table, but as soon as the game starts, you can reduce the animation complexity [Hack #70]. The user won't notice if you slowly drop the number of stars as the game gets faster and more difficult. He is more likely to be concentrating on getting to the next level!

Implementation

Once you decide on your priorities, you need to implement them in Action-Script. Since you can't just tell Flash that something is important, you instill priorities indirectly via the programming techniques and events you choose.

High-priority events can use either:

- An interval (created with *setInterval( )*) set to a period shorter than the frame rate [Hack #27]
- An *onMouseMove( )* event handler [Hack #26]

Because high-priority events occur more frequently than the frame rate, the high-priority event handlers must include an *updateAfterEvent( )* command to redraw the Stage between frames.

Normal-priority events can use an *onEnterFrame( )* event handler to perform operations at the same frequency as the frame rate.

Low-priority events can use either:

- An interval (created with *setInterval( )*) set to a period longer than the frame rate

- A listener event that is occasionally triggered from a normal-priority event's *onEnterFrame( )* handler

Figure 9-8 shows the interface for a scrolling video game. In this example, we'll set different priorities for different aspects of the game.

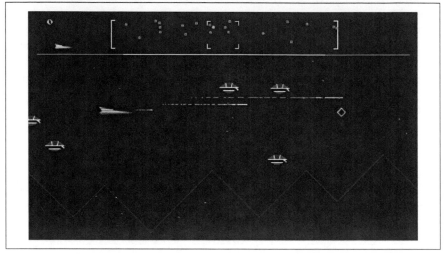

Figure 9-8. A scrolling video game interface

game01.fla from this book's web site shows the main routine for a typical FLA configured using a performance budget philosophy; look at the script on frame 2 of the movie clip mc.world for the main listing.

Although ActionScript purists might balk at the fact that a script is attached to a movie clip, game design is as much about animation as it is scripting, so you will find animation mixed with code, and very rarely will you find an entire game on a single frame. For example, if you look at the player's ship (symbol mc.ship in the Library), you will see that the explosion sequence is a keyframe animation rather than 100% scripted. Although you could use scripted timers to control the explosion animation, the timeline animation is easier to create, requires little forward planning, and is more likely to be comprehensible to designers who might have to edit it.

Here is how the three sets of priorities are handled in the FLA file's code.

The ship sprite is the only high-priority process. The following code sets up an interval that invokes *shipController( )* every 30 milliseconds to redraw the ship:

```
shipControl = setInterval(shipController, 30);
```

The background terrain update has a normal priority (to be updated at the frame rate of 18 fps), so it is scrolled every frame by setting the *onEnterFrame( )* handler to *terrainController( )*:

```
terrain.onEnterFrame = terrainController;
```

The score update is low priority, so it is refreshed only once per second:

```
scoreKeeper = setInterval(scoreController, 1000);
```

You can also see how the system works by simply playing the game (a far better option!). You will notice that:

- The star field scrolls more slowly than the terrain. The stars are assigned a low priority and update every quarter of a second. This fact is hidden somewhat by staggering the update—each star animates once every quarter second, but not all of the stars update at the same time.

- The radar display updates at around the same rate as the stars. The game is designed to make the slow update seem intentional—the old cathode ray tube radars worked on a slow scan update. A common trick is to fill blank areas of the screen with things that the user expects to move slowly, such as clouds and distant hills. The slow updates for these items seems natural.

- The player's ship moves much faster (and more smoothly) than the aliens. Most users won't perceive the difference because they are focused on their own ship. If they notice the difference, they are happy to be able to outmaneuver their sluggish enemies.

- The aliens, laser, and terrain all move at the frame rate.

- The score updates very slowly (every 1 second). This is the lowest-priority process in the game because the user is busy looking elsewhere. Updating text fields too frequently is one of the biggest performance killers in Flash. Even a modest amount of text takes a lot of vectors to draw, especially if Flash is redrawing it every frame!

This game example shows it is possible to create a fast Flash game with a reasonably large Stage size. Increasing the size of the browser window need not kill performance if you structure your games properly.

Final Thoughts

Using a performance budget doesn't make the Flash Player faster, but it gives the perception of faster performance, just as a preloader status bar makes the user feel as if the download is faster. You should identify the elements that need to update frequently and allocate more of the available performance budget to them. Likewise, identify the low-priority processes and run them more slowly to make more time available for higher-priority processes. If you increase the performance in the user's areas of focus, the game will feel responsive and the user won't notice the areas of slower performance.

Substitute Bitmaps for Vectors

Vectors download quickly but can take a long time to render. Use bitmaps instead of vectors to improve playback speed.

Vector images are drawn using mathematical formulas that define the shapes and fills. This means that vectors provide crisp and scalable graphics in a compact download size. However, rendering an antialiased vector shape can take more processing power than rendering a bitmap (pixel-based) image. A bitmap is simply a fixed block of data. Although this data is usually much larger than typical vector images, once it is downloaded, it can be drawn quickly. Regardless, the download filesize is reduced even further via compression when creating the SWF file. (SWF files automatically use *z-lib* compression, a lossless compression algorithm similar to that used by the PNG graphic format.)

Bitmaps offer a good trade-off in performance versus download size in several cases:

- When the vector image contains many points, the vector version can be larger that the equivalent bitmap. Vectors are usually better for line art whereas bitmaps are better for photographs and textures, neither of which can be easily represented using vectors.

- If you don't require scaling or antialiasing, bitmaps generally render faster.

- If running from a CD-ROM, for which download speed is not an issue, consider using bitmaps.

If you have static, vector-heavy backgrounds, using a background bitmap will usually improve rendering times. If you have complex vector drawings that use many grouped graphics, you may also see benefits by using bitmaps instead.

Example One: Bitmaps Move Faster than Do Vectors

In this example (available as *tileexample_vector.fla* on this book's web site), several movie clips move across the screen simulating a distance parallax effect (i.e., where depth in the z-axis is implied by objects getting both slower in movement and darker in color as the distance from the viewer increases). The movie clips used in the effect consist of faux 3D tile graphics created using only vectors, as shown in Figure 9-9.

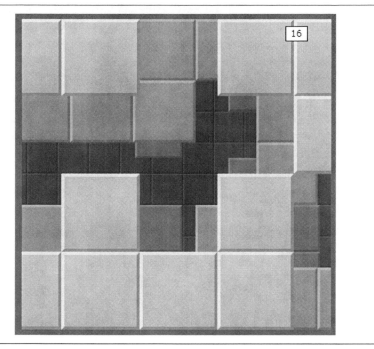

Figure 9-9. A tile animation created with vector images

A frame rate readout is displayed at the top left of the Stage, and you can use this to see how fast Flash renders the effect. When testing this vector-based version (test it in the browser by pressing F12 for the most representative results), you will see the Flash Player slow down significantly. Although the movie's target frame rate is set to 70 fps, a reasonably fast computer renders the movie at a rate of around 20–35 fps.

The solution in this case is to replace each vector image with a similar one that uses a bitmap graphic instead. The movie clips seen in the file *tileexample_bitmap.fla* (also available on this book's web site) appear the same as the vector version, but they:

- Are created using bitmaps tiles rather than vector ones
- Have the "darkening with distance" color effect already applied to them via a bitmap-editing application, which frees Flash from having to apply the effect during runtime

The improved version, using bitmaps, is faster than the original. The bitmap version will operate in the region of 40–70 fps when tested under the same conditions as the vector-based version. Note that the bitmap version also has the same filesize. Furthermore, because all elements are bitmaps using straight edges (and Flash doesn't antialias moving bitmaps unless you set the highest quality setting [Hack #67]), using low or medium quality would make the rendering process even faster. (And remember that changes in quality are difficult to see on a moving object, so even if the quality goes down, the user may find this difficult to spot!)

Example Two: Avoid Antialias Calculations

Often the most processor-intensive part of rendering vectors is the associated antialiasing. Converting the vectors to prealiased bitmaps can significantly increase performance.

Figure 9-10 shows a simple symbol on a background, with scrollable text and a few more copies of the same symbol above it. The file is available as *textexample_vector.fla* on this book's web site.

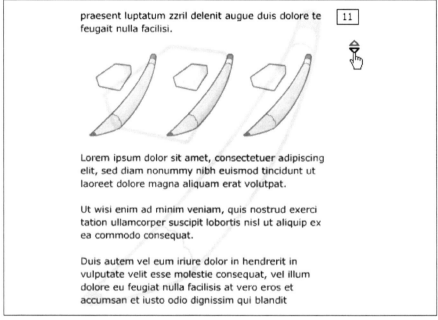

Figure 9-10. Symbols and a scroll text field

Moving the text via the scroll buttons results in significant drops in performance. Using a bitmap as the background would reduce the calculations Flash has to perform. Rendering a static bitmap image is faster than making Flash rerender the vector-based version each time the text scrolls.

Replacing the vector background with a bitmap (as seen in file *textexample_bitmaps.fla*) produces a speed gain of approximately 30%.

Final Thoughts

A bitmap image may be larger in filesize, but it has advantages. The visual information within a bitmap doesn't have to be calculated at runtime, and you can apply additional effects to a bitmap at authoring time using an application such as Photoshop, saving the need to calculate the same effect at runtime.

A vector-based image is usually (but not always) smaller in filesize. Regardless, drawing vector images can require the Flash Player to perform a large number of real-time calculations.

Although the Flash rendering engine works best with vectors, and bitmap animation is seen as the preserve of Macromedia Director, this is not always the case in practice. In a significant number of situations, bitmaps lead to a performance increase without a significant filesize increase.

If you're making a CD-ROM project and filesize isn't important (download time isn't a limitation), you can use bitmaps, unless you need to scale the content.

—Zeh Fernando

#73 Optimize Component Downloading and Usage

Flash ships with a large number of components, which are a useful solution to common Flash design tasks. Minimize the considerable download delay they can cause at the start of your SWF.

Many Flash presentations, especially business applications or movies meant to simulate desktop applications, require standard UI elements such as buttons and drop-down lists. These standard elements are provided by Macromedia in the form of prebuilt components, as shown in Figure 9-11.

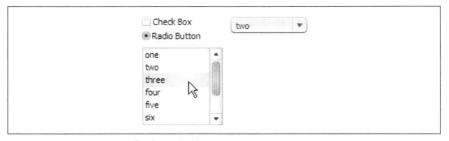

Figure 9-11. Various standard UI components

Components are a special type of movie clip that can be used as the building blocks of common UI elements or provide ActionScript classes to aid in the building of advanced interactivity or communication between Flash and other web technologies.

When you compile the FLA into a SWF, Flash scans through the timeline and makes a list of all the assets and the order in which they appear. It then adds the assets to the SWF in that order, so streaming can occur efficiently. If an asset never appears on the timeline, it never gets added to the list and therefore never gets exported, thus keeping the SWF filesize to a minimum.

That optimization works well, except when you use an asset or component via ActionScript but not in the timeline. You can force Flash to include assets even if they are not used in the timeline by selecting the Export for ActionScript checkbox in the Linkage Properties dialog box. Components have this option checked by default, so they are included in the SWF even if they aren't used in the timeline. If you place components on Stage (which adds them to the Library) and then later delete them from the Stage, they remain in the Library. This is the preferred way to add needed components to the Library. However, be sure to delete unused components from the Library (or uncheck their Export for ActionScript checkboxes) or they'll be included in the SWF even if you don't use them via the timeline or Action-Script.

Flash MX 2004 components (also known as *v2 components*) are a major redesign of the original Flash MX v1 components, but they require an initial download of around 25–30 KB, which occurs by default in the first frame of your SWF. The resultant delay for low-bandwidth users can be off-putting.

You can't avoid the download delay, but you can change when it occurs. Under File → Publish Settings → Flash, specify ActionScript 2.0 for the ActionScript Version (the v2 components are written in ActionScript 2.0). Click the Settings button next to the ActionScript Version drop-down list (Settings becomes selectable when you choose ActionScript 2.0). When the ActionScript Settings dialog box appears, in the Export Frame for Classes text entry box, change the value to **2**.

This setting forces Flash to export the component classes after frame 1 instead of before frame 1, allowing you to at least put something up in the browser as the classes load. This is useful if you want to create sites that work on low-bandwidth connections and use Flash MX 2004 components.

You shouldn't try to use any components until after their classes have loaded (including the Preloader component). If you want to use the Preloader component, you should add a dummy static graphic that looks like the preloader showing 0% on frame 1 and start animating it at frame 2.

Although the Flash MX 2004 components require a 30 KB preload before they start working, this figure doesn't increase measurably if you use more than one component. That is, the v2 component architecture is optimized for cases in which you use five or more components. The components are also skinnable, allowing you to create a more customized look. And they offer features like focus management and accessibility support.

If using a single component, especially if you don't need the new features, it probably isn't worth using the v2 components. Flash Player 7-compatible versions of the v1 components, which are not as bandwidth-heavy as the v2 components, are available from the Flash Exchange (*http://www. macromedia.com/exchange/flash*), in the User Interface category, under the title *Flash MX Components for Flash MX 2004*.

> Some of the original Flash MX v1 components don't work in Flash MX 2004 if you specify Flash Player 7 as the export format under File → Publish Settings → Flash → Version.

Some of the v1 components that come with Flash MX are not written with case-sensitivity in mind, so they cause compiler errors when you attempt to export them to Flash Player 7 format from Flash MX 2004, regardless of whether you're compiling them as ActionScript 1.0 or 2.0. The updated versions are case-sensitivity compliant, so they will work in Flash MX 2004 for any combination of ActionScript 1.0 or 2.0 and Flash Player 6 or 7 format export.

Many different component sets are available at the Flash Exchange. Also worth considering is the Macromedia Pocket PC CDK (Content Development Kit), available at *http://www.macromedia.com/devnet/devices*. The Pocket PC components that form a part of this kit are optimized for low file-size and work for the desktop-based Flash Player (they work for Flash Player 6 and appear to work well for Flash Player 7 when using ActionScript 2.0 export settings).

If you require very limited functionality, you should consider creating your own components. Most basic site designs require nothing more than a button and a scrollbar, both of which can be created via a couple of 1 KB movie clips. See also *http://www.flashcomponents.com* and *http://www. flashcomponents.net* for alternative components created by the Flash community, some of which are designed with low filesize in mind.

Final Thoughts

Although v2 components ship with Flash MX 2004, they are certainly not the only components you can use. The v2 components are geared toward higher-bandwidth web applications. For general design, you can use the Flash MX v1 components or even other Macromedia or third-party components, such as those designed for the Pocket PC.

CHAPTER TEN

ActionScript
Hacks 74–85

ActionScript adds true power to Flash. Without ActionScript, Flash can create only linear animation. With a little ActionScript, you can create basic navigation via clickable buttons and hotspots. Learning more advanced ActionScript techniques gives you access to features such as creating a local shared object (colloquially known as a "Flash cookie"). Without ActionScript, you cannot create Flash sites that communicate with the browser, exchange data with server-side applications, or download MP3 files.

Many new features in Flash MX 2004 and Flash MX Professional 2004 are implemented on the assumption that the developer knows ActionScript. Even features that assume no coding experience, such as Behaviors and Timeline Effects, can be implemented in a much more structured and flexible way if the developer has some knowledge of ActionScript.

Although timeline animation is easy to learn, what takes days or months to create by hand can often be coded in ActionScript in minutes or hours. And when designers want to implement applications with advanced interactivity, decision-making logic, or communication features, they need to learn ActionScript. Whether you are building Rich Internet Applications (RIAs), online games, or advanced GUIs, they all rely on scripting.

Although this chapter focuses on ActionScript, scripting appears in almost every hack in this book. The "Increase Code Performance" section in Chapter 9 addresses ActionScript optimization. This book also covers performance related-hacks, such as bytecode optimization [Hack #100]. So you can learn a lot of ActionScript by trying the hacks as presented and modifying them to create your own hacks. See also the discussion in the Preface regarding converting ActionScript 2.0 (used widely in this book) to ActionScript 1.0.

For a thorough introduction to ActionScript, see *ActionScript for Flash MX: The Definitive Guide*. For an extensive study on using ActionScript 2.0 for object-oriented programming, see *Essential ActionScript 2.0*. Both were written by Colin Moock and are published by O'Reilly.

Changes in Flash MX 2004

Flash MX 2004 is a major upgrade for ActionScript users. Major additions include syntax and structural changes that aid the building of large Action-Script applications, greater support for text formatting, and greater support for the control and running of media streams.

The Flash component framework has been upgraded to take advantage of class-based optimizations and new features in ActionScript 2.0, including strict datatyping.

Flash MX Professional 2004's new Slides and Forms features (collectively called Screens) allow development using a PowerPoint-like or Visual Basic-style authoring metaphor with a minimum of scripting.

Even the Flash MX 2004 authoring tool's interface can be customized using the Flash JavaScript API (JSAPI). See the JSAPI Documentation section of the Flash MX 2004 Documentation page (*http://www.macromedia.com/support/documentation/en/flash*) for links to documents that explain how to create commands and tools for use in the Flash authoring environment.

Furthermore, JSFL (Flash JavaScript), allows you to script authoring operations. Complete coverage of JSFL is outside the scope of this book, but here's a quick example of command-line compilation for Windows. This JSFL script from Colin Moock tells Flash to create the *.swf* file for each *.fla* file in your project:

```
// Code in exportPetSupplies.jsfl:
// Open the .fla file.
var doc = fl.openDocument("file:///c|/data/projects/pet/petsupplies.fla");
// Export the .swf file.
doc.exportSWF("file:///c|/data/projects/pet/petsupplies.swf", true);
// Quit the Flash MX 2004 authoring tool (optional).
fl.quit(false);

// Command issued on command line from /pet/ directory:
"c:\program files\macromedia\flash mx 2004\flash.exe" exportPetSupplies.jsfl
```

For this command to work, Flash MX 2004 must not be running. After the command is issued, the compiled *petsupplies.swf* movie appears in the directory *c:\data\projects\pet*.

Both Flash MX 2004 and Flash MX Professional 2004 support ActionScript 2.0 but also still support ActionScript 1.0 syntax (you can set which version of the ActionScript compiler to use under File → Publish Settings → Flash → ActionScript Version). So developers can stick with ActionScript 1.0 or switch to ActionScript 2.0, which is geared more toward object-oriented development, at their own pace.

New ActionScript in Flash Player 7

Numerous additions to ActionScript in Flash Player 7 are available whether you are using ActionScript 1.0 or ActionScript 2.0. Flash's online Help provides a detailed list of the ActionScript changes (Help → ActionScript Reference Guide → What's New in Flash MX 2004 ActionScript).

Here is a partial list of new features:

- Real-time error message feedback via the *Error* class, plus error handling via *try/catch/finally* and *throw*.

- The ability to customize the Flash Player context menu via the *ContextMenu* class and the new menu property (for the *Button*, *MovieClip*, and *TextField* classes).

- Support for the *Mouse.onMouseWheel* event, which detects changes in the mouse wheel position (Windows only) and an undocumented way to detect mouse wheel clicks [Hack #62].

- The *MovieClipLoader* class for creating preloaders (i.e., for displaying load status while the SWF file downloads).

- The *TextField.StyleSheet* class, which offers CSS support.

- SOAP support, which allows Flash Player 7 to access SOAP-based web services without requiring Flash Remoting to be installed on the server. (Prebuilt remote data connectivity components that implement SOAP communication are provided with Flash MX Professional 2004 only.)

- Some methods of the *MovieClip* class, most notably *getNextHighestDepth( )* and *getInstanceAtDepth( )* for depth management.

- The *PrintJob* class, which greatly simplifies Flash printing and gives much more control over printed output than the ActionScript 1.0 print functions.

Most Flash Player 6-format SWFs will play unmodified in Flash Player 7. However, Flash Player 7 also introduced a more stringent interdomain security policy, as described in Chapter 12, which may break certain Flash Player 6 content when viewed in Flash Player 7. The System.exactSettings property and the *System.allowInsecureDomain( )* method allow you to change some of the domain security measures back to the less stringent Flash 6 style, thus allowing more Flash Player 6-format SWFs to run in Flash Player 7.

Although many of Flash Player 7's features are also supported by Flash Player 6.0.65 (a.k.a. Flash Player 6r65), many others are not. For maximum compatibility (until more end users install Flash Player 7), you should export your Flash MX 2004 files in Flash Player 6 format (choose File → Publish Settings → Flash and select Flash Player 6 as the Version, then check Optimize for Flash Player 6r65), unless you are using Flash Player 7-specific features.

Case Sensitivity and Strict Typing

ActionScript 2.0 allows you to specify the datatype for any property, variable, parameter, or function return value. The datatype is used by the compiler to perform type checking. That is, the compiler validates that only data of the correct datatype is assigned to each item for which a datatype is specified. ActionScript 2.0 is also case-sensitive (as discussed at *http://swfoo.com/archives/000034.html*) to bring it in conformance with the ECMA-262 Edition 4 (ECMA 4) proposed standard as discussed in detail at *http://livedocs.macromedia.com/flash/mx2004/main/wwhelp/wwhimpl/common/html/wwhelp.htm?context=Flash_MX_2004_Documentation&file=01_what5.htm*.

Although many nonprogrammers will see ActionScript 2.0's strict typing and case sensitivity as something they can live without, it isn't hard to use, and it can help you avoid errors. For example, in ActionScript 1.0, we could quite happily assign any data to a variable, like this:

```
answer = "Einstein";
```

However, further along in your timeline, you might mistakenly write this:

```
answer = 6;
```

The preceding statement assigns a numeric value to what was supposed to be a string variable, which is probably a mistake. ActionScript 1.0 could not detect such potential errors nor warn you about them. However, using ActionScript 2.0's strict datatyping, your code would become:

```
var answer:String = "Einstein";
```

Note the datatype, String, following the colon (known as *post-colon syntax*). It specifies that the answer variable should contain a string and not a value belonging to another datatype. Whenever you define a datatype for a variable, the variable must be preceded by the *var* keyword.

Suppose that later in the timeline you use:

```
answer = 6;
```

When you try to compile the FLA, Flash warns you of the mistake by displaying a type mismatch error in the Output panel. Using strict typing thus tends to detect errors and help you create more robust code.

ActionScript datatyping occurs at compile time in the authoring environment only. ActionScript supports type checking only when you choose ActionScript 2.0 as the ActionScript Version under Flash → Publish Settings → Flash. Even when using the ActionScript 2.0 compiler, Flash does not perform type checking on any item for which you omit the post-colon datatype. This allows you to update legacy ActionScript 1.0 to ActionScript 2.0, even if you don't specify datatypes for every item.

LiveDocs

Keeping up with all the features in Flash and ActionScript isn't easy, especially since new bugs and updates mean the in-product documentation is not necessarily current. (Although if an Internet connection is available, Flash MX 2004 will periodically ask you whether it should download updated documentation.)

Although still in its early days, LiveDocs for Flash MX 2004 (*http://livedocs.macromedia.com/flash/mx2004/index.html*) offers users online access to the full Flash documentation. LiveDocs pages display other users' comments and include an Add Comments button that allows you to comment on a page's contents and usefulness.

Of particular interest is the online ActionScript dictionary—just the place to go if you are having trouble with getting a particular bit of code working and the in-product online Help isn't sufficient to address your question.

External Script Editors

Flash MX Professional 2004 comes with an editor capable of editing external files, but the standard edition of Flash MX 2004 does not. Increase your productivity with an external editor whether writing ActionScript, JavaScript, XML, or CSS.

Flash has supported the ability to include external ActionScript (*.as* files) since Flash 5. In both Flash 5 and Flash MX, external ActionScript files could be included using the #include directive. In Flash MX 2004 and ActionScript 2.0, the #include directive is still supported but it is often unnecessary.

The following paraphrases some important points on external ActionScript files from the book *Essential ActionScript 2.0*, by Colin Moock, which covers the subject in great detail.

In ActionScript 2.0, a class definition (defined with the class keyword) *must* reside in an external plain-text file. The external file must have an *.as* extension matching the class name (case sensitivity matters!) and can contain only one class definition. For example, the *Box* class must be stored alone in a file named *Box.as*.

ActionScript 1.0 had no formal *class* statement; classes were defined using the *function* statement, as in:

```
function Box ( ) {
}
```

ActionScript 1.0 class definitions were allowed to be stored in a frame or even on a button or movie clip but were conventionally stored in external *.as* files and brought into the SWF using the #include directive. In ActionScript 2.0, the class code in external *.as* files is incorporated into the SWF the first time the class is used.

So, for example, the following ActionScript 2.0 code, which constructs a *Box* class instance using the *new* operator, causes the compiler to automatically incorporate the code from *Box.as* into the SWF:

```
var someVar:Box = new Box( );
```

So, in short, if you are using ActionScript 1.0, you should put your class definitions in external *.as* files, and in ActionScript 2.0, it is mandatory that you do so.

In order to find the external *.as* class files, the ActionScript 2.0 compiler looks in the classpath or in a package specified via the *import* statement. You can add a folder to the ActionScript 2.0 classpath under Edit → Preferences → ActionScript → Language → ActionScript 2.0 Settings. (Under the Classpath section, click the plus sign (+) to add a new directory to the classpath.)

Classes that extend the *MovieClip* class can be associated with a movie clip symbol by setting the linkage properties under Linkage in the Library panel's pop-up Options menu. To export a movie clip subclass, select the Export for ActionScript checkbox in the Linkage Properties dialog box and specify the class name (without the *.as* extension) in the AS 2.0 Class field of the same dialog box.

If you are using Flash MX 2004, you'll need an external text editor to write *.as* files, and even if using Flash MX Professional 2004 (which includes an external file editor), you might want something more full-featured.

SciTE|Flash is a popular text editor for dedicated ActionScripters, and it is also useful for writing the text, XML, JavaScript, CSS, and other files that the professional Flash developer needs. You can use it to write server-side scripts in languages such as Perl or PHP, as well.

SciTE (*http://www.scintilla.org/SciTE.html*) is a general open source text editor beloved by many high-end coders (it supports Windows and Linux). SciTE|Flash (*http://www.bomberstudios.com/sciteflash*) is the (Windows-only) ActionScript editor based on SciTE and created by Ale Muñoz from bomberstudios, with a little help from Robin Debreuil. For Mac and Windows alternatives, see the "Final Thoughts" section at the end of this hack.

As of this writing, a Flash MX 2004 version of SciTE|Flash (i.e., one that supports ActionScript 2.0 classes) is planned but has not yet appeared. For those who would like to help the process along, visit *http://www. bomberstudios.com/sciteflash/status.php*. You can find a set of configuration files that supports ActionScript 2.0 code hinting and colorization for SciTE|Flash at mizubitchy (*http://mizubitchy.antville.org/stories/519068*).

The SciTE|Flash application has two main panes: editing on the left and output on the right, as shown in Figure 10-1. To jump between the SciTE|Flash panes, press Ctrl-F6.

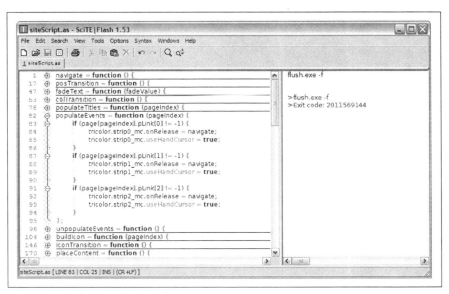

Figure 10-1. The SciTE|Flash editor

SciTE|Flash's editing controls are fairly self-evident and make writing code in the editor fast and easy. Particularly useful are:

- The collapsible/folding program blocks; each code block is represented in the lefthand margin by a long brace with a + or - circle in the center of it, as shown in Figure 10-2. Clicking this circle allows you to expand/ collapse the block, which is very useful for long, modular code, such as class-based *.as* files.

```
 97  ⊕  populateTitles = function (pageIndex) {
104  ⊕  populateEvents = function (pageIndex) {
119  ⊕  unpopulateEvents = function () {
127  ⊕  buildIcon = function (pageIndex) {
174  ⊕  iconTransition = function () {
198  ⊕  placeContent = function () {
212  ⊕  /*
218  ⊕  stripEvents = function () {
224  ⊕  stripCols = function () {
236  ⊕  stripPage = function () {
243  ⊕  /*
249  ⊕  navigationData = function () {
364  ⊕  /*
370     // Define screen extents for later use...
371     Stage.scaleMode = "exactFit";
372     border = 30;
373     bottom = Stage.height-border;
374     top = border;
```

```
 97  ⊕  populateTitles = function (pageIndex) {
104  ⊖  populateEvents = function (pageIndex) {
105         var pageIndex;
106  ⊖      if (page[pageIndex].pLink[0] != -1) {
107  ⟶        tricolor.strip0_mc.onRelease = navigate;
108  ⟶        tricolor.strip0_mc.useHandCursor = true;
109           }
110  ⊖      if (page[pageIndex].pLink[1] != -1) {
111  ⟶        tricolor.strip1_mc.onRelease = navigate;
112  ⟶        tricolor.strip1_mc.useHandCursor = true;
113           }
114  ⊖      if (page[pageIndex].pLink[2] != -1) {
115  ⟶        tricolor.strip2_mc.onRelease = navigate;
116           tricolor.strip2_mc.useHandCursor = true;
117           }
118     };
119  ⊕  unpopulateEvents = function () {
127  ⊕  buildIcon = function (pageIndex) {
```

Figure 10-2. Expanding and collapsing code blocks in SciTE|Flash

- The ability to format in a number of syntaxes other than ActionScript, including CSS, HTML, JavaScript, plain text, and XML. This allows you to create and edit all the code, data, and formatting files you need in a typical Flash project. All language options are available via the Syntax menu, as shown in Figure 10-3.

- Support for code bookmarks, allowing you to switch between lines within your listing (Ctrl-F2 to toggle bookmarking on or off for the current page, F2 to go to the next bookmark, and Shift-F2 to go to the last bookmark).

- The Edit menu allows you to comment and uncomment multiple lines of code in a single operation. There is also a nifty match braces feature

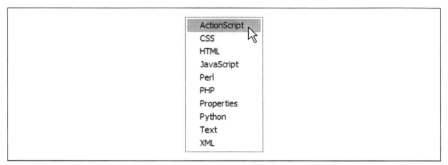

Figure 10-3. SciTE|Flash supports the syntax for multiple languages and file formats

in the Edit menu, allowing you to quickly debug situations in which you have one curly brace too many or too few.

- An autocomplete feature (well, okay, the Flash Actions panel has this, but it is nice to find an external editor that also has it).

- If you close the application with files still open, SciTE|Flash reopens the same files when you next start the application (you wouldn't believe how useful this is until you have tried it for a week!).

- Ability to change case (uppercase, lowercase, mixed case, etc.).

When using SciTE|Flash to write ActionScript 1.0 code (or ActionScript 2.0 code if you use the updated configuration files from mizubitchy), save your ActionScript classes in external *.as* files.

To test your script, open a new FLA and attach a script on frame 1 that includes the external *.as* file, such as:

```
#include "test.as"
```

Using a relative path allows the Flash compiler to find the external *.as* file, provided it is in the same folder as the *.fla* file. You can also specify a fixed path such as:

```
#include "c:\Documents and Settings\Sham B\Desktop\test.as"
```

If you are writing timeline code, you may prefer to copy and paste it into the timeline, but using an #include statement ensures that the latest version is pulled from the external *.as* file each time you recompile the FLA.

Furthermore, using an #include statement allows you to test and debug your script from SciTE|Flash!

To jump to Flash and view the running SWF in the Test Movie window, select Tools → Test Movie from SciTE|Flash's menu bar.

To capture the output from Flash's Output panel in SciTE|Flash's Output pane, select Tools → Capture Output from SciTE|Flash's menu bar. Flash enters Test Movie mode but doesn't receive window focus or become maximized because the output is being sent to SciTE|Flash.

To both test the movie and capture output, select Tools → Test and Capture Output from SciTE|Flash's menu bar. The SciTE|Flash window stays in front, but the Flash authoring tool enters Test Movie mode and becomes maximized. This is my preferred mode of working when developing long scripts.

SciTE|Flash also supports a command-line interface. The right pane in SciTE|Flash acts as both the Output pane and command-line text-input area. Click on the right pane to enter command-line mode, or press Ctrl-F6 to toggle between code-editing (left pane) and command-line (right pane) modes. You can press Shift-F5 at any time to clear text that may be present in the Output pane.

To test the SWF and capture output, type the following on the command line:

```
flush.exe-w
```

Final Thoughts

Developers who need a fast and light external editor to write code-heavy applications should give SciTE|Flash a whirl. It's blindingly fast for those who find the Flash Actions panel claustrophobic for long scripts (the SciTE|Flash code folding really helps navigate mammoth scripts). It is also much lighter weight than Dreamweaver whose external editor is overkill if you just want to write a bit of XML.

Of course, SciTE|Flash isn't the only external editor in town. Other popular editors include SE|PY (*http://www.sephiroth.it/python/sepy.php*), a free, open source editor supporting both Mac and Windows, and PrimalScript (*http://www.sapien.com/primalscript.htm*) starting at $179 (a 30-day fully functional trial version is available). Both editors offer ActionScript 2.0 code completion and an ActionScript 2.0 class browser.

Strict Typing and Casual Scripters

#75   ActionScript 2.0 introduces strict typing to check for incorrect datatypes. Strict typing can help motion graphics developers spend less time debugging and more time being creative.

ActionScript 2.0 introduces strict typing to detect datatype mismatches at compile time. Should you use strict typing if you're a motion graphics scripter and not a hard-core application developer creating object-oriented programs using classes? The answer is a resounding "yes." Motion graphics is predominantly about speed and responsiveness, and all developers want to spend less time debugging and more time being creative. Strict typing lets you perform less runtime checking, which improves performance, and the compile-time checks catch potential errors that would cause silent failure in Flash MX.

So you get better, more robust code using ActionScript 2.0 type checking, even if your code is brief and doesn't use object-oriented techniques. The additional type checking makes it more likely your code will work correctly once it compiles successfully, and there is no runtime performance hit [Hack #100].

How Strict Typing Helps

Let's have a look at how to implement some ActionScript 2.0 code and how strict typing helps when scripting motion graphics.

```
function makeDot(clip:MovieClip):Void {
  // Make a dot within clip
  clip.lineStyle(10, 0x0, 100);
  clip.moveTo(0, 0);
  clip.lineTo(1, 0);
}
function mover( ):Void {
  // Move the dot
  this.sX = checkLimits(this.sX, this._x, 0, 550);
  this.sY = checkLimits(this.sY, this._y, 0, 400);
  this._x += this.sX;
  this._y += this.sY;
}
function checkLimits(speed:Number, limit:Number,
                     low:Number, high:Number):Number {
  // Reverse direction when the dot hits an edge of the screen
  if ((limit < low) || (limit > high)) {
    return -speed;
  } else {
    return speed;
  }
}
var ball:MovieClip;
for (var i:Number = 0; i < 100; i++) {
  ball = this.createEmptyMovieClip("dot" + i, i);
  ball._x = Math.random( ) * Stage.width;
  ball._y = Math.random( ) * Stage.height;
  ball.onEnterFrame = mover;
  ball.sX = Math.random( ) * 8 + 2;
  ball.sY = Math.random( ) * 8 + 2;
  makeDot(ball);
}
```

Notice that var ball:MovieClip; declares the ball variable to be an instance of the *MovieClip* class (this is synonymous with saying that ball is of type *MovieClip* because a class declaration effectively defines a custom datatype of the same name). Specifying ball's type as *MoveClip* tells the compiler that the variable must contain a movie clip reference. We later use the ball variable to store a reference to the clip created at runtime with *createEmptyMovieClip( )*, such as clips dot0, dot1, and so on.

Notice that the datatype is specified after a colon, and whenever you define a datatype for a variable, the variable must be preceded by the *var* keyword.

If we try to assign a value that is not a movie clip reference, such as:

```
ball = 0;
ball = "dot+i";
```

the Flash compiler displays a type mismatch in the Output panel. Fixing it during authoring is easy and fast, whereas omitting the type checking would leave us staring at a blank Stage at runtime, wondering where the problem might lie.

Notice in the preceding example that the functions and event handlers are also typed. A function that doesn't return any value should be given a return type of Void (with a capital "V"):

```
function myName( ):Void {
  // Do stuff
};
```

If the preceding function returns a value, which it shouldn't, Flash displays an error at compile time.

A function that accepts arguments and returns a value is written like this:

```
Function myName(argument:argType):returnType {
  // Do stuff
  return someValue;
};
```

If we try to pass it an argument that is of the wrong datatype or if it returns the wrong datatype (i.e., if someValue isn't of the datatype specified by *returnType*), Flash again provides a compile-time error.

Using strict type checking helps the Flash compiler catch many bugs that would have caused runtime problems in Flash MX. ActionScript 2.0 strict typing helps to confine errors to one code block (such as a function or event handler) to prevent errors from propagating to other code that calls the problematic code.

Limitations of Strict Typing

Strict typing can't be quickly and easily used in all cases. Let's look at some of the limitations of compile-time type checking.

Dynamic properties are not type checked. Notice that in the preceding example, `ball.sX` and `ball.sY` are specified without a datatype. You cannot use the *var* keyword when you attach custom properties to a clip dynamically at runtime. Not being able to use *var* also means that you can't specify their datatype. Furthermore, because an untyped variable is allowed to be of any datatype, the Flash compiler wouldn't complain about the following (even though we intend `ball.sX` to hold a number not a string):

```
ball.sX = "cat";
```

Even though `ball.sX` is eventually accessed as `this.sX` inside the *mover( )* function and passed to the *checkLimits( )* function as a parameter named speed, where it is strictly typed as `Number`, Flash's compile-time validation can't detect such indirect errors. An untyped variable passes through all checks with no errors.

If you want to use strict typing to validate the datatype of properties, you have to create a custom class. You can then define the type of each class property or instance property within the class definition. For example, you can place this code in an external *Ball.as* file to create a custom *Ball* class that subclasses the *MovieClip* class:

```
// This ActionScript 2.0 code must go in an external Ball.as file
class Ball extends MovieClip {
  var sX:Number;
  var sY:Number;
}
```

Then, revising the earlier code example, you can declare the `ball` variable to be of type *Ball* instead of type *MovieClip*:

```
var ball:Ball;
```

Because of the class definition, Flash will perform type checking on instance properties such as `ball.sX` and `ball.sY`.

Conditional statements confuse type checking. Flash supports only compile-time type checking, so it does not run the code when it performs type checking. Therefore, it cannot detect cases involving *return* statements within conditional expressions. If an *if* statement is structured as follows, the *checkLimits( )* function won't return a value even though its return datatype is specified as *Number*:

```
function checkLimits(speed:Number, limit:Number,
                     low:Number, high:Number):Number {
```

```
    if (false)) {
      return -speed;
    }
  };
```

But Flash checks only the datatype of the expression following the return key-word, in this case -speed, and the preceding code does not cause a compile-time error.

Final Thoughts

ActionScript 2.0 provides type checking unavailable in ActionScript 1.0, without affecting runtime performance or complaining about untyped vari-ables (i.e., it won't choke on legacy ActionScript 1.0 code that hasn't been updated to ActionScript 2.0). Type checking helps you write correct, robust code by catching errors you might otherwise miss.

Although ActionScript 2.0 doesn't perform type checking at runtime and author-time type checking can't be quickly implemented in all cases, using type checking whenever possible saves scripters of all levels considerable time and aggravation.

Code Hints

#76

Flash's Actions panel provides code hints to ease scripting and prevent typographical errors. Take advantage of code hinting without having to name your variables with datatype-specific suffixes.

Flash MX introduced a code hints system in the Actions panel (F9). Code hints appear as a context-sensitive drop-down list that suggests relevant method names and property names appropriate to the current item's datatype. Flash MX used an item name's suffix to determine its datatype. For example, to activate code hinting for a *Color* class instance, the instance name had to end with the "_color" suffix. Pressing the period (.) key after an identifier with an appropriate suffix displays the code hint drop-down list as shown in Figure 10-4.

Figure 10-4. The code hint drop-down list is activated in response to the item's suffix, such as "_color"

Of course nobody likes having to name his color instance myColor_color or his sound instance siteSound_sound. Even Macromedia didn't bother to use suffixes in much of its own documentation. Furthermore, the dependency on suffixes required you to remember the code hinting suffix for each class ("_mc" for the *MovieClip* class, etc.).

A little-known feature in Flash MX is that you could force code hinting without using a suffix by specifying a variable's type using a comment instead. For example, a comment of the following form—the semicolon is mandatory—activates code hinting for the identifier, in this case foo, as if it belonged to the specified class, *MovieClip*:

```
// MovieClip foo;
```

If you are using either suffixes or comments to activate code hinting, with less effort you can get both code hinting and strict typing in ActionScript 2.0 [Hack #75]. In ActionScript 2.0, simply specify the datatype using post-colon syntax, as shown in Figure 10-5, to activate both code hinting and strict typing regardless of the identifier's name (or lack of suffix).

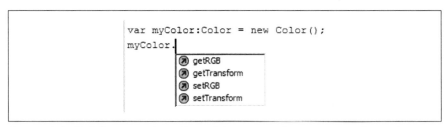

Figure 10-5. Code hinting in ActionScript 2.0 is activated in response to the item's declared datatype

Cool. So now you don't have to mess around with suffixes to make use of code hinting. You can even declare datatypes for instance names specified for movie clips, text fields, and buttons in the Properties panel. (Remember, these assets can be dragged from the Library onto the Stage in addition to being created via ActionScript.) Simply declare the datatype for the clip, text field, or button using a *var* statement as shown in Figure 10-6.

```
var myClip:MovieClip;
myClip.
        _accProps
        _alpha
        _currentframe
        _droptarget
        _focusrect
        _framesloaded
        _height
        _lockroot
```

Figure 10-6. You can declare the datatype for instance names defined in the Properties panel for movie clips, text fields, or buttons

This hack saves time when using class instances, especially instances of the *MovieClip* and *Button* classes, which have many methods with long names such as *createEmptyMovieClip( )*!

HACK #77 Clone an Object

ActionScript copies objects by reference rather than by value. Clone an object to create an independent copy rather than a reference to the original.

In many situations, you will store values as properties of a single object, instead of as separate variables, because the first technique offers a cleaner, more structured approach. However objects are not always treated the same way as simple variables. Consider the following code:

```
var x = 5;
var y = x;
trace(y);    // Displays: 5
x += 1;
trace(x);    // Displays: 6
trace(y);    // Displays: 5
```

We set x equal to 5, assign the value of x to y, and then increment x. After the example, the value of x is 6 and the value of y is 5. As expected, they are independent; changing the value of x after the assignment statement var y = x; doesn't alter the value of y. Therefore, variables that hold primitive values such as numbers are said to be *passed by value* because ActionScript copies the value held in variable x at the time it is assigned to the variable y.

Let's try the analogous operation with objects:

```
var obj1 = new Object( );
obj1.prop = 5;
var obj2 = obj1;
trace(obj2.prop);  // Displays: 5
obj1.prop += 1;
trace(obj1.prop);  // Displays: 6
trace(obj2.prop);  // Displays: 6
```

This time, we create object obj1, add property prop to it, and set obj2 equal to obj1. Do we have two separate objects? Immediately after the assignment, obj2.prop is 5, as we'd expect. However, if we increment obj1.prop and then trace the value of obj1.prop and obj2.prop, we find they are the same—they are both 6. Did you expect obj2.prop to still be 5 even after obj1.prop was set to 6?

The explanation is that we have not created two separate objects, but two references to a single object (both obj1 and obj2 hold a pointer to the same location of the object's data in memory, not a primitive datum such as the number 6).

Because both obj1.prop and obj2.prop point to the same thing in memory, changes made to the value via either reference are reflected in both. This is akin to the way that you can drag a single symbol to the Stage multiple times to create multiple movie clip instances. If you change the Library symbol of the movie clip, all instances reflect the change. (However, the analogy doesn't hold 100%. Movie clip instances, although dependent on the Library symbol, are independent of one another. Changes to the instance properties of one clip are not reflected in other clips derived from the same Library symbol.)

Complex datatypes such as objects and arrays are said to be *passed by reference*. Complex datatypes can be very large, so passing them by reference is more efficient. For example, to operate on an array, Flash need pass only a pointer to the array rather than all the data within it.

This can be a problem, however, if you want the duplicate to be a separate copy rather than a reference to the original. You could clone an object by defining each property explicitly:

```
var obj1 = new Object();
obj1.prop1 = 5;
obj1.prop2 = 12;
var obj2 = new Object();
obj2 .prop1 = obj1.prop1;
obj2 .prop2 = obj1.prop2;
trace(obj2.prop1);    // Displays: 5
obj1.prop1 += 1;
trace(obj1.prop1);    // Displays: 6
trace(obj2.prop1);    // Displays: 5 (not 6)
```

The two objects, obj1 and obj2, and their properties, such as obj1.prop1 and obj2.prop1, are now independent.

We can build our own method to create a unique copy of an object rather than a reference to it, by adding the following *clone()* method to the *Object* class. This is ActionScript 1.0 code, but it will work in ActionScript 2.0 as well.

```
Object.prototype.clone = function() {
  if ( (typeof this) != "object" || (this instanceof Button) ||
      (this instanceof TextField) ) {
    // Return the original reference if this is a movie clip,
    // button, or text field (i.e., don't clone these types).
    return this;
  }
  var c = new Object();
  for (var n in this) {
    var o = this[n];
    if ( (typeof o) == "object" &&
          !(o instanceof Button || o instanceof TextField)) {
```

```
      // Property is itself an object, so clone it recursively
      c[n] = o.clone( );
    } else {
      // Properties that are primitives are copied by value.
      // Otherwise, it's a reference to a function, MovieClip,
      // Button, or TextField, which we'll copy by reference
      // because we can't easily create an onscreen representation.
      c[n] = o;
    }
  }
  return c;
}
// Keep clone instance method from showing up in for...in loops,
// and protect it from deletion:
ASSetPropFlags(Object.prototype,["clone"],5,1);
```

The preceding code adds a new *Object.clone( )* method to the *Object* class. It also works with most classes that inherit from *Object*, as all ActionScript classes do. The preceding code does not, however, attempt to clone movie clips, because the built-in *MovieClip.duplicateMovieClip( )* method can already create an independent copy of a clip. Although you could use *duplicateMovieClip( )* within the preceding code to clone nested clips, typically you wouldn't want to duplicate a clip just because more than one object has a property that refers to it. Similarly, you won't ordinarily want to clone existing text fields or buttons. You're more likely to use, say, *MovieClip.createTextField( )* to create a new text field rather than clone an existing one.

Given the preceding definition of the *clone( )* method, the following snippet creates an independent copy (i.e., clone) of obj1 and stores a reference to the new, independent object in obj2:

```
obj2 = obj1.clone( );
```

Contrast the preceding with:

```
obj2 = obj1;
```

which simply makes obj2 store a reference to the same object as obj1.

Notice that:

- If the *clone( )* method is invoked on one of the graphical classes (a movie clip, button, or text field), it returns a reference to the object instead of cloning it. If the original is a primitive object, such as a number, it returns the value.

- Likewise, the *clone( )* method creates references rather than clones when an object property is a primitive or an instance of one of the graphical classes.

- Only enumerable properties are attached to the cloned object. Enumerable properties include those you would usually want to search through within a *for...in* loop (such as custom properties and methods created by the developer) but not preset properties that define how the class works internally or ActionScript methods.

- We use the undocumented *ASSetPropFlags( )* [Hack #82] to protect our new *Object.clone( )* method from deletion and hide it from *for...in* loops.

You can test the *clone( )* method as follows:

```
// Create an object containing a nested object for testing
obj = {name:"test", num:10, bool:true,
  childObj:{childName:"original child name", childNum:5}, root:_root};
// Clone the object
cloneOfObj = obj.clone( );

// Change a value in the new object
cloneOfObj.childObj.childName = "changed child name";

// Check to see if the two values are independent (they are)
trace("obj.childObj.childName = " + obj.childObj.childName);
trace("cloneOfObj.childObj.childName = " + cloneOfObj.childObj.childName);
```

The preceding code demonstrates how both the clone object and its child object are independent of the original object or its child object. The *clone( )* method saves you from having to copy properties and user-defined methods manually if you want a new copy of an object.

Cloning for Motion Graphics

Call me old-fashioned, but I prefer to look at data and its effects visually, so here's another example in which you can see the difference between data that has been cloned versus data copied by reference.

The following code creates an sData ("sprite data") object, which is used to control several semi-transparent circular clips to produce a particle effect. The effect works by creating many identical movie clips, each of which has an independent instance of sData on its timeline.

```
function animate( ):Void {
  this.sData = sData.clone( )
  this._x = this.sData.x;
  this._y = this.sData.y;
  this.lineStyle(10, 0x404040, 10);
  this.moveTo(-0.5, 0);
  this.lineTo(0, 0);
  this.onEnterFrame = function( ) {
    this.sData.x += Math.random( ) * this.sData.s - sData.s / 2;
    this.sData.y += Math.random( ) * this.sData.s - sData.s / 2;
    this._x = this.sData.x;
    this._y = this.sData.y;
```

```
   };
}
var sData:Object = new Object( );
sData.x = 275;
sData.y = 200;
sData.s = 4;

for (var i:Number = 0; i < 500; i++) {
  var dot:MovieClip = this.createEmptyMovieClip("dot" + i,
                      this.getNextHighestDepth( ));
  dot.onEnterFrame = animate;
}
```

Notice that the preceding code contains an example of a common and proper use of copying a movie clip by reference. The dot variable holds a reference to the movie clip instance dot*i*. It always points to the movie clip created within the loop without making a clone of the clip.

Each clip is unique and maintains its independent properties, such as size and position. The code creates a simple Brownian motion (random particle movement) simulation, as seen in gases and in Figure 10-7. All 500 clips are independent.

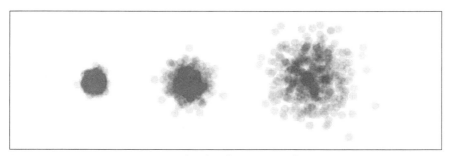

Figure 10-7. Brownian motion simulated with 500 movie clips

If you change the first line in the *animate( )* function so that it copies by reference instead of cloning:

```
this.sData = sData;
```

you get a totally different result, as shown in Figure 10-8.

Figure 10-8. Failing to clone (separate) the sData results in a clumpy animation

In the independent example, each clip has its own sData object with separate x and y coordinates, so the dots move independently. In the non-independent version, a single sData object is used throughout (i.e., all the local versions of this.sData contain a reference back to the original, sData).

Therefore, changing the properties of sData via one reference changes the properties of every this.sData. Instead of a random distribution, you get a constrained squiggle shape that dances around the Stage. All the particles act as part of a single, larger graphic entity because their controlling data is now related; they have lost their individuality.

Final Thoughts

References to existing clips are often used in loops when you'd rather avoid referring to separate clips by separate names. For example, in the following loop, we want to refer to the current movie clip that was just created with *createEmptyMovieClip( )*. It is much easier to refer to the new clip using the reference myClip rather than write code that refers to the movie clips (clip0 to clip9) by their specific instance names.

```
for (i = 0; i < 10; i++) {
  var myClip:MovieClip = this.createEmptyMovieClip("clip" + i, i);
  // Code that uses current clip, myClip goes here
  myClip._rotation = 50;
}
```

In some cases, using a reference is typically an error on the programmer's part—she might want to create independent objects instead; the *Object. clone( )* method presented here allows you to easily create independent objects. In motion graphics, swapping between independent (unique) data and references allows you to create vastly different final effects with very little effort.

—*Grant Skinner*

An Idle Timer (Timeout Event)

#78   When performance is critical, you don't want to waste processor time checking for user interactivity. Add a "no-interaction" timeout event that does not interfere with performance-sensitive multimedia delivery during periods of interaction.

I was asked to develop a Flash-based questionnaire application that ran on the screens on the backs of aircraft passenger seats. When the questionnaire was left idle, Flash should start playing some video. It should switch back quickly to the questionnaire if the user moved or clicked the mouse, so I set up some idle-detection code. However, the video playback became jerky if the idle-detection code wasn't highly optimized.

Macromedia Director has an *idle* event that fires whenever Director is not doing anything, allowing you to use this spare time doing something constructive via a background task. It's normal for Flash designers to increase the frame rate until Flash doesn't have any idle time (it is significantly lower than the Director idle time in any case because Flash performance is slower than Director's). So Flash doesn't provide built-in support for an idle event to be triggered when no other processing is being performed, because it isn't really appropriate to the way Flash is used.

That set me thinking. I needed an idle event that looks for no user interaction, which would be a more appropriate time for Flash to do some different processing. If no activity is detected, the SWF could, say, display an appropriate animation or an audible prompt. (In Director, these are called *timeout* events, but again, Flash has no native support for detecting when the user is inactive.)

It is common for users to leave Flash sites open while rich media elements (such as video or sound) load and then do something else in another browser window. Rather than have the SWF wait on a "content loaded" message screen when the download is complete, it would be nice for the SWF to provide an audible cue if the user hasn't responded to the fact that content loading has completed.

In kiosk applications, you might want the SWF to return to an attract loop (i.e., a screen displaying a video or animation intended to attract passers-by) when no user activity has been detected within the timeout period.

The key is creating an idle-detection routine that doesn't consume processing power when the user *is* interacting with the SWF. The most obvious event for detecting user activity is *onMouseMove* (a user who is moving the mouse is presumed to be breathing). However, when the user is actively using the application, the *onMouseMove* event occurs often enough to affect performance of the main SWF, so we should avoid relying on this event when designing a background event handler.

A more processor-friendly way to detect interaction is to use two *setInterval( )* timers as follows:

- Use a short interval that checks for interaction every one to two seconds (not often enough to adversely affect performance).

- Use a long interval (typically 15 to 120 seconds) that specifies the timeout period length. This interval is reset whenever the short interval detects user activity.

So, we have two intervals that occur relatively infrequently compared to events like *onEnterFame*, which occurs once for each Flash frame. The key is to make the code as minimal as possible to avoid a performance hit; too much background processing will make Flash sluggish.

Here's a short code listing that shows the two intervals in action. The more frequent of our two intervals executes minimal code (only one *if* statement). The commented *trace( )* statements can be uncommented to see what the code is doing during the interval periods (be aware that *trace( )* statements are time consuming, so you don't want them in your final version).

```
function idleTime( ) {
    // Play the attract animation
    //trace("playing the animation")
    gotoAndStop("attract");
}
function idleS( ) {
    // See if there has been any mouse movement in the last two seconds
    if ((_root._xmouse + _root._ymouse) != mousePos) {
        // If there has, restart the check for the idle timer
        //trace("resetting");
        gotoAndStop("noAttract");
        clearInterval(idle);
        idle = setInterval(idleTime, 28000);
    //} else {
        //trace("no movement this period");
    }
    // Store an integer representing the mouse position
    mousePos = _root._xmouse + _root._ymouse;
}
function startIdle( ) {
    mousePos = -100000;   // Initialize it to a dummy value
    idleSample = setInterval(idleS, 2000);
}
startIdle( );
stop( );
```

The first interval, idleSample, checks the mouse position every two seconds (it is better to check for mouse movement this way rather than *onMouseMove*, because *onMouseMove* happens sufficiently often to possibly slow down your Flash application). If the sum of the mouse x and y positions do not remain the same between two interval invocations, the user has moved the mouse, so we reset the second, longer interval, idle. If no interaction occurs before the idle interval reaches its timeout value (28 seconds), the *idleTime( )* function executes and sends the playhead to the attract frame (which typically displays a looping animation or possibly a video).

If desired, you can modify the code so that the *idleTime( )* function starts a wait animation and the *idleS( )* function stops it. The wait animation would typically be a screensaver-style animation or a "where have you gone?" animation.

This preceding code carries on indefinitely until 30 seconds (2,000 + 28,000 ms) of inactivity causes Flash to invoke the *idleTime( )* function, which jumps to the attract frame. Presumably, an *onMouseDown( )* event handler on that frame aborts the attractor animation and starts the presentation anew when the user clicks the mouse.

Final Thoughts

To maintain Flash performance, you have to minimize background tasks operating when rich media (video, sound, or complex animation at fast frame rates) are also being delivered. This means that your background tasks have to be highly optimized. The "check for idle user" code presented doesn't run often, so that when the user is interacting with the site, it does not slow down the main content.

When the user has not been interacting for some time, the code allows switching to an attract loop or screensaver-style animation. This would be useful for kiosk applications in which you want the Flash movie to reset to the beginning if no user is presently interacting with it. One caveat: be sure that your timeout period (such as 30 seconds) is longer than, say, any animation sequence you expect the user to sit through. If the user is watching your kiosk run, you don't want it to suddenly time out. So you might have to lengthen your timeout to allow for expected periods of inactivity even when a user is present and otherwise active. If you expect a user to sit passively through something for more than, say, 90 seconds, it is probably time to rethink your kiosk design instead of merely increasing the timeout duration.

Similarly, it is a good idea to have keypress events reset the timeout period. Otherwise, if the user is entering text in a form but not moving her mouse, the movie might unceremoniously jump to the attract loop. Therefore, if your kiosk has a keyboard, use *Key.addListener( )* to invoke an *onKeyDown( )* event handler that resets the idle interval.

Fast ActionScript Searches

#79 Searching through arrays and text in ActionScript can be slow. Create fast text search code with some string manipulation tricks.

Although Flash Player 7 performs faster than its predecessors, text and array processing can still take considerable time. When creating code that performs searches, it is typical to use a *while* or *for* loop. The trouble with repeated operations such as loops is that Flash isn't truly a compiled language; when publishing a SWF, Flash converts human-readable Action-Script into bytecode that the Flash Player can understand. For every loop iteration, at runtime, the Flash Player has to convert each line of bytecode into executable instructions before it is run.

The code may run faster if you avoid repeated operations in a loop, as shown in the following listing. It implements three versions of a simple search through an array.

```
method1 = function ( ) {
  // Search through array sequentially
  for (var i = 0; i < arr.length; i++) {
    if (arr[i] == nr) {
      return true;
    }
  }
  return false;
};
method2 = function ( ) {
  // Search through array as an object
  var i:String;
  for (i in arr) {
    if (arr[i] == nr) {
      return true;
    }
  }
  return false;
};
method3 = function ( ) {
  // Search through array by first converting its
  // elements to a single string.
  var searchPos:Number = arr.join(" ").indexOf(nr.toString( ));
  if (searchPos != -1) {
    return true;
  }
  return false;
};
// Create array containing the sequence 0 to 999 to search through
var arr:Array = new Array( );
var elem:Number = 1000;
for (var i = 0; i < elem; i++) {
  arr.push(i);
}
// Determine random number to search for
var nr:Number = Math.floor(Math.random( ) * elem);
trace("searching for:" + nr);
// Test method 1
var sT = getTimer( );
method1( );
eT = getTimer( ) - sT;
trace("time method 1 : " + eT);
// Test method 2
var sT = getTimer( );
method2( );
eT = getTimer( ) - sT;
trace("time method 2 : " + eT);
```

```
var sT = getTimer( );
method3( );
eT = getTimer( ) - sT;
trace("time method 3 : " + eT);
```

First, the code defines an array containing the sequence 0 to 999. Then it picks a random number, nr, between 0 and 999 to search for.

```
var nr:Number = Math.floor(Math.random( ) * elem);
```

Our test executes three functions, *method1( )*, *method2( )*, and *method3( )*, which search the array for the number.

The first function, *method1( )*, is a simple *for* loop search. It looks at each array element in turn and tests whether it is equal to the number for which we are searching. If the number is found, the function returns true. The second function, *method2( )*, uses a *for...in* loop. Finally, the third method, *method3( )*, doesn't use a loop at all; instead, it builds a string consisting of all entries in the array, separated by spaces (so we will have "0 1 2 3 4 5... 997 998 999"). It then searches for the value nr within it as a string.

You can see the speed of each search by running the code a few times. Optimizing code by benchmark testing [Hack #69] helps diagnose a huge variety of problems.

The third search function, *method3( )*, is the fastest overall and maintains a constant and low search time. Rather than using loops, it converts our data into strings and uses Flash's string manipulation methods on the result. Because it runs the fewest lines of code (it is the only search out of the three that doesn't use a loop), it is somewhat faster than the other searches. (The *Array.join( )* operation required to convert the array into a string is relatively fast because it is executed in C++, the compiled language in which native Flash functions are written.) The *String* and *Array* class methods on which this hack relies give relatively fast results in Flash Player 6 and 7. Earlier versions of the Flash Player yield poorer results.

The preceding implementations tell you whether the target value is in the array but not *where* it is within the array. The speed of the search, however, depends on where in the array the sought-after value is found.

The *for* loop is the faster of the two loop-based search functions, if the match is found early in the array:

```
searching for:153
time method 1 : 2
time method 2 : 7
time method 3 : 2
```

If the search match is made near the middle of the array, then the two loop searches come out even:

```
searching for:418
time method 1 : 5
time method 2 : 5
time method 3 : 2
```

If the search match is made toward the end of the array, the second search function is faster than the first. This is because the *for...in* loop searches properties (array elements in this example) in the reverse order they were created in the searched object, with the last elements created being the first ones searched.

```
searching for:777
time method 1 : 8
time method 2 : 4
time method 3 : 2
```

But in all three cases, the third search method is the fastest and has the most consistently predictable search time. If you know the contents of the array aren't changing, you can make it even faster by storing the result of the *join( )* method and reusing it in future invocations.

The string search approach slows down when the data set is large, but it is still faster than the other methods for searches up to about 10,000 array elements. Realistically, if you are searching data sets of that magnitude, you should perform the search on a remote server and return the results to Flash via, say, Flash Remoting.

Final Thoughts

Looping is a common way to carry out a repetitive set of operations, but Flash loops can be very time consuming. Recognizing the strengths and weaknesses of these three types of search—element search loop, property search loop, nonlooping string search—allows you to create optimized code for any given application.

—Suggested by Edwin Heijmen

HACK #80   Lock the actions Layer

ActionScript can be placed almost anywhere on the timeline. Keep your scripts on a dedicated, locked *actions* layer to promote separation of code from assets.

In animation applications, the timeline represents the passage of time. Flash generates an event (*onEnterFrame*) every time the next frame interval has started. That makes perfect sense until you start adding code into the mix.

Unlike other scripting languages in which scripts are stored centrally, Flash code can be attached to keyframes anywhere on the timeline, usually in the order in which it needs to run, using the Actions panel.

Some developers choose to centralize their ActionScript on frame 1 of the main timeline, but in many projects, at least some code is attached to keyframes other than frame 1. Many developers even attach code to buttons and movie clips on various layers. As the timeline becomes long and many layers are added with code scattered throughout, the Flash movie becomes more difficult to debug and maintain. Developers often need to use the Movie Explorer (Window → Other Panels → Movie Explorer) just to locate their code!

To minimize the problem, name the first layer in your timeline *actions* (or *scripts*) and attach all your scripts only to that layer. Using a dedicated layer just for scripts helps to centralize your code (you can use the same layer for any frame labels you add via the Properties panel or create a *labels* layer for that purpose).

Instead of attaching code directly to buttons and movie clips on other layers, give your buttons and movie clips instance names using the Properties panel. Then you can "attach" code to a movie clip indirectly by using its instance name in code written elsewhere. The ActionScript code should be placed on the *actions* layer, not on the layer containing the clip, nor on the clip's timeline. For example, if a movie clip has the instance name `ballClip`, you can refer to it from code on the *actions* layer of the main timeline and set its x coordinate as follows:

```
var ballClip:MovieClip;
ballClip._x = 50;
```

Locking a Layer

One simple trick to keep your *actions* layer as a script-only layer is to keep it permanently locked. Flash allows you to lock any layer in the timeline by clicking the dot in the padlock column that appears adjacent to the layer, as seen in Figure 10-9. To unlock a layer, click the padlock icon that indicates a locked layer (in Figure 10-9, *Layer 2* is locked). Locking a layer doesn't prevent the layer from being edited, as you might assume; however, it does prevent anything from being added onto the Stage in the locked layer.

Even when the layer is locked, you can:

- Add keyframes to the locked layer (scripts can be attached only to keyframes). To add a keyframe, select a frame on the locked layer and press F6 (or choose Insert → Timeline → Keyframe) as you would with any unlocked layer.

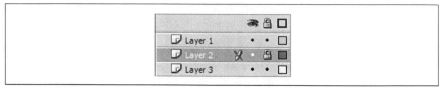

Figure 10-9. To lock a layer, click the dot in the padlock column

- Attach or edit scripts associated with keyframes on the layer using the Actions panel (F9).

- Insert frames on the locked layer. To add a frame, select a frame on the locked layer and press F5 (or choose Insert → Timeline → Frame) as you would with any unlocked layer. Subsequent frames are pushed to the right by the newly inserted frame.

So, locking the *actions* layer prevents you from drawing graphics in it or attaching symbols to its keyframes (thus keeping it a script-only layer). However, you can add and edit keyframes and scripts, even though it remains locked.

Final Thoughts

Although storing code in external *.as* files is appropriate and recommended in many applications, as is storing all your code in the first frame of the main timeline when possible, this is just not practical when:

- You are creating a full-length animation with ActionScript control of timelines, such as for *The Goober Story* (*http://www.humbugz.com/hela.htm*).

- You want to create simple timeline control. For example, it's overkill to write a custom class to stop a movie clip at frame 12. It's far better (and more performance efficient) to simply add a *stop()* action at the required frame!

- You want to attach an event handler to a movie clip instance that doesn't exist on the first frame. You cannot attach an event handler on an instance before it exists. If a movie clip doesn't exist on the timeline until frame 34, you can attach the event handler to it using a script on the *actions* layer in frame 34, but not in frame 33.

Even when such issues tend to spread out your code, you can still keep the majority of your code on frame 1 of the *actions* layer if you write all your scripts and event handlers as functions and call the functions on the frames on which they are required. This keeps most of your ActionScript on frame 1.

Debug with trace( )

The *trace( )* action displays text in the Output panel. Use the *trace( )* action to maximum effect as a debugging tool.

Although the debugger (Window → Development Panels → Debugger and Control → Debug Movie) is useful for real-time debugging, it is often easier to use the *trace( )* action to display output in the Output panel. However, *trace( )* accepts only one expression for output. To display more (and more useful data), use string concatenation (the + operator) to build a more complex expression for output.

Suppose you want to output information on the following data:

```
var x:Number = 10;
var y:Number = 20;
var z:Array = [10, 20, 30, 40];
var w:Object = {p1:10, p2:"hello", p3:true};
```

If x and y contain coordinates, you might display them in (x, y) format on a single line using:

```
trace("(" + x + ", " + y + ")");
```

which displays:

```
(10, 20)
```

You can use multiple *trace( )* statements or the "\n" escape sequence to split the output over more than one line. This:

```
trace("x is: " + x);
trace("y is: " + y);
```

and this:

```
trace("x is: " + x + "\n" + "y is: " + y + "\n");
```

both display:

```
x is: 10
y is: 20
```

When working with arrays, simply tracing the array (i.e., passing the array to the *trace( )* function) will display a list of all the elements in the array. Assuming the earlier value assigned for z, this code:

```
trace(z)
```

displays:

```
10,20,30,40
```

Notice that there are no spaces in the output display for array contents. To format the output in a more appealing manner, you can specify a delimiter using the *Array.join( )* method:

```
trace (z.join(", ");
```

which displays:

```
10, 20, 30, 40
```

This code:

```
trace (z.join("\n");
```

adds line breaks between items:

```
10
20
30
40
```

When working with objects, you need to use a *for...in* loop to view the enumerable properties of the object. Assuming the earlier value assigned for w, this code:

```
for (var i in w) {
    trace("w." + i + " = " + w [i]);
}
```

displays:

```
w.p1 = 10
w.p2 = hello
w.p3 = true
```

Note that the nonenumerable properties (such as built-in methods and properties that ActionScript has hidden) can be displayed using the undocumented *ASSetPropFlags( )* function [Hack #82].

Often your ActionScript doesn't do what you hoped and you don't know why. The culprit is often an invalid instance (you think that a variable holds a valid movie clip or object instance when in fact it does not), which could be caused by a programming error or because you mistyped (or forgot) the instance name in the Properties panel. Unfortunately, the Flash Player fails silently if it can't perform an operation because the specified instance is invalid. This can be a difficult problem to debug because:

- It usually occurs when you are creating movie clips dynamically or when you have a full timeline hierarchy, so the debugger may be too cluttered to make the problem apparent.

- Although the instance may be shown in the debugger, it may not have existed at the start of the frame, or the variable may not have the scope you expect. To debug this type of problem with the debugger, you have to set breakpoints and manually step through the code, line by line, which can be time consuming.

An easier way to see whether your instance is valid at the point your code expects it is to use a *trace( )* debugging statement of the form:

```
for (var i in this) {
  if (i.indexOf("myClip", 0) != -1) {
    trace(myClip._name + " is on timeline " + this);
  }
}
```

If the instance myClip can be seen on the main timeline, the line will display
"myClip is on timeline _level0" in the Output panel. Otherwise, it will display nothing. Notice that the output message is very precise about what was
found and where, the hallmark of a good debug message. The message
"found it!" may not mean that much six months down the line. Similarly,
make sure that each of your *trace( )* statements prints out different text to
distinguish which *trace( )* statement was reached. For example, this code
displays the type of the incoming argument. If incoming is an object, it displays, "Incoming object in checkObject( ) is of type: object."

```
function checkObject(incoming) {
  trace("Incoming object in checkObject( ) is of type: "
    + typeof incoming);
}
```

You can add an identifying string and a ">" to your *trace( )* messages in
order to make the program's execution and results easier to understand:

```
survey.fla > Starting up.
xmlutils   > Loaded.
view       > Loaded. Let's draw  the display.
display    > Drawing.
```

Final Thoughts

Debugging information is usually required at authoring time only, and you
can force Flash to omit all *trace( )* actions by checking the Omit Trace
Actions option under File → Publish Settings → Flash. This prevents *trace( )*
statements from being exported and is the same as globally commenting out
all *trace( )* statements in the FLA.

For more complex debugging and to prevent being overwhelmed by the output from *trace( )* statements, you can create a custom, centralized tracing
function. Then, you can manually comment out the body of the debugging
function when you publish the final site. (For optimal performance, you
could comment out each individual function invocation.)

The following code shows a simple system to assign a verbosity level to
debugging messages. Debugging messages are queued using the function
cTrace(message, priority). If priority is below the verboseLevel threshold,
the message is not displayed in the Output panel. In the following example,
both messages are seen if you set verboseLevel to 0, but only the first is seen
if you set verboseLevel to 1.

```
cTrace = function (message, priority) {
  if (priority >= verboseLevel) {
    trace(message);
  }
};
// Usage:
verboseLevel = 1;
cTrace("Important message", 1);      // Displayed
cTrace("Low-priority message", 0); // Not displayed
```

Another enhancement would be to create message filtering. For example, if you have a file with many errors, you may want to fix the most important issues first, followed by the less important ones. The following code hides all messages that are of a lower priority than the last most important one. This allows you to hone in on the debug information that is most likely needed to fix your code. In the following example, the last message is not seen because a higher priority error appears to be the one causing the problem.

For example, if the very important message was, "XML file not loading," the less important message, "Unexpected characters found in XML file," would be filtered out until you have the XML loading in the first place!

```
cTrace = function (message, priority) {
  if (priority >= verboseLevel) {
    verboseLevel = priority;
    trace(message);
  }
};
// Usage:
verboseLevel = 0;
cTrace("XML file not loading", 2);
cTrace("Unexpected characters found in XML file", 1);
```

Finally, you can also output messages using text fields if you want to test outside the authoring environment (such as in the browser). The following code modifies the previous listing to redirect diagnostics information to a text field instance, myText, presumed to exist on the Stage (changes are shown in bold). The easiest way to stop such output is to change the layer the text field is on into a guide layer.

```
cTrace = function (message, priority) {
  if (priority > verboseLevel) {
    verboseLevel = priority;
    myText.text += message + "\n";
  }
};
```

Undocumented ActionScript

#82

Everyone likes knowing about undocumented ActionScript. Discover the goodies in the `_global` property that Macromedia isn't ready to officially support.

You'll often want to examine the properties of an object to achieve a larger goal. For example, you might want to list an object's property values in the Output panel for debugging purposes. Or you might want to decode the unknown properties of an object returned by, say, a server-side database call so you can parse the data intelligently. But this is a hacks book, so of course we want to *enumerate* (list) hidden properties of ActionScript to see if we can find any undocumented goodies.

ActionScript's basic *for...in* loop effectively says to the Flash interpreter, "Look at the object of interest, and for each of its properties (including its methods stored within properties), execute the body of the loop once. And while you're at it, tell me the name of the current property. Love the shoes, babe."

However, many of ActionScript's built-in methods and properties aren't enumerable within a *for...in* loop by default. Macromedia assumes you want to see the objects and properties that your code creates, not the ones that underpin ActionScript, so they hid a lot of the built-in properties from being enumerated with *for...in*. However, the undocumented *ASSetPropflags( )* function can make properties and methods visible even if they aren't ordinarily enumerable within a *for...in* loop.

Macromedia has a habit of adding new functionality to late builds of earlier major releases. For example, many new Flash Player 7 features were undocumented and unsupported (but work!) in Flash Player 6.0.65.0. I check whether anything noteworthy has been added whenever Macromedia releases a new Flash Player, particularly if it's late in the product's lifecycle.

As its name suggests, *ASSetPropFlags( )* allows you to set property flags within ActionScript. These flags tell the Flash Player whether to enumerate the specified methods and properties within a *for...in* loop.

You can also use *ASSetPropFlags( )* to make your custom objects' properties and methods unwritable (or unenumerable), so that no one can inadvertently overwrite them. This is especially true of global properties you might use in components you distribute to prevent conflicts with other third-party components used in the same SWF.

Okay, let's have a quick look at how it works.

ASSetPropFlags( ) takes the following form:

```
ASSetPropFlags(object, properties, setTrue, setFalse)
```

where:

object

Is the object or scope that you want to examine.

properties

Is the properties/methods of *object* for which you want to change the protection flags. You also have the option of setting *properties* to null, which acts as a wildcard that means "all properties."

setTrue

Is an integer bitmask specifying the configuration flags. The last 3 bits of this integer are the important ones and represent (rightmost bit to leftmost) the "protect from overwrite," "protect from deletion," and "hide" flags. For example, setting *setTrue* to 110 binary (06 in hex or 6 in decimal) keeps them protected from overwrite and deletion but unhides the properties specified by *properties*.

setFalse

Is another integer bitmask that works like *setTrue*, except it sets the attributes to false. The *setFalse* bitmask is applied before *setTrue* is applied.

The FlashCoders Wiki (*http://chattyfig.figleaf.com/flashcoders-wiki/?ASSetPropFlags*) includes a chart describing various bitmasks used with *ASSetPropFlags( )*.

The properties/methods we want to make visible are those of the _global scope, which contains all the built-in ActionScript classes. We can thus make the entire set of classes within ActionScript enumerable via a *for...in* loop:

```
ASSetPropFlags(_global, null, 6, 1);
```

The following code unhides all of ActionScript and then looks to see what classes it can find:

```
// Set protection flags to 110 for _global to unhide everything
ASSetPropFlags(_global, null, 6, 1);
// List all objects in _global
for (thisObject in _global) {
  trace(thisObject);
}
```

To see if there is anything interesting within the classes, we can look at each property of the classes in turn. If we hit upon the prototype property—where methods and properties are stored for the class (whether using

ActionScript 1.0 or 2.0)—looking at its properties and methods should reveal whatever interesting tidbits lurk there:

```
// Set protection flags to 110 for _global to unhide everything
ASSetPropFlags(_global, null, 6, 1);
// List all objects in _global
for (thisObject in _global) {
  ASSetPropFlags(_global[thisObject], null, 6, 1);
  trace("\n" + thisObject);
  for (props in _global[thisObject]) {
    trace("  " + props);
    // List subitems found under prototype.
    if (props == "prototype") {
      ASSetPropFlags(_global[thisObject].prototype, null, 6, 1);
      for (protoChain in _global[thisObject].prototype) {
        trace("    " + protoChain);
      }
    }
  }
}
```

If you attach the preceding code to frame 1 and test the movie in Flash MX 2004, you'll see a lengthy display (which would stretch 10 pages in this book). The listing includes documented classes and their methods and properties, such as for the *String* class:

```
String
  fromCharCode
  __proto__
  constructor
  prototype
    substr
    split
    substring
    slice
    lastIndexOf
    indexOf
    concat
    charCodeAt
    charAt
    toLowerCase
    toUpperCase
    toString
    valueOf
    __proto__
    constructor
```

Note that this lists class methods and class properties followed by instance methods and instance properties indented under the prototype property.

You can try to access the methods and properties of the class using *trace( )* statements to see what they return. Here, I access the *String.fromCharCode( )* method, which I know accepts one numeric argument because it is a documented method:

```
trace(String.fromCharCode(65));   // Displays: A
```

However, the listing also includes undocumented classes, such as:

```
Cookie
  setCookie
  getCookie
  __proto__
  constructor
```

You'll have to guess whether a list item is a property or a method, and if it is a method, you might have to guess the expected parameters. For example:

```
trace(Cookie.getCookie( ));
```

displays the following:

```
Error opening URL "file:///C|/WINDOWS/PROFILES/SHAM%20B/
APPLICATION%20DATA/MACROMEDIA/FLASH%20MX%202004/EN/
CONFIGURATION/Mmfdata/mmfdata3ff9f1df.xml"
```

which tells me that it is trying to open a particular file even without me specifying a filename as a parameter!

So then I tried to create a cookie using *Cookie.setCookie( )*:

```
Cookie.setCookie("footest data");
```

Then, I tried calling *getCookie( )* again:

```
trace(Cookie.getCookie( ));
```

This time, there was no error! So the *setCookie( )* method must have successfully stored the file that *getCookie( )* was looking for.

So I fished the *mmfdata3ff9f1df.xml* file out of the folder cited in the preceding error message, opened it in a text editor, and sure enough, it contained my cookie text:

```
footest data
```

But trace(Cookie.getCookie( )); wasn't displaying anything in the Output panel, so I checked the datatype of the return value:

```
trace(typeof Cookie.getCookie( ));
```

Sure enough, it displayed "object" in the Output panel, so *getCookie( )* was returning an object! A quick *for...in* loop test displayed the object's properties, which, not surprisingly, were properties of the *XML* class (plus a few others). Here is the code confirming the object is an instance of the *XML* class (although more likely a custom subclass of the *XML* class). Test it in Flash MX 2004 to see the properties it displays.

```
Cookie.setCookie("footest data");
result = Cookie.getCookie( );
trace (typeof result);
trace (result instanceof XML);
for (props in result) {
  trace (props);
}
```

Decoding the XML structure to recover the original text ("footest data") specified in the original *setCookie( )* call, is left as an exercise for the reader.

Happy hunting!

Final Thoughts

Of course, undocumented features of the Flash Player are undocumented and unsupported for a reason. They may be beta features that don't work properly or haven't been thoroughly tested. There is no guarantee that undocumented features will be present in future versions of the Flash Player, so use them with caution. Even if it works on one browser and platform, it might not work on all of them.

H A C K #83 ASnative( ) Back Door

All ActionScript method calls are mapped to a table of internal functions built into the Flash Player. Directly access the internal function table via the undocumented *ASnative( )* method.

The Flash Player supports methods that are not exposed in the ActionScript API. That is, not only are some functions undocumented, they don't even have names! Instead, they are stored in a function table and accessed by indexing into that table.

The undocumented *ASnative( )* function can access internal ActionScript methods, including those not findable using *ASSetPropFlags( )* [Hack #82]. It appears to access functions in a lookup table by using two indexes:

```
ASnative(a, b);
```

or, in some cases, an optional argument list:

```
ASnative(a, b)(args);
```

where index *a* is an integer correlated to an ActionScript class, index *b* is an integer correlated to a method within the class, and args is one or more argument(s) associated with the method.

For example, using 200 for index *a* seems to access the *Math* class, so varying index *b* offers access to the *Math* class's methods. Try these:

```
trace(ASnative(200, 0)(-4.567)); // Displays 4.567
trace(ASnative(200, 9)(144));    // Displays 12
```

From these tests, you can conclude that *ASnative(200, 0)* accesses the *Math. abs( )* method, and *ASnative(200, 9)* accesses the *Math.sqrt( )* method. That's fine, but why would we want to use a cryptic *ASnative( )* call to access documented ActionScript methods?

Most (*a, b*) indexes into *ASnative( )* yield something that is exactly equivalent to a documented method of a documented class. However, some indexes have no exposed ActionScript equivalent, in which case the only way you can access them is via the *ASnative( )* back door.

ASnative(800, b) is one such set of indexes. Index 800 seems to access input/output functions, including undocumented methods of the *Mouse* class [Hack #62].

Final Thoughts

The "find the undocumented Flash Player features before Macromedia tells us about them" game is a favorite among longtime Flash users. See the FlashCoders Wiki (*http://chattyfig.figleaf.com/flashcoders-wiki/index. php?ASNative*) for a blow-by-blow account of this hunt to date and additional insights into the *ASnative( )* method and the parameters it accepts.

Obscure Operators
#84

Undocumented ActionScript isn't the only fertile hunting ground for the curious coder. Discover nonobvious uses for several obscure ActionScript operators.

Although ActionScript is large, typical developers can solve 90% of their problems using 10% of the available features. The remaining ActionScript is used only rarely or for very specific purposes. Some ActionScript is used rarely because developers don't know how to use it or it has a nonobvious use.

Here are a few alternative uses for obscure ActionScript commands and operators.

Modulo: Clamp and Snap

The modulo operator, %, returns the remainder of a division operation assuming no decimal part. For example, the result of 15 modulo 6 is 3, which is the remainder of 15 divided by 6:

```
trace(15 % 6); // Displays: 3
```

What is it good for? Because the result of a%b can never be greater than b, you can use modulo division to limit (*clamp* or *clip*) an expression a to the range 0 to b.

The following animation helps visualize the results. If you attach the following code to the first frame of a new movie, you will see that the center point of the ball movie clip never goes beyond the line at x = 300. The *clamp( )* function, which acts as the *onEnterFrame( )* handler for the ball clip, uses (this._x + speed)%300 to set the position of the ball. This limits ball._x to the range 0 to 300.

```
function clamp( ):Void {
  this._x = (this._x + speed)%300;
}
// Create ball
var ball:MovieClip = this.createEmptyMovieClip("ball",
                    this.getNextHighestDepth( ));
ball.lineStyle(20, 0x0, 100);
ball.lineTo(0, 1);
ball._x = 0;
ball._y = 200;

// Create line
this.lineStyle(null, 0x0, 100);
this.moveTo(300, 190);
this.lineTo(300, 210);
var speed = 4;

// Set up animation
ball.onEnterFrame = clamp;
```

Another use of modulo is in snapping a value to a particular multiple of a number. If x = a%b, you can constrain x to whole values that are divisible by b by either adding or subtracting x%b from x. These lines display 300 and 400:

```
x = 350;
trace(x - x%100); // Next closest lower number divisible by 100
trace(x + x%100); // Next closest higher number divisible by 100
```

The following code uses snapping in a simple drag-and-drop example. The ball movie clip follows the mouse, snapping to the nearest 30-pixel multiple.

```
ball.onMouseMove = function( ) {
  this._x = _xmouse - _xmouse%size;
  this._y = _ymouse - _ymouse%size;
  updateAfterEvent( );
};
size = 30;
```

The *dragger.fla* file on this book's web site uses the snapping code to create a series of tiles that can be arranged only along a grid. If you run the example and drag and drop the colored squares, you will see that they snap to the nearest whole position, allowing you to stack them edge to edge, as seen on the right side of Figure 10-10.

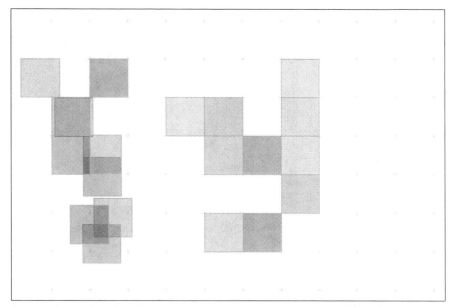

Figure 10-10. The colored squares snap into position as you drag and drop them

This sort of feature would be useful in:

- Flash puzzle games, especially sliding block games and jigsaws
- Flash tile-based action games (platform games)
- Flash board games
- Icon-driven Flash OS-type interfaces (in which you create a site that looks like an operating system desktop, typically driven by point, click, and drag-and-drop icons)

Optimize Range Checking

The *Math.abs( )* method returns an expression's absolute value. Math.abs(5) and Math.abs(-5) both return 5. Not the most exciting method, but it is an efficient way to limit a number at both ends of a scale. Simply offset the scale so that the top and bottom ends of the scale are the same absolute number (such as -5 and +5 instead of 0 and 10).

Checking the upper and lower limits for the x and y coordinates of a clip traditionally requires four conditionals. You can hack this down to two conditionals by moving the origin to the center of the Stage. In the case of a default Stage size (550×400), the leftmost and rightmost x positions are -275 and 275 (instead of 0 and 550) and the topmost and bottommost y positions are -200 and 200 (instead of 0 and 400).

This optimization isn't apparent unless you need things to run really fast, as in the following code. It uses *setInterval( )* with a one-millisecond interval to force Flash to run the animation as fast as it can. The optimized range-checking functions are shown in bold.

```
function anim(target:MovieClip):Void {
  if (Math.abs(target._x) > 275) {
    target.xSpeed = -target.xSpeed;
  }
  if (Math.abs(target._y) > 200) {
    target.ySpeed = -target.ySpeed;
  }
  target._x += target.xSpeed;
  target._y += target.ySpeed;
  updateAfterEvent();
}
// Create balls
for (var i = 0; i < 20; i++) {
  var ball:MovieClip = this.createEmptyMovieClip("ball"+i,
                       this.getNextHighestDepth());
  ball.lineStyle(5, 0x0808AF, 100);
  ball.lineTo(0, 1);
  ball.xSpeed = Math.random() * 10;
  ball.ySpeed = Math.random() * 10;
  this["fastAnim"+i] = setInterval(anim, 1, ball);
}
// Capture screen extents
var temp:String = Stage.scaleMode;
Stage.scaleMode = "exactFit";
var sWidth:Number = Stage.width;
var sHeight:Number = Stage.height;
Stage.scaleMode = temp;
// Move Stage's original origin to center
this._x = sWidth / 2;
this._y = sHeight / 2;
// Mark out Stage
this.lineStyle(undefined, 0x0, 100);
this.beginFill(0xF0FAFF, 100);
this.moveTo(-sWidth, sHeight), this.lineTo(sWidth, sHeight);
this.lineTo(sWidth, -sHeight), this.lineTo(-sWidth, -sHeight);
this.endFill();
```

The still image of the output shown in Figure 10-11 doesn't do the effect justice. On a modern computer, the dots fly quickly around the Stage. If you do not have a high enough monitor refresh rate, you will not see many of the dots at all, but rather the trails they leave behind!

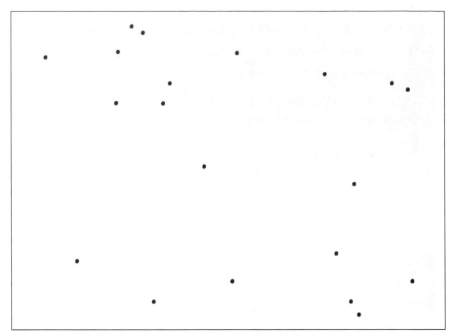

Figure 10-11. Flying dots demonstrating optimized range checking

On my machine, I see around 15% to 20% faster animation using optimized range checking with 5-pixel wide circular movie clips. The speed increase depends heavily on the speed of your computer and the complexity of the movie clip graphics (remembering that screen redraw, not the code, is usually the performance bottleneck).

The following code uses the *Math.min( )* and *Math.max( )* methods to "clip" a value to a particular range. It skips the conditional expression and simply forces the value into the desired range. (The code assumes you haven't shifted the origin as in the previous example.) It works well when you want to restrict an object's range of motion, say a puck along a slider, but not for objects that need to "reverse course," such as a bouncing ball. Here, the calculation prevents the movie clip from traveling off stage:

```
function anim(target:MovieClip):Void {
  target._x = Math.max (0, Math.min (target._x + target.xSpeed, 550));
  target._y = Math.max (0, Math.min (target._y + target.ySpeed, 400));
  updateAfterEvent( );
}
```

Or, more generally:

```
function clip(input:Number, minVal:Number, maxVal:Number):Number {
  return Math.max (minVal, Math.min (input, maxVal));
}
```

```
function anim(target:MovieClip):Void {
  target._x = clip(target._x + target.xSpeed, 0, 550);
  target._y = clip(target._y + target.ySpeed, 0, 400);
  updateAfterEvent( );
}
```

Optimize Inertial Motion with Bit Shifting

Flash's base unit of measure is a twentieth of a point (a "twip"). Flash allows you to define pixel values with precision down to .05 pixels (smaller increments are ignored), so drawing a pixel at the point (10.5, 10.5) is legal. Flash displays graphics at fractional locations using antialiasing. By blurring the pixel, Flash attempts to give the impression that the pixel is at the fractional position, even though the video card can address pixels only at integer positions, such as (10, 10). The problem is that you can lose detail through the blurring effect, so it is best to position graphics at whole-pixel intervals.

Inertial motion [Hack #39] is one of the most oft-used tricks in Flash. However, the standard inertia algorithm returns fractional pixel values. For example, the following code creates the ubiquitous ball movie clip and animates it with an inertial motion toward the mouse position (a.k.a. the Cheesy Flash Mouse Follower effect):

```
inertia = function ( ):Void {
  this._x -= (this._x - _xmouse) / 4;
  this._y -= (this._y - _ymouse) / 4;
  trace(this._x)
};
// Create ball
var ball:MovieClip = this.createEmptyMovieClip("ball",
    this.getNextHighestDepth( ));
ball.lineStyle(20, 0x0, 100);
ball.lineTo(0, 1);
ball.onEnterFrame = inertia;
```

Almost none of the traced values (this._x) give an integer, which means that the clip can appear blurry because it is positioned on the Stage between physical pixel positions. More typically, if you are adding inertia effects to drop-down menus or scrollbars, it will make any associated text fuzzy and wreak havoc with pixel fonts.

Instead of dividing by 4 in the preceding example (which, incidentally, is an arbitrary value, chosen because it gives a pleasing inertial effect at my chosen frame rate of 18 fps), you can instead bit-shift the value to the right by 2 binary digits via the following:

```
inertia = function ( ):Void {
  this._x -= (this._x - _xmouse) >> 2;
  this._y -= (this._y - _ymouse) >> 2;
  trace(this._x)
};
```

The >> 2 operation tells Flash to shift the bits in the answer 2 positions to the right, effectively dividing the result by 2^2, or 4, using integer division. This is faster than the standard ActionScript division operator, /, which performs floating-point division. Now the *trace( )* statement displays integer values only, which keeps your animated content much sharper, assuming that the content is snapped to the nearest pixel (View → Snapping → Snap to Pixels) and all your graphics are rendered in exact pixel sizes (you can ensure this by specifying integer values for Width and Height in the Properties panel).

Final Thoughts

As you can see, there are many ways to use the more obscure features of ActionScript, which are often more optimized or shorter than mainstream solutions. It pays to keep an eye out for alternative ActionScript when performance is at a premium.

H A C K #85 Import ASC Files as XML

Read non-XML text files using methods of the *XML* class for basic file loading. Then parse the text out of the single resulting XML node.

XML is a well-known format for sending and receiving data to and from the Flash Player. When you want to load a smaller amount of data (or unstructured data), the *LoadVars* class is another popular route. XML is common in web design and web-related technologies but many non-web applications use proprietary data formats not supported by the Flash Player. Two common options for loading nonstandard data into Flash are to convert the data into XML or ampersand-delimited text files (for *LoadVars*). Both approaches force you to reformat the data every time you update the source data, making for an inefficient workflow and possibly introducing errors during conversion.

A better route is to import the source application's original file format if possible. Here we import the ASC file format, which is common to many applications.

ASC Files

The ASC file format consists of any sequential ASCII file structured as a series of lines of space-delimited data, each line being terminated with a carriage return (or other delimiter), such as:

```
data data data data data<CR>
data data data data data<CR>
...
data data data data data<CR>
```

ASC files and ASC-style files are typically used as a general file format that is easy to read by other applications. Many 3D applications support plug-ins that allow them to import and export ASC files, although fewer have this native capability.

ASC files are easy to hand-edit in any text editor because:

- The data file is simple ASCII.
- The data does not contain any nonprintable characters or escape sequences (a.k.a. control codes).
- The data is ordered in a regular table format that is easy for humans to read.

This format should not be confused with the Flash-specific ASC (ActionScript Communications) file format used by Flash Communication Server MX.

This hack uses an ASC file created by 3D Studio Max. As you can see, it is essentially a table of data:

```
Ambient light color: Red= 0.0 Green= 0.0 Blue= 0.0

Named object: "Torus01"
Tri-mesh, Vertices: 100     Faces: 200
Vertex list:
Vertex 0:  X:-0.4     Y: 0.0      Z:61.1
Vertex 1:  X:-0.4     Y:-11.8     Z:57.3
...
Vertex 98:  X:-27.5    Y:19.0      Z:38.5
Vertex 99:  X:-33.4    Y:11.8      Z:46.6
Face list:
Face 0:    A:0 B:11 C:10 AB:0 BC:1 CA:1
Smoothing: 1
Face 1:    A:0 B:1 C:11 AB:1 BC:1 CA:0
Smoothing: 1
...
Face 198:   A:99 B:0 C:9 AB:0 BC:1 CA:1
Smoothing: 1
Face 199:   A:99 B:90 C:0 AB:1 BC:1 CA:0
Smoothing: 1
```

The data forms a 3D torus (doughnut), as seen in Figure 10-12.

The problem is how to load our ASC file into Flash. One of the easiest (and downright sneaky) ways is to trick Flash into thinking the file is an XML file. The fact that the file isn't really XML causes Flash to assume that the file contains only one node. This single node is a string containing the entire contents of the file, which we can parse using standard string-handling (rather than XML node-parsing) functions.

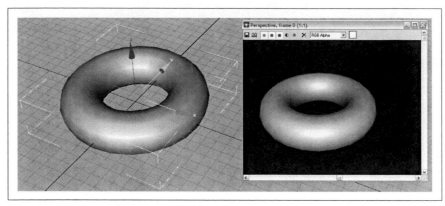

Figure 10-12. The torus shape in 3D Studio Max

Import and Parse the ASC File

The functions *handleIncoming( )* and *readXMLstart( )* in the following list-ing cause Flash to load the ASC file as an XML file and place the contents of the file into a string, my3dFile, if the load is successful.

We know that each line of the ASC file contains related data and ends with a carriage return ("\n" or Key.ENTER in Flash). To split the ASC file into sepa-rate lines of data, we simply search through the file looking for each occur-rence of "\n" (we don't use *String.split( )* because we want to loop through the array anyway to look for the data of interest, as discussed later). The *readASC( )* function separates the ASC file into lines and stores them in an array named shape:

```
handleIncoming = function (success) {
  if (success) {
    readXMLstart( );
  }
};
readXMLstart = function ( ) {
  my3dFile = xObj.firstChild.nodeValue;
  readASC( );
};
readASC = function ( ) {
  var oIndex:Number = 0;
  var rIndex:Number = 0;
  var elem:String = "";
  while (rIndex != -1) {
    rIndex = my3dFile.indexOf("\n", oIndex);
    elem = my3dFile.substring(oIndex, rIndex);
    // Skip any lines that are padding (less than 30 characters)
    if (elem.length > 30) {
      shape[shape.length] = elem;
    }
```

```
        oIndex = rIndex+1;
    }
};
var xObj:XML = new XML();
var my3dFile:String = new String();
var shape:Array = new Array();
xObj.onLoad = handleIncoming;
xObj.load("torus.asc");
```

The *String.substring( )* method searches my3dFile and extracts the characters between the start of the first unsearched character position, oIndex ("old index"), and the position of the next "\n", rIndex ("return index"), as a line of data:

```
rIndex = my3dFile.indexOf("\n", oIndex);
elem = my3dFile.substring(oIndex, rIndex);
```

The value of rIndex is found by looking for the next "\n" via the *String.indexOf( )* method. The code knows when the end of the ASC file is reached because *String.indexOf( )* returns -1 when the search string cannot be found.

Some lines of the ASC file are not of interest to us (i.e., they contain data other than the raw point and line data we are looking for), and we can get rid of these by checking for some identifying characteristic before we treat the current line as valid. In our case, if the line length is greater than 30 characters, the currently found line is assumed to be valid data and stored as the next element in array shape:

```
if (elem.length > 30) {
    shape[shape.length] = elem;
}
```

Figure 10-13 shows the first 10 elements of the shape array as created by the code presented. We'll filter out anything that isn't vertex data momentarily.

⊟	shape	
	0	"Ambient light color: Red= 0.0 Green= 0.0 Blue= 0.0\r"
	1	"Tri-mesh, Vertices: 100 Faces: 200\r"
	2	"Vertex 0: X:-0.4 Y: 0.0 Z:61.1\r"
	3	"Vertex 1: X:-0.4 Y:-11.8 Z:57.3\r"
	4	"Vertex 2: X:-0.4 Y:-19.0 Z:47.3\r"
	5	"Vertex 3: X:-0.4 Y:-19.0 Z:34.9\r"
	6	"Vertex 4: X:-0.4 Y:-11.8 Z:24.9\r"
	7	"Vertex 5: X:-0.4 Y: 0.0 Z:21.1\r"
	8	"Vertex 6: X:-0.4 Y:11.8 Z:24.9\r"
	9	"Vertex 7: X:-0.4 Y:19.0 Z:34.9\r"

Figure 10-13. The first 10 elements of the shape array

Parse Each Line in an ASC File

Normally, we don't want to store the individual lines but rather the relevant data contained within them. Given that the ASC file in question represents a 3D shape, we want to extract the vertex point data (x, y, z) of this shape.

A typical data line that contains 3D point data in our imported file looks like:

```
Vertex 98:  X:-27.5     Y:19.0      Z:38.5
```

From this line, we can deduce that:

- All lines that contain vertex data in the ASC file are at least 30 characters long and start with "Vertex."

- Within these lines, the x data is preceded by "X:" (similarly for the y and z data).

We can add these rules to the code as follows. We can determine whether the current line contains vertex data by looking for a "V" as the first character of the current line:

```
if (elem.substring(0, 1) == "V") {
```

If this is the case, we search through the line for the offset of "X:", "Y:", and "Z:":

```
posX = elem.indexOf("X:", 0);
posY = elem.indexOf("Y:", posX);
posZ = elem.indexOf("Z:", posY);
```

These offsets are the same for all lines starting with "Vertex" in the example file, but that is not guaranteed, so we have to search for the start positions rather than assuming them.

We use these offsets to extract the x, y, and z coordinates. We add 2 to the starting offset to account for the letter and colon, such as "X:".

```
pX = Number(elem.slice(posX + 2, posX + 6));
pY = Number(elem.slice(posY + 2, posY + 6));
pZ = Number(elem.slice(posZ + 2, posZ + 6));
```

Finally, we can add the (x, y, z) point as structured Flash data that can be used by ActionScript to build the 3D shape [Hack #37]. Here, I add the 3D point data as properties to the shape array, as shown in Figure 10-14.

```
shape[sPointer] = new Object();
shape[sPointer].x = pX;
shape[sPointer].y = pY;
shape[sPointer].z = pZ;
```

The full code to extract the (x, y, z) point data from our 3D Studio Max ASC file is:

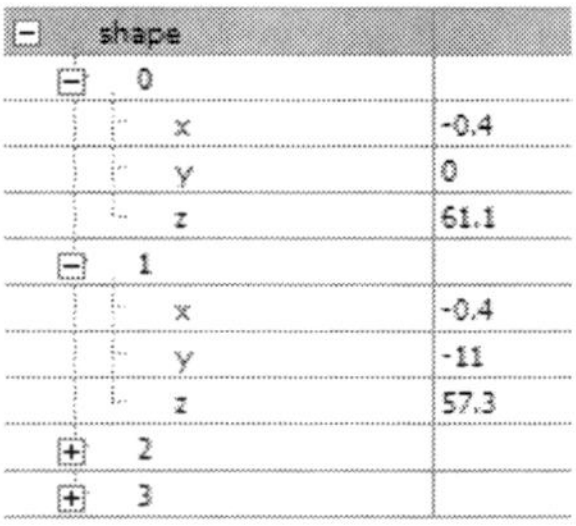

Figure 10-14. The 3D data points stored as x, y, and z properties of each shape element

```
handleIncoming = function (success) {
  if (success) {
    readXMLstart();
  }
};
readXMLstart = function () {
  my3dFile = xObj.firstChild.nodeValue;
  readASC();
};
readASC = function () {
  var oIndex:Number = 0;
  var rIndex:Number = 0;
  var elem:String = "";
  var posX:Number = 0;
  var posY:Number = 0;
  var posZ:Number = 0;
  while (rIndex != -1) {
    rIndex = my3dFile.indexOf("\n", oIndex);
    elem = my3dFile.substring(oIndex, rIndex);
    if (elem.length > 30) {
      if (elem.substring(0, 1) == "V") {
        posX = elem.indexOf("X:", 0);
        posY = elem.indexOf("Y:", posX);
        posZ = elem.indexOf("Z:", posY);
        pX = Number(elem.slice(posX + 2, posX + 6));
        pY = Number(elem.slice(posY + 2, posY + 6));
        pZ = Number(elem.slice(posZ + 2, posZ + 6));
        shape[sPointer] = new Object();
        shape[sPointer].x = pX;
        shape[sPointer].y = pY;
        shape[sPointer].z = pZ;
        sPointer++;
      }
    }
    oIndex = rIndex+1;
  }
};
```

```
var xObj:XML = new XML( );
var my3dFile:String = new String( );
var shape:Array = new Array( );
var sPointer:Number = 0;
xObj.onLoad = handleIncoming;
xObj.load("torus.asc");
```

You can see Edwin Heijmen's version of this file in the Experiments section at *http://www.poeticterror.com*. The full version uses the 3D point data to create an interactive 3D wireframe viewer, as shown in Figure 10-15.

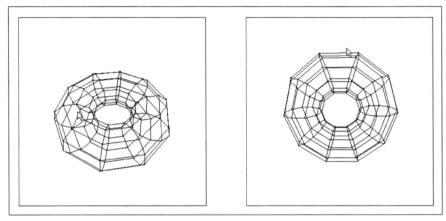

Figure 10-15. Wireframe data imported from an ASC file into Flash

Final Thoughts

As Flash becomes more of a general web multimedia platform, you are increasingly likely to want to import data into a SWF from nonstandard or non-web-based applications. Even if this data is not XML, you can use the *XML* class to load the data (Flash doesn't care whether a file you ask it to treat as XML is actually XML). This is one of the better ways to import structured text files that are formatted in a way that Flash does not understand, because you gain many of the features of the *XML* class, such as notification via the *onLoad* event that the file is loaded.

Furthermore, the raw ASC file format makes it particularly easy to import data not intended for Flash (such as 3D point data or database recordsets) into a running SWF, so there may be little gain in converting to native Flash formats such as XML.

Avoid the temptation to always convert data into XML. Doing so unnecessarily adds steps to the production workflow if the source application updates the data, however infrequently.

—Edwin Heijmen

CHAPTER ELEVEN

Browser Integration

Hacks 86–96

Since its inception, Flash has been intimately tied to web browsers. Granted, Flash can create Projectors that use the Standalone Player to play SWF files, but most Flash content is viewed through web browsers, courtesy of the ubiquitous Flash Player browser plugin (for Internet Explorer on Windows, it is an ActiveX control).

Ironically, part of the world's love-hate relationship with Flash is based on misconceptions. Many web developers and users don't realize the extent to which Flash works with browsers. In this chapter, we'll see how to integrate Flash with standard browser conventions, such as the Back button [Hack #94], and search engines like Google.

This chapter also discusses a unique way to check for the Flash Player browser plugin [Hack #87]. If the Flash Player is installed, it can periodically check for Player updates on the macromedia.com site. As described in the Macromedia Flex documentation *Managing Flash Player Auto-update (http://livedocs.macromedia.com/flex/1/flex_docs/wwhelp/wwhimpl/common/html/wwhelp.htm?context=Flex_Documentation&file=38_dep42.htm#wp154069)* the auto-update settings can be configured via an *mms.cfg* file in the user's home directory or via the user settings as described next.

Security and privacy are important to Flash's acceptance as a distribution platform. Most developers are aware of the Flash context menu accessed using right-click (Windows) or ⌘-click (Macintosh). The most important option on this menu is Settings, which opens the Macromedia Flash Player Settings dialog box. This dialog box has tabs that allow the user to manage settings for Privacy, Local Storage, Microphone, and Camera access. However, few developers and even fewer users realize that additional Flash Player settings are available only via Macromedia's web site. Users can access the Settings Manager (*http://www.macromedia.com/support/documentation/en/flashplayer/help/settings_manager.html*) using the Advanced button on the

Privacy tab of the Settings dialog box. Once at Macromedia's site, the user can configure additional settings regarding privacy, storage, security, and update notifications.

As has been the case for many years, browser standards and compatibility continue to fluctuate as new versions of various browsers are released for the major operating systems. Legal influences often trump technical ones, however. A company called EOLAS (Embedded Objects Linked Across Systems) has several patents covering playing content in a browser. You may have heard of the EOLAS patent case in which Microsoft was sued to prevent it from seamlessly launching the Flash Player ActiveX control in Internet Explorer for Windows. At the time of this writing, Microsoft has won a preliminary ruling to invalidate the patent, but the litigation is still pending. See *http://www.eolas.com/news.html* for the latest news on this issue from EOLAS. Search *http://www.microsoft.com* for the word "EOLAS" to find any implications of recent rulings to Internet Explorer. See *http://www.macromedia.com/devnet/activecontent* for any issues raised for Flash and other rich media developers. Any late-breaking news will be updated on this book's site, as noted in the Preface.

It remains to be seen whether Microsoft will ultimately prevail, but we assume it will. Although it is not implemented here, we researched a possible workaround even if EOLAS prevails. The patent claim revolves around the use of plugins that work seamlessly with the browser. When <object> and <embed> tags that require the browser to load non-HTML content (such as a Flash SWF) are found on a page, the process of loading the Flash Player is largely transparent to the user and developer. If the EOLAS patent is upheld and Microsoft doesn't license the patent, Internet Explorer will be prohibited from loading the Flash Player plugin directly. The solution is to use non-plugin-based technology (such as JavaScript) to load non-HTML content, including loading the Flash Player to play SWFs. For convenience and sanity's sake, let's hope it doesn't come to that.

Of course, the Flash Player is not just for web browsers. There is also the Flash player for PocketPC, Flash Lite for cell phones, and hardware-specific versions of the Flash Player for a number of other devices (see *http://www.macromedia.com/devnet/devices*). Note that the version of the Flash Player supported by most mobile or standalone devices will lag behind the latest version of the Flash Player for desktop PC web browsers. Most non-browser-based versions of the Flash Player support either Flash 4, 5, or 6 features, whereas the latest Flash Player for Macintosh and Windows browsers is Flash Player 7.

The Flash authoring tool is not open source, but the SWF format is public. Third parties can license the Flash SWF file format for free (see *http://www. openswf.org* and *http://www.macromedia.com/software/flash/open/licensing* for more details). Not surprisingly, a number of third-party tools play SWF files in nonstandard environments or produce SWF output without requiring the Flash authoring tool [Hack #29].

Keep Your Site Browser Friendly

#86

The standard Flash site creation workflow does not create the most web-friendly output. Make your designs much more browser friendly with a little HTML hand-editing and web savvy.

More than 80% of web users use Internet Explorer (IE 5 or later) according to W3Schools (*http://www.w3schools.com/browsers/browsers_stats.asp*), and more than 93% of all users have the Flash Player 6 or later installed according to Macromedia's Flash Player census (*http://www.macromedia.com/ software/player_census/flashplayer/version_penetration.html*). Regardless, your site should deal as gracefully as possible with users with various configurations. Customers with complaints are more vocal than customers with no complaints. So a minority of site visitors, say 5%, who are turned away for no good reason may be providing 100% of the site feedback to your client (in which case it will all be negative). In real life, each unhappy customer is rarely cancelled out by one happy customer, and a dissatisfaction rate of more than a few percent is disconcerting to many clients.

You should keep up with current web user statistics. For example, W3Schools (*http://www.w3schools.com/browsers/browsers_stats.asp*) provides browser trends by month and thecounter.com (*http://www.thecounter. com/stats*) provides browser statistics for the large number of visitors it gets each day (for a browser breakdown, click on a month, then click the Browsers link on the righthand side of the web page that appears).

Remember that compatibility statistics tend to underestimate the likelihood for complaints by the minority of users who can't access your site.

Use a Flash Plugin Sniffer

The best user experience will occur when your online content is able to detect what resources are available on the user's machine and display content that will run on that system (or give the user explicit information on what he needs to do to view the content). There are almost as many methods to test for Flash plugin support as there are designers who have attempted the feat, but some of the more popular are:

Colin Moock's fpi (Flash plugin inspector)
http://moock.org/webdesign/flash/detection/moockfpi

Web Monkey: Detecting Plugins
http://hotwired.lycos.com/webmonkey/99/40/index3a.
html?tw=programming

O'Reilly WebDev center
http://www.oreillynet.com/pub/a/javascript/2001/07/20/plugin_detection.
html

See also our JavaScript-free plugin sniffer [Hack #87].

Test Using Many Browsers

Contrary to some reports, you can have a number of different browsers
installed on the same system and even running at the same time. For example, I have Internet Explorer, Netscape Navigator, Opera, and Mozilla
installed on the same machine, as shown in Figure 11-1.

*Figure 11-1. Windows XP system with (back to front) Internet Explorer, Netscape
Navigator, Opera (free version), and Mozilla all running at the same time*

The problem you will most often see when you have several browsers
installed is that they tend to fight one another for the title of default
browser. As long as you choose the custom install option and avoid the
"make this the default browser" option, you should be okay.

Also look out for any extras that new browser installers try to add. Deselect-
ing all installation options except the basic browser is usually a good idea,
unless you want your default email application, messenger, and MP3 player
to change! Netscape Navigator is particularly zealous in its overreaching, so
always go for a custom install when adding this bad boy. Likewise, beware
of automated Internet Explorer updates that might, say, upgrade your Windows Media Player as well.

Although having multiple browsers is a requirement for all web designers, it is particularly important for Flash sites because you also need to test what happens if the correct plugin is not available. In my case, I always make sure that at least one browser in my set does not have the Flash Player plugin installed and that most of them have the most popular version of the Flash Player plugin installed (rather than necessarily the latest). So most of my machines have Flash Player 6 installed because Flash Player 7 hasn't yet reached ubiquity (as of June 2004).

You can quickly and easily change the plugin version installed on some browsers with a free application called Flash Plugin Switcher [Hack #88]. Legacy versions of the Flash plugin are also available online to allow you to change among all the major Windows/Mac Flash Player revisions.

Note that there are Flash Player versions for alternative operating systems such as Linux and OS/2. To download the Flash Player for all your non-Windows/Mac OS machines, see the rather well hidden page at *http://www. macromedia.com/shockwave/download/alternates*.

An additional useful "browser" is AnyBrowser. This utility emulates a stripped-down, minimum browser (HTML 3.2 with support for tables that supports neither Flash nor JavaScript). Although Flash content cannot be displayed in AnyBrowser, it is a good resource to test the worst-case "no Flash installed" condition on your site. If your web page can tell the user what is wrong and what they need to do through this browser, you are doing well!

To get hold of AnyBrowser, click the Site Viewer link on *http://www. anybrowser.com*, where you will see a download link. An online version may also be found via the same link.

Design and Test for Search Engine Compatibility

The AnyBrowser site also has a useful tool to see how a search engine crawler will see your site. Click on the Engine View link from the main Any-Browser page.

The easiest way to add text that a search engine can read is to incorporate it within a comment field <!-- --> within the <body> tag of your HTML page. You would typically fill the comments with an initial paragraph of text describing what the site is, followed by a list of keywords. Don't list the keywords first; if you do, the keywords will appear as the site description on most search engine results pages!

Flash will add commented text in the HTML page automatically when using many of the HTML templates that ship with Flash (including the Flash Only template), but the HTML exporter is not that clever. It cannot differentiate between UI text and content text and, therefore, usually exports gibberish that is not suitable for search engine viewing or keyword creation. Your best option by far is hand-editing the Flash-generated HTML file yourself to include the proper description and keywords.

I know of at least one search engine consultant who suggested putting your Flash movie's content in external files whenever possible, claiming that your text and XML files will sometimes be indexed by search engines. I don't know if its true, but if you are using dynamic external files, it might improve your site's searchability

The Flash Context Menu

I'm often asked, "How do I get rid of the Flash context menu when the Flash site is viewed in a browser? I need to use the right mouse button for something else and even if I didn't, the pop-up menu appears unprofessional." The Flash context menu (right-click on Windows or ⌘-click on Mac) is something that you cannot normally turn off completely. Even if you set Stage.showMenu to false or select File → Publish Settings → HTML and uncheck the Display Menu option, the context menu still includes the Settings and About Macromedia Flash Player options. Some less than useful ways of removing the menu have been suggested in the past. One was to cover the Stage with a selectable text field (which, rather perversely, brings up the text-editing context menu instead and also has the side effect of making it impossible to click on anything else on the Stage!).

I've seen the question enough times in Flash newsgroups to warrant giving the only sensible solution some airtime. You can remove the context menu completely via some clever HTML and JavaScript, as seen on Gregg Wygonik's site (*http://www.broadcast.artificialcolors.com/stories/2003/09/21/ disableFlashMovieRightclickMenu.html*). Better still, you can download Gregg's gwContextKiller component (*http://www.artificialcolors.com/ experiments/gwContextKillerInfo.html*) that disables right-click menu functionality for IE 6+ and Mozilla 1.3+ browsers (it also works in IE 5 but not IE 5.5). Simply drop the component on Flash's Stage, typically off screen, and then set the Window mode in the File → Publish Settings → HTML tab to Windowless Opaque. Note, however, that windowless, opaque Flash movies appear as black squares for users who have disabled floating Flash ads, as described at *http://www.jessewarden.com/archives/000507.html*, or turned off auto-updating, as described at *http://livedocs.macromedia.com/ flex/1/flex_docs/wwhelp/wwhimpl/common/html/wwhelp.htm?context=Flex_ Documentation&file=38_dep42.htm#wp154069*.

Final Thoughts

You can make your Flash sites more browser friendly in a number of ways. In most cases, you can significantly reduce the final percentage of users who cannot view your site, even if you have only one machine, by:

- Testing with a number of browsers
- Hand-editing the HTML to make your site appear in search engines with meaningful descriptions and keywords
- Assuming that the user will not have the Flash plugin installed and making sure your site acts sensibly under these conditions

A Universal Flash Plugin Sniffer

Build a non-JavaScript-based Flash plugin sniffer that won't need to be updated each time Macromedia releases a new version of the Flash Player.

A Flash plugin sniffer is something that tries to detect whether or not the Flash content within the current web page is viewable by the browser. It does this by looking for a particular installation of the Flash Player. The problem is that prerequisites may have to be addressed before the sniffer itself works correctly. Flash content that would have worked perfectly well without a sniffer may never be reached if the sniffer itself fails! This hack shows how to build a sniffer that has fewer prerequisites and is thus very likely to work.

Traditional sniffers usually have to be updated whenever a new version of the Flash Player is released. Worse still, traditional sniffers are written in JavaScript and have notorious browser dependencies. As the Hacks series editor Rael Dornfest once said, "We contemplated a JavaScript Hacks book, but everything in JavaScript is a hack." I can't even look at a JavaScript manual any more without giggling.

The upshot is that a JavaScript-based Flash sniffer has a number of Achilles' heels:

- The variability of JavaScript support in different browsers and the differences in ways browsers identify (or fail to identify) the presence of a given plugin. For example, detecting an ActiveX control in Windows Internet Explorer is different than detecting a Netscape-style plugin in Netscape and other browsers that don't support ActiveX.
- Variability in the Flash plugin. Your sniffer may not recognize more recent versions of the Flash plugin or versions for alternative platforms, even if they can actually run your SWF.

- Whether the user has turned JavaScript support off in the current browser (quite common in commercial organizations because it reduces the probability of malicious JavaScript-based virus infections or hacker Trojans), which will defeat any JavaScript-based sniffer script altogether!

What we would really like is a Flash sniffer that doesn't rely on JavaScript at all. Wouldn't that be a cool hack to know?

Five Seconds and Counting...

The <meta> tag is an HTML header tag that allows you to send information to the browser or specialized browser plugins (such as screen readers for the sight impaired). It is also used to present information for search engine indexing purposes. This hack uses a particular ability of the <meta> tag, the *client-pull*. For more information, see *HTML & XHTML: The Definitive Guide*, fourth edition, by Chuck Musciano and Bill Kennedy (O'Reilly), especially section 13.2.1, "Uniquely Refreshing."

Here is the syntax for the <meta> tag to implement a client-pull:

```
<meta http-equiv="refresh" content="n; URL=newdoc.html">
```

A client-pull is simply a request for the browser to load a new HTML document, in this case *newdoc.html* (which may also include the full path to a new document, such as *http://www.myDomain.com/mydoc.html*) after a certain time delay, *n*, in seconds. Its effect is much the same as if the user clicked on a hyperlink to *newdoc.html* after the *n* second time delay. For this hack, we set the time delay to five seconds and specify that the browser should load the document *noflash.html*.

We also embed a SWF inside our original HTML file. The SWF uses the *getURL( )* action to load an HTML page, *flash.html*, containing our final Flash content. Figure 11-2 shows the general process at work.

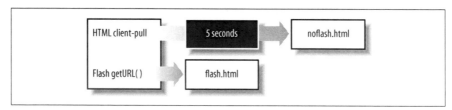

Figure 11-2. Flash sniffer

So what we have is an attempt to run a Flash SWF that executes a *getURL( )* action, which loads the Flash content embedded in the *flash.html* web page. If that works, we know Flash Player is installed. If it doesn't execute, we know the appropriate Flash Player is not present. But no worries—if Flash doesn't change the current web page (using *getURL( )* to load *flash.html*), the client-pull fires after five seconds, loading our non-Flash HTML page, *noflash.html*. Best of all, none of it is dependent on JavaScript—the browser, OS platform, or user preferences.

Asking Flash to Run Itself

Let's look more closely at the requirements for this hack.

Here are the steps:

1. Create a new Flash document and add the following script to frame 1 of the main timeline:

   ```
   getURL("flash.html", "_self");
   ```

2. Save the file as *index.fla*.

3. Publish the document with File → Publish Preview → Default (HTML). This option creates the files *index.html* and *index.swf* in the same folder where you saved *index.fla*. The two together will form our Flash sniffer.

4. Open *index.html* in your HTML or text editor of choice.

5. The <head> section of the file will look like this:

   ```
   <head>
   <meta http-equiv=Content-Type content="text/html;  charset=ISO-8859-1">
   <title>index</title>
   </head>
   ```

6. Add a new <meta> tag as shown in bold:

   ```
   <head>
   <meta http-equiv=Content-Type content="text/html;  charset=ISO-8859-1">
   <meta http-equiv="refresh" content="5; URL=noflash.html">
   <title>index</title>
   </head>
   ```

Create your *noflash.html* file. It should be one of the following:

- An HTML-only version of your site
- An HTML-only page advising the user to update to the latest Flash plugin
- A page prompting the user to click a button to go directly to the Macromedia Flash plugin download site (*http://www.macromedia.com/shockwave/download/download.cgi?P1_Prod_Version=ShockwaveFlash*)

In any case, your page should explain that Flash was not detected. The page should also include a link for the user to run your Flash-based site if she is sure she has the plugin installed. Nothing so frustrates an end user as being told she doesn't have the plugin because your automatic detection failed. So don't unceremoniously send the user to the Macromedia site to obtain the Flash plugin; leave it up to the user to choose an appropriate course of action.

Place your *flash.html* and *someFlashMovie.swf* (your Flash site) in the same folder as *index.html*. To test your sniffer locally, open *index.html* in a web browser. If you're having trouble, see the basic files provided on this book's web site.

Once that seems to be working, upload the files to your web server and point your web browser to the URL where you uploaded the HTML page, such as *http://www.yourdomain.com/sniffertest/index.html*.

To emulate a basic browser without any plugins, visit *http://www. anybrowser.com*. This site emulates a plugin-free HTML 3.2-compatible browser—a perfect place to test a Flash sniffer.

Making It a Bit More Discerning

Sometimes, you may find that early versions of the Flash Player recognize the *getURL( )* command, which has been supported since Flash Player 2, but can't play all the content in your Flash SWF-based site. An example of this might be if you want to use Flash video, supported in Flash Player 6 and later, but the user has Flash Player 5 installed. Flash Player 5 supports *getURL( )* but will not play the video embedded in a SWF file. In this case, you need to check for a minimum Flash Player plugin version.

Your Flash movie that checks the Flash Player version should itself be a Flash Player 4- or Flash Player 5-format *.swf* file. It can check the Flash Player version and then load another *.swf* file, perhaps in Flash Player 6 or Flash Player 7 format, that contains your real Flash content.

To check the Flash Player version, use the Flash environment variable $version. You can see the version in the Variables tab of the Debugger panel, as shown in Figure 11-3, if you test a movie in debug mode.

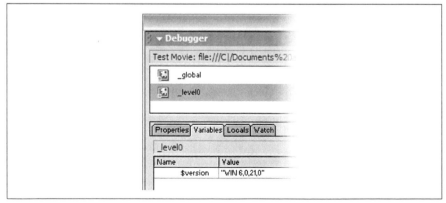

Figure 11-3. The Variables tab of the Debugger panel, showing the Flash version

The $version property is supported in Flash Player 4.0.11.0 and later. It returns a version string of the form "*platform major,minor,build,patch*", where *platform* is either WIN, MAC, or UNIX and the other items are numbers, such as "WIN 6,0,21,0". Don't use more modern methods to retrieve the version, such as the *getVersion( )* function (supported in Flash 5 and later) or the System.capabilities.version property (supported in Flash 6 and later), unless you can ensure that the user has a more recent version of the plugin. It is a pretty safe bet that users have at least Flash Player 5 if they have any version installed, and more than 90% of users have Flash Player 6 or later as shown in the Flash Player census (*http://www.macromedia.com/software/player_census/flashplayer/version_penetration.html*).

Regardless, $version, *getVersion( )*, and System.capabilities.version, when supported, all return the same string on a given platform.

The major revision number is at an offset of 4 (the fifth character) in the $version string for Mac and Windows. Here we use *String.substr( )* to check whether the user has at least Version 5 of the Flash Player. If so, it replaces the current page with the *flash.html* site. Otherwise, it goes to an error page that says, "You need to update your Flash Player to at least Version 5."

```
if ($version.substr(4, 1) >= 5) {
  getURL("flash.html", "_self");
} else {
  getURL("old_flash.html", + "_self");
}
```

This script will fail and simply continue playing the SWF on Flash Player 1, 2, and 3, but those versions are extremely old and represent less than 1% of the installed base. The cool thing about this hack is that you don't have to update this detection system for users with Flash Player 6, Flash Player 7, or future versions. If you want to support platforms that return "UNIX" in the version string, extract the major version number following the first space in the string rather than assuming it starts at the fifth character.

Final Thoughts

The hack here relies on the absence of the Flash Player, which is easier than actively determining the presence of the Flash Player. We check the Flash Player version (if we need to) once we know that Flash Player is present. Instead of trying to check the Flash Player via JavaScript, we ask the Flash Player to identify itself.

Our sniffer is not susceptible to either JavaScript support or revisions nor dependent on the version of the Flash Player plugin. At a minimum, it relies only on the <meta> tag, supported by Version 3.x browsers and later. At a maximum, it requires a Flash Player plugin that can recognize the *if* statement and $version property, namely Flash Player 4 or higher.

Admittedly, the approach presented here is a hack—this is *Flash Hacks*, after all—and is not necessarily foolproof. Depending on their configuration, Internet Explorer users without the Flash Player ActiveX control may be prompted to install it. Depending on the timing (how long it takes for the prompt to appear and for the user to respond), the user might not be forwarded to your no-Flash page.

Plugin-detection scripts are always controversial and none are perfect. Consider this technique one more arrow in your quiver rather than a silver bullet (how's that for a mixed metaphor!). See the resources in the introduction to this chapter for more traditional browser-sniffing techniques.

Test Multiple Flash Plugins

#88

Test against multiple versions of the Flash Player without moving between computers or having to manually install/uninstall Flash ActiveX or plugin versions.

Many clients require sites to be compatible with the previous version of the Flash Player (at the time of this writing, Flash Player 6) until the current version (Flash Player 7, for now) reaches an installed base of around 90%. This degree of ubiquity is achieved around 18 months after the release of a new Flash Player.

Although the Flash authoring environment allows you to create content for previous versions of the Flash Player, it has no facility to allow you to test your SWFs using previous versions; it simply assumes that viewing content on the latest version of the Player (currently Flash 7) is fine. Fortunately, Macromedia does a good job of ensuring that the current Flash Player plays older-format *.swf* files the same as earlier Flash Player versions.

A good designer will also test with the latest Flash Player version. However, testing a site using previous versions of the Flash Player is a prudent exercise, and it can be a messy one.

Because your browser can have only one version of the Flash Player installed at one time, there are four options:

- You can install the Flash Player version you want to test every time you need it and reinstall the latest version before you finish.
- You can test on several computers, each of which has a different version of the Flash Player installed. Many design houses have several computers set up with different configurations to test in this way. But for

smaller teams, if you lack computers or the space to house them, this solution may not be possible.

- Ask friends to test it for you. This isn't a terrible idea, but your friends are probably other Flash developers with the latest plugin installed, and friendship goes only so far.

- Use the wonderful donationware program Flash Plugin Switcher (*http://www.kewbee.de/FlashPluginSwitcher*) by Alex Blum, which avoids the need to install and uninstall the Flash Player plugin or ActiveX control.

Because we're not gluttons for punishment, this hack uses Flash Plugin Switcher (FPS), whose excellent logo is shown in Figure 11-4. FPS can force the browser to go back to the previous version of the Flash Player. Unfortunately, the application is Windows-only, so you'll have to resort to the other methods for Macintosh testing.

Figure 11-4. The Flash Plugin Switcher's rune

Although Alex's site is in German, the application and its help files are in English.

Macromedia archives older versions of the Flash Player (back to Flash Player 2) on its site specifically to facilitate testing:

> *http://www.macromedia.com/support/flash/ts/documents/oldplayers.htm*

This URL leads to Technote 14266: *Archived Macromedia Flash Players available for testing purposes.* Simply entering "14266" in the search box on Macromedia's home page should get you the current URL if Macromedia changes it.

Using Flash Plugin Switcher

Once you have unzipped the Flash Plugin Switcher download, start the application. Click the Help button to access information on how to install the plugins and ActiveX controls. Once you have it up and running, as seen in Figure 11-5, you can:

1. Change the browser plugin or ActiveX control (Netscape and Internet Explorer are supported).

2. Change the Standalone Flash Player version.

3. Change the plugin used in Test Movie mode in the Flash IDE for all versions of the Flash authoring environment you have installed.

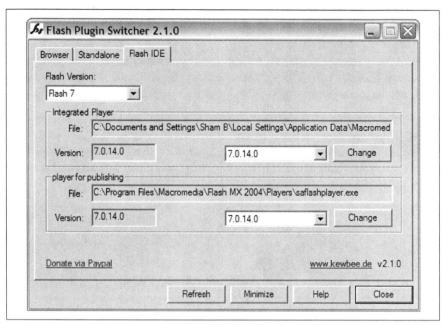

Figure 11-5. Flash Plugin Sniffer browser configuration

The general procedure to change a plugin or ActiveX control is to:

1. Make sure that the browser, Standalone Player, or Flash authoring application (IDE) for which you want to change the plugin or ActiveX control is closed.

2. Select the appropriate tab in FPS (Browser, Standalone, or Flash IDE).

3. Uninstall the existing Flash Player if the option to do so is there.

4. Select and install the new Player. Simple, but ingenious!

5. To test the case in which no Flash Player plugin is installed, uninstall the current plugin or ActiveX control in the Browser tab, as in Step 3, but don't install a new one.

Final Thoughts

As it is donationware, please thank Alex via PayPal if you make use of the Flash Plugin Switcher application.

Preferences and Publishing Defaults

Change the Flash IDE defaults to suit current hardware and/or your preferred workflows, plus utilize a few tips and tricks for good measure.

Flash has several default settings that haven't changed since the early versions of the software, although current hardware usually has enough memory and/or performance to warrant an increase. Additionally, you may not know about several important little checkboxes and requesters that are hidden in the Flash interface.

Changing the Preference Defaults

Select Edit → Preferences to alter the default preferences using the Preferences dialog box.

Let's look at some of the default preferences you may want to change under each tab.

General tab. Our first stop is the undo cache under the General tab as seen in Figure 11-6. This is set to 1000 levels of undo in Flash MX 2004, but in Flash MX, it is set to a paltry 100. If you have the memory to spare (and who doesn't these days?), set it to 1000.

Editing tab. Although the Flash MX 2004 patch updater (*http://www. macromedia.com/support/documentation/en/flash/mx2004/releasenotes. html#Update*), which was released in November 2003 and updates the authoring tool to Version 7.0.1, fixes many of the issues seen in the initial 7.0 release, it has some issues of its own. You may find that some or all of the Drawing Setting defaults are blank (no default), which stops the Smooth, Straighten, and Ink drawing modes for the Pen tool from working properly. If you see this, set the blank options to Normal. In late summer 2004, the 7.2 updater should be available at the aforementioned URL.

Clipboard tab. The Clipboard limit is set to a measly 250 KB, which is far too small for copying bitmaps from Photoshop and other graphic editing applications directly into Flash. Bump it up to 5000 KB (the equivalent of 5 MB) if you edit a lot of bitmaps in Photoshop and import them into Flash. Rather than saving them in Photoshop and then importing the image into Flash with File → Import, you can now use the Ctrl-C and Ctrl-V (Windows) or ⌘-C and ⌘-V (Mac) to copy and paste. Flash will name your pasted bitmaps "Bitmap *n*" when they appear in the Library.

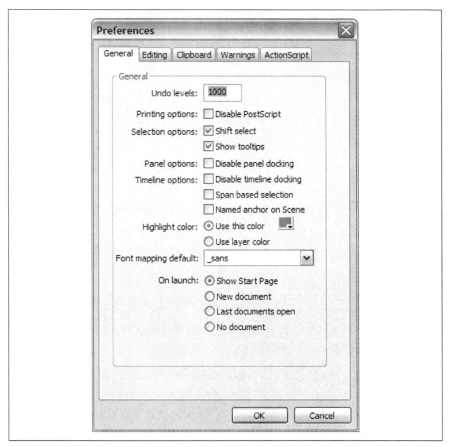

Figure 11-6. The General tab in the Preferences dialog box

Warnings tab. There's nothing on the Warnings tab we need to change. It's a good idea to leave every warning option checked (the default).

ActionScript tab. In Flash MX 2004 and Flash MX Professional 2004, the font used to display ActionScript can be set via the font drop-down list in the Text section of the ActionScript tab. Earlier versions of Flash offered no choice; you had to use a default font, Lucinda Console. Because Lucinda Console is a particularly clear and well-proportioned font for code, you may want to select it from in the font drop-down list.

Changing the Publishing Defaults

Unlike the Preference settings, which apply to the entire authoring tool, the Publish Settings are set (and remembered) individually for every FLA you edit. Choose File → Publish Settings to access the Publishing Settings dialog box. The most commonly used tabs are HTML and Flash.

HTML tab. The Flash authoring tool will create an HTML page in which your SWF is embedded. The HTML tab controls how the HTML is created. (Flash MX 2004 and Flash MX Professional 2004 generate XHTML, but the file still uses the *.html* extension.)

You can create a nonscaling SWF centered in the browser window [Hack #90] using the options under the HTML tab.

Flash tab. Under the Flash tab, you can set the ActionScript compiler version to either ActionScript 1.0 or ActionScript 2.0. ActionScript 2.0 compilation offers strict datatyping, compile-time case-sensitivity, and access to newer OOP syntax, such as the class keyword. You can also set the version of the SWF file format for export, such as Flash Player 6 or Flash Player 7, as shown in Figure 11-7.

Figure 11-7. Set the compiler version or the SWF export format version under the Flash tab

If you set it to export for Flash Player 6 via the Version drop-down list, the Optimize for Flash Player 6r65 checkbox becomes selectable. Flash Player 6r65 behaves very much like Flash Player 7, so you can get increased compatibility until Flash Player 7 becomes ubiquitous.

Note that Flash Player 6r65 does not support all of the new ActionScript added to Flash Player 7, as described in Chapter 10. See BIT-101 blog (*http://www.bit-101.com/blog/archives/000047.html*) for details on v2 component compatibility with recent Flash Players.

Other Panels and Tabs

The Output panel is useful for debugging scripts, but it opens at the position and size it was last opened in Flash. The first time you enter Test Movie mode after launching the Flash authoring tool, the Output panel usually obscures the Stage of the SWF you're testing. To keep it from getting in the way, you can dock the Output panel in the righthand docking area (Windows only). Whenever the Output panel is called up by a *trace( )* action in your scripts, it now appears to the right of the Stage in Test Movie mode, rather than appearing over your Stage. Flash for Mac OS does not support docking panels.

The Flash MX 2004 interface has some neat new tabs at the top of the authoring tool window (a la Dreamweaver). Not only do these allow you to move quickly between different open windows, there is a rather useful new context menu that you might miss. Right-click (Windows) or ⌘-click (Mac) on a tab to bring up a contextual menu that allows you to open new files or save the file associated with the tab.

Center Your SWF Without Scaling
#90
Center unscaled content in the browser window without using tables or CSS.

Although everyone knows vectors (unlike bitmaps) do not lose quality when you zoom into them, almost all commercial Flash sites use a small, nonscaling SWF centered in the browser. The reasons for this are:

- Flash performance is based on the number of pixels that change every frame. By keeping the SWF movie's area modest and forcing nonscaling, you are able to create a fast site with a more or less constant frame rate. You don't want to let the user scale the SWF up to full screen size (especially 1280×1024 and larger), because such a large area would make Flash run really slowly.

- Many commercial Flash sites use bitmaps, which don't look good scaled.

- You should also avoid scaling video. Scaling both reveals optimization artifacts and slows performance (sometimes drastically), although Sorenson-encoded video can reduce this problem significantly.

- A smaller Stage area requires fewer graphics, and that makes for smaller bandwidth requirements.

The *Stage.onResize( )* listener event allows you to detect resize events and scale or reposition individual elements in a custom manner, negating the need for one-size-fits-all scaling.

One of the most commonly asked questions for new users to Flash is, "How do I generate a nonscaling SWF that is always centered in the browser?" None of the out-of-the-box templates under File → New → Templates includes this option, and even some longtime Flash users instead use an HTML table or CSS formatting. However, the easiest way to create a centered, nonscaling SWF is using File → Publish Settings. Simply set the Horizontal and Vertical options under Flash Alignment to Center, and set the Scale option to No Scale, as shown in the Publish Settings dialog box in Figure 11-8.

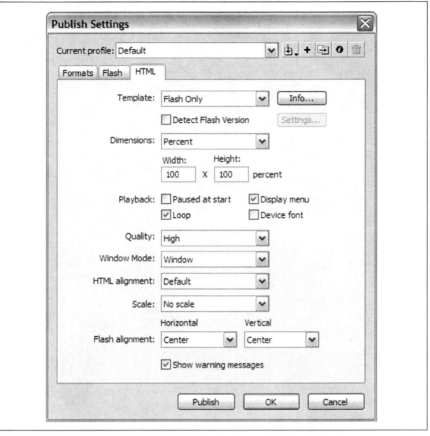

Figure 11-8. The Publish Settings dialog box

However, this technique allows off-stage content to be visible. We'll address this drawback in the next hack, which uses CSS formatting [Hack #91].

HACK #91 CSS-Based Browser Centering

Centering an unscaled Flash SWF can inadvertently expose off-stage content. Center a Flash SWF using XHTML and CSS for excellent results without displaying off-stage content and in a standards-compliant way.

One of the most common initial problems a new designer faces is centering the SWF in the browser [Hack #90]. Although there are several ways to do this, all have at least some issues. This hack shows the options and the hacks needed to get them working better.

Centering Using the Publish Settings

Consider the SWF shown in Figure 11-9.

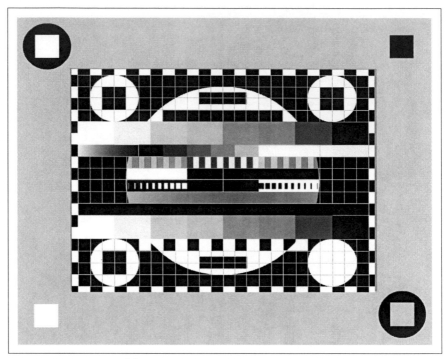

Figure 11-9. A center calibration pattern

The central calibration pattern (a.k.a. test card) covers the Stage, and the four outer shapes (the two circle-squares and two squares) are outside the Stage area. The light gray frame is also outside the Stage area.

If you allow the Stage to scale to fit the browser window (using File → Publish Settings → HTML, then set the Dimensions to percent), you won't see the four outer shapes.

The problem with scaling a SWF in the browser is that, if the user opens a large browser window, the large size of the resulting SWF can dramatically reduce performance of the site. Setting the Horizontal and Vertical options under Flash Alignment to Center and setting the Scale option to No Scale, as shown in Figure 11-8 (in the preceding hack), gives you the centering shown in Figure 11-10.

The SWF is now centered, but you also see all the off-stage content. This is fine for some sites, but many sites have content hidden off stage or partially off stage. It is normal to want to hide content that is currently off stage when creating animation in Flash because this allows panning shots and zoom shots.

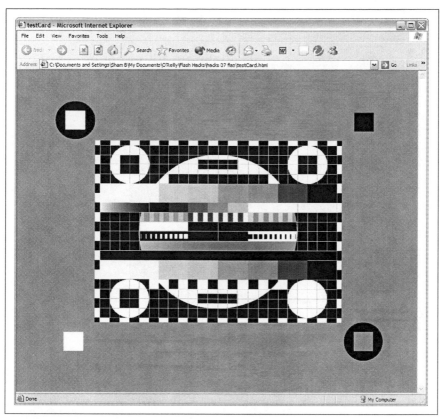

Figure 11-10. A centered, unscaled calibration pattern

For example, consider the SWF in Figure 11-11. This is an animation in progress by Adam Philips, a sometime collaborator of mine.

So, although we can center a SWF in the browser window via the Publish Settings alone, it has a significant disadvantage in that off-stage content is also visible.

Our goal is to hide all off-stage content. As you can see from the shot of the same frame in the final animation, shown in Figure 11-12, only the on-stage content is visible. We can achieve this effect via a little HTML hand-coding.

Centering Using HTML

The way to center a SWF in Flash Player 6 and earlier is simple—use an HTML table. Flash MX produces HTML code that uses the <object> and <embed> tags to embed the SWF in the web page. All you have to do is enclose these two tags with a simple <table> tag with horizontal

Figure 11-11. A SWF unintentionally showing off-stage content

Figure 11-12. The final SWF, hiding off-stage content

(align="center") and vertical (valign="middle") attributes, as follows (hand-coded additions are shown in bold):

```
<html>
<head>
<title>myTitle</title>
</head>
<body bgcolor="#FFFFFF">
<!--URLs used in the movie-->
<!--text used in the movie-->
<table width="100%" height="100%" border="0">
<tr align="center" valign="middle">
<td>
<object...

...</object>
</td>
</tr>
</table>
</body>
</html>
```

This change not only centers your SWF, it also hides the off-stage content. The trouble is that this method doesn't work for Flash MX 2004. Flash MX 2004 exports XHTML, not HTML, and HTML table vertical centering does not work well in XHTML. Regardless of the fact that we could fix the problem by embedding our Flash 7 files in HTML, we should really be embracing XHTML and using CSS <div> and <span> tags instead of deprecated <table> tags and alignment attributes.

Centering a Flash MX 2004 SWF Using CSS

Because Flash MX 2004 exports XHTML, the valign attribute is a no-no, and, although tables are supported, it is better to perform all our formatting in CSS.

The trouble with CSS is that there is no direct way to center anything vertically—we have to hack it.

Ignoring the detailed <object>, <embed>, and <param> tag attributes, a typical Flash MX 2004 XHTML file looks something like this:

```
<!DOCTYPE html PUBLIC "-//W3C//DTD XHTML 1.0 Transitional//EN"
"http://www.w3.org/TR/xhtml1/DTD/xhtml1-transitional.dtd">
<html xmlns="http://www.w3.org/1999/xhtml" xml:lang="en" lang="en">
<head>
<meta http-equiv="Content-Type" content="text/html; charset=iso-8859-1" />
<title>myFlash</title>
</head>
<body bgcolor="#999999">
```

```
<!--URLs used in the movie-->
<!--text used in the movie-->
<object...

...</object>
</body>
</html>
```

To center our Flash content, we first need to hand-edit the XHTML to add a style definition.

To quickly edit the XHTML associated with a Flash SWF that is being viewed locally on IE, select View → Source. Of course, this depends on your file associations opening a plain-text editor such as Notepad and not Word!

Add the following style definition between the <head> and <\head> tags:

```
<style type="text/css">
<!--
body
{
 margin: 0px
}
#centercontent
{
 text-align: center;
 position: absolute;
 top: 50%;
 left: 50%;
}
-->
</style>
```

This should theoretically place your SWF 50% from the lefthand and top edges of the browser (as well as getting rid of any gutters around the edge of the page), but wouldn't you know it, CSS takes the registration point of the SWF to be its top-left corner. You can see this misalignment if you enclose the <object> and <embed> tags with a <div> tag using the centercontent attribute, as follows (additions are shown in bold):

```
<div id="centercontent">
<object ...

...</object>
</div>
```

CSS has centered the SWF, but it's the top-left corner of the SWF that is centered, as shown in Figure 11-13.

Employing the little-known fact that CSS allows negative margins, we can have our cake and eat it too. If we offset the left and top margins by an

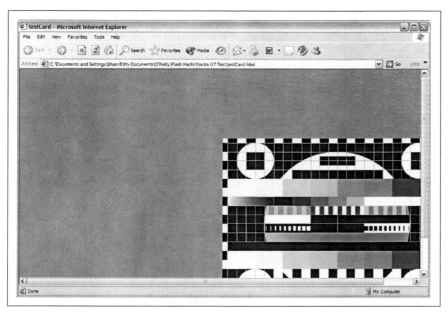

Figure 11-13. The SWF's upper-left corner is in the center of the browser window

amount equal to half the height and width of the SWF's Stage, we also off-set the SWF in such a way that the center point of the SWF and browser coincide, as shown in Figure 11-14.

Add the following to the #centercontent CSS definition in the XHTML file, assuming a default Flash Stage size (550 × 400 pixels):

```
#centercontent
{
margin-left: -275px;
margin-top: -200px;
text-align: center;
position: absolute;
top: 50%;
left: 50%;
}
```

The margin-left and margin-top attributes are set equal to minus half the width and height of your Flash Stage, in pixels. This technique centers your SWF in any browser that understands XHTML and CSS (and XHTML and CSS go together like, um, two things that are pretty much useless without each other).

The final result, in which the SWF is centered and unscaled without revealing off-stage content, is shown in Figure 11-15.

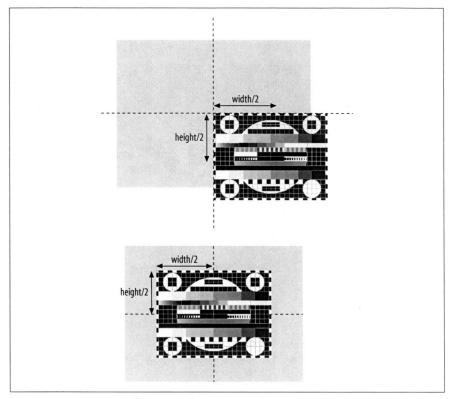

Figure 11-14. Centering the SWF with negative margins in CSS

Final Thoughts

As Flash designers, we should not stick to the old ways when it comes to HTML versus XHTML/CSS. Although properly centering a SWF using only CSS is not obvious, it's not a problem now that you know one or two hacks to make the browser behave.

HACK #92 Dynamically Resize Content

Ideally, your Flash content will display at the desired size even if the user resizes the browser window. Dynamically size your Flash content in response to the browser window to preserve the original design.

Although dynamically resizing the SWF to fit the browser window may seem simple, not many people seem to be able to make it work properly. So let's get hacking.

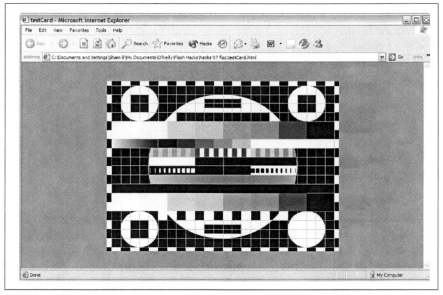

Figure 11-15. The SWF is centered and unscaled without showing off-stage content

Although the Flash Player has the ability to resize the SWF to match the size of the browser window, you wouldn't want to do this for a number of reasons:

- If you allow Flash content to resize too big, it can affect performance drastically, especially on a large screen.

- Allowing Flash sites containing bitmaps to scale up can reveal the imperfections of the bitmaps.

- Allowing Flash sites to resize too small can make them unusable from a user interface perspective.

- Many parts of a typical Flash site are designed to be viewed at a particular size, and the graphical look and feel of the site can be compromised by viewing it at large sizes. For example, pixel fonts are designed to be viewed at a small size and start to look odd when viewed in a larger than intended SWF. Also, you may find that sans-serif and typewriter fonts may not scale proportionally.

A more desirable technique is to allow only parts of your site to be resized or to limit the degree to which they can be resized.

Although the designer may not want her site resizable out of concern for the look and feel, there are two problems. A site that looks cool on a big 21-inch screen may be unreadable on a 17-inch screen. Conversely, a Stage that fits on a 17-inch screen may appear quite small on a large screen, which has more, but smaller, pixels. A good compromise is to allow the site to scale 10% to 20% up or down. This keeps the site legible on a range of screen sizes without compromising the site design aesthetic.

Measuring the Stage

You can read the Stage dimensions very easily with the *Stage* class's static properties:

```
trace(Stage.width);
trace(Stage.height);
```

Although the *trace( )* statements have no effect in the browser, you can see the results in Test Movie mode after resizing the Stage.

If the HTML scale attribute is set to anything other than the literal string "noScale", the Stage.width and Stage.height properties always return the internal Flash Stage dimensions (550×400 by default), although you can override this in ActionScript with:

```
Stage.scaleMode = "noScale";
```

You can also set the scale mode manually via the Scale drop-down list under File → Publish Settings → HTML. With the scaleMode set to "noScale", your Stage.width and Stage.height give the dimensions of the browser window.

The "noScale" mode tells Flash not to resize, but it allows you to control scaling through ActionScript. Note that if you set scaleMode to "showAll", "noBorder", or "exactFit", Stage.width and Stage.height return the Flash Stage size shown under Modify → Document, regardless of the browser window size.

The next problem is that we don't want to be constantly checking the Stage or browser dimensions every frame, but only when they change (i.e., when the user resizes the browser). To do this, we read the dimensions within a listener event, as follows:

```
var stageListener = new Object( );
stageListener.onResize = function( ) {
  trace(Stage.height);
  trace(Stage.width);
};
Stage.scaleMode = "noScale";
Stage.addListener(stageListener);
```

Suppose we have two movie clips. The first is called scaleable_mc, which we want to act as a background and always fill the browser window. The second is called centered_mc, which we want to always stay centered and not scale.

In Figure 11-16, the light gray background gradient is our scaleable_mc clip, and the rectangle with the text "content" in the center represents our site content, centered_mc.

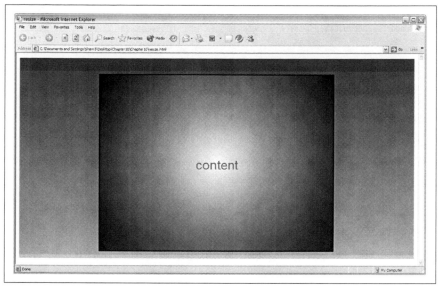

Figure 11-16. A background gradient with superimposed content

Note that having our Flash content completely fill the Stage allows us to add all sorts of features that using a Flash site in front of an HTML tiled GIF background would not. We can easily add transparency effects (drop shadows or an irregularly shaped main site) without relying on Internet Explorer-only ActiveX controls, or we can add incidental animations or effects in the background. Using a vector gradient instead of a bitmap one also gives a smoother pattern. Although we are allowing a SWF with large dimensions, performance slows down only if you change large areas of the screen per frame. Our background area stays essentially constant, so the background does not affect performance.

The following code (available from this book's web site as *varyStage.fla*) will keep content_mc in its original position at its original scale, while scalable_mc will vary in size to fill the browser window:

```
function stageResize( ) {
  scalable_mc._width = Stage.width + 50;
  scalable_mc._height = Stage.height + 50;
}
Stage.scaleMode = "noScale";
myListener = new Object( );
myListener.onResize = function( ) {
```

```
    stageResize( );
};
Stage.addListener(myListener);
```

The last six lines are the ones that execute first (the other lines are a function definition), so let's consider those now. They set scaleMode to "noScale" and then set up a listener to respond to browser resize events.

The main work is done by the *stageResize( )* function, which is invoked whenever the user resizes the browser window. The *stageResize( )* function sets the background clip, scaleable_mc, to the same dimensions as the current browser window, in pixels, or rather the browser dimensions plus a bit more (+50) to also cover as much of the browser gutter as possible.

For the effect to work, select File → Publish Settings → HTML and set Dimensions to Percent and set the Scale to Default (Show All). To prevent the gutter around the browser window (and allow as much of our +50-pixel overlap to show up in the browser window, hand-edit the <body> tag in the HTML file to:

```
    <Body marginwidth="0" marginheight="0" topmargin="0" leftmargin="0">.
```

(Alternatively, you can set the body margins with CSS.)

Final Thoughts

A number of sites that emulate a "Flash operating system within the browser window" consist of a single, large background SWF that always covers the browser window overlain with smaller, nonscaling SWFs. This same technique can also be used successfully for traditional sites, substituting a GIF background tile pattern for a much more flexible and crisp vector background. Allowing a site to scale slightly aids readability immensely without cramping the style of the ubiquitous small (pixel font) text Flash site. There is no limit to adapting your interface to the browser window size. See *http://www.it2004.jp/index2.html* for an example of a complex interface that automatically reconfigures itself in response to browser window resizing. For a discussion of improving performance by buffering *Stage.onResize* events using an interval, see *http://chattyfig.figleaf.com/ezmlm/ezmlm-cgi?1:msn:62851:dggpkifkacibblilcmok*.

Create HTML Links in Flash
#93

Flash content doesn't typically include HTML-style links, but there's no reason it can't. Create HTML-style hyperlinks that control the Flash timeline within Flash.

Flash MX 2004 allows you to use CSS formatting, which supports text that looks like standard HTML links. Unfortunately, they also act like standard

HTML links—they will jump to pages outside the Flash SWF. That is, unless you know how to use *asfunction* to allow the links to control the interface with ActionScript, as shown shortly.

The first step is to create the appearance of hyperlinks in Flash, which is relatively straightforward.

Create a *.css* file in your favorite text editor (mine is SciTE|Flash [Hack #74]) with the text shown in Figure 11-17. Save the file as *flash.css*.

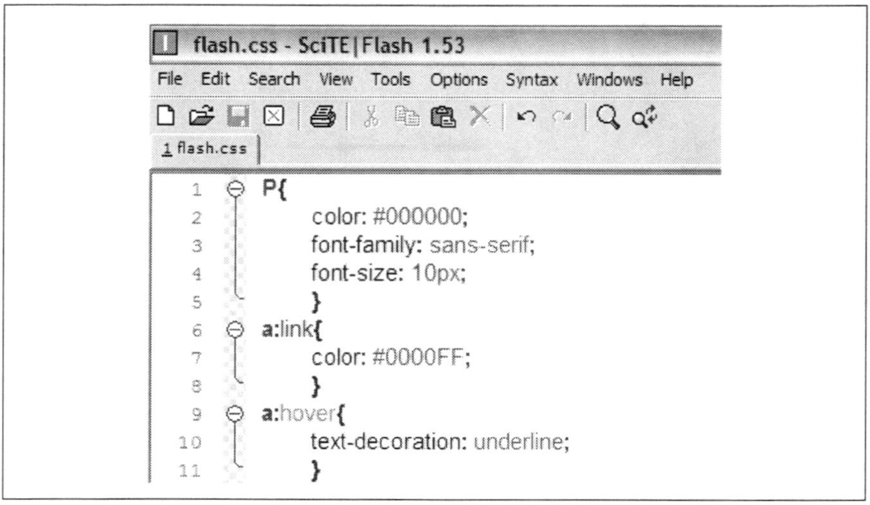

Figure 11-17. The contents of the .css file

Next, create a multiline text field named myHTML_txt on the Stage. Add the following code to create our HTML text inside myHTML_txt, complete with a hyperlink to *http://www.oreilly.com*:

```
var myCSS = new TextField.StyleSheet( );
myCSS.load("flash.css");
myCSS.onLoad = function(success) {
  if (success) {
    myHTML_txt.styleSheet = myCSS;
  }
};
myHTML_txt.html = true;
myHTML_txt.htmlText = "<p>This is a <a href =
  'http://www.oreilly.com'>link</a> to my site.</p>";
myHTML_txt.htmlText += "<p>Click it and see!</p>";
```

The hyperlink appears, as shown in Figure 11-18.

Although a pure HTML hyperlink within a Flash SWF is cool for navigating to external pages, it isn't much use in controlling the current Flash timeline. To control the Flash timeline, we have to use asfunction. The following

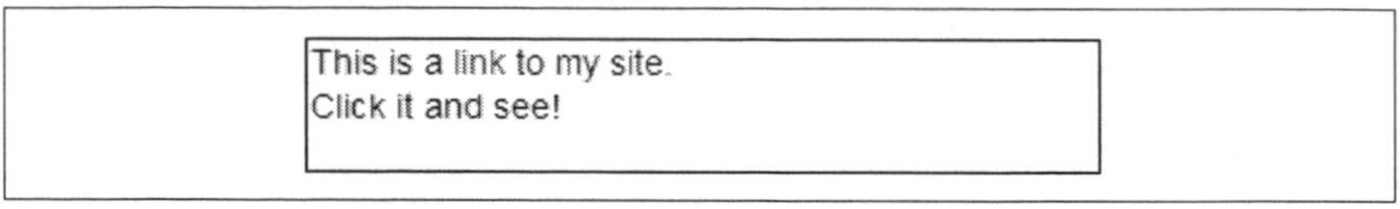

Figure 11-18. A hyperlink as a true HTML link in Flash

code uses asfunction to invoke the function *asLink( )* with an argument of
10 when the link is clicked, causing the playhead to jump to frame 10 in the
current SWF's timeline. Note that asfunction: is a protocol that is specified
as the link, just as mailto: and http: are protocols. The browser passes any
URLs starting with asfunction: to the Flash Player plugin or ActiveX control. And the Flash Player invokes the function specified in the first argument following asfunction: and passes subsequent arguments to the
function.

```
function asLink(goto) {
  gotoAndPlay(goto);
}
var myCSS = new TextField.StyleSheet( );
myCSS.load("flash.css");
myCSS.onLoad = function(success) {
  if (success) {
    myHTML_txt.styleSheet = myCSS;
  }
};
myHTML_txt.html = true;
myHTML_txt.htmlText = "<p>This is a <a href =
    'asfunction:asLink, 10'>link</a> to frame 10.</p>";
myHTML_txt.htmlText += "<p>Click it and see!</p>";
stop( );
```

Final Thoughts

Because Flash MX 2004 supports HTML text and a subset of CSS formatting, HTML-style links can be mixed with standard Flash buttons. This hack
shows the route to using such links to provide internal Flash navigation
from outside Flash (or simply to run ActionScript code). Of course, it can be
used for the more typical hyperlink to external pages.

Knowing how to do this is pretty important, given that Flash can now
include images as well as HTML-formatted text within a text field [Hack #46],
making it a way of presenting mini-HTML pages within a Flash SWF. Text
fields can even contain other SWFs, which is a cool alternative to *loadMovie( )*
or *loadMovieNum( )*!

Integrate the Back Button with Flash

A long-standing complaint against Flash's usability is that it didn't work with the browser's Back button. Dispel this myth—use the browser Back button to navigate back in a non-timeline-based Flash site.

Part of the design intent of Flash MX (and Flash Player 6) was to make Flash more accessible. Among other things, Macromedia added support for named anchors.

Most designers know anchors by their HTML-based implementation. An anchor is a link within a document (usually) to another part of the same document. It is often used in long text documents in which significant parts of the document scroll outside the visible area of the browser window. Rather than having to scroll up and down the page, an anchor allows users to jump to the required section via an intrapage link. The anchor name is preceded by a #, such as *http://www.oreilly.com/index.html#faq*.

In its implementation of anchors, Macromedia equated the HTML document to the SWF's main timeline, so anchors allow you to jump back and forth along _root using the browser Back button (assuming an accessibility-enabled browser). Naturally, within Flash, you can still use typical Flash navigation (i.e., Flash buttons with *gotoAndPlay( )* actions as part of their *onRelease( )* event handlers).

One major problem is that most Flash sites do not use frames on the _root timeline as anchor points. When the user clicks on a button, he doesn't jump to a frame on _root because that approach makes the SWF difficult to maintain and has a number of issues when you start using bandwidth-heavy content. Instead, a Flash interface for a typical commercial application uses an ActionScript-based system that employs *loadMovie( )* and nested movie clips or attaches content directly to the main timeline.

The only way to hack around this is to have hidden HTML pages that change in step with the Flash site; it is these hidden pages that populate the browser history. When the hidden HTML pages change due to the browser Back and Forward buttons, JavaScript is used to send variable values to the Flash site telling it about the page changes, and the Flash site is configured to catch and respond to these changes.

You can't use JavaScript to simply read the browser history and send it to Flash because it isn't accessible to JavaScript (or anything else) for security reasons (i.e., keeping your browsing preferences outside the reach of advertisers).

Creating the HTML

By far the easiest way to set up your hidden HTML pages is to include them in the same page as the Flash site using a frameset. Given that many Flash users have the Macromedia Studio MX package, we will use Dreamweaver MX (you can enter the HTML listings shown in an editor of your choice).

Dreamweaver MX has something close to the frameset we need as a standard template, so select File → New and select the Fixed Bottom frameset as shown in Figure 11-19.

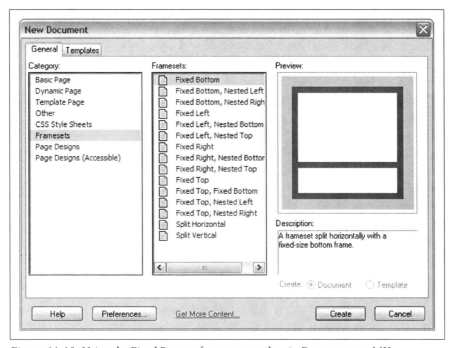

Figure 11-19. Using the Fixed Bottom frameset template in Dreamweaver MX

Our Flash HTML file will populate the top frame, and the hidden HTML pages will be implemented as blank pages (containing only JavaScript) in the lower frame.

Using this template (or similar), create the following HTML. The lines I have changed from the Dreamweaver MX defaults—the title, the two frame source files, and the noframes content—are highlighted in bold. Save the frameset as *frame.html*.

```
<!DOCTYPE HTML PUBLIC "-//W3C//DTD HTML 4.01 Frameset//EN" "http://www.w3.
org/TR/html4/frameset.dtd">
<html>
<head>
```

```
<title>:: Flash with Browser History ::</title>
<meta http-equiv="Content-Type" content="text/html; charset=iso-8859-1">

</head>
<body bgcolor="#FFFFFF">
<frameset rows="*,80" frameborder="NO" border="0" framespacing="0">
  <frame src="flash.html" name="mainFrame">
  <frame src="one.html" name="bottomFrame" scrolling="NO" noresize>
</frameset>
<noframes><body>
You should really get a more up-to-date browser before they phase out steam
power.
</body></noframes>
</html>
```

Next up, our hidden pages. Create five blank HTML files named *one.html*, *two.html*, *three.html*, *four.html*, and *five.html*, and save them in the same folder as *frame.html*.

Modify the first file, *one.html*, as shown (changes from Dreamweaver MX defaults are shown in bold):

```
<!DOCTYPE HTML PUBLIC "-//W3C//DTD HTML 4.01 Transitional//EN">
<html>
<head>
<title>one</title>
<meta http-equiv="Content-Type" content="text/html; charset=iso-8859-1">
</head>
<body bgcolor="#FFFFFF">
  <script language='JavaScript'>
    parent.mainFrame.flash.SetVariable('history', 1);
  </script>
</body>
</html>
```

Note that the <title> tag should change for each file, in this case one, and the line of JavaScript should specify the file number, in this case 1, as the second parameter passed to *SetVariable( )*. We explicitly set the background color of the bottom frame pages, so that they aren't noticeable if the user has a different default background color set.

Modify the remaining four HTML files similarly. For example, here are the changes to *five.html*:

```
<!DOCTYPE HTML PUBLIC "-//W3C//DTD HTML 4.01 Transitional//EN">
<html>
<head>
<title>five</title>
<meta http-equiv="Content-Type" content="text/html; charset=iso-8859-1">
</head>
<body bgcolor="#FFFFFF">
  <script language='JavaScript'>
    parent.mainFrame.flash.SetVariable('history', 5);
```

```
    </script>
    </body>
    </html>
```

Your frameset won't work just yet because it is missing the *flash.html* section, so let's create that next.

In Flash, create a new Flash Document with File → New. Select File → Publish Settings and set these options under the HTML tab of the Publish Settings dialog box: set the Horizontal and Vertical options under Flash Alignment to Center, and set the Scale option to No Scale, as shown in Figure 11-8 in [Hack #90].

Save the Flash file as *flash.fla* in the same folder as the previously saved HTML files (but remember to upload the SWF, not the FLA, if you decide to put the files online!). Publish the file (File → Publish) to create *flash.html* and *flash.swf*.

Creating the Flash Content

We will create a simple embedded timeline to show the principle of the hack.

Create a new movie clip symbol with five keyframes (it doesn't matter what the symbol is named), as shown in Figure 11-20, each of which shows a different page of our Flash application, as shown in Figure 11-21.

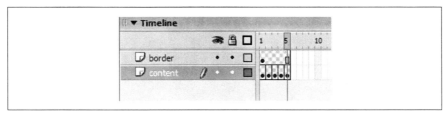

Figure 11-20. A clip with five keyframes representing different pages of our Flash application

Place the clip onto the Stage at frame 1 of the main timeline, and give it the instance name content using the Properties panel. Next, add a menu of five buttons with instance names b1 (the 1 button) to b5 (the 5 button).

Finally, create a new layer above the current one, calling it *actions*. Attach the following script to frame 1 of this new layer:

```
b1.onRelease = function( ) {
  fillBottom("one.html");
  content.gotoAndStop(1);
};
b2.onRelease = function( ) {
```

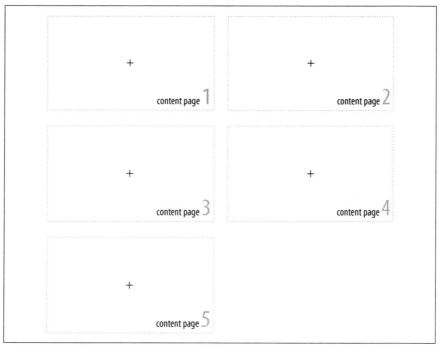

Figure 11-21. Pages of our Flash application

```
    fillBottom("two.html");
    content.gotoAndStop(2);
  };
  b3.onRelease = function( ) {
    fillBottom("three.html");
    content.gotoAndStop(3);
  };
  b4.onRelease = function( ) {
    fillBottom("four.html");
    content.gotoAndStop(4);
  };
  b5.onRelease = function( ) {
    fillBottom("five.html");
    content.gotoAndStop(5);
  };
  function setHistory( ) {
    if (history == 1) {
      hisEnabled = true;
      content.onEnterFrame = function( ) {
        if (history != 0) {
          this.gotoAndStop(history);
          history = 0;
        }
      };
    }
```

```
    clearInterval(startHistory);
  }
  function fillBottom(doc) {
    if (hisEnabled) {
      getURL(doc, "bottomFrame");
    }
  }
  var history;
  var hisEnabled = false;
  startHistory = setInterval(setHistory, 500);
  content.stop( );
```

When you click each of the buttons, not only does Flash jump to the appropriate frame in the Flash timeline, but the function *fillBottom( )* jumps to a corresponding HTML page in the lower frame of the final web page. Although the user doesn't see these HTML pages (they contain no visible content), the browser adds them to the browser history.

As the user clicks the browser Back and Forward buttons, the same HTML pages are reloaded from the browser history, and the JavaScript inside them changes a Flash variable, history, to a value between 1 and 5, depending on the page.

The *onEnterFrame( )* handler catches this change and forces content to change its appearance in sync with the HTML page change, thus propagating the browser history to the Flash movie.

Note that when you are using the Flash buttons for navigation, you actually tell the movie clip content to jump to the required frame twice, once from ActionScript and once from JavaScript. Rather than remove the Action-Script jumps, it's better to leave them in for redundancy; this ensures that the navigation still works, even if JavaScript isn't available.

The ActionScript is written so that:

- The navigation still works if JavaScript is not available in the current browser (or the SWF is running in a Standalone Player). Flash knows if JavaScript is not working via the if (history==1) check within *setHistory( )*. If JavaScript is disabled, history is undefined, and Flash addresses this by not setting up the *onEnterFrame( )* handler so that no checks on browser history are made.

- A delay of 0.5 seconds is included before ActionScript starts talking to JavaScript. The HTML doesn't seem to start setting the Flash variable history until after a short delay. The ActionScript therefore delays the creation of the *onEnterFrame( )* handler for 0.5 seconds using *setInterval( )*.

Final Thoughts

If you set up a history by moving back and forward using the Flash navigation buttons, you will see the browser Back and Forward buttons become
active. Clicking on either of the browser buttons allows you to go back/
forward through this history.

A lack of Back button functionality is one of the major usability problems
normally pinned on Flash. Someone tell Jakob we've fixed it!

Of course, there are still a few issues here for advanced Flash users, like the
fact that you need to create (and maintain) a blank HTML page for every
Flash page you use, which can be a real pain and which breaks one of the
really cool things about Flash design (i.e., it isn't page based). This brings up
an irony of using the Back button in Flash. The question arises, where
should the user go back to in the current Flash application? In an HTML-
based site, each page represents the application state at a given time. But in a
Flash application, each "scene" might span many frames and contain animations or time-based media. For example, if the user clicks the Back button to
return to the previous scene, should the Flash designer rewind and replay
the animation, audio, and video in the scene? Think carefully about your
application's state when deciding which pages to use to represent a point in
time.

A possible enhancement to this hack is to generate the HTML pages in the
hidden frame dynamically via JavaScript. This way, the number of pages you
can add to the browser history is not hardcoded, allowing for a more flexible solution for more complex Flash sites.

JavaScript-to-Flash communication is not supported in all browsers, as discussed at *http://www.macromedia.com/support/flash/ts/documents/java_
script_comm.htm*. This hack works in Netscape and IE, but at least one user
reported a JavaScript error when using Mozilla 1.6. You can test various
browsers at Macromedia's JavaScript-to-Flash communication example
page, at *http://www.macromedia.com/support/flash/ts/documents/java_script_
comm/javascript_to_flash.html*.

Give the Flash SWF Keyboard Focus

#95

Flash can't detect keystrokes or accept text input unless the SWF has
keyboard focus. Force keyboard focus onto your Flash SWF without requiring
the user to click manually.

The browser does not give your SWF browser focus until you select the
SWF, usually by clicking on it.

This means that your SWF cannot respond to keypresses until it has been clicked on at least once, something that can be undesirable in a number of situations. For example, you may have just loaded a video game in which the player must take control using the arrow keys. Unless the user is made to click on the SWF before the game commences, the arrow keypresses are not detected. The usual workaround is to force the user to click once on the SWF, usually by clicking a Start button put there solely for this purpose. It is better to have a large clickable area and text instructions such as "Click anywhere to proceed," but it is even more elegant to not require the user to click at all.

Fortunately, you can force browser focus from within Flash using the following ActionScript (it works best when tested in a browser, rather than from Test Movie mode within the Flash authoring application):

```
getURL("javascript:me.focus( );void 0;");
```

Using *getURL( )*, the line invokes the JavaScript *Window.focus( )* method, targeting a file called *me*. As long as your SWF is called *me.swf*, it will gain focus automatically.

Final Thoughts

Although this is a very short hack, it's one of those little touches that makes your Flash presentation's look and feel much more professional. Users expect to be able to fill in and tab between the text fields in a pop-up form without first having to click on it. If keypresses don't register, users get confused. As with the preceding hack, this technique doesn't work in browsers that don't support JavaScript-to-Flash communication, such as Mozilla.

Add Key Shortcuts to Your Site

#96

To make your application easier and faster to use (and more like a desktop application), associate a keystroke or key combination with each button in your SWF.

Adding keyboard shortcuts to each of your buttons makes your site more accessible. This hack shows how to implement shortcuts with a minimum of code. Detecting keypresses is a little more complex than just looking for a key being pressed. We have to be able to detect keyboard combinations, such as Ctrl-Q, and detect both when the key is pressed and when it is released.

Detecting Keypresses

To detect the state of the keyboard, you first have to set up a listener object that listens to the *Key* class. The following code traces a message every time it detects a keypress:

```
function down( ) {
  trace("detected!");
}
var keyListener:Object = new Object( );
keyListener.onKeyDown = down;
Key.addListener(keyListener);
```

Note that the *Key* class does not differentiate between uppercase and lower-case letters when looking for keyboard inputs. For example, the *Key* class returns the same keycode regardless of whether you have the Shift key down or the Caps Lock key enabled when you press the A key.

The trouble with our code is that it runs our function for as long as a key is held down, which makes it unsuitable for detecting keyboard shortcuts, because pressing and holding a key down will generate multiple events. To fix this, we need to switch our event handling around so that we see only one "detected!" message for each key down-up cycle. The following code does this:

```
function down( ) {
  trace("detected!");
  delete this.onKeyDown;
  this.onKeyUp = up;
}
function up( ) {
  this.onKeyUp = undefined;
  this.onKeyDown = down;
}
var keyListener:Object = new Object( );
keyListener.onKeyDown = down;
Key.addListener(keyListener);
```

As soon as a *keyDown* event is detected, the code switches to looking for the corresponding *keyUp* event. The *keyUp* event causes the cycle to restart, creating a set of events that respond to the full keystroke toggle.

Note that this code works even if you attempt a keystroke combination, such as Ctrl-A. In that case, you will see a "detected!" message for each key.

Turning Keystrokes into Inputs

So far, we have only the ability to detect keystrokes. We really need to be able to detect which keys were pressed. We can do this with the *Key. isDown( )* and *Key.getCode( )* methods. The first tells you whether a particular key is pressed, and the second tells you the keycode of the last key that caused a key event (i.e., the last key that changed its state, which will not necessarily be the key that is currently held down). For example, if you hold down the A and S keys at the same time, then release the A key, the *getCode()* method returns the code for the A key, even though the S key is still down.

Note that the *Key* class returns keycode values for the physical keys themselves and does not take modifiers into account. For example, pressing the X key will give you the same code regardless of the state of the Shift or Ctrl keys.

The online help has a table listing the alphanumeric keycodes. Search on "Keyboard keys and keycode values" to find them. For nonalphanumeric keys, such as the arrow keys and spacebar, you can use the constant properties of the *Key* class. For example, Key.SPACE contains the keycode for the spacebar and Key.CONTROL contains the keycode for the Ctrl key.

For example:

```
x = Key.isDown(65); // x is true if the "A" key is pressed
y = Key.getCode( );  // y is 65 if the last key to cause an event was "A"
```

Knowing a key's keycode, we can quickly write ActionScript that detects single keystrokes. Assuming you have three buttons on the Stage with instance names buttonA, buttonB, and buttonC, the following code causes each button's *onRelease( )* handler to execute if you click button A, B, or C. It also gives selection focus to the button associated with a keystroke, which (among other things) causes a yellow rectangle to be drawn around the button:

```
function aHandler( ) {
  trace("you clicked A");
}
function bHandler( ) {
  trace("you clicked B");
}
function cHandler( ) {
  trace("you clicked C");
}
function down( ) {
  if (keys[Key.getCode( )] != undefined) {
    keys[Key.getCode( )].onRelease( );
    Selection.setFocus(keys[Key.getCode( )]);
  }
  this.onKeyDown = undefined;
  this.onKeyUp = up;
}
function up( ) {
  this.onKeyUp = undefined;
  this.onKeyDown = down;
}
```

```
//
var keys:Array = new Array( );
var keyListener:Object = new Object( );
keys[65] = buttonA;
keys[66] = buttonB;
keys[67] = buttonC;
buttonA.onRelease = aHandler;
buttonB.onRelease = bHandler;
buttonC.onRelease = cHandler;
keyListener.onKeyDown = down;
Key.addListener(keyListener);
```

The preceding code creates an array called keys whose indexes are used to identify associated Flash buttons. For example, keys[65] contains a reference to buttonA, so when the A key (keycode 65) is pressed, the event handler *buttonA.onRelease( )* is run. In Figure 11-22, the left and right images show the buttons buttonA, buttonB, and buttonC before (left) and after (right) the keyboard A key is pressed. When the A key is pressed, the message "You clicked A" appears in the Output panel.

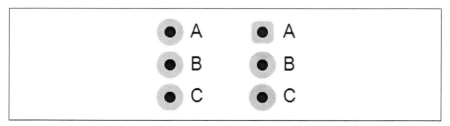

Figure 11-22. Unselected buttons (left); buttonA selected (right)

For the Flash Player to be able to capture keystrokes, the SWF must have browser focus [Hack #95]. The SWF maintains focus if the SWF within the browser has been clicked on, until other content outside the SWF is clicked on. Simply moving the mouse causes a button to lose browser focus, so you may never see the yellow bounding rectangle if you are holding the mouse when pressing A.

To test a SWF that needs to capture keystrokes, you should select Control → Disable Shortcuts once in Test Movie mode. This prevents the Flash application from capturing keyboard inputs for its own keyboard shortcuts and masking them from the SWF under test.

Turning Combos into Inputs

As well as having single keystroke shortcuts, many applications have multiple keystroke combinations (also known as combos), such as Ctrl-F1. Flash is sometimes used as a standalone desktop application, so it would be reasonable to use combos as Flash inputs.

However, you need to be careful about using combos as inputs into Flash, given that Flash is rarely at the top of the pecking order for receiving combos. Most of the common combos are already taken by the operating system or the browser, so Flash will not receive them all.

We can make our code look for combo keystrokes by specifying an array that defines a number of keys that need to be held down to form an input.

Suppose we wanted to make:

- A the keystroke for buttonA
- Ctrl-B the combo for buttonB
- Ctrl-D the combo for buttonC

We can define this information in an array of objects:

```
keys[0] = {btn:buttonA, combo:[65]};
keys[1] = {btn:buttonB, combo:[Key.CONTROL, 66]};
keys[2] = {btn:buttonC, combo:[Key.CONTROL, 68]};
```

Each of our keys entries is now an object consisting of two properties:

- The keys[].btn property tells us the Flash button with which to associate the combo.
- The keys[].combo property is an array containing the individual keys that make up each combo.

The following code uses this data structure to add the keyboard combos for our three buttons, buttonA, buttonB, and buttonC. The hacky part of this code is the way we check whether the full combo is down. For each combo, the code:

- Sets a Boolean, allKeys, to true prior to searching through each combo entry, keys[j].combo.
- For each key in the combo, tests whether each key is down via Key.isDown(keys[j].combo[i]). This expression is true if the key is down and false if it is not. This value is ANDed (&&) with allKeys. If any key is not down, allKeys becomes false and remains so until the end of the loop.
- At the end of the search, if allKeys is still true, we know that the full combo was depressed.

The cool thing about using the && logic operator in this way is that allKeys doesn't care in which order the keys were pressed or how many keys there are. We test whether they are all down whenever we carry out the test. If allKeys is true, the code carries on in much the same way as the preceding single keystroke code. The following code demonstrates (changes are shown in bold):

```
function aHandler( ) {
  trace("you clicked A");
}
function bHandler( ) {
  trace("you clicked B");
}
function cHandler( ) {
  trace("you clicked C");
}
function down( ) {
  var allKeys;
  //trace("--------------");
  for (var j = 0; j < keys.length; j++) {
    allKeys = true;
    for (var i = 0; i < keys[j].combo.length; i++) {
      allKeys = allKeys && Key.isDown(keys[j].combo[i]);
    }
    if (allKeys) {
      Selection.setFocus(keys[j]);
      //trace("combo detected");
      this.onKeyDown = undefined;
      this.onKeyUp = up;
      keys[j].btn.onRelease( );
      break;
    }
  }
}
function up( ) {
  //trace("up");
  this.onKeyUp = undefined;
  this.onKeyDown = down;
}
//
var keys:Array = new Array( );
var keyListener:Object = new Object( );
keys[0] = {btn:buttonA, combo:[65]};
keys[1] = {btn:buttonB, combo:[Key.CONTROL, 66]}; // Ctrl-B
keys[2] = {btn:buttonC, combo:[Key.CONTROL, 68]}; // Ctrl-D
buttonA.onRelease = aHandler;
buttonB.onRelease = bHandler;
buttonC.onRelease = cHandler;
keyListener.onKeyDown = down;
Key.addListener(keyListener);
```

I have left in some useful *trace( )* actions, which I used in developing this code in the listing. If you want to see how (and in what order) the code detects and sets off the *keyDown( )*, *keyUp( )*, and *onRelease( )* event handlers, you can uncomment the *trace( )* statements and view the order of events in the Output panel. It should make the code much easier to understand.

The Ctrl-B shortcut won't work when you test the movie in Flash unless you disable keyboard shortcuts, because Ctrl-B opens the Bandwidth Profiler. Ctrl-C doesn't work because it is captured by other applications, most likely your operating system's copy feature so we use Ctrl-D as the keyboard combination for buttonC.

If you test the SWF in the browser, you will also see that Ctrl-B may cause problems (it is the shortcut for organizing your Favorites links in Internet Explorer). The moral of this is to check that your combos are not used by anything else that might be running at the same time as the Flash SWF; otherwise, Flash will not see them!

Final Thoughts

Accessibility is becoming more of a required feature as time goes on. Making your site respond to the keyboard as well as the mouse makes it more useful to the sight impaired but also makes it more accessible to the command-line twitch-typer. Surprisingly few Flash sites support keyboard shortcuts, probably because the code to do this is not totally obvious. Well, it is now, so there's no excuse!

Security
Hacks 97–100

With HTML-based web sites, a user can quickly download a site's source files and review them without permission (by definition, the HTML page is just a text file that is sent to the user's browser or any client that requests it). A web browser or "site-sucker" program can also easily download any text and images displayed on a web page. Unfortunately, copyright laws offer scant protection, especially outside the United States and Europe, so most site owners accept that content will be copied or try to adopt technological defenses against it. On the mild end of the spectrum, a developer might add a visual copyright watermark to her images, forcing would-be pirates to at least edit out the watermark to cover their tracks. On the more aggressive end of the spectrum, files can be invisibly digitally watermarked to prevent their playback on unauthorized systems (of course, all such digital protection is prone to cracking, and we don't deal with that extensive technical and politically charged subject here).

The SWF file format is binary, so it cannot be read as easily as a text file, but this offers little extra protection. It simply requires software designed to read the SWF file format, which Macromedia makes publicly available at *http:// www.macromedia.com/software/flash/open/licensing/fileformat*. (The license is free, but the SWF format is still proprietary to Macromedia, not open source.) For those interested in writing software to create SWF files, see OpenSWF.org (*http://www.openswf.org*), a resource site for developers working with the SWF format.

A number of Flash SWF decompilers and content extractors—including ActionScript Viewer (*http://buraks.com/asv*), the first one to hit the market a few years back—are available.

So SWF files suffer from the same vulnerability as traditional web assets. There is no way to prevent the resourceful cracker from looking at your assets and code, so don't store sensitive information, such as passwords, in your SWF file. However, you can at least make theft more difficult for the cracker because many will give up rather quickly when faced with obstacles or pursue a more vulnerable site.

Aside from content theft, a bigger issue is security. In traditional web design, no sensitive information should appear in any downloadable files or any file that can easily be opened or copied. Instead, secure information should be transmitted directly between the client browser and the web server. Such transmitted data is not saved by the browser, but it can still be captured.

Flash doesn't implement its own security protocol but rather piggybacks onto the browser's support for encryption. So when you use URLs starting with the "https:" protocol, Flash uses the browser's HTTPS services, if available, to transmit the data. Therefore, you should ensure that the user's browser supports HTTPS and uses an HTTPS server to encrypt all transmitted information. For example, a so-called Password field (available as an option for Input Text fields via the Properties panel) offers no security. It simply obscures the input with asterisks but still allows the plain-text password to be transmitted to the server. Readers unfamiliar with over-the-wire security should understand that sending sensitive information, such as credit card numbers or passwords, as plain text instead of in encrypted form across an open channel is inviting trouble. A packet sniffer can easily intercept your client-server traffic as it wends its way across the Internet. Encrypted information can also be intercepted, but it can't be decoded as readily as plain text, so intercepting it does the cracker little good.

There are related security concerns when using adjuncts to Flash, such as Flash Communication Server MX (FlashCom server). A FlashCom stream, such as audio or video, should not be considered secure because the transmission protocol used (Real Time Messaging Protocol or RTMP) is not secure. FlashCom applications can still use a secure server for normal (non-media) HTTPS transmissions. The *Macromedia Flash Communication Server MX Security Overview* whitepaper at *http://www.macromedia.com/devnet/mx/flashcom/articles/security_overview.html* discusses FlashCom security.

Likewise, server-side code that is improperly protected can represent a security risk. When using Flash Remoting, developers can write their server-side code in various languages, including Server-Side ActionScript (SSAS), which is supported for ColdFusion and JRun installations. Like many server-side scripting languages, SSAS code is stored in a plain-text file on the server (the code is stored in ActionScript Remote files with an *.asr* extension). However, in their default configurations, many web servers, including Apache and Microsoft IIS, don't specify the *.asr* file extension in their list of non-browsable file types. Therefore, if a user browses to the URL of an *.asr* file, he can download it and read the code in plain text! This is a real security flaw because some ColdFusion and JRun developers use SSAS to query a database or work with the filesystem on the server. If a cracker can read the contents of an *.asr* file, he can learn about your database and file structure and likely exploit your system's vulnerabilities.

 To plug this major security gap, Server-Side ActionScript developers should configure their web servers so that *.asr* files aren't served as plain text.

Flash security is a big topic that cannot be covered exhaustively here but is well documented elsewhere. The Macromedia Flash Developer Center security page at *http://www.macromedia.com/devnet/mx/flash/security.html* provides links to additional security whitepapers that cover Flash MX and Flash MX 2004 (Flash Player 6 and 7) and the *security sandbox* in which they operate (to prevent virus attacks, denial of service attacks, etc.).

Although Flash shares the same security issues as many other web technologies, Flash presents several special cases:

- Flash Player 6 and 7 can retrieve data from a locally connected microphone or video camera. Flash can also store information on the local hard drive, but because Flash is a media delivery plugin, the stored information may be much larger than a typical browser cookie. Flash's *privacy settings* allow the user to limit Flash Player's access to the microphone, camera, and hard drive.
- Macromedia's uses *cross-domain policy files* to control the ways in which Flash content on one domain can access content on another domain.
- Flash can run as an application in a Standalone Player, independent of the browser as described under "Handling Local Executables."

Privacy Settings

Flash can access media streams available to the local (client) computer, including data from any connected microphone and video camera. Flash can also store persistent information (files or other preference data) [Hack #44] locally via the *SharedObject* class (so-called *local shared objects* or LSOs). For details on the *SharedObject* class, see pages 760–768 in *ActionScript for Flash MX: The Definitive Guide*, by Colin Moock (O'Reilly), and Recipe 16.4—"Saving a Local Shared Object"—in the *ActionScript Cookbook*, by Joey Lott (O'Reilly).

The ability for a site to receive input from a microphone or camera attached to your computer or store information on your hard drive raises privacy and security issues. Therefore, the Flash Player must have the user's permission before it allows the SWF to do anything that may infringe on the user's privacy. Such permission is sought on a per-domain basis (the Flash Player 7 System.exactSettings property specifies whether to use superdomain or exact-domain matching rules when accessing local settings) via the Macromedia Flash Player Settings pop-up window shown in Figure 12-1.

Figure 12-1. The Flash Player Settings window

This pop-up window appears atop the running SWF in several situations:

User interaction
> The user can right-click (Windows) or ⌘-click (Mac) on the SWF and select Settings from the context menu that appears.

As required by the content
> The Flash Player displays the pop-up window if the running SWF attempts to access any feature that may compromise user privacy, unless the user has previously given permission for the domain and checked the Remember option.

Via ActionScript
> Invoking *System.showSettings(tab)* where *tab* is 0, 1, 2, or 3 brings up the Settings panel with the corresponding tab open: Privacy (0), Local Storage (1), Microphone (2), or Camera (3). Omitting the *tab* argument opens the Settings panel to the last opened tab. You could, for example, add this feature as part of a button handler or before attempting to store local data.

The Settings dialog box has tabs that allow the user to manage settings for Privacy, Local Storage, Microphone, and Camera access. Additional Flash Player settings are available only via the Settings Manager on Macromedia's web site (*http://www.macromedia.com/support/documentation/en/flashplayer/help/settings_manager.html*).

Users can access the web-based Settings Manager by clicking the Advanced button on the Privacy tab of the Settings dialog box. Once at Macromedia's site, the user can configure global and domain-specific options regarding privacy, storage, security, and update notifications.

The following script shows the skeleton code to handle permissions for the default local microphone hardware. The other Flash features that require permission vary slightly in implementation but are very similar in overall technique.

The code assumes the presence of a dynamic, multiline text field with instance name myStatus. You will see best results if you test it in the browser using File → Publish Preview → Default - (HTML) or by pressing F12.

```
1   function micPermission( ) {
2     if (myMic.muted) {
3       myStatus.text = "User denied permission.";
4     } else {
5       myStatus.text = "User gave permission.";
6     }
7   }
8   // Create a Microphone object and attach it to the
9   // current timeline.
10  var myMic:Microphone = Microphone.get( );
11  this.attachAudio(myMic);
12  // Check current microphone muted value
13  if (myMic.muted) {
14    myMic.onStatus = micPermission;
15    myStatus.text = "Either user will always deny access to the " +
16      "microphone, or user is looking at the Microphone Settings panel " +
17      "and function micPermission( ) will soon run.";
18  } else {
19    myStatus.text = "User has already given permission.";
20  }
```

Lines 10 and 11 set up the *Microphone* instance (note that although Flash allows you to select from a list of possible connected microphones, you are strongly advised to use the code shown, which selects the default microphone).

Flash assumes any hardware capable of having a microphone connected to it in fact has a microphone attached, and this includes each sound card Flash finds. On most computers, the default device is defined as such for a very good reason. It is the only one to have a microphone actually attached!

When you try to access the microphone using *Microphone.get( )*, Flash automatically opens the Settings panel if the user has not previously granted permission. If you prefer, you can invoke *System.showSettings(2)* to open the panel manually (for example, if you prefer to ask at the beginning of the application rather than waiting until the application tries to access the microphone). If the user has previously given permission to allow use of the microphone to your site, `myMic.muted` is `false`, the script displays the text "User has already given permission.", and the microphone is available to Flash. If `myMic.muted` is `true`, the user has either not yet allowed permission for your site to use the microphone or has set privacy permissions to always deny your site access. If appropriate, Flash displays the Settings panel, and the code waits to see if the user changes the permission.

Once the user closes the Settings panel, the function *micPermission( )* is invoked and code will run depending on whether the muted property is `true` or `false`. If, however, the user has already denied permission during a previous visit to your site, you will not be given permission and *micPermission( )* will never run (because no status change occurs). Your code will exit, displaying the message on lines 15–17 (which is all one long statement). You have the option to pester the user to give permission by forcing the Player Settings window to appear (using *System.showSettings(2)*), but it's better to give a brief message as to why nothing is happening and then let the user decide what to do next.

Cross-Domain Policy

Macromedia has defined very stringent policies (called the *security sandbox* by Macromedia) for the control and management of how SWF files can interact with one another and with executable files on the Web or your hard drive. Most of these policies are more stringent in Flash Player 7 than in previous versions (and more stringent than many other web technologies implement). You may find that some sites that work with Flash Player 6 do not work in Flash Player 7 due to added security restrictions, as described at *http://www.macromedia.com/devnet/mx/flash/articles/fplayer_security.html*.

Macromedia's cross-domain policy determines whether a SWF can load or communicate with other SWFs or content from other domains. In particular, for Flash Player 7, the default policy is as follows:

- A SWF is not allowed to load another SWF unless it is loaded from exactly the same domain.

- A SWF is not allowed to communicate with any other SWF (i.e., using the *LocalConnection* class) unless both SWFs come from exactly the same domain.

- A SWF is not allowed to load assets from a different domain than the one from which the SWF is running.

You can modify this default policy to allow SWFs from other domains to interact with your SWFs:

- moock.org's *Cross-Domain Policy File* technote (*http://moock.org/asdg/ technotes/crossDomainPolicyFiles*) discusses the conditions that cause a warning dialog to appear when playing Flash Player 6-format (and older) SWF files in Flash Player 7 and cause data loading to fail in Flash Player 7–format SWF files.

- Flash technote *Macromedia Flash Security Sandbox* (*http://www. macromedia.com/support/flash/ts/documents/security_sandbox.htm*) explains the Flash Player 7 security sandbox. The sandbox provides a restricted area that "surrounds" the Flash Player to restrict access to private data and prevent a SWF from executing potentially damaging applications.

- Flash technote 16520 *Loading Data Across domains* (*http://www. macromedia.com/support/flash/ts/documents/load_xdomain.htm*) explains what operations are allowed and disallowed when attempting to load assets from a different domain than the one from which the SWF is running.

- Macromedia technote 14213 *External data not accessible outside a Macromedia Flash movie's domain* (*http://www.macromedia.com/support/ flash/ts/documents/loadvars_security.htm*) explains the limitations on loading data, typically via the *LoadVars* class, from domains other than the one hosting the SWF.

- The *LocalConnection.allowDomain( )* event handler described in Recipe 17.4 ("Accepting Communications from Other Domains") in the *ActionScript Cookbook* allows you to specify other domains from which SWFs can create local connections to the current SWF.

- Recipe 15.6 ("Loading Remote Content by Proxy") in the *ActionScript Cookbook* explains how to evade the cross-domain limitations for loading content by using a proxy server.

- The *System.Security.allowDomain( )* method described in Recipe 15.2 ("Loading an External SWF from a Trusting Domain") in the *ActionScript Cookbook* allows you to specify which domains are allowed to load your SWF file.

- If a Flash movie served via HTTP attempts to access secure HTTPS content, the operation fails silently by default. Flash MX 2004 adds a *System.security.allowInsecureDomain( )* method, which allows a SWF published for Flash Player 7 to permit HTTP-to-HTTPS access. (This is not recommended because it compromises HTTPS security, but it may be required to permit access to HTTPS files published for Flash Player 7 or later from HTTP files published for Flash Player 6.)

- Users can access the web-based Settings Manager by clicking the Advanced button on the Privacy tab of the Settings dialog box. Once at Macromedia's site, the user can configure global and domain-specific options regarding cross-domain policies.

Handling Local Executables

Users who are not suspicious of executables received over the Web won't have fully functioning computers for long. To prevent the Flash Player from running virulent code, the ActionScript environment is under strict control. A SWF running in the Flash Player plugin or ActiveX control in a browser is not allowed to run an executable on the user's machine, such as by using *fscommand("exec")*.

However, a SWF file running in the Standalone Flash Player (a separate executable sometimes called a Projector) is allowed to execute external applications using *fscommand("exec")*, as described at *http://www.macromedia.com/ support/flash/ts/documents/fscommand_projectors.htm*. Like any desktop application, the Standalone Flash Player constitutes a potential security risk. To reduce the risk, Macromedia allows *fscommand("exec")* to execute a file only if it is stored within a subfolder named FSCOMMAND (case-insensitive) within the folder containing the Flash Projector.

Now that you understand some of the security issues surrounding Flash, let's look at some of the hacks to help you protect your content [Hack #98] against likely angles of attack [Hack #97].

Recover Content from a SWF

#97   SWF decompilers can be used to "crack" a SWF file. Use them to recover your own content if you lose the source FLA.

Picture the scene. You have been given the job to update a Flash site. If you are fortunate enough to be the original developer and have a robust backup system in place, you should have all the source files you need. In reality, that is rarely the case.

Before we look at protecting your SWFs from content thieves [Hack #98], let's review situations in which decompiling SWFs has a legitimate purpose.

You might not have the latest source files because:

- The client made changes to the version you provided, so you need to obtain the latest version as a starting point.
- You weren't the original developer and the previous developer has left multimedia development to pursue a career in Hollywood.

- The client had the foresight to request the FLA files as part of the original contract, but the sys admin assumed the source files were on the server, so he deleted all files that don't do anything cool when you double-click them. Anyway, he says, "You should be able to download and update the online files like you can with HTML and Notepad, right?" Ummm, no.

- You are the original developer, but you have changed offices twice since the original site design, and the last backup CD-ROM you can find has an incomplete/older version of the site on it. You archived all the files, including JPEGs and MP3 files, as a ZIP file and the whole archive is corrupted and its contents irretrievable. Or you backed it up on a DAT tape and can't retrieve the files successfully.

So, often, you'll have only the SWF and HTML files on the server from which to work. Although there is no way you can get back the complete FLA file—Flash eliminates significant portions of the information in the FLA when it compiles down to the SWF—you can get enough of it back to make rebuilding the FLA via a decompiler far easier than starting again from scratch.

 If the SWF hasn't been saved with the Protect From Import checkbox selected (under File → Publish Settings → Flash), it can be opened directly in the Flash authoring tool. This is good news for you if you're trying to recover content and bad news if you are trying to hide your content from others [Hack #98].

Although you could roll your own based on the publicly documented SWF format, a number of SWF decompilers are publicly or commercially available. They include:

- ActionScript Viewer (*http://buraks.com/asv*) was the first to hit the market and is well–respected.

- Flash Decompiler (*http://www.flash-decompiler.com*) claims to be fast and easy to use.

- Sothink Decompiler (*http://www.srctec.com/flashdecompiler*) offers support for ActionScript 2.0 and a SWF Catcher feature to retrieve files from the browser cache.

- Flare (*http://www.nowrap.de/flare.html*) is free (as in beer), runs on Windows, Linux, and Mac OS X (command-line versions available), and the Windows version supports decompiling from the context menu (right-click).

A decompiler uncompiles the SWF bytecode and extracts parts of the compiled SWF back to the original source files (a.k.a. reverse compilation) or to a form that allows you to make them editable again.

We will look at using ActionScript Viewer (ASV). You can download a free trial of ASV 3.0 from *http://buraks.com/asv*. Although the trial version is feature-limited (it decompiles only the first 5 frames in each timeline and the first 25 lines in any script) and it does not support Flash 7 (the latest full version, ASV 4.0, does), it is enough to give a flavor of the decompilation workflow and what you can (and cannot) do. Even if the SWF has been protected from import, ActionScript Viewer allows you to unset the "protected" flag in a SWF (under the Special Tags tab), making it possible to import the file into Flash.

The ASV 3.0 Interface

When you open a SWF in ASV, you will see a window similar to Figure 12-2, although you may see fewer tabs because some tabs may not be appropriate for the current SWF.

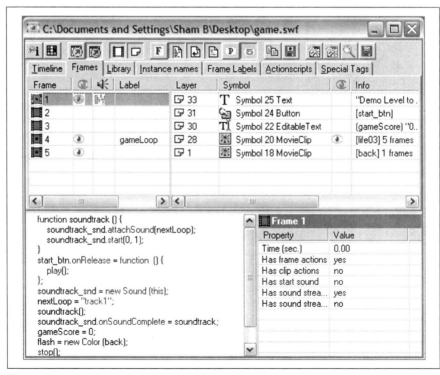

Figure 12-2. The ActionScript Viewer 3.0 interface

Although a large number of options are available, you need to do only three
things to get back to the FLA:

- Extract the ActionScript listings.
- View what the original timeline looked like, including the contents of
  each keyframe. You also need to know all instance names.
- Extract the Library, complete with any linkage identifiers.

We will look at how to do all of these quickly in the following sections.

Extract ActionScript

To view all ActionScript contained within a SWF, select ASV's Action-
Scripts tab, as shown in Figure 12-3, and select any of the scripts listed in
the top pane. The code appears in the bottom-left pane. To save this script
as a text file, you can choose Utility → Save ActionScript (as Text). Or, if you
also have Flash open, you can copy and paste the ActionScript from ASV
into an open FLA document.

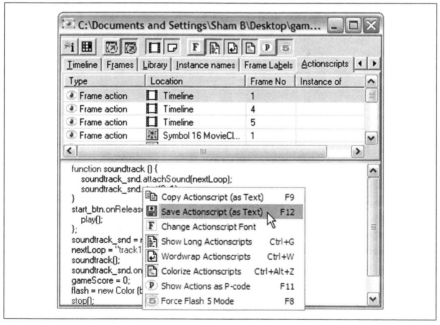

Figure 12-3. ActionScript Viewer 3.0's ActionScripts tab

View the Original Timeline

Click on ASV's Timeline tab to view the reconstructed timeline, as shown in
Figure 12-4.

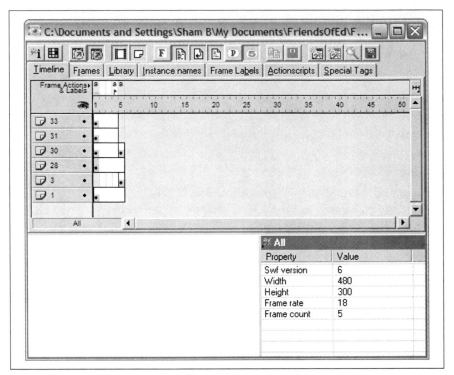

Figure 12-4. ActionScript Viewer 3.0's Timeline tab

The first layer of the timeline shows all frame labels and ActionScript attached to frames. The remaining layers constitute ASV's best guess as to what the content-holding layers need to look like to reconstruct the working FLA. You can export the timeline as a series of SWFs (one per reconstructed layer). For simple layers containing no tweens or numerous keyframes, you are better advised to simply replicate the layers in a new FLA. If you prefer to replicate the timeline manually, you also need to know each instance name on the timeline. You can review a list of instance names via the Instance Names tab (if this does not appear, it is because no instance names were used, as is typical in a SWF that contains no scripting).

ASV cannot retrieve the original timeline layers and the Library symbol names, which exist in the FLA as authoring aids only. The decompiler makes best guesses to reconstruct the missing information (such as to assume one layer per symbol or graphic and use default names such as *Symbol 23* and *Layer 6*). Layers that held no content in the original FLA (including guide layers and layer folders) are not exported into the SWF, so the decompiler cannot reconstruct them.

Extract the Library

To export the Library, select ASV's Library tab, as shown in Figure 12-5, then right-click (Windows) or ⌘-click (Mac) on any symbol and select Save All Library Symbols as SWF.

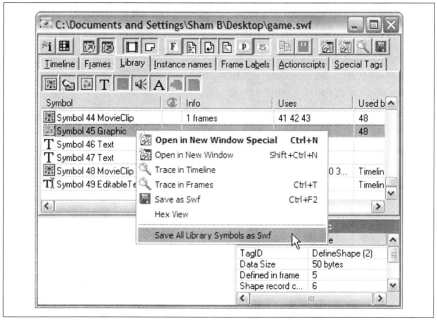

Figure 12-5. ActionScript Viewer 3.0's Library tab

You can import the SWF symbols back into Flash using File → Import → Import to Library. After importing them, you must rename the symbols into something meaningful and manually define the linkage identifiers for each symbol (linkage identifiers are not exported from ASV even though they appear within square brackets in the ASV Library tab adjacent to each symbol name).

Final Thoughts

Although the decompilation process can be time-consuming for large or complex SWFs, it is still much faster than starting from scratch. You are able to retrieve the two most important assets from the SWF: the ActionScript and the Library symbols. Even if they are the only assets you extract, this will save considerable time.

Another use of SWF decompilation is to see exactly what your SWF contains and whether you are making the best use of the filesize. Furthermore, decompilation is useful if you want to get a better understanding of how Flash content works in general and exactly what the Flash Player sees.

Of course, decompilation can also allow others to steal your content or (more likely) to deconstruct your ideas without permission.

Once a content thief has your SWF open via a decompiler or code changer (such as URL Action Editor, *http://buraks.com/uae*), the potential for stealing your work (and reasons for doing so) are possibly even greater than that offered by HTML because:

- A Flash SWF can contain a major portion of your site's contents in very few files, making them easy to locate.

- Media assets are more costly to develop than static web pages. The media, graphics, and scripts contained in your Flash masterpiece require a broader set of skills (musical, animation, scripting, video) to create than would an HTML page consisting of images and text.

- A Flash site is usually more configurable than a standard HTML page. By tweaking the code contained within a SWF, a content thief can quickly repurpose a stolen Flash web site to look and feel different. I have seen a number of sites that look suspiciously as if the designer had copied symbols and scripts from two or three other well-known Flash sites and just combined them to create something "new"!

When presented with the tools and opportunity to decompile SWF files, you often have a moral decision to make. If the developer did not provide publicly available FLA files, she probably doesn't want you reverse-engineering her code, although doing so for research purposes isn't necessarily illegal. If you are going to look to other developers for inspiration (as many hacks in this book do!), you can get that by simply running the SWF in the Flash Player. Take the high road and do original work rather than misappropriating the work of others without their permission. If you want to learn how to program in ActionScript, read a good book like *ActionScript for Flash MX: The Definitive Guide* or *Essential ActionScript 2.0*, both by Colin Moock (O'Reilly).

Remember that if a client sends you SWF files and says he couldn't get the FLA files from the original developer, you are right to ask questions. The original developer's contract might indicate that the source FLA files were not part of the deliverables. You could be liable for copyright infringement if you misappropriate the original developer's work. At a minimum, make a good faith effort to verify the client has the rights to the FLA files, especially if he doesn't possess copies of them. And make sure the client indemnifies you in your software development contract so that any materials he provides improperly are his liability and not yours.

Protect and Obfuscate Your Flash Files

Make it difficult for others to steal or reverse-engineer your online Flash content.

Your carefully honed Flash designs may not be as safe from theft [Hack #97] as you'd like to believe. For example, the URL Action Editor (*http://buraks. com/uae*) allows someone to change the arguments of any URL-based actions that a SWF uses. Someone could take a SWF that loads in your content and rework it to load in his content, or worse yet, pass of your content as being his own.

In at least one clear-cut case, a well-known designer decompiled the code of another well-known designer and passed it off as his own on a resource site. (Hint to the thief: next time, change the variable names to avoid suspicion!)

Protect the SWF

The Flash authoring tool allows anyone to load an unprotected SWF directly. You can protect your SWFs from import into Flash by checking the Protect From Import checkbox (under File → Publish Settings → Flash tab). However, other applications (such as a text editor) can still open your file, and decompilers such as ActionScript Viewer (*http://buraks.com/asv*) can unset the protected flag [Hack #97] so that it can be imported back into Flash. Compressing the SWF (File → Publish Settings → Flash → Compress Movie checkbox) helps obfuscate your work because the compressed data is harder to decode than the raw SWF.

Technological protection is never foolproof. A clever cracker—we reserve the term "hacker" for innocent tinkerers such as ourselves—can break any protection scheme given enough time. The trick, therefore, is to present the cracker with sufficient obstacles—each one making the solution more obscure and time-consuming—so that he simply gives up.

Games and commercial applications often use a single protection scheme they consider unbreakable, but crackers seem to enjoy the challenge. And the Flash Player browser plugin must ultimately display the SWF content. So if you are going to publish your SWFs, they are unencrypted on the user's machine, even if you serve them from an HTTPS server. Even if browsers supported encrypted playback, a resourceful cracker could capture the images as they are sent to the video card or the audio as it is sent to the sound card.

So our first technique is *obfuscation*. The aim is to dissuade or delay the cracker by hiding the nature of the protection scheme rather than using an obvious mechanism that seeks to be 100% secure.

Obfuscate ("Dummy") the File Types

We know that all the files for our site will end up in the cracker's browser cache. To find a SWF file or MP3 file, the cracker simply has to look for the right filenames. To make life difficult for the cracker, even at this initial stage, change the file extensions and filenames of crucial files.

For example, consider a streaming MP3 file asset loaded at runtime:

```
my_sound = new Sound (this);
my_sound.loadSound ("song.mp3", true);
```

Suppose you are writing a Flash-based music jukebox for a recording artist. To avoid a cracker finding your MP3 file and immediately putting it in his *Napster/WinMX* file-sharing folder, simply change the MP3's filename to an obfuscated name such as *top_header_02.gif* and modify the code to read:

```
my_sound = new Sound (this);
my_sound.loadSound ("top_header_02.gif", true);
```

Flash ignores file extensions when loading external files (it assumes that you are loading a sound file regardless of the filename and file extension passed to the *Sound.loadSound( )* method). Unless the cracker's operating system looks at the files' contents to confirm file extensions are as advertised (and the last computer I used able to do this was the Commodore Amiga!), he cannot easily determine the file's type.

Readers who have done traditional web design probably already have a big wide smirks thinking about the downright dirtiness of this hack, but here's a rundown for everyone else.

When the cracker looks in his browser cache for any useful media goodies, he will see *top_header_02.gif* and:

- He will most likely not even look at it further, because its name implies a rather mundane GIF slice for an HTML table.
- If he decides to open it, his GIF-reading software will tell him it is a corrupt GIF file, and he will most likely give up.

If the cracker starts looking at the domain and time properties of each file in the browser cache or has specifically saved the whole web page and its embedded media (in IE this can be done using File → Save As), he may smell something fishy. Even once he is onto the trick, it may take a long time for him to realize the so-called GIF is in reality an MP3 file. The altered file extension will wrong-foot both the cracker and his operating system. He has to be prepared to open every file in the site to find a file to steal, or he has to decompile the SWF and look for, say, *loadSound( )* commands.

If you are feeling particularly evil (and this is a real hack from the dark side), you can rename the filenames using system file types that would tend to crash the cracker's operating system if he double-clicked them. Windows actually warns users who try to fish around in the browser cache that double-clicking on anything there could have dire consequences, so consider your victim to have had fair warning. Naturally, some of these techniques don't apply directly to the Mac OS, but changing the file extensions will confuse crackers on both platforms.

 If you use this hack, keep a record of each file's true type. Keep your "dummied file versions for upload" separate from your development files. Make sure you have a backup policy because the protection may backfire on you one day when you're the one who needs to decompile the SWF.

Final Thoughts

The designer who takes inspiration from your work is doing nothing wrong. Even if you do not take this as a compliment, there is little in law and reality you can do about it. You can copyright your expression of an idea but not the idea itself. Although a *utility patent* can protect an idea, most ideas are not unique enough to be patented, and applying for patents is too expensive and time-consuming to be of practical use. In many cases, even patents offer little protection. A little-known class of patents called *design patents* can protect designs such as the shape and translucent color case of the original iMacs. But even Apple's legal department couldn't prevent PC manufacturers from quickly imitating the product design.

Although your content theoretically enjoys copyright protection the moment you put it in tangible form, and you can register your copyright for marginal extra benefit, it is next to impossible to enforce copyrights in an international medium such as the Web. And in most cases of misappropriated Flash designs, there is no provable economic damage from copyright infringement, so there is little restitution to be recovered and little use in crying foul.

A better route is the technical one, mixed with a little social engineering. If a cracker wants to save time by using your assets, the trick is to make stealing your content take so long as to not be cost effective.

Make Your SWF Phone Home

Protect your content from being displayed anywhere but on your site—make it location-dependent.

If a cracker can find your SWF file [Hack #98], before decompiling your work [Hack #97], he will most likely try to run your SWF from his local machine to see what it does. The Flash Player prohibition against loading content from other domains merely forces a cracker to change all the URLs in the SWF (which is the first thing he would do to repurpose your site with minimum modification).

By making your SWF run only if it finds itself in the expected place (i.e., on your server), you make sure the SWF cannot be run (or easily repurposed) without the cracker spending some time trying to break your protection.

The MovieClip._url property tells a SWF where it is being run from. Using this property, your code can check whether the SWF is being run from the correct location on the Web, namely your domain, or whether it is being run locally (which is one indication that someone is trying to repurpose some or all of your SWF). For example, if you use the following code:

```
var myLocation = this._url;
```

the myLocation variable stores a URL if the SWF is accessed from the Web (e.g., "http://www.futuremedia.org.uk/test/test.swf") or a local file path if it is viewed locally (e.g., "file://C:\Documents and Settings\Sham B\Desktop\test.swf"). If myLocation doesn't contain the expected location, you can take appropriate defensive action.

Cause the SWF to Fail

If the Flash Player detects a loop that carries on for a large number of iterations lasting more than 15 seconds, it will stop executing scripts (or issue a warning and give you the option to exit if you are testing a movie within the Flash authoring environment). The following code causes the SWF to enter an infinite loop if it finds itself being run from unfamiliar territory:

```
myLocation = this._url;
if (myLocation != "http://www.futuremedia.org.uk/test/test.swf") {
  do {
    // This infinite loop will hang up the Player
  } while (true);
}
```

This disabling code will cause the cracker some trouble in working out what the SWF does. You can obscure it even further by inserting long delays that do not cause the warning dialog but still make the SWF seem hung up. Here we execute a delaying function every millisecond:

```
myLocation = this._url;
if (myLocation != "http://www.futuremedia.org.uk/test/test.swf") {
  // Invoke our delaying function every millisecond
  setInterval (delayMe, 1);
}
function delayMe () {
  // Perform 10,000 calculations just to slow the Player down
  for (var i = 0; i < 10000; i++) {
    x = Math.random();
  }
}
```

Jump to Your Home Site

You can use *getURL( )* to jump to your site if the SWF is being run from the incorrect location. The cracker, noticing that the SWF keeps launching your site, will likely assume you are using *getURL( )* to go to a different URL. So he will search for the URL string (using something like URL Action Editor, *http://buraks.com/uae*), although it will still take him time to work it out. To make it harder for the cracker, you can write the code so that it jumps to a new URL only occasionally, such as "If I find myself in an unfamiliar place and it is Thursday, jump to Sham's home site via *getURL( )*." The cracker will be thinking that he has gotten away with his crime until Thursday comes along. If you want to be really nasty, you can have it jump to a pornography site or something likely to get him in hot water with the client.

The following code jumps to *http://www.futuremedia.org.uk/test/test.swf* (not a porn site) if the current SWF is not located at that URL and the day is Thursday (4 is the code for Thursday when using the *Date.getDay( )* method). Notice the cryptic variable names. Ideally, p, q, r, and s should be defined elsewhere to further obfuscate what is happening.

```
var p:String = this._url;
var q:String = "http://www.futuremedia.org.uk/test/test.swf";
var r:Date = new Date();
var s:Number = 4;
if (r.getDay() == s) {
  if (p != q) {
    getURL(q);
  }
}
```

Use Cross-Protection

It's easier for the cracker to work on a single file than it is for him to work on a site that is divided into a number of SWFs, particularly if you have also given dummy names to some of your SWFs [Hack #98] and made them all location-dependent. Also worth considering is placing your protection code in a

SWF other than the one it is actually protecting (I call this *cross-protection*). For example, place the following code in a SWF loaded in by the main SWF:

```
myLocation = _level0._url;
if (myLocation != "http://www.futuremedia.org.uk/test/test.swf") {
  do {
  } while (true);
}
```

The protection scheme can appear in a SWF that the cracker is not likely to want (e.g., place it in a SWF containing content rather than the main SWF containing your oh-so-cool UI, so he won't find it easily).

Using *setInterval( )* to run the protection code (rather than running it as soon as the SWF loads) makes locating the protection code much harder for the cracker because he will not be able to deduce which loaded SWF contains the protective payload. For example:

```
function test( ) {
  clearInterval(m);
  var myLocation:String = _level0._url;
  if (myLocation != "http://www.futuremedia.org.uk/test/test.swf") {
    do {
    } while (true);
  }
}
var m:Number = setInterval(test, 30000);
```

You can add the protection scheme at the end of your development cycle, leaving yourself to develop the protection-free main SWF in peace.

Final Thoughts

As soon as SWF decompilers became available, a spate of copycat sites and example FLAs that looked suspiciously familiar to previously unpublished code appeared. Take steps to prevent your carefully created work from being paraded where it shouldn't be!

Flash developers often ask how to protect themselves from clients who fail to pay after receiving all deliverables. Withholding the source FLA files until final payment is received is a common approach (the client gets the SWF to post to his site but the developer maintains some leverage by withholding the FLA). You can't use the phone home trick to disable the SWF in such a case because the SWF is supposed to run from the client site, but you can put an XML file on a remote server over which you (the developer) has control. The Flash movie (on the client's server) should check the remote XML file each time it initialized. This gives the developer the ability to "turn off" the application by setting an appropriate flag in the XML file if the client doesn't pay on the agreed schedule. However, such validation schemes may be contrary to your development contract and can get you in hot water if they malfunction. For example, if the SWF cannot access the remote server providing the XML file (which may become inaccessible due to downtime), the default behavior should be for the SWF to work without it. Use such "time bomb" schemes with caution and be sure to deliver an unfettered version of the SWF and/or FLA once the client pays up.

Review Compiled ActionScript

Use Flasm to create low-level code optimizations or develop a general optimization-friendly coding style by examining compiled code.

A SWF decompiler allows you to recover uncompiled ActionScript [Hack #97] based on the bytecode in a SWF.

SWF decompilers are helpful when you want to recover (or steal!) the ActionScript source code, but sometimes you want to see the compiled byte-code, such as when you are optimizing your code for either speed or filesize. The open source Flasm utility (*http://flasm.sourceforge.net*) allows you to view bytecode compiled from ActionScript.

A different breed of tool from decompilers, Flasm is for the hard-core ActionScript guru who wants to optimize his code. It also satisfies general geek curiosity about what has become of your code by the time the Flash Player sees it. The Flasm documentation goes into how the Flash Virtual Machine within the Flash Player processes compiled ActionScript in some detail, which you might find both interesting and instructive.

The latest version of Flasm (Version 1.51) can handle Flash MX 2004 files. This is useful to compare how Flash Player 7 optimizes code versus Flash Player 6 (given that it is faster than previous versions) and helps you write code that lends itself to easy optimization. Flasm is a really useful application and not just a hacky curiosity.

Flasm

Flasm (FLash ASseMbler) is a free SWF compiler and decompiler initially written by Dave Hayden (*http://www.opaque.net*) and Damian Morton and currently developed/maintained by Igor Kogan.

It is a command-line-based tool, so you have to use either the command line (Windows) or an open terminal window (Mac). A Windows user interface called WinFlasm by Shariff Aina (the latest URL can be found in the Flasm docs or at *http://flasm.sourceforge.net*), which we use here for simplicity, avoids the command line altogether.

To install Flasm, simply download the ZIP file and expand it into a location of your choice. To install WinFlasm, expand its ZIP file and drop the application into the same location as Flasm. Mac users are (unfortunately) stuck with the command-line interface.

More detailed instructions for integrating Flasm into the Flash authoring environment, useful for developers with a keen interest in creating highly optimized code, are available in the Flasm docs.

After compiling your SWF file using the Flash authoring tool, run Win-Flasm and select Open to browse for your SWF.

Specify what you want to do with the SWF using the radio buttons in Win-Flasm's lower pane, as shown in Figure 12-6.

Figure 12-6. The WinFlasm interface for Flasm

I usually choose Decompile and Edit Directly, which, despite its name, doesn't decompile the SWF so much as display the compiled SWF. Click Execute to open the compiled SWF in WordPad, as shown in Figure 12-7.

Using the Compiled Listing

The compiled listing is your best indication of the final code that the Flash Player sees at runtime. The ActionScript in your FLA is converted to a

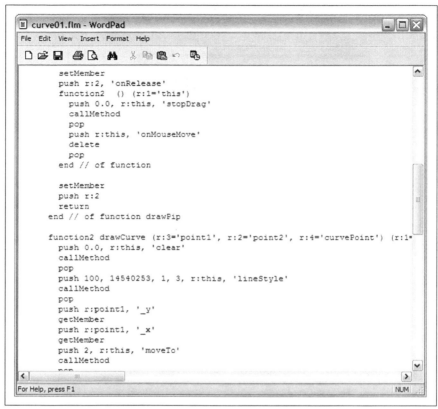

Figure 12-7. A compiled ActionScript file shown in WordPad

stream of bytes called bytecode, the purpose of which is to compress the code by converting actions and methods into shorter byte-based tokens and to convert more complex actions and methods into the longer series of simpler bytecodes that the Flash Player actually understands.

Anyone who has had experience with assembly language will see that the internals of the Flash Player Virtual Machine are very much like the old 8-bit microprocessor architectures. It includes a *stack* onto which values to be manipulated (added, subtracted, etc.) are placed (*pushed*) before being processed. The results are then taken from the stack (*popped*). Hence, the Flash Player is stack-based rather than using absolute memory locations. To store intermediate values, registers are used, and these speed up the process significantly for long or repetitive calculations. The alternative to registers appears to be constants, where "constant" probably refers to a constant location.

Working with Flasm

Let's look at how Flasm can help you create efficient modular code. The other day, I wanted to see the effect on overall performance of using functions. Although functions make for more modular and structured code, I wasn't too sure about using function calls in performance-critical areas because common sense told me the function invocation itself would take extra time. Anyway, I thought it would be a good idea to investigate it in Flasm.

Here is the code using no functions:

```
var x = 5;
var y = 6;
var z = x*y;
trace(z);
```

for which Flasm yields the following Flash Player 7 bytecode:

```
frame 0
  constants 'x', 'y', 'z'
  push 'x', 5
  varEquals
  push 'y', 6
  varEquals
  push 'z', 'x'
  getVariable
  push 'y'
  getVariable
  multiply
  varEquals
  push 'z'
  getVariable
  trace
end // of frame 0
```

If I use ActionScript 2.0 datatyping:

```
var x:Number = 5;
var y:Number = 6;
var z:Number = x*y;
trace(z);
```

I get exactly the same output, telling me that there is no performance or file-size hit caused by using typed code (as would be expected because type checking is performed at compile time and not runtime). On my machine, both typed and untyped versions execute in approximately 0.06 ms (excluding the *trace( )* command because output statements tend to be slow). I timed the execution using code of the following form (we test for 1000 iterations to get an average speed):

```
// Time how long a for loop itself takes
startTime = getTimer();
for (var i = 0; i < 1000; i++) {}
endTime = getTimer();
measureTime = endTime - startTime;

// Run some simple code, and trace how long it takes
startTime = getTimer();
for (var i = 0; i < 1000; i++) {
  // Put code under test here
}
endTime = getTimer();
codeTime = endTime - startTime - measureTime;
trace(codeTime/1000);
```

Here is a version that uses a function to perform the earlier operation:

```
function multiply() {
  return x * y;
}
var x:Number = 5;
var y:Number = 6;
var z:Number = multiply();
trace(z);
```

Again, Flasm yields the following bytecode version. As expected, it is longer in terms of bytecode and elapsed time (0.16 ms, more than twice as long as the non-function-based version). Not good.

```
frame 0
  constants 'x', 'y', 'z', 'multiply'
  function multiply ()
    push 'x'
    getVariable
    push 'y'
    getVariable
    multiply
    return
  end // of function multiply

  push 'x', 5
  varEquals
  push 'y', 6
  varEquals
  push 'z', 0.0, 'multiply'
  callFunction
  varEquals
  push 'z'
  getVariable
  trace
end // of frame 0
```

I then tried it with a function invocation with arguments, thinking that this would create the longest bytecode of all:

```
function multiply(a, b) {
  return a * b;
}
var x:Number = 5;
var y:Number = 6;
var z:Number = multiply(x, y);
trace(z);
```

But this version runs marginally faster (0.12 ms)! We can see why when we look at the Flasm bytecode. Using function arguments generates bytecode that accesses the arguments directly rather than having to look for the variables holding the values. This results in shorter bytecode and faster execution.

```
frame 0
  constants 'x', 'y', 'z', 'multiply'
  function2 multiply (r:2='a', r:1='b') ()
    push r:a, r:b
    multiply
    return
  end // of function multiply

  push 'x', 5
  varEquals
  push 'y', 6
  varEquals
  push 'z', 'y'
  getVariable
  push 'x'
  getVariable
  push 2, 'multiply'
  callFunction
  varEquals
  push 'z'
  getVariable
  trace
end // of frame 0
```

If you write your code using functions that pass values via arguments, the Flash Player makes greater use of direct registers rather than memory locations (which have to be pushed into registers or onto the stack before they can be used, doubling access time). This is a very interesting finding because it implies that Macromedia is aiming ActionScript toward a more structured coding style that tends to use functions, references, and parameters rather than separate variables.

Experimentation shows that the time required to invoke functions is made up for as you place more code within each function; writing clear, modular code actually increases performance in many applications.

Thus, the Flash Player 7 optimizations that Macromedia advertises are actually most seen when you use the sort of OOP coding style that ActionScript 2.0 promotes.

If you try our examples here with Flash Player 6 (Flash MX) you will see a different result, unless you use Flash Player 6r65 (check the Optimize for Flash Player 6r65 in File → Publish Settings → Flash tab), which seems to act very much like Flash Player 7 (probably because it fundamentally is Flash Player 7, apart from the new ActionScript classes added in Flash MX 2004). Looking at previous versions of the Flash Player using Flasm, it becomes obvious that the Flash 7 and Flash Player 6r65 code optimizations are strongly linked to the way that your bytecode makes efficient use of registers and the stack.

But you have to write code that takes advantage of the optimizations, such as by:

- Passing arguments to functions
- Using local variables
- Passing the target of an animation routine as an argument rather than using the this property

Another set of tests you may want to make is the differences between ActionScript 2.0 class declarations and ActionScript 1.0-style timeline-based code or prototype-based inheritance.

Hint: ActionScript 2.0's strict datatyping comes at compile time (so there's no performance cost) and class-based OOP uses well-defined functions and local data (both of which lead to code optimizations in the bytecode through use of registers rather than memory). This means that class-based Action-Script 2.0 code produces highly optimized bytecode, as does any structured coding style that uses functions and localization of data within functions and arguments.

Final Thoughts

Flasm is very useful to investigate what becomes of your ActionScript in the final SWF. Although it may initially seem a little difficult to understand, you can easily get a feel for it if you start with short, simple scripts as we have done in the preceding examples.

Flasm is also useful for checking for any ActionScript bottlenecks. Be aware that for motion graphics applications, the performance bottlenecks are caused by Flash's graphic-rendering engine [Hack #68] and not bytecode.

This hack has, of course, only scratched the surface of Flasm and code optimization. If you are an advanced ActionScripter looking for new avenues with which to hone your game, digging into Flasm to see what you can learn about the Flash Player environment will turn up more than a few gems that enable you to squeeze a little more performance out of your SWFs.

Index

We'd like to hear your suggestions for improving our indexes. Send email to *index@oreilly.com*.

Colophon

Our look is the result of reader comments, our own experimentation, and feedback from distribution channels. Distinctive covers complement our distinctive approach to technical topics, breathing personality and life into potentially dry subjects.

The tool on the cover of *Flash Hacks* is a spotlight. The modern spotlight descends from an invention at the beginning of the nineteenth century by British army officer Thomas Drummond. Drummond produced "limelight" by burning a cylinder of calcium oxide (lime) in an oxyhydrogen flame. As the lime was oxidized by the flame, it produced a brilliant light that could be directed into a beam by a glass lens. Although its original use was to make survey stations more visible at night, limelight quickly became a part of stage lighting; its first appearances were in the Paris opera houses, and it was used widely throughout Europe and the United States until the 1890s.

The etymology of the expression "in the limelight"—being at the center of attention—comes from this beam of light, which was used to direct the audience's attention to an important person or event on stage.

As technology improved, limelight became less popular as a means to light theatres because it produced intense heat, started fires, emitted a noxious gas-like odor, and cast a greenish tint. Its brief successor was the carbon arc lamp, which was quickly replaced in the 1920s by the newer and safer incandescent spotlight that used a modern 1000-watt lamp. Of course, that lamp was possible because Thomas Edison continued to make advances in electrical technology that led, in 1911, to the introduction of the "concentrated filament" lamp designed for use in a lens hood. Thus, the modern spotlight was born.

Marlowe Shaeffer was the production editor and proofreader for *Flash Hacks*. Norma Emory was the copyeditor. Reg Aubry and Darren Kelly provided quality control. John Bickelhaupt wrote the index.

Hanna Dyer designed the cover of this book, based on a series design by Edie Freedman. The cover image is a photograph taken from the Classic PIO Entertainment CD. Emma Colby produced the cover layout with QuarkXPress 4.1 using Adobe's Helvetica Neue and ITC Garamond fonts.

Melanie Wang designed the interior layout, based on a series design by David Futato. This book was converted by Andrew Savikas to FrameMaker 5.5.6 with a format conversion tool created by Erik Ray, Jason McIntosh, Neil Walls, and Mike Sierra that uses Perl and XML technologies. The text font is Linotype Birka; the heading font is Adobe Helvetica Neue Condensed; and the code font is LucasFont's TheSans Mono Condensed. The illustrations that appear in the book were produced by Robert Romano and Jessamyn Read using Macromedia FreeHand 9 and Adobe Photoshop 6. This colophon was written by Marlowe Shaeffer.

CPSIA information can be obtained at www.ICGtesting.com
Printed in the USA
BVOW021639030112

279714BV00003B/19/P